FALSE NATIONALISM
FALSE INTERNATIONALISM

Class Contradictions in the Armed Struggle

E. Tani & Kaé Sera

KER
SPL
EBE
DEB
2021

False Nationalism False Internationalism: Class Contradictions in the Armed Struggle
by E. Tani & Kaé Sera

First Published in 1985 by Seeds Beneath the Snow

ISBN 978-1-989701-08-9
This edition copyright Kersplebedeb 2021

To order copies of the book:

        Kersplebedeb
        CP 63560, CCCP Van Horne
        Montreal, Quebec
        Canada
        H3W 3H8

        info@kersplebedeb.com
        www.kersplebedeb.com
        www.leftwingbooks.net

My whole life has been a series of failures, and the history of my country has been a history of failure. I have had only one victory—over myself. This one small victory, however, is enough to give me confidence to go on. Fortunately, the tragedy and defeat I have experienced have not broken but strengthened me. I have few illusions left, but I have not lost faith in men and in the ability of men to create history. Who shall know the will of history? Only the oppressed who must overthrow force in order to live. Only the undefeated in defeat who have lost everything to gain a whole new world in the last battle. Oppression is pain, and pain is consciousness. Consciousness means movement. Millions of men must die and tens of millions must suffer before humanity can be born again. I accept this objective fact. The sight of blood and death and of stupidity and failure no longer obstructs my vision of the future.

Kim San

To

Atiba Shanna

and

Oyaya (Oya) Ayoluha

Contents

Young migrants, running away from Honduras to the United States, cross the river on the Mexico-Guatemala border.
Photo: Jan Sochor / Alamy Stock Photo.

INTRODUCTION

Political events of the last twenty-five years have shown that the revolutionary movements born in the 1960s still believe that white people (i.e. the US oppressor nation) are the answer to the problems of the oppressed nations. The decline of these old movements has also shown that these beliefs lead to bitter defeats, both militarily and politically. This view that white people are the answer to the problems of the oppressed nations is neo-colonial and Eurocentric, and is one of the main forms of false internationalism.

On a world scale, neo-colonialism as a stage of imperialism has proven to be very dangerous because of its flexibility and powers of camouflage as compared to colonialism. Even people who are opposed to imperialism can get misdirected by neo-colonial influences.

REVIEWING NEO-COLONIALISM

So there are not misunderstandings, right at the beginning we want to take the time to spell out what certain key concepts are. Neo-colonialism (literally "new colonialism") is a more sophis-ticated, disguised form of the classic capitalist colonialism. Originally, the European capitalist nations and their settler offshoots ("u.s.a.," Canada, Australia, Azania, "Israel," New Caledonia, Northern Ireland, etc.) militarily seized oppressed nations, which they ruled and looted as national property. However, to deflect anti-colonial revolutions the imperialist powers found it expedient to grant "flag independence" to new governments representing the oppressed nation petty-bourgeoisie.

So Kenya before independence in 1960 was an outright British Crown Colony, where the economy was owned by major European corporations and settler plantation owners, and where political dissent and rebelliousness were brutally put down by Britain's puppet "native police." Today, Kenya is a British neo-colony, governed by a well-paid Afrikan elite who are in alliance with imperialism against their own people. The same European and US corporations and the same settler planters dominate the economy, while the same puppet troops repress the masses. So the "flag independence" is democratic only in outward form, a change of faces, but in essence the Kenyan neo-colony is still a nation oppressed by another nation (and by imperialism as a system).

Implicit in everything we say is the communist understanding that the **imperialist** stage of capitalist development is characterized by the complete division of the world into oppressor and oppressed nations. By the start of the 20th century, the imperialist powers of Europe, the "u.s.a.", and Japan had divided among themselves claim to every square inch of the earth's surface. Every person was supposed to be owned by one imperialist nation or another. While today we generally think of oppressed nations as Third World or non-European, there have been numerous exceptions—Ireland (oppressed by Britain), the Basque (oppressed by Spain), Albania (oppressed by Italy), and so on.

Neo-colonialism uses a facade of democracy ("native rule," "one man one vote," etc.) to conceal continued domination. This need not take the form of independence, but can also take the form of phony citizenship in the oppressor nation. French imperialism gave "democracy" to its small New Caledonian colony in the Pacific, for example, by annexing it into France. All Kanak people, the true inhabitants, were involuntarily given paper French citizenship with "voting rights." Of course, even in Kanaky elections the garrison of French settlers on the island outvotes the Kanak "minority," while assassinating or imprisoning those who get too militant. New Caledonia is a "democratic" neo-colony, in the same way as Puerto Rico or New Afrika. New Afrika was originally a **colony** of chattel slaves, but was converted to a **neo-colony** in 1865 when New Afrikan colonial subjects were invol-

untarily given phony US citizenship as a pretense of democracy, a substitute for independence as a nation.

While neo-colonialism is a phenomenon of imperialism, that does not mean that only the capitalist class practices it. **Neo-colonialism is a part of the general relations between oppressor nations and oppressed nations. Often noble sentiments and concerns are twisted or exploited, in the same way that "democracy" or "voting rights" are used to deny real democracy through independence.** For example, in 1985 one of the major events in the US was the popularity of aid to Afrika campaigns. While pre-

venting starvation in drought areas is humanitarian, the campaigns were also clearly neo-colonial propaganda. The implicit message was always put out that Afrikans are too savage and too stupid to feed themselves, so that their survival depends on white people. It is our point that in many ways neo-colonialism has pervaded relations between revolutionary movements in the US Empire, however masked by lofty words like "solidarity" and "internationalism."

There is a relationship between neo-colonialism and class, just as there is between false internationalism and class. Genuine proletarian internationalism between revolutionaries of different nations is based on our class stand. We recognize that the oppressed and exploited masses of the world, led by the proletariat as the most modern and revolutionary class, not only have common interests but are remaking the world through socialist revolution. False internationalism is a pretense of this, in the same way that neo-colonialism is the pretense of true independence. When we think about it, examples are easy to find.

In the late 1960s Euro-Amerikan radicals and liberals raised tens of thousands of dollars,

BLACK PANTHER · PEACE & FREEDOM

FREE HUEY

RALLY

FOR: HUEY NEWTON ELDRIDGE CLEAVER SUN. SEPT. 22 1:00 P.M. BOBBY HUTTON MEMORIAL PARK 18th & ADELINE, OAK.

walked picket lines in front of courthouses, and helped make a big public issue of the defense trials of Black Panther Party leaders Huey Newton and Bobby Seale. **Newton and Seale were projected by the media and the white Left as the most revolutionary leadership for the New Afrikan movement.** Was that campaign an example of genuine internationalism? No. Many Euro-Amerikan students may have been subjectively sincere in a desire for internationalism, but objectively what took place was the reverse. Because at the same time that the Euro-Amerikan Left was promoting Huey and Bobby, they were also ignoring—and thus implicitly condoning—imperialist counterinsurgency against real revolutionary nationalists, such as Fred Ahmed Evans in Cleveland or the Republic of New Afrika 11 in Mississippi. In other words, no solidarity with those explicitly fighting for New Afrikan independence. What passed for "solidarity" was really a settler Left attempt to once again pick Black leaders more suitable to them. Not internationalism but false internationalism.

While false internationalism involves deception, it is more than a trick. It is a class alliance between petty-bourgeois and lumpen opportunist elements from both oppressor and oppressed nations. Misleadership and continued dependency on the oppressor nation is promoted, against the interests of the oppressed. And the collaboration is concealed under the label of revolutionary "solidarity" or internationalism.

THE ROLE OF CLASSES IN FALSE INTERNATIONALISM

At this point we want to break down the class question. Classes are social groupings of people that occupy a common role in economic production and distribution, and therefore share a common way of life, a common position in society, common political interests, and common social goals. In general we recognize four main world classes, two of them laboring classes and two of them non-laboring classes: the bourgeoisie (capitalists), petty-bourgeoisie (small business owners, managers, intellectuals, and other privileged middle-persons), proletariat (workers), and peasantry (small farmers). We say "in general" because in each nation the actual class situation reflects that nation's own particular historical development.

It is necessary to keep in mind that class structure can be very different from nation to nation. It is not true that every nation has the same classes, based on the European 19th century model of Marx and Engels' day. For example, although the New Afrikan nation has a very large proletariat and a small petty-bourgeoisie, it has no bourgeoisie. There is a New Afrikan **pseudo-bourgeoisie**, made up of a handful of individual millionaires, car dealers, entertainers, politicians, funeral home owners, etc. That is, while there are **individual** New Afrikans who are wealthy or own businesses, they do not make up a real capitalist class of their own. The reason for this is that the position and role of the capitalist class in the New Afrikan oppressed nation is taken up by the US oppressor nation bourgeoisie. The handful of wealthy New Afrikan **pseudo-bourgeoisie**, while they can buy stocks, sports cars, and yachts, do not employ the New Afrikan proletariat, do not own any significant capital, and do not control in any way the economic activities of their own nation. All that is done by the settler bourgeoisie. In other words, the pseudo-bourgeoisie are wealthy individually, but do not own their nation's means of production and distribution (steel mills, airlines, chemical plants, utilities, etc.). **So the class structure itself has been shaped by the contradiction between Imperialism and the oppressed nation.**

Conversely, on the other side of the same national contradiction, there are many individual Euro-Amerikan workers but they do not make up a genuine proletariat. That is, settler workers are a non-exploited labor aristocracy, with a privileged lifestyle far, far above the levels of the world proletariat. **They might be called a pseudo-proletariat, in that individual settlers do work in factories and mines, but as a group they do not perform the role of a proletariat.** Settler workers neither support their society by their labor, nor is their exploitation the source of the surplus value (or profit) that sustains the US bourgeoisie. The life-giving role of the proletariat in the US Empire is relegated to the proletariats of the oppressed nations, which is why "nations become almost as classes" under imperialism. The shrinking number of settler workers actually

In an attempt to lure black voters to the Republican ticket, boxers Muhammad Ali, George Frazier, and Floyd Patterson appeared with President Reagan on a Reagan-sponsored billboard in Chicago's South Side. Tribune photo by Frank Hanes.

live as part of the lower petty-bourgeoisie, and have no separate political existence. **Classes in the US Empire themselves reflect the primary contradiction between imperialism and the oppressed nations.**

The petty-bourgeoisie (literally "little bourgeoisie") is an in-between class, that neither owns the means of production and commands society, as the bourgeoisie does, nor sustains society by its labor as the proletariat does. Nor can this class successfully make revolution itself. **Politically the petty-bourgeoisie is a vacillating and intermediary class, shifting its position back and forth between imperialism and socialism.** Like other classes it is divided into sectors. There are, for instance, social and political differences between the small retail-shop owning sector and the intellectuals. Yet, there is even more in common.

There was a tendency in the '60s movements to glorify the petty-bourgeoisie (and the lumpen). Some folks even said that in the New Afrikan nation the intellectuals (teachers, lawyers, doctors, college students, etc.) were national revolutionary as a whole. When we examine the political careers of people from this class, however, we can see that while some committed class suicide within the Revolution, many other Black intellectuals, whatever their rhetoric, only had the ultimate goal of "equality" with their settler class-mates—foundation grants, professorships,

American GI parties with Grenadian women in St. Georges.

government positions, neo-colonial reforms that benefitted them as a privileged sector.

The main political ally of the petty-bourgeoisie in the old '60s–70s movements were the lumpen (lumpen-proletariat). There has been much confusion about this class or semi-class. Classically, the lumpen have been described as the "rag-tag" grouping of individuals uprooted and dislocated from the main classes, and who consequently no longer have any relationship at all to productive society.

The lumpen have many different origins. In pre-Nazi Germany many of the lumpen came from the bankrupted petty-bourgeoisie while others came from the peasantry and lower proletariat. Their primary political expression was in the paramilitary "Brown Shirts" (Sturmabteilung or Storm Troopers) of the Nazi Party, and they were the class base for the "radical" wing of that party (which sought to terrorize and rule over both the bourgeoisie and the proletariat). After the "Brown Shirts" were purged in a 1934 blood-bath by Hitler, many of the lumpen survivors became exiles from Germany. In that stage the ex–Storm Troopers became the main element in the Thälmann Battalion, the German Communist Party unit that fought in the Spanish Civil War against the fascists. We can see that the lumpen should not be carelessly characterized without social investigation in the individual case.

In the 1960s–1970s movements within the US Empire the lumpen were glorified, sometimes to the point of proclaiming them as the leading or even the only revolutionary class. This was widespread. **A misunderstanding was pushed which falsely identified the lumpen as the poorest and unemployed.** As we shall see, this was not an accident. Most of the folks whom the old movements called lumpen were really from the bottom, most-oppressed layer of the proletariat.

In general under capitalism roughly 50% of the proletariat are unemployed, forming the reserve army of the unemployed. This was true in England in 1848 and Watts in 1985. Mass unemployment is a normal, fixed situation for much of the real proletariat (unlike the Euro-Amerikan labor aristocracy). Capitalism needs the reserve army of the unemployed to give them more choice in hiring workers, to help push down wages and maintain competition for scarce jobs, and to be there ready-at-hand when economic expansion creates an instant need for more labor. Marx referred to them as the proletariat's "Lazarus-layers," after the Biblical character revived from the dead by Jesus. In the same way the bourgeoisie, when it needs more labor, suddenly revives the "Lazarus-layers" into economic life. That millions must therefore live lives of desperation, lives fragmented with chaos and cut short by the conditions of the streets, is only a regular feature of capitalist "civilization." So the poor and unemployed are not per se the lumpen, although lumpen may be poor and unemployed.

What characterized the lumpen as a class or semi-class is their individualistic separation from

both the class and society they came from. They have no loyalty to the oppressed, although they may hate the oppressor. To merely be poor and unemployed still leaves one within the working classes, but to be lumpen is to see your life as preying on the working classes. The individualism, political vacillation, and subjectivity that characterize the petty-bourgeoisie are only more so for the lumpen, although we can see how these classes can work hand-in-hand with each other.

The political rootlessness of the lumpen is one of their main attributes. In pre-Revolutionary China some former peasants, forced off their lands and hence out of the farming communities they came from, took part in anti-landlord rebellions and formed secret societies for mutual self-protection. But in most cases these initially righteous secret societies—the Triad Society, the Green Band, the Big Sword Society, and many others—quickly evolved into armed gangs preying on the people, and then became mercenary gangs doing the dirty work for the imperialists.

It was only in militarily beating the mercenary gangs and puppet army units, both mainly lumpen, that the Chinese Red Army could remold lumpen, proletarianizing them as part of the Revolution. We can see this rootlessness and alienation from their people in the careers of lumpen who were former leading figures in the '60s Black Movement, but who turned to drug dealing, petty hustling, or fronting for the CIA once things got difficult. The street force or what was called the lumpen was a mixture of classes, with lumpen elements within a primarily proletarian mass.

It is not a question of the lumpen being "good" or "bad." Many lumpen fighters, as everyone knows, played a militant role in the revolutionary movements. **But to falsely glorify the class as such is to undermine the necessary understanding that the Revolution requires lumpen to transform themselves, to become**

proletarian. No lumpen can successfully serve their people without committing class suicide. In Revolutionary China the Red Army gladly recruited lumpen bandits or mercenaries, but systematically assisted them to adopt a proletarian outlook—in putting collective interests first, in learning scientific military practice, in doing productive work instead of living off of others, and in serving the oppressed. When the 1960s–1970s movements here mistakenly glorified the lumpen and glorified criminality as such, they were rejecting the task of helping the lumpen become true fighters for the people. False praise just covered up for slighting the legitimate political needs of these rads.

As a class or semi-class the lumpen in the old 1960s–1970s movements became pawns in neo-colonial alliances with the white Left. That is, the politically active Black lumpen, Puerto Rican lumpen, and so on, were allied to the Euro-Amerikan petty-bourgeoisie.

This produced distortions and setbacks for the oppressed nations. In 1969–70 some groupings within the Euro-Amerikan New Left, most notably the National Office of SDS (Students for a Democratic Society), began promoting a Chicago youth gang as the leading Puerto Rican revolutionary organization in the US. An alliance was formed, with SDS activists providing political guidance. This gang, the Young Lords, made an impressive sight when they turned up in berets and jackets at radical demonstrations, on occasions hundreds strong. The Young Lords' early actions, such as building takeovers to protest gentrification, won them respect and much publicity.

But while they were being heavily promoted by the white Left, internally the youth gang was becoming preoccupied with heroin use. The top leaders, then public figures in Chicago supposedly representing Puerto Rican independence and socialism, were themselves slaves to their drug habit. And in the community too many gang members were abusing people while committing petty crimes to support heroin addiction.

Soon the "Organization" just fell apart. In retrospect, the Young Lords (who initially inspired but were separate from the Young Lords Party in New York) as a revolutionary leadership were the artificial creation of the petty-bourgeois white Left and the imperialist media, out of an alliance with lumpen elements leading oppressed youth. False theories glorifying the lumpen as the most revolutionary class were no accident, emanating from the radical Euro-Amerikan petty-bourgeoisie and like-minded class-mates in the petty-bourgeoisies of the oppressed nations.

FROM THE OLD TO THE NEW

We are in the transition period between the old revolutionary movements of the 1960s and 1970s, and the new movements that are coming into being. The remnants of the old movements, unable to face their crippling weaknesses, try to hold things together by denying the reality of defeats. **Their practice has been reduced to repeating what hasn't worked before, over and over.** Now, the two-line struggle between socialism and neo-colonialism is manifested in the struggle to find and overturn the sources of those defeats.

False internationalism had been a factor in the leadership crisis within the revolutionary movements. This can be seen just in the effect of maintaining the idea that **white people are the answer to the problems of the oppressed nations.** We maintain that this backward idea had a stranglehold on the old revolutionary movements.

Simultaneously, the inevitable corollary to that idea also became dominant: that the US oppressor nation Left could avoid the difficult challenges within its own non-revolutionary society by becoming political parasites on the oppressed nations. "Allies" is a noble word that has, like "democracy" and other fine words before it, taken on a sour taste in Babylon.

There is a direct connection between the defeats suffered by the old 1960s–1970s movements on the one hand, and neo-colonial relationships that have existed between revolutionaries of the oppressor and oppressed nations on the other hand. It is necessary to understand this connection scientifically.

Also, it is true that genuine internationalism is invaluable for us, and that anything that undermines this must be viewed as a danger. We are fighting in the continental US Empire, "the prisonhouse of nations," a very center of world imperialism crowded with nations and peoples. Alliances between revolutionaries and movements of different nations are not only positive, but are in practice inevitable. Therefore, these alliances must be consciously built in a correct way, in both word and deed.

This study sums up experiences from the development of the 20th-century communist movement; that is, of world communism in the epoch of imperialism and proletarian revolution. It deals with both past and present (as of 1985, when it was first published). In the first half of the study examples of revolutionary alliances both false and genuine are examined. To start with, we see how Finland, a small oppressed nation, played a key role in the overthrow of the Czarist Empire. The genuine alliance between the Finnish nation and the Bolsheviks enabled that young party to survive and build the armed struggle from 1900 onwards.

Following the victory of the Bolshevik Revolution the new Soviet state built the Communist International, the most ambitious experiment

in international alliances we have yet seen. Out of this, for reasons we shall explain, came episodes of false internationalism that severely tried the first generation of oppressed nation (colonial) communists: the China–USSR alliance in the 1920s–1930s; the Communist Party USA (CPUSA) relationship to Asian nationalities in that same period; finally, the role of the CPUSA's Black cadres in the 1935 New Afrikan solidarity movement with Ethiopia.

While it is sometimes hard to study earlier revolutionary experiences, these struggles prove that false internationalism is not a brand new problem nor one unique to the "u.s.a." It is especially useful to see the full meaning of national movements succeeding or failing to overcome false internationalism. **The seriousness of what is at stake should impress itself on us.** Armies, parties, and entire national movements suffered setbacks and in cases complete defeats. "Those who do not learn from history are doomed to repeat it."

The second half of our study deals with false internationalism in the US Empire during the 1960s–1970s. It particularly examines the relationship between the New Afrikan National Liberation Movement and the Euro-Amerikan New Left on the terrain of armed struggle, the highest and most decisive form of struggle.

This study is not in itself a new, higher level in our understanding of the world. But it is more evidence that we need to reach for such a new stage. Recent crisis not only in movements within the US Empire, but within world socialism is pushing us relentlessly to change. Cabral's accurate prediction of "neo-socialism" as a higher form of neo-colonialism in Afrika, the Capitalist Road in China, are just cases in point. Imperialism can no longer hold power, but we have not been able to always build socialist power. Imperialism loses but then sometimes retakes countries. Confusion about communism in the US Empire mirrors and is part of a world two-line struggle in peoples' movements between socialism and neo-colonialism.

GROWING CONTRADICTIONS WITHIN THE CONTINENTAL EMPIRE

This is a time when changes are taking shape that will eventually shatter this Empire and break up the "u.s.a." itself. Our basic understanding of the "u.s.a." is that it is an illegitimate nation. This was summed up in *Settlers: Mythology of the White Proletariat*, which is the historical-materialist analysis of the Euro-Amerikan masses:

"We all know that the 'United States' is an oppressor nation; that is, a nation that oppresses other nations. This is a characteristic that the US shares with other imperialist powers. What is specific, is particular about the US oppressor nation is that it is an illegitimate nation.

"What pretends to be one continental nation stretching from the Atlantic to the Pacific is really a Euro-Amerikan settler empire, built on colonially oppressed nations and peoples whose very existence has been forcibly submerged. But the colonial crime, the criminals, the victims, and the stolen lands and labor still exist. The many Indian nations, the Afrikan nation in the South, Puerto Rico, the northern half of Mexico, Asian Hawaii—all are now considered the lands of the Euro-Amerikan settlers. The true citizens of this US Empire are the European invaders and their descendants. So that the 'United States' is in reality not one, but many nations (oppressor and oppressed).

"We see the recognition of Amerika as a 'prison-house of nations' as the beginning—no more, no less—of the differences between revisionist and communist politics here. We hold that once this outward shell of integration into a single, white-dominated 'USA' is cracked open—to reveal the colonial oppression and anti-colonial struggle within—then the correct path to a communist understanding of the US Empire is begun.

"We hold that settlerism is the historic instrument created by the European ruling classes to safeguard their colonial conquests with entire, imported populations of European invaders. In return for special privileges and a small share of the colonial loot these settlers became the loyal, live-in garrison troops of Empire ..."

The primary contradiction within the US Empire is between imperialism and the oppressed nations. National and class contradictions, which are not completely separate but interrelated, continue to grow sharper within the US Empire. Indeed, the ebbing of the '60s protest movements could not stop or even slow the growth of national contradictions.

The shell of the G.P.O. on Sackville Street (later O'Connell Street), Dublin in the aftermath of the 1916 Rising. May 1916.

I. The Importance of National Struggles to Communism: the european experience

Internationalism has always played a central role in modern revolutionary struggles for independence and socialism. We cannot go fully into the history of the "national question" here, but we will show how the importance of struggles for national self-determination and independence was emphasized by communists early on in the 20th Century European experience.

It is necessary to begin our study here, in order to refute two bourgeois political lines that have confusing influence, though of varying degrees, within the Movements in the US Empire. The first is US oppressor nation revisionism. It argues that all "nationalism" is "narrow" and ultimately reactionary. New Afrika is compared to Israel, revolutionary nationalism is said to be like Zionism. These revisionists make "class" holy, and argue that merging the New Afrikan proletariat with the settler masses is the only road to liberation. As a corollary in this Eurocentric view, only the "u.s.a." is considered to be a "real" nation. Hawaii, the Navajo nation, Puerto Rico, and so on are not thought to be real nations, or in any case are not thought to be very important politically. We can see the widespread effect of this attitude in Third World comrades who think "ally" only means Euro-Amerikans.

The second bourgeois line believes that liberation for the oppressed nations can only come from developing their own capitalism (Black capitalism, etc.). The apostles of this put down modern class-consciousness as unnecessary, and picture communism or Marxism-Leninism as a "racist European philosophy" whose leaders always ignored the rights of small nations and colonies. These two bourgeois lines keep reinforcing each other back and forth, keep mutually pitting "class" and "nation" against each other, and both support the continued ideological domination of the US oppressor nation over its captive nations and peoples. Modern communism in the imperialist era recognizes the dialectical interpenetration of class and nation, not just in theory but in revolutionary practice. It was Lenin who said of this era that **nations become almost as classes.**

We should know that this ideological struggle is not new, but has been going on since the emergence of scientific socialism. Today the revisionists falsely wrap themselves in the banner of the Bolshevik Revolution, misquote Lenin on "ultra-leftism," and claim to represent proletarian politics. But in the early imperialist period in Europe it was precisely Lenin and the Bolsheviks who led the fight to recognize and support the world importance of national liberation struggles—**even in the case of premature, unsuccessful struggles in small oppressed nations.** This has always been the communist stand.

The issue in Europe came to a head over the Easter 1916 Irish Rebellion. That Easter Day a few hundred Irish revolutionaries, mostly from the petty-bourgeoisie, staged a brave but ill-conceived uprising. They took over the Dublin Post Office and declared Irish independence. Within hours they were crushed; most of the Irish rebels were hanged by the British. There was no general rebellion. Yet that event marks the historic beginning of the present Irish Republic. This small armed action was mocked by the European revisionists, who put it down as a "putsch ... which notwithstanding the sensation it caused, had not much social backing."

Lenin publicly defended the unsuccessful Irish military action, showing the vital interconnection between the international class struggle and the movements for the independence of oppressed nations. In 1916 the European workers' movements as a whole were still weak and politically not very revolutionary. Lenin admitted this, and reminded everyone of the world importance of the independence struggles of small oppressed nations, who were helping create a world imperialist crisis:

"In the colonies there have been a number of attempts at rebellion, which the oppressor nations naturally did all they could to hide by means of a military censorship. Nevertheless, it is known that in Singapore the British brutally suppressed a mutiny among their Indian troops; that there were attempts at rebellion in French Annam [i.e. Indochina] and in the German Cameroons [i.e. Afrika]; that in Europe, on the one hand, there was a rebellion in Ireland, which the 'freedom-loving' English, who did not dare to extend conscription to Ireland, suppressed by executions ...

...

"This list is, of course far from complete. Nevertheless, it proves that, **owing** to the crisis of imperialism, the flames of national revolt have flared up both in the colonies and in Europe, and that national sympathies and antipathies have manifested themselves in spite of the Draconian threats and measures of repression. All this before the crisis of imperialism hit its peak; the power of the imperialist bourgeoisie was yet to be undermined ... and the proletarian movements in the imperialist countries were still very feeble."[1]

In showing the importance of small oppressed nations to the world revolution, Lenin was also dismissing the misleading doctrine of "pure" or abstract working-class revolution. In his period as well as ours, the proletarian movement could not be the revolution, but could only **lead** a revolution composed of differing class, national, and political forces:

"To imagine that social revolution is **conceivable** without revolts by small nations in the

RUSSIAN PEASANTS   4157-10

colonies and in Europe, without revolutionary outbursts by a section of the petty bourgeoisie **with all its prejudices**, without a movement of the politically non-conscious proletarian and semi-proletarian masses against oppression by the landowners, the church, and the monarchy, against national oppression, etc.— to imagine all this is to **repudiate social revolution**. So one army lines up in one place and says, 'We are for socialism', and another, somewhere else and says, 'We are for impe-

rialism', and that will be a social revolution! Only those who hold such a ridiculously pedantic view could vilify the Irish rebellion by calling it a 'putsch.'"[2]

When the Russian Revolution itself is examined we can understand Lenin's heated insistence on the importance of national liberation struggles to the world future. The 1917 Bolshevik Revolution was world-historic, marking the communist movement's breakthrough in creating the **first modern communist party**, organized on a professional revolutionary basis and guided by pro-letarian ideology. For years this party had done political struggle with European revisionism, upholding the right of oppressed nations to self-determination in both theory and practice. It was a party that had consciously struggled internally for a correct understanding of internationalism.

Lenin's fight against false internationalism within the movement and especially within his own party was important. Like the "u.s.a.", Czarist Russia was not really a nation but an empire. The dominant Great Russian oppressor nation had annexed many smaller nations into its continental Empire. False internationalist views downgraded the importance of these oppressed nations, with many in the Russian movement wanting to simply continue the old Empire under new "socialist" management. As Lenin kept pointing out, the Party was calling itself "Russian" in its name even though it was not Russian, but an all-Empire party with much of its membership non-Russian. Great Russian chauvinism and hidden attraction to Russianism even had many followers among communists from the oppressed nations. It was only because the party managed to hold to a correct line on internationalism that it was able to develop.

What we are told about this revolution is that it remains the model of a "pure" workers uprising. Supposedly the militant workers' councils in Petrograd, Moscow, and the other main cities, led by the Bolshevik Party, overthrew capitalism by suddenly storming the palace and other cen-ters of power. These are the images popularized by the Hollywood movie "Reds." All this is shallow—to the point of being misleading half-truths.

To understand the Bolshevik Party we have to look at its early practice, the reality of long years of surviving and building an illegal (and armed) underground apparatus. One key to their initial organizational survival was the fact that the **Bolsheviks had a rear base area only a few miles from the Russian capital of**

RUSSIA AND EUROPE 1801 - 1825

Area in which all landless serfs were given their freedom 1816

Estates between Novgorod and Vologda from which 1600 male serfs and their families were sold to the owner of iron factories near Viatka; they resisted their transfer with arms, 1812-1813. In 1814 they were put down by armed force

Centres of conversion to Judaism 1796-1825. In 1825 all settlements were destroyed and the converts banished to Siberia and the Caucasus

Provinces in which Alexander I established Military Colonies 1810-1825. He hoped to create a permanent, self-sufficient military class, and turned complete villages of peasants into army camps. All male adults under 45 in selected areas had to wear military uniforms; children over 7 were given special military training

Conferences at which Russian influence was paramount, first in refusing to allow the desmemberment of defeated France; then in setting up a Polish state under Russian control; finally in upholding the supremacy of autocratic states

National revolutions outside Russia, to which Alexander I was opposed, and against which he supported Great Power intervention

Territory annexed by Russia, 1809-1815, Tarnopol was annexed in 1801 but returned to Austria in 1815

European frontiers in 1815

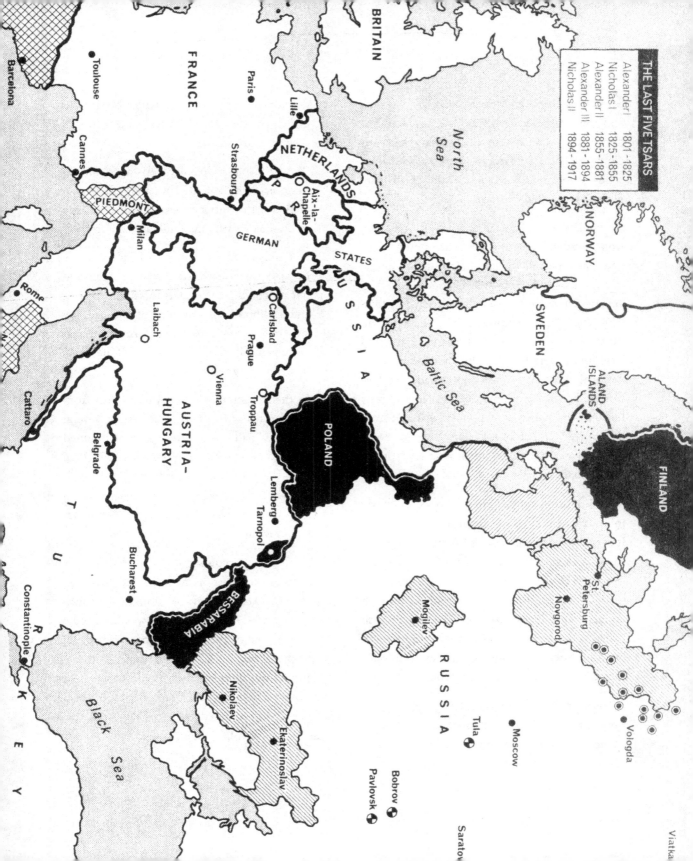

THE LAST FIVE TSARS

Alexander I	1801 - 1825
Nicholas I	1825 - 1855
Alexander II	1855 - 1881
Alexander III	1881 - 1894
Nicholas II	1894 - 1917

BRITAIN

FRANCE

Barcelona

Toulouse

Paris

Lille

Cannes

Strasbourg

NETHERLANDS

Aix-la-Chapelle

PIEDMONT

Milan

GERMAN STATES

P
R
U
S
S
I
A

NORTH Sea

NORWAY

SWEDEN

Rome

Cattaro

Laibach

Carlsbad

Prague

Vienna

Troppau

Baltic Sea

ALAND ISLANDS

FINLAND

AUSTRIA-HUNGARY

POLAND

Belgrade

Lemberg

Tarnopol

RUSSIA

St. Petersburg

Novgorod

Mogilev

T
U
R
K
E
Y

Bucharest

BESSARABIA

Nikolaev

Ekaterinoslav

Black Sea

Constantinople

Tula

Moscow

Vologda

Bobrov

Pavlovsk

Saratov

Viatka

St. Petersburg. This was as life-giving to Lenin and the early Bolsheviks as the mountain border regions were to Mao, Zhu De, and the early Chinese Red Army. Their rear base was Finland, a semi-autonomous but subject nation to Czarism. Finland was called "the Red base."

Finland was a Russian possession, (obtained from Sweden), but one which for ninety years had been permitted to retain much internal autonomy—with its own legal code, police, university system, and so on. That changed in 1898, when the Russian Empire appointed a new colonial Governor-General, Nicholas Bobrikov, and gave him orders to gradually strip away all the national rights the Finnish people had. This gave birth to a broad movement of anti-Russian resistance by the Finns, of all political leanings from left to right. In that atmosphere Russian revolutionaries received the sympathetic help of the Finnish nation.

The Finnish capital, Helsinki, was only forty miles from the Czarist capital of St. Petersburg. It became a sanctuary where Russians wanted by the Czarist secret police could quickly hide out. More important, for years much of the practical work of the Bolsheviks was organized through Finland. One historian describes how Finnish patriotic reaction to Great Russian tyranny swiftly evolved from non-violent to violent resistance, including support for Russian revolutionaries:

"Passive resistance to Bobrikov's policy was organized by a group known as the Kagal. One of its leading members, Adolf Torngren, developed close contacts with Russian liberals, but also occasionally helped Russian revolutionaries.

"The principle of passive resistance was to stand firm on Finland's laws and refuse cooperation with arbitrary measures, such as, especially, the new system of military conscription.

"… Finnish officials were in a difficult position; Russian pressure was steadily intensified, and not all could be expected to sacrifice career and livelihood. The meaning of duty and loyalty, of law and conscience, formed an ever more painfully tangled knot, which there was no agreed way to unravel.

"In this situation, a few began to turn from passive to active resistance. After several schemes had been tried and abandoned, Bobrikov was eventually assassinated in June 1904. In November of that year, the Finnish party of active resistance was formed, with a programme of collaboration with Russian revolutionaries."[3]

This scholarly account goes on to describe how Finland lived up to its name as the "Red base," given it by the Bolshevik Vladimir Smirnov. As Smirnov was half-Finnish, he was assigned as an organizer of the support base, in coordination with the armed underground. Although Smirnov was working visibly among the masses, building solidarity, his style of work was different from that considered by us as "legal" or "public." He used a false identity and full cover, for example, and communicated clandestinely. The Bolsheviks' mass work was regularly done with the use of clandestine methods and coordinated with all other areas of work (even those that were underground and armed). In other words, mass work and being "aboveground" didn't mean lack of precautions, secrecy, etc. "Above" and "under" were more a question of compartmentalization rather than the widespread error in our movements that regards mass work as needing no security precautions or clandestinity.

"The description of Finland by Smirnov as 'the Red base' is borne out by many documents in the archives of the governor-general of Finland. On the whole, Finnish police and officials performed their duties in accordance with Finnish law, and were reluctant to accept Russian direction. The Russians had their gendarmerie in Finland, but its powers were limited. The Finnish police would hold suspects only for a certain time; arrested Russian revolutionaries were set free after a month, unless proper documentation of the crimes they were alleged to have committed in Russia was received from the Russian authorities within that time.

"This Finnish law saved the chief underground organizer of the Russian social democrats, Leonid Krasin ('Nikitich'), by profession an electrical engineer (and a brilliant one, as he was later an outstanding Soviet diplomat; at his death in 1926 he was Soviet representative in London).

"Arrested in Finland in March 1908, Krasin was imprisoned in Viipuri. Several attempts to escape failed. But after a month he was freed, as the Russian authorities had not supplied the necessary documentation to justify his continued detention.

"The staff and students of a bolshevik school and workshop for explosives, situated in Finland, who were arrested in 1907, were given up to Russia only after a prolonged legal battle between Finnish and Russian authorities.

…

"Smirnov and his colleagues could count on help from many ordinary Finns, in addition to socialists and active resisters, in the work of forwarding literature (ferried from Stockholm) from Turku and Helsinki to St. Petersburg.

"Among the most useful helpers were Smirnov's old mother, in whose knitting secret messages were always safely concealed, and Finnish engine-drivers, manning the trains that went through to the Finland station in St. Petersburg. Arrived there, literature was taken away by workmen in their tool-boxes.

"A Finnish railway official in St. Petersburg gave Smirnov contacts among station staffs along the whole line between Viipuri and the frontier station of Beloostrov. For urgent messages, it was even possible to use the private channels of the railway telegraphic system.

"When revolutionaries are described as being 'in Finland' at this time, it should be remembered that this often meant small places, such as Terijoki and Kuokkala, on the railway line close to the Russian frontier, only a few miles from St. Petersburg. Not all writers seem aware of this; one sometimes reads for example of Lenin retreating 'deep into Finland', when his refuges were usually within about forty miles of the Russian capital, and his couriers could commute almost as quickly as though between London and St. Albans, Stockholm and Sodertalje, or Copenhagen and Roskilde.

Vladimir Smirnov

"At the beginning of 1903, Smirnov became a teacher in Russian at the University of Helsinki. With the widespread anti-Tsarist mood in Finland, he had no difficulty in finding assistance. Sometimes he received useful information from the deputy police chief of Helsinki, through friends in shipping he could obtain cut-price steamer tickets, and later had Lenin's manuscripts typed in Finnish government offices. His home in Helsinki became the chief intermediate stage for revolutionaries travelling to or from Russia, including Lenin and (in 1907) Trotsky.

"Revolutionaries could even assemble in Finland in fair safety, and many large and small meetings were held there, such as the bolshevik conference at Tampere in December 1905, when Stalin met Lenin for the first time."[4]

The support network organized by Smirnov delivered funds to a section of the underground responsible for military affairs. Finnish radicals became familiar with a young Russian pianist whose real name was Nicholas Burenin:

"Burenin was known in Finland as an amateur impresario, arranging charity concerts for needy Russians. Finnish resisters knew him as 'Victor Petrovich', one of the mysterious Russians who kept appearing in Helsinki. Adolf Torngren described him as a pleasant young man evidently of wealthy family, son of a Moscow cotton king, and added condescendingly that he seemed somewhat vague and unpractical.

"This talented pianist Burenin, after the bolshevik revolution for a time director of the Soviet State Opera, must often have smiled his agreeable smile when telling Finns as little as possible of his real affairs. From early 1905, he was head of the bolshevik fighting organization in St. Petersburg, under Krasin's direction. As Smirnov was the expert in smuggling literature through Finland, so was Burenin the specialist in weapons and explosives.

…

"Burenin, too, advanced far in the underground. When the bolsheviks began to prepare for uprising in St. Petersburg and established early in 1905 a fighting organization with Burenin, responsible to Krasin, at its head, the main task was finding arms.

"They were scarce. But miscellaneous weapons, and particularly explosives for bombs, could sometimes be obtained in Finland—there were many reports of stores of explosives being raided—and rifles were sneaked out of the arms factory at Sestroretsk, near the frontier, where several workers in the factory assisted.

"The transport of such valuables to the capital occupied several specialists, of both sexes. Afterwards, women particularly recalled the harsh reek of dynamite (known conspiratively as 'uncle', and worn in belts and bandages close to the body)—overpowering when sweating in a close atmosphere. They used to apply strong scent heavily, and travelled for preference on the open platform at the end of the railway carriage, even in hard frost.

"Rifles were divided into barrels and stocks, and the pieces suspended from a towel or cord tied around the neck. Some girl students became virtuosos in this art, and could carry up to eight rifles.

"A transporter laden with rifles in this way was not able to bend. This could be awkward. One girl, known as 'Fat Fanny', was once rigged out with rifles together with a male colleague, 'Molecule'. Suddenly Molecule noticed that a piece of cord, part of Fanny's apparatus for carrying rifles, was trailing from beneath her skirt. Neither could bend, and the street was full of people. The threat of discovery was averted by boarding a double-deck tram and Fanny mounting the stairs to the top deck first, while Molecule wound up the cord behind her.

…

"Not all the adventures of Burenin and his group were so whimsical. Several enthusiastic amateurs set about producing bombs. Burenin was once presented with a basket containing home-made infernal machines. An expert he consulted was horrified at their primitive construction, and told him to get rid of them at once, no easy task. So half an hour before he was to play at a concert, Burenin found himself scrabbling on the steep and slippery bank of a canal, trying to drown a dangerous bomb.

"The situation was improved by setting up a bomb workshop and chemical group, which had a distinctly scholarly atmosphere—leading members were 'Alpha' and 'Omega', while the expert advisor was a professor known as 'Ellipse'. On Krasin's instructions, Trotsky, a leader of the St. Petersburg Soviet in 1905, was supplied with two powerful hand grenades by this group. Plans for a satisfactory bomb were obtained from a Bulgarian expert in Macedonia, and large quantities of fuses, bought in France, were imported through Finland. 'Natasha' specialized in this job, travelling with her infant daughter as cover.

Russian hangman

"For the comings and goings in Finland of Burenin's group, the chief meeting-place was a well-known liquor shop in Helsinki run by Valter Sjoberg. This was an ideal centre, easy to find with its conspicuous sign, and visited by all sorts of people. Sjoberg was unfailingly helpful, whether the job was corseting Natasha with fuses, contacting shipping firms, or passing on tips from the Finnish police. Another advantage was that next door was a barber's shop, useful for quick changes.

"... It may seem strange that revolutionaries were able to leave or enter Finland with little difficulty. For this they had to thank particularly their Finnish friends like Sjoberg in Helsinki, and a socialist, Valter Borg, in Turku, who had influence with shipping firms. Passport control, too, was normally carried out not by Russian gendarmes, but by the Finnish police."[5]

This look at the practical details of the Bolshevik Party shows how they were not super-human revolutionary figures. They were a handful of young rebels, overcoming their inexperience and struggling to build an organization that was not only clandestine but professional. Before the 1905 Revolution there were less than two hundred Bolshevik cadre. Their tactics were crude and makeshift. But they were able to build a revolutionary vanguard against a powerful Empire because they joined with the rising tide of Finnish national consciousness. **Only those who refuse to see revolution as it actually is, can**

fail to see the connection between the breakthrough of world socialism and the rebellion of a very small, oppressed nation. The Finns combined a struggle against their own bourgeoisie and the oppressing Czarist Empire with aid to the revolutionaries of the Great Russian oppressor nation. They were practicing internationalism, which in turn aided their own struggle for independence. Who can say that the Finnish national struggle, which never reached the stage of successfully overthrowing its own bourgeoisie, still had not made an important contribution to world revolution?

Even after the bitter defeat of the 1905 Revolution and the increased severity of Czarist rule, the Finnish people aided the Bolsheviks whenever possible. When the chief Bolshevik organizer in Finland was arrested in 1908, the Finnish police released him (so he could escape) on technical grounds.

In 1907 the Czarist repression had become so fierce that Lenin's underground security was no longer good enough. He was forced to leave for Western Europe. Since it was unsafe to try and take ship passage straight from Helsinki, Lenin hid out in the remote Aland Islands, between Sweden and Finland, until he could get an outbound ship. Alone, Lenin was taken care of by Finnish farmers and workers. Even the policemen patrolling one island helped take care of him. Lenin told the Finns that a nation whose police fought oppressors would surely get independence. Ten years later Lenin again had to take

shelter in Finland. This time, in July 1917 when the bourgeois Kerensky government, which had briefly filled the void when Czarism fell, ordered Lenin's arrest as an alleged German agent. Lenin was secretly protected by the chief of the Helsinki militia (which was then functioning as the local police), the very person who was supposed to be leading the hunt for Lenin.[6]

This seldom-discussed story is only one chapter in the relationship between the proletarian struggle in Russia and the liberation struggles of oppressed nations. It refutes an abstract picture

Nadezhda Krupskaya, coordinator of the Bolshevik underground network

of the Bolshevik Revolution that has been spread here in the US Empire. Not only was the role of the small oppressed nations much greater in the Bolshevik Revolution than we have been told, **but their struggle was more like ours than we may think**. Making revolution was not just orating before crowds of factory workers. The problems of correct political line and the problems of practical work drove the young Bolsheviks.

Starting with nothing but will, every step involved innumerable new practical challenges—from underground security problems, to distributing political literature to the masses, to recruiting people to carry raw explosives past the Czarist customs inspectors (similar to the Battle of Algiers). We should not forget that their small party was underground, hardened by years of practical work and terrible setbacks—virtually wiped out after the defeats of 1906–1907. It was precisely such a party that could grasp the interrelationship of national liberation to socialist revolution—especially inside "their own" empire.

Here history gives a warning—no one and no party can simply rest on their laurels. The two-line struggle on the national question within the Bolshevik Party reversed itself after the new Soviet government was formed. Great Russian national chauvinism in false internationalist disguise crept back into power. Lenin, who had led the principled battle against this new deviation, was increasingly isolated politically within the Party in his last few years of life. He was in a small minority within the Party. The other major Party leaders, including Stalin and Trotsky, all opposed his views. Lenin, ever forthright, wrote: **"Scratch a Bolshevik and you'll find a Great Russian chauvinist."** His death in 1923 marked a nodal point. Henceforth, Russian oppressor nation chauvinism would do its work disguised as internationalism. This had an unanticipated effect on the development of the world revolution.

In the making of their Revolution the Bolsheviks not only showed internationalism in practice, but provided lessons for us about the importance of small nations as well as large ones. There is a tendency within the US Empire, fostered by colonial domination, to consider only the "u.s.a." a "real" nation. Small nations such as Hawaii, New Afrika, Independent Oglala Nation, etc. are widely—even by Third World people—not thought of as either very real or politically decisive. The notion that small oppressed nations are as real as large oppressor nations is one that still needs reinforcing here. And practice proves that small nations such as Finland or Guinea-Bissau or Vietnam can, at decisive points in the struggle, exercise a world-historic influence.

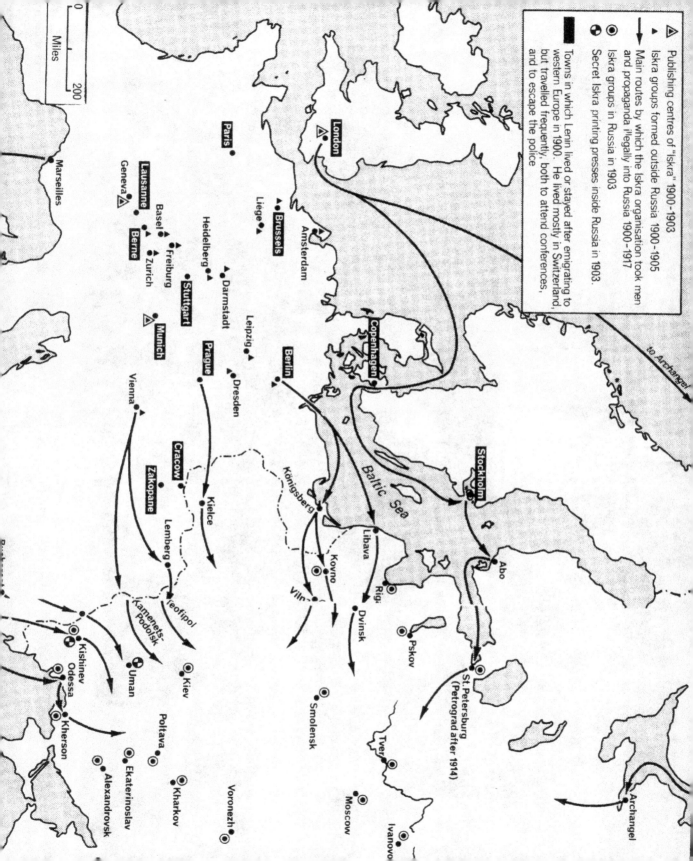

Publishing centres of "Iskra" 1900-1903

Iskra groups formed outside Russia 1900-1905

Main routes by which the Iskra organisation took men and propaganda illegally into Russia in 1903

Iskra groups in Russia in 1903

Secret Iskra printing presses inside Russia in 1903

Towns in which Lenin lived or stayed after emigrating to western Europe in 1900. He lived mostly in Switzerland, but travelled frequently, both to attend conferences, and to escape the police

II. False Internationalism in China

False internationalism is a dangerous weapon against revolution in the hands of revisionism, because it uses genuine respect for proletarian unity in order to reintroduce oppressor nation hegemony. Proletarian unity is the recognition that the oppressed and exploited masses of the world, led by the proletariat as a world class, not only have common interests but make up a world socialist revolution. False internationalism tries to manipulate this need for unity across national lines in different ways: in Eurocentric or oppressor-nation dominated politics, in liquidating national liberation activities into "international" forms unresponsive to the masses, and so on. **What is common in this is that despite the good intentions of so many revs who get caught up in such things, the results are really neo-colonial. We can see this in our own histories.**

Within the communist movement, there was a period when the issue of false internationalism took on world significance. That was the Comintern period of 1920–1943, when modern communist parties were first being born throughout the world under the direction of the Soviet Union. In every case these young parties had to undergo many trials. Communists who could not understand false internationalism were in all cases defeated by revisionism. **In Europe, Afrika, Asia, Latin Amerika, and North Amerika, those national movements and communist parties which could not pass that trial were destroyed.** The defeat of proletarian movements in Algeria, Mexico, Italy, New Afrika, and many other nations then is recorded in history. The experiences of this Comintern period allow us to throw light on our own movements today.

Again, we must remember that false internationalism is an **alliance** between petty-bourgeois/lumpen elements in both oppressor and oppressed nations. In this alliance the "allies" are used to promote opportunist elements into leadership over the colonial peoples. This is not an unfamiliar mechanism when practiced by imperialism itself. After all, indigenous nations continually have to struggle against "tribal chiefs" and "tribal chairmen" installed by the US government as neo-colonial puppets. And New Afrikans are also used to having the US Empire finance and publicize selected leaders for them (ministers, bourgeois politicians, civil rights leaders, etc.) instead of any they might choose themselves.

But this is not, unfortunately, a distant phenomenon; rather, one that is politically too near to us. For even within revolutionary movements, "allies" are found to help promote one petty-bourgeois/lumpen group or another as the supposed leaders of the oppressed nation. In the mid-1970s, US settler Left groups were falling all over themselves to proclaim the Puerto Rican Socialist Party (PSP) as the leadership of the Puerto Rican liberation struggle—although that party was only **one** of a number of PR revolutionary organizations and not necessarily the most correct. The same thing happens within the New Afrikan Liberation Movement, in which petty-bourgeois/lumpen cliques are partially sustained and pushed forward by various settler Left "allies," who proclaim them as their selected leadership for the New Afrikan nation. The Comintern experience shows us how common such false internationalism has been in world politics.

How powerful a revisionist tool is false internationalism? Picture the following scenario: A young communist leader named Mao Zedong was suddenly thrown out of the Red Army, although he had successfully fought for six years to build a worker-peasant guerrilla army of a new type. Overnight Mao was removed from his post as political commissar of the Red Army, removed as secretary of the Soviet area united front committee. A new party security apparatus purged those cadre who tried to still practice Mao's political-military doctrines. Some guerrillas who supported Mao were summarily dealt with as supposed security risks.

To replace the "opportunist" Mao Zedong, the party leadership introduced an obscure German "communist" as the new secret leader of China's Red Army. This untried European had great authority, since he had just been sent from the Comintern to oversee the Army. He was supposedly much more "Marxist" than Mao, a top European military expert. The German's military writings, published under a Chinese pseudonym, were hailed by the party leaders as an improvement on Mao's. Red cadres and soldiers were set to studying the German leader's strategy, which was to replace all the strategy and tactics learned in a hundred battles by the Red Army.

Unfortunately, that German's military learning came from a classroom in Moscow; he had never been in an army or won a battle. His Chinese allies didn't care how many defeats he led the Chinese people into, since with his backing they could at last isolate Mao Zedong and his ideas. Finally the criminally incompetent generalship of the German and his Chinese allies led to the loss of the entire liberated zone—hundreds of thousands of peasants died, and in the German leader's panicked flight half the central Red Army was lost. In one stupid river crossing the German got 30,000 Red fighters killed. Red commanders had found their units decimated in a few weeks. Within six weeks he had lost two-thirds of the revolutionary army. That was a time of bitter losses, of possible extinction.

To us this scenario may sound so strange that it is little short of science-fiction. It was real, however. Those incredible events did take place in China during the years of 1932–1935. Party, army, and national liberation movement took terrible blows, and faced extermination, before that epidemic of false internationalism was broken. Even a strong party and an army of three hundred thousand soldiers was brought almost to its knees. It would be arrogant for us to believe that we are somehow so advanced that false internationalism is no problem for us. As we shall see, People's War in China could only develop, step by step, in intense two-line struggle within the Revolution.

There are several things about the Comintern (Communist International) that we should notice. First, that it was the most sweeping experiment in organizational internationalism the communist movement has ever seen. **One single structure united communists in over sixty nations, deliberately disregarding national distinctions**. Although people were very careful to publicly say that the Comintern's relationship to individual communist parties was only "advi-

Delegates at the Second Congress of the Comintern.

sory," the Comintern was in reality a disciplined world super-party. The member communist parties were even referred to as "national sections." While day-to-day leadership rested in the hands of the various national communist parties, the Comintern's center in the USSR ultimately led every communist in the world.

The Communist International was part of a European socialist tradition, and was the third of the internationals. Starting from the days of Marx and Engels, it was the practice of European revolutionary parties to all unite in continental associations. It was therefore quite natural for the Bolsheviks to initiate a new ("Third") international to oppose the already existing Second International of the reformist Social-Democratic Parties. Although the Comintern was founded in 1919 by the Russians, it didn't become a true world body until the 2nd Congress in June 1920. The Bolsheviks had issued a call for left socialists in Europe to split their parties and regroup into new communist parties around their new socialist state. In colonial nations they called upon revolutionaries to join the new international first individually, and later as whole parties. To join the Comintern was a heavy matter, and one by one, in nation after nation, new communists joined in the spirit of internationalism, to become full participants in the world communist movement. In many nations this decision took time. In Vietnam, for example, revolutionaries were not able to form a communist party and decide to join the Comintern until 1930.

While the Comintern was first organized to coordinate the Europe-wide revolution (particularly in Germany) that communists expected within a few years, from the start Third World revolutionaries were involved. Ho Chi Minh, in exile in France, became a founding member of the French Communist Party in 1920. Sen Katayama, the founder of Japanese communism, was likewise a founding member of the Communist Party USA in 1919. New Afrikan revolutionaries had gone to Moscow for consultation with Lenin and the other Bolshevik leaders.

In form nothing appeared more internationalist to young communists than that. It was a very ambitious step, and in the 1920s and 1930s the Comintern seemed to give the oppressed a world army, complete with proven general staff, fully strong enough to take on imperialism. Comintern representatives from the Moscow center crisscrossed the world secretly bearing orders for new strategies and needed funds, bringing foreign experts to guide strikes, publications or uprisings. Even when the Chinese Red soldiers had no other insignia, they wore simple armbands with two slogans—**"Support the Communist International"** and **"Make the Land Revolution."** The enthusiasm among the revolutionary masses for the Comintern in the beginning years was tremendous.

The second thing about the Comintern was that it represented one form of unity, arising from a concrete historical situation. Many comrades regard internationalism as something like universal brotherhood and sisterhood. To the contrary, internationalism is always realized in specific relationships, with a definite historical and political character. The Comintern was born in the drive of the USSR, the world's first socialist state, to rapidly generalize its revolutionary breakthrough from a regional to a world scale. So the Comintern was set up to actually carry out the world revolution. **It was hoped that by using the historic example, the already-proven leadership, and the material resources of the USSR in a giant short-cut, capitalism could be swept away entirely in a few years.** A completely socialist world was envisioned as an immediate goal, led by industrial Europe. Were this to fail, the Bolsheviks feared that imperialism might crush their infant socialism with military and economic encirclement. V. I. Lenin wrote in June 1920 for the 2nd Congress of the Comintern:

> "The world political situation has now placed the dictatorship of the proletariat on the order of the day, and all events in world politics are inevitably revolving around one central point, viz., the struggle of the world bourgeoisie against the Soviet Russian Republic, around which are inevitably grouping, on the one hand, the movement for Soviets among the advanced workers of all countries, and, on the other, all the national liberation movements in the colonies and among the oppressed nationalities ... Consequently, one cannot confine oneself at the present time to the bare recognition or proclamation of the need for

closer union between the working people of the various nations; it is necessary to pursue a policy that will achieve the closest alliance of all the national and colonial liberation movements with Soviet Russia ..."[1]

This Comintern of the Bolsheviks made positive contributions to the world revolution in the early 1920s, initially helping to spread modern communism to many peoples. But it quickly became a new roadblock to revolution. A Russian-oriented organization and a Russian-oriented political strategy was unable to meet the needs of widely diverse national situations. Far worse, the explicit dogma of Russian superiority in political matters fostered a revival of crude European chauvinism in new revolutionary dress. The supposedly internationalist form of the Comintern too often boiled down to arrogant foreign agents "meddling in our affairs" (to use Mao's words); their alliances were with petty-bourgeois revisionists who were only too glad to trade away the self-reliance of their own people. Russian intervention did not mean that there was a frank, respectful, two-way exchange of views on political matters, or that criticism on possible errors was shared. The Comintern had one-way criticism, which tried to impose Russian views on anti-colonial struggles whether the oppressed nation agreed or not.

The most important effect of Russian oppressor nation intervention was not the pushing of wrong policies—it was the symbiotic relationship with opportunist cliques within the national

Li Dazhao (1888-1927), one of the founders of the Chinese Communist Party. "Li Dazhao became, during his relatively brief life, which ended in execution by strangulation, the single most important radical political influence in his time, the first impressive Chinese interpreter of Marxism, and the first major contributor to a system or ideology which may be called Chinese Marxist thought. To say that without Li Dazhao there could have been no Mao Zedong may be an overstatement, but some of the main features of Mao's thought are explicit or implicit in the writings of Li Dazhao, which Mao implements in action."

liberation movements. Just as the remote peasant areas were the sheltering rear base for Mao Zedong and the correct revolutionary line, **so the Comintern and Russia became the rear base for petty-bourgeois opportunism within the Chinese revolution.** False internationalism was thus welcomed and promoted by certain types of Chinese leaders who were petty-bourgeois nationalists. This has parallels to the struggles within the US Empire, where the US settler Left has acted as the rear-base area to aid and promote opportunist Black leadership that has misled their liberation struggle.

Comintern internationalism was ultimately false, because it was both an unequal unity based on oppressor nations still dictating to the oppressed nations, and an incorrect perspective of building movements whose leadership was not responsible to the masses. **Correct relations between revolutionaries of different nations must be based on the principle of equality and mutual respect; this means respect for the right of self-determination of the oppressed nations in all matters.** Communists must uphold the principle that the masses of an oppressed nation are the masters of their own destiny, and must be responsible to them by adhering firmly to their interests, to the foundation and objectives of the liberation struggle, and by "committing class suicide" in firmly merging themselves into the new proletariat.

While modern communism spread "like a prairie fire" across the colonial world, the Com-

毛泽东　　董必武　　李达　　刘任静　　王尽美　　陈公博

何叔衡　　陈潭秋　　李汉俊　　张国焘　　邓恩铭　　周佛海

Delegates at the First National Congress of the Communist Party of China, 1921.
First row from left: Mao Zedong, Dong Biwu, Li Da, Liu Renjing, Wang Jinmei, Chen Gongbo.
Second row from left: He Shuheng, Chen Tanqiu, Li Hanjun, Zhang Guotao, Deng Enming, Zhou Fohai.

intern's European-centered outlook fostered a fad of Third World imitation Russians. To these eager students everything European was scientific, while everything to do with their own national struggles and story was backward. Revolutionary leaders like Ho Chi Minh and Mao Zedong were labeled "bourgeois nationalists." Even in Vietnam it had reached the point by 1934 that the *Bolshevik,* theoretical journal of the Indochinese Communist Party, proclaimed that Ho Chi Minh **"advocated erroneous reformist and collaborationist tactics ... based on his bourgeois nationalism."**[2] Ho's "error" was urging his comrades to lead in building a broad national liberation front against the colonial enemy. Far from providing advanced international leadership to new communist parties, the Comintern was wittingly or unwittingly an international structure to accelerate the most unrealistic and opportunistic tendencies within the national movements. We can accurately judge the level of political confusion by the sight of even our Vietnamese comrades denouncing their nation's greatest revolutionary leader.

CHINA: THIRTEEN YEARS OF STRUGGLE

Correct leadership for the revolutionary war in China was forged in a two-line political struggle that lasted twenty-five years (thirteen years of which saw the correct ideas in the minority). False internationalism played a major role against that liberation struggle. This was the clearest possible example of an opportunism that covered itself with false internationalism, and its effect on the armed struggle.[3]

In this current season we can learn a lot from that two-line struggle. All too often comrades become discouraged because advanced ideas have not yet prevailed inside the struggle. Others dismiss the worth of advanced ideas at all, arguing that these ideas have been passed around but folks in the movement for whatever reason won't pick them up. Yet Mao Zedong, one of the greatest revolutionary leaders in history, was in the political minority within his party for 13 years. Several times he was dismissed from the leadership of the party. More than several times he lost command of the army. His advanced ideas were opposed by the combined past and present leadership of the party, plus all "foreign friends," despite the fact that for many years he could prove that the customary, "regular" way of doing things was a disaster.

New answers, new ideas, cannot get taken up by acclamation on first hearing, and are in fact not even developed at first. **Advanced ideas here have not been successful in large part because they have not been so advanced, still being a mixture of old bourgeois ideas, revolutionary ideas applied in a mechanical way, and so on.** Only protracted struggle, which definitely includes real scientific methods of analysis, can arrive at correct answers. What separated Mao from the established Movement leadership was not thirteen years: his thinking was in a different place; his outlook was proletarian in that it was firmly rooted amidst the oppressed while applying real scientific methods to create the conditions for success.

To understand the influence of false internationalism we have to see how powerful the impact of the Bolshevik Revolution was on the Chinese people. Their liberation struggle had gone on for generations, yet still the "dark night of slavery" held China in its grip. While China was the largest nation on earth, and one which had reached a high stage of civilization when Europe was still in the Dark Ages, she was by 1920 a backward neo-colony of imperialism. The old Manchu Dynasty still sat on the imperial throne in the palace in Beijing, but each foreign power had its own enclaves, bases, its own economic enterprises, and its own troops on Chinese soil. Britain, France, Germany, Belgium, Italy, Russia, the USA, and Japan jealously ruled China together. Chaos and misery grew. China's own native handicraft industries had been wiped out by cheaper industrial imports, while minerals and even the railroads were owned by Western imperialism. Since China was very large, but with a decaying society and a weak central government, vast areas had fallen into chaos. Much of China was ruled by one or another warlord army. These warlord armies were like giant street gangs, swelled by homeless peasants and engaging in looting for survival. The warlords themselves were wealthy, paid by the local landlords and the foreign interests. China was a scene of constant civil war between all these armies, and no national unity at all.

Dr. Sun Yat-sen

During the fifteen year Taiping Rebellion a rebel army distributed land to the peasants and unbound women's feet before being finally crushed by the Western-aided imperial forces at the Dadu River in 1864. In 1911 the Great Revolution took place, ending the decadent imperial government. But the new bourgeois democratic government of Dr. Sun Yat-sen, the "father of modern China," tried in vain to establish a democratic republic by paying some warlords to serve as an army for his government of unification. Masses of Chinese patriots had taken part in these national wars. Young Mao Zedong first became a patriotic soldier in the nationalist armies of 1911, ten years before he became a communist. After almost a century of uprisings, mass movements and civil wars, the Chinese people were still searching for the correct path that would lead them to victory.

The Bolshevik Revolution, which not only overthrew capitalism but also successfully defended itself against the invading armies of the US, France, Britain, Japan, and other capitalist nations, attracted much interest in China. Many democratic-minded patriots saw in this communism the long-sought-after answer for China's future. In June 1922 Dr. Sun Yat-sen met with one of China's most brilliant commanders, Brigadier General Zhu De. He wanted Gen. Zhu De to rejoin his forces and help lead another military expedition to subdue the northern warlords who held Beijing. Zhu De and his companion, another nationalist officer, fraternally refused. Zhu De, who went on to command the Red Army, recalled:

"… I had lost all faith in such tactics as the alliances which Dr. Sun and his Guomindang followers made with this or that militarist.

Such tactics had always ended in defeat for the revolution and the strengthening of the warlords. We ourselves had spent eleven years of our lives in such a squirrel cage. The Chinese Revolution had failed, while the Russian Revolution had succeeded, and the Russians had succeeded because they were Communists with a theory and a method of which we were ignorant.

"We told Dr. Sun Yat-sen that we had decided to study abroad, to meet Communists and study Communism, before re-entering national affairs in China."[4]

Communism took root in China, gradually becoming a material force as it was taken up by the workers and peasants. Soon in some areas peasants noticed that even the mention of this new word made the hated landlords afraid—and took to shouting communist slogans at them even when they didn't know who or what this communism was, just to enjoy the effect it had. Dr. Sun Yat-sen had turned all China over by putting forward his new program, the famous Three People's Principles to save the nation: national independence, political democracy, socialism. In 1923 Dr. Sun led the nationalist movement into a historic alliance with the Soviet Union and the small Chinese Communist Party. This was the first United Front, when bourgeois nationalists and communists openly worked together in the Guomindang government.

In the 1923–1927 period of the First United Front the two-line struggle emerged very sharply within the ranks of the Revolution. The Party secretary-general was then Chen Duxiu, one of the most prestigious of China's Mandarin intellectuals. He was someone who feared struggle. Chen Duxiu was just a front-man, however. The de facto leader of Chinese Communism was Mikhail Borodin, the famous special representative of the Bolshevik Party Politburo to the Guomindang. Borodin was a Bolshevik who had spent the ten years before the revolution in Valparaiso, Indiana (where he went to college) and Chicago, where he and his Euro-Amerikan wife had been active in the movement. After the 1917 Revolution he had returned to Russia, and on the basis of his foreign experience was made an important Comintern agent. Borodin was no closet figure in China. He held court in Guangzhou, the nationalist capital; he spoke at mass meetings, negotiated with all political groups, was openly enjoying his role as one of the most powerful leaders over the Chinese nationalist movement. All the Chinese communist leaders, including Mao Zedong, had to come to Borodin to get their policies approved.

This European meddler made common cause with the conservative Chen Duxiu tendency within the Chinese Communist Party. Their joint policy was one of "all unity and no struggle" with the Chinese bourgeoisie. Comintern policy saw the first priority as the defeat of the reactionary warlords, with China reunified and made independent under the leadership of the bourgeoisie. The Comintern opposed a separate communist army, class struggle against the

Mikhail Borodin, Russian advisor to the Guomindang, speaking in Hankou, March 1927.

landlords, or communist uprisings. The nationalist united front was just, and desperately wanted by the masses. But when Borodin and Chen Duxiu so freely gave the bourgeoisie everything, with no communist army or giving power to the masses, they were really signing death warrants for millions.

Mao Zedong acidly summed Borodin up: **"Borodin stood just a little to the right of Chen Duxiu, and was ready to do everything to please the bourgeoisie, even to the disarming of the workers, which he finally ordered."** False internationalism literally ripped the guns out of the hands of the Chinese workers and peasants, and left them defenseless before the imperialist terror.

The USSR built up the Guomindang military to counter the warlords; although this nationalist army had many communist and patriotic officers and soldiers, in its overall character it was still a bourgeois warlord army. Borodin organized Whampoa, a new Guomindang military academy initially staffed with thirty Russian officers. A Russian general was sent to become the actual battle commander of the army. Even the small—and strongly patriotic—nationalist navy was commanded by a Russian officer. Borodin sent a young aide of Dr. Sun Yat-sen to Moscow for military training, grooming him to become commander-in-chief of the Guomindang military. This Chinese general professed his love for Russia and socialism in return for the Comintern's backing. His name was Chiang Kai-shek.

This nationalist united front expanded revolutionary consciousness among the masses, with worker and peasant unions and anti-imperialist organizations enlisting millions in the nationalist areas. Membership in the Communist Party grew in the first eleven months of 1925 from less than 1,000 to over 10,000 activists. With the sincere support of Dr. Sun Yat-sen, communists by 1925 took over leading roles in all branches of the nationalist movement. This was, however, a castle built on sand. The left–right split within

Peng Pai and Mao Zedong

the nationalist movement was not overcome, but was deepening.

During these eventful years the correct line of peasant revolutionary armed struggle under proletarian leadership began to emerge, under the leadership of Mao Zedong and Peng Pai (the great leader of the first peasant Soviet, who was killed by the imperialists in 1929). The achievements of this 1923–1927 period were considerable: the first scientific class analysis of Chinese society; the first revolutionary peasant organizers' school; the first militant peasant branch of the party.

While this correct revolutionary breakthrough was led by communists, it was opposed by their own Communist Party. Borodin's ally Chen Duxiu pushed the Party to spit on the peasant masses, saying: "… over half the peasants are petty bourgeois landed proprietors who adhere firmly to private property consciousness. How can they accept Communism?" Mao was forced out of the Party's Central Committee in 1925. At a special Politburo meeting the next year Mao tried to discuss the need for mobilizing the peasants before it was too late, but Secretary Chen Duxiu cut him off and denied him the right to speak. Looking back we can see why Mao summed up Chen, the Comintern's favorite leader at the time, as **"an unconscious traitor."** The Chinese Revolution did not smoothly and easily find the correct path to liberation; even basic "commonsense" ideas only prevailed after the most bitter political struggle over years.

The correct communist line, under attack from their own Party, grew in the environment of the broad nationalist movement. In 1924 the Guomindang agreed to set up a Peasant Institute, where peasants could receive full-time training to become nationalist organizers. Peng Pai was the first director. By 1925 Mao had returned to his native Hunan Province, where he conducted social investigation of the countryside, and began the first peasant branch of communists. The 32 cadres of the branch met in Mao's family home. In August 1926 Mao took over as director of the Guomindang Peasant Institute. Poor peasants from all over China got trained as communist organizers, with 128 class-hours out of the course's 380 hours secretly devoted to military training. Mao's peasant activities were regarded as so unimportant by both the Guomindang warlords and his own Party that they were overlooked. Simultaneously Mao became head of the Propaganda Department of the Guomindang, as well as an alternate member of the Guomindang Central Executive Committee. Quietly he was training a network of rural organizers to span China, to give the communist movement a real national mass base. His first class at the Peasant Institute had peasants from 21 provinces and Mongolia.

Suppressed by the Comintern-Chen bloc within the Party, Mao used the nationalist movement to prepare the liberation road to come. In March 1926 Mao wrote the first important theoretical work of the Chinese Revolution—*Analysis of Classes in Chinese Society*. It was the first scientific class analysis of the Chinese nation, as opposed to the ignorant rhetoric of Chen and his petty-bourgeois clique. This work also was used by Mao as a tool to teach cadres the need for actual social investigation to solve questions. The Communist Party rejected *Analysis of Classes in Chinese Society*, refusing to even let it be printed in the official Party publication. So Mao, who was editing several revolutionary nationalist political magazines, printed it in *Peasant Monthly* (the journal of the Peasant Institute). It was then reprinted in *Chinese Youth*, a revolutionary nationalist young soldier's journal edited by communist Zhou Enlai. The fundamental scientific analysis of the Chinese Revolution was thus first published within the broad nationalist movement, not by the Comintern-led Communist Party.

Mao's prolonged investigation of the countryside had led him to see the peasant masses as the key to liberation. "Formerly, I had not fully realized the degree of class struggle among the peasantry." In Hunan, Mao's home province, the peasants had a rich tradition of uprisings. They had played a large part in the Taiping Rebellion that raged for fifteen years in the 19th Century. In 1906 the Gelaohui, a secret peasant society, led an attempt to overthrow the old imperial government. Another armed uprising took place just three years later, leaving in its defeat a bloody wake of executions. In Mao's own village of Shaoshan he had witnessed the same secret society leading a revolt against a landlord, the rebel peasants having to flee to the mountains to survive as roving bandits.

In 1925 peasant unions and patriotic struggles spread rapidly in Hunan Province. The peasants not only fought the landlords, but demanded the liberation of their nation from colonialism. When the peasants couldn't understand the communist slogan "Down With Imperialism!"—imperialism was first translated into Chinese as "emperor-countryism"—Mao simply explained that it just meant "Down with rich foreigners!" A 1926 spontaneous peasant revolt in Hunan was crushed. Mao pointed out that the peasants not only displayed revolutionary consciousness, but that **"all the lumpen proletariat joined them very courageously."** He saw the main lesson of their defeat was that **"they did not have the proper leadership."** Mao in 1926 saw the oppressed masses as more advanced than their supposed leadership. He told a friend that if the Party would use the peasant cadres training at the Peasant Institute to start guerrilla war it would save the Revolution.

But the Comintern-Chen clique had no plans to go against the Chinese national bourgeoisie. Their right deviation undermined the revolution in all areas. Leadership of the national liberation movement was given to the bourgeoisie, who were supposed to lead the struggle against imperialism. The Land Revolution was chained by their policy of exempting families of allied Guomindang officers and warlords from expropriation; since all landlord families had such political connections, in practice the Comintern-Chen program was using the authority of the Revolution to protect the oppressors.

While Russian experts and guns poured into building the bourgeoisie a large national army, the Party itself had no military organization. Proclaiming that the main threat to the united front was "excesses" by angry workers and peasants, the Comintern-Chen clique kept the masses disarmed. Mao was ordered repeatedly to follow the line of "limitation of peasant struggle," to stop his peasant comrades from arming and mobilizing. Although the two-line struggle was very sharp, most communists were fooled by the authority of the "internationalist" clique.

This period ended in mid-1927. The fools' paradise of the Comintern-Chen clique collapsed as the bourgeoisie put its own class dictatorship into effect. So long as Dr. Sun Yat-sen had lived, his noble influence protected the patriotic united front. But in early 1925 he died of cancer, touching off a power struggle for control of the Guomindang. General Chiang Kai-shek, commander-in-chief of the army, seized power at gun point. Borodin and Chen Duxiu went along with him. For two confused years Chiang and his reactionary grouping gradually pushed communists and patriots out of key positions. Prominent patriots, particularly those formerly close to Dr. Sun Yat-sen, began to flee or were assassinated.

When the first arrests of communists by Chiang Kai-shek troops began in 1926, Borodin quickly explained it as due to communist "**excesses**." He ordered the Chinese communists to restore the united front by giving in to

Chiang Kai-shek on all matters. One of Chiang's first orders was to remove Zhou Enlai as political commissar at Whampoa military academy. The Comintern felt sure that Chiang Kai-shek was trustworthy, for they were bribing him with the money, arms, and international backing to become head of China. It never occurred to them that Chiang Kai-shek was negotiating for even bigger bribes from British, French, and US imperialism (who were his natural masters).

Chiang Kai-shek out-thought and out-maneuvered Stalin and the Comintern. To buy time he sent his son to Moscow as a hostage. Knowing that the Comintern-Chen clique would swallow any pretense of his loyalty to them, he gave fiery speeches manipulating their own fantasies: **"The Communist International is the headquarters of the world revolution ... We must unite with Russia to overthrow Imperialism."** At a Comintern meeting in December 1926, Stalin personally rebuked uneasy Chinese communists. They had reported that the masses, far from feeling liberated by Chiang's warlord troops, felt "disillusionment" with this new bourgeois army. Stalin replied that "the same thing had happened in the Soviet Union during the civil war," thus putting the Guomindang army on the same plane as the Soviet Red Army!

As long as Chiang Kai-shek still needed communist help to conquer the northern warlords and bring all China under his thumb, he toler-

On April 12, 1927, Chiang initiated a purge of Communists from the Shanghai Guomindang and began large-scale killings in the "Shanghai massacre of 1927."

ated a show of unity. But once he held Nanjing and Shanghai, his dictatorship recognized by the Western Powers as the sole legitimate Chinese government, he turned on the revolutionary masses in a savage bloodbath. In Shanghai, communist workers led by Zhou Enlai staged an uprising, capturing the police station, railroad station, and other strategic points. For three weeks the communists controlled Shanghai, but followed Comintern orders to turn power peacefully over to the advancing army of Chiang Kai-shek.

On April 12, 1927, the bloodbath started. Unprepared and unarmed, the workers, patriots, and communists were slaughtered by the thousands in public executions that went on for months. In all the regions held by Chiang Kai-shek and his warlord allies the mass killing went on. Many patriots, especially liberated women, met death only after the most barbaric public tortures. The death count has never been exactly known, but is usually held to be well over one hundred thousand that year.

Facing the most terrible defeat since the crushing of the Taiping army in 1864, the shaken leadership of the Chinese Communist Party met at their Fifth Congress just as the mass repression began. The Comintern-Chen clique decided that their only way out lay in even further concessions to the bourgeoisie. The Shanghai massacres were blamed on Zhou Enlai, who was said to have "provoked" Chiang Kai-shek by not completely disarming the workers there. The Guomindang was offered supreme command of all the workers' unions and peasant associations if they would spare the Party. As Mao said: "The Central Committee made complete concessions to landlords, gentry, everyone."

And all during that Spring, as the slaughter went on, the peasants had tried to form self-defense militia and fight back. The Comintern-Chen leadership ordered all peasant weapons surrendered to the landlords. The All-China Labor Federation disarmed workers militias. When 20,000 angry peasants and miners in Hunan marched on the provincial capital to avenge the machine-gunning of two hundred unarmed peasant militiamen, the Comintern-Chen clique ordered Mao and the other Hunan leaders to disarm them. The disarmed patriots were then promptly massacred themselves—over 30,000 that Summer in Hunan. On June 4, 1927, the Central Committee answered the pleas for help from Hunan peasant unions with a new directive blaming the killings on poor peasants who had allegedly provoked the Guomindang armies by "encroachments" on the lands of the rich warlord families. The Comintern-Chen clique went on to order: "To forbid such juvenile actions is an important task of the peasant associations." Borodin's last act before being kicked out of China was to try and find Mao Zedong, in order to get him to "restrain" the Hunan peasants some more.

In five years the Comintern had completely betrayed the trust of the Chinese people, had backed counter-revolutionary leadership for Chinese communism, and had failed the test of revolutionary practice. In no way can these errors be placed on Mikhail Borodin as an individual, although he later admitted: **"I was wrong, I did not understand the Chinese Revolution … I made so many mistakes."** The Comintern had sent virtual legions of politically-confused "experts" to China. In a typical case, one Euro-Amerikan was made a Comintern "expert" over the Chinese workers because of his experience as a trade-union organizer in Wisconsin. Another Euro-Amerikan, Earl Browder, was made head of the Comintern's entire Pan-Pacific Labor Secretariat on the basis of having once organized a local bookkeepers' union in his office in Kansas City. The Comintern thought that being European and following their orders were enough for being an "expert" over the Chinese Revolution.

The strategic guidelines laid down in Moscow center itself were invariably wrong, usually revolutionary-sounding platitudes that couldn't be translated into sound practice because they were impractical, mis-timed, or contradictory. One good example is Stalin's secret telegram in June 1927, in the middle of the disaster. The telegram ordered the Chinese Communists to push forward the peasant revolution, but use the peasant associations to stop land expropriations ("excesses") by the masses; the bourgeois leaders must be out-voted on the Central Committee of the Guomindang by somehow adding "a large number of new peasant and working class leaders"; the Party should quickly gather 70,000 revolutionaries "and organize your own reliable army before it is too late."

Chinese communists could not spread the peasant revolution by stopping the class struggle against the landlords, obviously had no way of taking over the Guomindang leadership, and had already lost most of their cadres and active supporters to the repression because the Comintern had spent five years arming the bourgeoisie while disarming the revolutionary masses. It was already "too late" for Stalin's further meddling.

The right deviation was finally overturned in July 1927, when a new Party Front Committee decided on armed struggle. **On August 7, 1927, a provisional Central Committee, including Mao Zedong, ousted Chen Duxiu and confirmed the new policy of revolutionary war.** There is no mystery in the ability of the liberation struggle to turn things around while in a difficult position. To save the nation the revolutionary cadres paid heavily in the only resource they had. Peng Pai, the first great revolutionary leader of the peasant struggle, was captured and executed without breaking. Of those 32 original peasant cadres who founded the communist cell in Mao's home village of Shaoshan, all gave their lives in the next few years. Mao's entire family had gone into the revolutionary struggle. Yang Kaihui, who was a leading organizer and was married to Mao, held out under torture and was executed. Mao Zejian, adopted sister of Mao Zedong, was killed doing underground work in 1929. Both of Mao's brothers, Mao Zetan and Mao Zemin, had brilliant histories of patriotic work before they were killed by the Guomindang (in 1935 and 1945 respectively). One brother's son, Mao Chuxiong, was adopted by Mao, became a communist guerrilla cadre, was captured in 1945 and buried alive by the Guomindang. Mao himself was captured in 1927 by landlord soldiers, and barely escaped as he was being taken for execution, ducking bullets as he broke away into the rice fields.

The period between the Nanchang Uprising of August 1, 1927, and the Long March in 1935 was not only a time of armed struggle, but of continued two-line struggle around political-military questions. Nor had false internationalism been finally laid to rest. It was in this period that Chinese communism, under the leadership of Mao Zedong, worked out the strategic and tactical answers that led to liberation, finding their "center of gravity" in the armed struggle.

Even though the central Red Army under Mao Zedong's political leadership had worked out a sound political-military line, these views for some years were only a minority within the revolution. Mao's new policies were not welcomed by the established leadership. And the Comintern, although publicly praising Mao as a military leader, kept up their disruptive meddling, determined to run the Chinese nation. While the communist cadres and the peasants were fighting to build the Red Power in the countryside, even in the revolutionary low ebb, the Comintern was discouraging their armed struggle. The Comintern directive to the Chinese Communist Party on June 7, 1929, said:

"... our tactics in the countryside should correspond to the work of the Party in winning over the urban proletariat in the process of its day-to-day economic struggles. It is not at all necessary to begin the peasant movement immediately with calls for carrying out an agrarian revolution, with guerrilla warfare and uprisings."

Even after the Red Army had built liberated zones and proved the soundness of the Mao line, the Comintern was still discouraging. The Comintern directive in October 1929 defined **"all these peasant activities"** as only **"an important side-current in the revolutionary wave."** In the name of internationalism the Comintern was undermining what was then the most important communist advance in the world struggle.

Mao had once again been removed from the Central Committee (and even the Province Committee) after 1927. From 1927 to 1935 there were a series of "Left" deviations, under different Party leaders, which were by no means identical but had certain features in common. **They tended to be militarily adventuristic; they tended to view the oppressed masses as only a resource to be exploited instead of correctly seeing them as the element of change; they did not unite the nation correctly in a liberation front.** These "Left" deviations had led the armed struggle up to and over the brink of disaster.

By 1930 the Comintern center in Moscow was impatient to once again take over total control of the struggle in China. The incumbent Chinese Party leader was removed by the simple method of ordering him to Moscow for an inquiry, and then detaining him there for "education" for 15 years! In January 1931, a special Comintern-trained faction seized the leadership of the revolution. It was headed by new Party Secretary-General Wang Ming, foremost among the group of Chinese "returned students" from Russia (who are ironically known in Chinese history as "the 28 Bolsheviks").

Wang Ming

Wang Ming was a landlord's son, a former student at Shanghai University, who joined the Chinese Communist Party in 1925 while studying at the Sun Yat-sen University in Moscow. He became a translator for the Comintern. This was the man, with no ties to the masses and without so much as one hour's experience in the real struggle of his nation, that the Comintern shoved in as the would-be leader of the Chinese people. Wang Ming's faction called a partial meeting of the Central Committee in Shanghai, without notifying Mao, Zhu De, or other guerrilla leaders, and voted themselves in. The Comintern backed this clearly illegal coup. Again, Mao and the revolutionary line were in the minority.

The years of the Wang Ming line (the "Third 'Left' Deviation") were a great disaster for the Chinese people. Perhaps the worst damage might have been avoided had the Wang Ming leadership confined itself to Shanghai and the other big cities, throwing cadres away in periodic "city-taking" adventures. But by the late Summer of 1931 the repression in Shanghai was closing in on the Party leadership. In order to survive most of them had to join the Red Armies in the rural base areas. Wang Ming returned to safety in Moscow.

Mao Zedong, Zhu De, and their communist forces had built a Central Base, a large liberated zone in Jiangxi-Fujian Provinces with a soviet government. The soviet governed three million people, 70% of them poor peasants, over 19,000 square miles (an area equal to the states of Massachusetts and Maryland combined). Unlike earlier bases, the Central Base by 1931 had shown enough strength, when correctly applied, to smash full Guomindang armies. Three "encirclement and suppression" campaigns, each larger than the last, were smashed by the Red Army in quick succession. In the third campaign Chiang Kai-shek personally commanded 300,000 attacking soldiers, but was still soundly beaten by the Red Army. 10,000 rifles were captured.

The Wang Ming faction took over the Central Base in late 1931 and early 1932, by the simple expedient of declaring it the capital of a newly proclaimed Soviet Republic, a new national government. This paper maneuver effectively put the local base committee out of business, since an all-China government had to be led by the Central Committee itself. Conveniently for Wang Ming, the Russians had just "advised" the Chinese to set up a new national government.

The Comintern-Wang Ming clique were no good at winning battles, no good at building the people's Red Power, no good at building the Party, but plenty good at petty-bourgeois intrigue, coups, and takeovers that were parasitic on the work of others. The only fly in their ointment was that they couldn't avoid elections for the new government—such was the mass recognition of his leadership that Mao was elected Chairman of the Soviet government. Still he was in the minority, and the Comintern-Wang Ming clique were rapidly destroying everything, in particular the political-military line. Mao later summed up:

"But beginning from January 1932, ... the 'Left' opportunists attacked these correct principles, finally abrogated the whole set and instituted a complete set of contrary 'new principles' or 'regular principles.' From then on, the old principles were no longer to be considered as regular but were to be rejected as 'guerrilla-ism.' The opposition to 'guerrilla-ism' reigned for three whole years. Its first stage was military adventurism, in the second it turned into military conservatism, and, finally, in the third stage it became flight-ism ... The new principles were 'completely Marxist,' while the old had been created by guerrilla units in the mountains, and there was no Marxism in the mountains ... And anyone who did not accept these things was to be punished, labeled an opportunist, and so on and so forth.

"Without a doubt these theories and practices were all wrong. They were nothing but subjectivism. Under favorable circumstances this subjectivism manifested itself in petty-bourgeois revolutionary fanaticism and impetuosity, but in times of adversity, as the situation worsened, it changed successively into desperate recklessness, conservatism and flight-ism. They were the theories and practices of hotheads and ignoramuses; they did not have the slightest flavor of Marxism about them; indeed they were anti-Marxist."

The Wang Ming leadership set up a security program, in which suspects would be eliminated on the spot. Many good revolutionaries were purged (Mao had all such victims restored posthumously to the Party's rolls after 1945). Mao himself was gradually stripped of all his posts save his elected position as Chairman. His connection to the Army was severed at the Ningdu conference of August 1932. At the same time a new nationalist groundswell had been sweeping China. The Japanese invasion of Manchuria in September 1931 had shown that Japanese imperialism intended to be master over all China. Mao, as Chairman of the Soviet government, and Zhu De, as commander-in-chief of the Red Army, signed a declaration of war against Japan. Mao's program for a new patriotic united front, which later was to prove to be the means by which communists could unite the nation behind their leadership, was rejected. The Comintern-Wang Ming clique attacked Mao's "nationalism."

The final mockery of the Chinese people's armed struggle came in early 1933, when a Comintern military expert arrived to take over strategic command of the Red Army from Mao. He was Otto Braun, who used the Chinese alias "Li De." Braun knew nothing about China and nothing about warfare. He was not even a soldier, although the Comintern had given him a military course before sending him to China. Any ignorant European was superior to Mao, in the eyes of false internationalism. **And now the Comintern-Wang Ming clique could take full hold of the army, with the visible presence of a big European expert to endorse their claim for leadership.**

Otto Braun became the head of a new Military Commission, which included Zhu De and Zhou Enlai, that dictated all military plans. Braun sent the Red divisions off to engage the Guomindang armies in regular positional warfare. Instead of guerrilla fluidity, Red units were told to dig trenches and fight to the last man before giving up one inch of ground. Instead of Mao's policy of concentrating superior strength to surprise the enemy with locally superior forces, the new Braun policy was to split up and fight in all directions, with each smaller Red unit expected

Otto Braun

to confront enemy forces up to ten times its size (under the slogan: "pit one against ten, pit ten against a hundred").

By September 1934 the immobilized Red Army was suffering defeat after defeat, as the Soviet area choked within the closing ring of Chiang Kai-shek's fifth "encirclement and suppression" campaign. Panicked, Otto Braun and the rest of the Comintern-Wang Ming clique decided to abandon the Central Base and break out for another base area (which had, in fact, already fallen to Chiang Kai-shek's armies). Although, as Mao pointed out, the Jiangxi-Fujian base would still hold out for months, giving the Red Army precious time for rest, planning, and preparing for the extended Winter march, Otto Braun was too panicked to wait. In October 1934, on a week's notice, half of the Red Army moved out, 120,000 soldiers and cadre without destination, a military plan, winter clothing, or adequate food. 8,000 porters were also taken. The Comintern-Wang Ming clique, used to playing at bureaucracy, had the soldiers and peasants carry government files, furniture, machinery, and all the other trappings. Mao sarcastically called this the "house-moving operation." That confused flightism was the beginning of the famous Long March.

Otto Braun aimed the bulky columns of the Red Army straight at the encircling Guomindang fortifications. 25,000 Red soldiers died in the breakout. Pursued constantly and strafed from airplanes, the huge Red Army slowly marched day and night. At the Xiang River, Otto Braun ordered the Army to clumsily cross under the direct fire of a Guomindang army. There 30,000 Red soldiers, cadre and patriots fell in the seven day long crossing. Ninety percent of the Red Army had been lost—killed, captured, wounded and left behind, or dispersed. Over nine out of ten Party cadres had gone as well. The largest liberated area the Party had yet seen, with three million peasants and workers, had been lost. These were bitter fruits of false internationalism, of "international" meddling that propped up "hotheads and ignoramuses" who were unfit to save the Nation.

Mao writes: "It was not until the Central Committee held the enlarged meeting of the Political Bureau at Zunyi, Guizhou Province, in January 1935 that this wrong line was declared bankrupt and the correctness of the old line reaffirmed. But at what a cost!" At the conference Zhou Enlai criticized himself for having gone along on the Military Committee with Otto Braun, and moved that Mao take the leadership of the Revolution: "He has been right all the time and we should listen to him." The Conference declared: **"the Chinese Soviet revolution, because of its deep historical roots, cannot be defeated or destroyed ... The Party has bravely exposed its own mistakes. It has educated itself through them."**

Mao explained to the 30,000 surviving soldiers and cadre at Zunyi why the "Left" deviation military policies were wrong, analyzed their recent struggles. Most importantly, he explained that the Long March had a new objective. Not simple flight or personal survival, but to march to the far Northwest to save the Chinese nation, to found a new center for all patriotic resistance to the foreign invaders. Their new destination would become Yan'an. The rest we know. The two-line struggle still went on, of course, although under qualitatively changed conditions.

We may ask why the correct revolutionary line was a minority in the Revolution for thirteen years? Why even obvious blunders and repeated military defeats were endured for so long by the ranks of the liberation struggle? We must keep in mind that people grow up under imperialism. Even the oppressed are used to believing in others, and not themselves. Even the rebellious are awed by the bourgeois way of doing things, and are habituated to the yoke of leaders who reflect this. Many soldiers and cadre felt that all those highly-placed leaders, with big reputations and similar ideas, must be right. Who was this Mao Zedong anyway, with his ragged clothes and unfamiliar ideas that weren't like anyone else's? When the correct revolutionary line takes root among the masses it becomes a material force, a great human storm that can topple Pharaoh and build a new Nation—but this is not a casual or an easy thing to accomplish.

False internationalism took advantage of this, and took advantage of the genuine international-ism and respect the Chinese people had for the Russian Revolution. The general line of Chinese communism has been to lay no public blame for errors on anyone but themselves. After all, if some Chinese communists allowed foreigners, no matter how well-meaning or important, to use them against their Revolution, then the main problem is on the Chinese side. Still, the full truth has never been a secret. Much later Mao wrote:

"Stalin did a number of wrong things in connection with China. The 'left' adventurism pursued by Wang Ming in the latter part of the Second Revolutionary Civil War Period and his Right opportunism in the early days of the War of Resistance Against Japan can both be traced to Stalin. At the time of the War of Liberation, Stalin at first wouldn't let us press on with the revolution, maintaining that if civil war flared up, the Chinese nation ran the risk of destroying itself. Then when fighting did erupt, he took us half seriously, half skeptically."[5]

When the Comintern formally dissolved in 1943 Mao Zedong and his comrades were already at that point; they had long since determined that their Revolution could only survive by ending "such meddling in our affairs." Most particularly by confused revolutionaries or would-be revolutionaries of other nations. If Chinese communism had not conquered false internationalism they would have been destroyed, root and branch.

Our criticism of the Comintern as an experiment in internationalism is not about errors of judgment. The relationship itself was incorrect in ignoring national distinctions between oppressor and oppressed nations, in ignoring the inescapable duty of each revolutionary movement to struggle out its own answers, reflecting the particularities of its own national situation, and in ignoring the right of each people to demand that its revolutionary leadership be held accountable to it. In other words, self-reliance.

We should never forget that false internationalism promotes political corruption, inevitably shielding slavish attitudes. What kind of contempt for their own people did the Wang Mings have, that they would promote the slavish notion that in all the many tens of thousands of Red commanders, soldiers, and cadre—communists who had been tested and remolded in the great furnace of People's War—there was not one Chinese comrade who could do the job given to Otto Braun?

False internationalism is not outside the oppressed nation, but is within. It actually divides the oppressed nation, shielding false leaders while subtly promoting the slavish attitudes of the oppressor. This was the lesson of thirteen years of political struggle to find the correct path of armed struggle and national liberation in China.

Yan'an

WAR
IN AFRICA

ITALIAN FASCISM PREPARES
TO ENSLAVE ETHIOPIA

By JAMES W. FORD and HARRY GANNES

5c

III. Afrikan Anti-Imperialism in the 1930s

Are the problems that challenged the Chinese Revolution fifty years ago meaningful to us, halfway around the world and in an entirely different historical period? To overturn false internationalism is one key to unlocking the door before us. **The time of the Comintern is not just "ancient history," but is directly related to the molding of our own political consciousness and our own movements.**

In 1960 the Southern Sit-Ins marked the beginning of a great period of mass struggle, not only for the New Afrikan National Revolution but across the continental US Empire as a whole. One feature of that new awakening was the twisted shape of political consciousness. **Nowhere in the Black Nation in 1960 was there a New Afrikan communist organization.** While there was a revolutionary nationalist political current centered then within the Nation of Islam, there was no communist organization. Neither were there communist organizations in Aztlan or the Asian-Amerikan communities. This has been unquestioningly accepted as normal. But isn't such a state of affairs not normal but abnormal?

The Afrikan Blood Brotherhood, the first New Afrikan communist organization, was formed in 1919 at the same time as the first Vietnamese communist study groups and the Chinese Communist Party. Yet some forty years later, in a new generation of struggle, New Afrikans once again faced the necessity of building a communist center from ground zero. What happened to the work of thousands of New Afrikan communists of the 1920s and 1930s—those who fought the planters, organized unions, and took part in a militant wave of national consciousness?

The first generation of Third World communists here in the US Empire were destroyed, just as the Chinese comrades would have been if they hadn't defeated false internationalism. That is why they inherited nothing organized, why they had to learn the A-B-Cs of revolution from scratch, making so many mistakes on the way. The defeat of the previous generation was not State repression alone. What made the setback so devastatingly effective was that it was also carried out by the communist movement of the US Empire.

Disarmed politically by false internationalism, Third World communists here during the 1930s allowed themselves to be "united" into the settleristic Communist Party USA (CPUSA). This was the approved "national section" of the Communist International in the US. The CPUSA recruited tens of thousands of Third World revolutionaries, but only to break them, disarm and scatter them.

We can say that, whether knowingly or not, the CPUSA served the interests of US Imperialism by: 1. Leading the oppressed away from armed struggle, away from joining the world revolution. 2. Convincing people that national liberation and communism were opposed to each other. 3. Using Third World "communists" to disunite the oppressed nations, while also placing the activities of the oppressed under the constant monitoring and meddling of Euro-Amerlkans. "Left" settlerism worked as a counter-revolutionary police for their Empire. And their most loyal Third World "communists" became "unconscious traitors" to their own people.

USING THE ATTRACTION OF INTERNATIONALISM

The Communist Party USA won the allegiance of Third World "communists" by appearing so different from the rest of settler Amerika (this was the Jim Crow 1930s). Theirs was a Party that played up the importance of anti-colonial struggles, the integration of all races and peoples, and readily confessed how it had to overcome the "white chauvinism" of even its own members. **This party wrapped itself in the mantle of John Brown, formed John Brown Clubs, put out John Brown pamphlets, and held meetings to praise John Brown as its model for white people.** The Party not only said that it supported

the right of New Afrikans to their own Nation in the Black Belt South, but in 1931 held a public showpiece trial in Harlem (the "Yokinen Trial") to discipline a Finnish-Amerikan Party member for racism at a Party social event. This was "the Party of Lenin and Stalin," with all the authority then that such a claim carried, the official party of world communism.

Third World revolutionaries finding this surprising Party were often won over by "the generous intoxication of fraternity." The CPUSA seemed to be what they needed. Angelo Herndon, the Alabama worker and organizer whose defense case under the old slave insur-

rection law became a national issue, said: "The education I longed for in the world and expected to find in it I surprisingly began to receive in my Communist circles. To the everlasting glory of the Communist movement, may it be said that wherever it is active, it brings enlightenment and culture... My new white friends ... gave me courage and inspiration to look at the radiant future ... The bitterness and hatred which I formerly felt toward all white people was now transformed into love and understanding. Like a man who had gone through some terrible sickness of the soul, I mysteriously became whole again."[1]

The CPUSA, unlike all previous "Left" settler parties, was very active in Third World struggles. It became the self-proclaimed "Champion of Negro Rights." We can see how this drew folks. Hosea Hudson, the Birmingham steel worker, has told us how he became attracted to the CPUSA in 1931:

"The Communist Party was putting out leaflets, but I didn't know nothing about the Party ... I didn't pay no attention to any leaflets til the Scottsboro case, when they took the boys off the train, and then the sharecroppers' struggle

in Camp Hill. These two was about the first thing that claimed my interest.

"The first break I know about the Scottsboro boys was in the *Birmingham News* on Sunday morning, had big, black headlines, saying nine nigger hobos had raped two white women on the freight train, and Attorney General Knight said he was going to ask for the death penalty ...

"Whenever Negroes was frame-up, I would always look for someone else to say something about it. I wouldn't say nothing because I didn't think there was nothing I could say ... until the Scottsboro case, when these people from all over the world began to talk. Then I could see some hope.

...

"Then they had this gun battle, these Negroes down there had that shoot-out at Camp Hill. The papers came out about it, and about fifteen of the leading Negroes, preachers and some businessmen in it, issued a statement in the paper condemning the action of the Sharecroppers' Union down there in Camp Hill. They put up a $1500 cash award for the capture and conviction of the guilty party who was down there 'agitating and misleading our poor, ignorant niggers.' (Later I learnt that Matt Cole was the man who was down there, that they put up the $1500 reward for, and he was a Negro from the country just like me, couldn't read or write.) I thought the bet-

ter class ought to have been putting money up trying to help the Negroes who's trying to help themselves. I had some wonders about it. I couldn't understand it.

"They had filled the jails at Camp Hill full of these Negroes, and telegrams began to come in from all over, demanding they not be hung. I wanted to know what's happening to them, what's going to happen to them, what's going to be done? It was the first time I ever known where Negroes had tried to stand up together in the South. I tried to keep up with it, asking people about it, and 'what you think about it?,' getting other people's opinions among my friends and people of my stature, all working people. I didn't have no contact with no better class of Negroes. A whole lot of them was sympathetic to the sharecroppers. They wanted to see something done, too, to break up the persecution against the Negro people."[2]

By supporting and then leading such breakthroughs as the armed sharecroppers movement, the CPUSA maintained its position as a false substitute to prevent an independent New Afrikan communism.

LEADING
THE OPPRESSED AWAY
FROM ARMED STRUGGLE

The 1935–1936 mass movement around the Italian invasion of Ethiopia was a turning point for New Afrikan rebellion in the 1930s. In October 1935 Italian imperialism sent its armies into Ethiopia, the last remaining independent Afrikan nation. Italian imperialism had sought to add Ethiopia to its other Afrikan colonies, Libya, Eritrea, and Italian Somalia. Even before the fighting began it was clear that Italy was going to invade; the Ethiopian government of Emperor Haile Selassie had begun war mobilization and had sent out a call for international aid. The response and excitement were worldwide. In the continental US Empire, the New Afrikan Nation was caught up in the cause of Ethiopia. It was to them in 1935 what the Vietnam war was to us in 1968. The militant solidarity movement was spearheaded by the nationalists, with everyone from the Baptist churches and the NAACP to the Garveyites and Communists joining together.

The CPUSA played a conspicuous role in this Ethiopian solidarity movement. The largest single event of the campaign, a 25,000-person integrated protest march in Harlem on August 3, 1935, was initiated by the Party. The main Euro-Amerikans opposing the Italian invasion were the Party's Italian nationality sections in New York-New Jersey. In Harlem alone the CPUSA had hundreds of New Afrikan members spread-

ing propaganda about the issue, while the Party published a steady stream of pamphlets, leaflets, and newspaper articles denouncing the Italian fascist dictator Mussolini and the war. All this let the Party claim that it had proven its promise of "full support in this united defense."

But here again there were two opposing lines, two diverging political directions of **how** to unite with Ethiopia and **what** internationalism meant. One line was represented by the CPUSA; **the other line, most fully developed by the Chinese Communist Party, was also the line taken by the New Afrikan masses here. That**

line was the path of rebellion and national liberation; the other line was the path of defeatism and submission to the US Empire.

The Communist Party USA defined the struggle as an "anti-fascist united front," in which **the main task facing New Afrikans was uniting with Euro-Amerikans and Europeans**. Under the discipline of the Party, Black members were sent out into the community to stop angry militants from violent attacks on fascist supporters here. Likewise the Party's Black cadres had to denounce the Volunteer Movement, the spontaneous nationalist upsurge of many thousands of

New Afrikans (in particular many World War I veterans) who wanted to go fight in Ethiopia.

Party spokesman James W. Ford, while forced to admit that **"The Volunteer Movement is another idea that has wide support among the Negro People,"** put it down as **"thoroughly impractical."** He then went further to say that the Volunteer Movement was a trick by **"those who wish to talk but do nothing in reality to help Ethiopia."** The program for the movement put forward by the Party had only two points: peaceful picket lines at Italian consulates and other legal demonstrations; sending money to Ethiopia.[3] Black members and supporters of the CPUSA were disciplined to a program precisely tailored to Amerikan liberalism. Ethiopia was treated in a half-hearted way as a charity case.

Our Chinese comrades were then deep in remote regions of the countryside, struggling for survival by mastering armed struggle. Far from being uninterested or half-hearted about Ethiopia, Chinese patriots took up the issue of Ethiopia in the true spirit of internationalism. Not as another Third World charity case or "good cause" for liberals in their spare evenings. The Chinese patriots embraced the far-away

Ethiopian liberation war as a positive example, a model to the Chinese nation. Internationalism to the Chinese people meant **learning** from Ethiopia, and uniting with the Afrikan people by **also picking up the gun against world imperialism.**

While the settleristic CPUSA looked down on Ethiopia as a backward victim who should be tossed some spare change, the Chinese people **looked up to the Ethiopian masses** as heroic pioneers whose example should be followed. Here we can see the difference between false internationalism and genuine internationalism.

We must focus for a moment on this: the Chinese people, from young students to Mao Zedong, had genuine respect for Ethiopia and her war. China itself was being invaded by Japanese imperialism, and the Guomindang government refused to lead the nation to recover their independence. China, too, knew well the problems of being weak, feudalistic, and unorganized. Agnes Smedley, the famous journalist, was in China during those years. She was in Beijing when the Italo-Ethiopian war began:

"**The Chinese people writhed under the humiliation of defeat and impotence. Students who had demonstrated against the Japanese and demanded war were beaten in the streets and imprisoned ...**

"**When, later, Italy copied Japanese technique and occupied Abyssinia [Ethiopia was also known as Abyssinia then] the**

resistance of the Abyssinians lit new fires of patriotism in the Chinese people. If little Abyssinia could fight a powerful invader so courageously, so could China, argued all Chinese patriots ... Each weekend men and women students gathered by hundreds in the Western Hills on what they called 'picnics.' I heard anti-Chinese foreigners accuse them of sexual debauchery. What they were really doing was practicing mountain-climbing and guerrilla warfare. Sticks were their weapons, and stones were their hand-grenades."[4]

Should it be a surprise that a small Afrikan nation fifty years ago helped the Chinese people rise to their feet?

On December 23, 1935, Gen. Zhu De of the Red Army issued an open letter to the officers of an opposing Guomindang Army from Sichuan province, challenging them to follow the Ethiopian people:

"**For two months now the Abyssinians have been fighting for the independence of their country. Though Abyssinia has a population of only 10 million and a territory of only 300,000 square miles, its people are still fighting an imperialist power many times their numerical and military strength ... You, Szechwan officers, have many millions of soldiers, and you have good modern weapons. Why can't you even dream of following the example of little Abyssinia whose dark soldiers are fighting**

gloriously for their independence? Why should not brave and gallant men in our country also step out to fight for national survival?"[5]

Compare these fighting words with the words of James W. Ford, the CPUSA's main spokesman on Ethiopia, in opposing armed struggle: "It would seem, therefore, that the more practical thing to do in this connection would be to send every penny we could raise to help the people of Ethiopia ... We can flood the Italian consulates and Embassies with telegrams and resolutions of protest."[6] There is, of course, nothing abstractly wrong with these tactics as such. **But to insist that an oppressed people who want to rise up should limit themselves to liberal protests is "to preach submission to the yoke."**

The Italian invasion was a triumph due less to imperialist strength than to poor military strategy by the Ethiopians. 800,000 Italian troops armed with tanks and air squadrons, using poison gas, pushed aside the brave but ill-led Afrikan soldiers who tried to stop them in direct positional warfare. On June 2, 1936, Emperor Haile Selassie and his leading officials evacuated Addis Ababa, the capital, and fled to exile. The war was not over, however.

Italian imperialism, which had indeed imposed a brutal fascist dictatorship on the Italian proletariat, proceeded to go far, far beyond this in Ethiopia. There again the difference between political repression and national genocide was demonstrated. Mussolini's son Vittorio was a fighter pilot in the invasion, and he regaled European reporters with his accounts of how hunting Afrikans from the safety of the air was "magnificent sport." He poetically described how "... one group of horsemen gave me the impression of a budding rose as the bomb fell in their midst and blew them up."[7]

The invaders tried to destroy Ethiopia as a nation. Just before the invasion the first modern school system had been started, with the first class of Afrikan school teachers just finishing training. Rome ordered all of them killed. Throughout occupied Ethiopia every educated Afrikan that could be found was executed. The Italian troops, bored with firing squads, killed many Afrikans by soaking them in gasoline and burning them alive (in public ceremonies, of course). Because Italy feared even the memory of Ethiopian Emperor Menelik, whose armies had smashed the first Italian invasion of 1896, they ordered his name obliterated. Menelik's statues and the imperial tombs (along with many cultural monuments) were dynamited. When hidden arms caches were found in a search of Ethiopia's most famous monastery, Italian Viceroy Graziani had 400 Ethiopian monks and deacons slaughtered.[8]

Unable to control seething Ethiopia, the Italian occupation conducted daily arrests and executions of suspected patriots. Mussolini personally ordered that remote rural villages be wiped out with "maximum use" of poison gas.[9] To say, as the CPUSA did, that both Ethiopians and Italians were equal victims of Italian fascism together, made a mockery of the nationally oppressed (and smeared over the communist insistence on the distinction between oppressor and oppressed nations).

ETHIOPIA & NEW AFRIKA— SAME STRUGGLE

When the nationalists saw a special relationship to Ethiopia they were, of course, quite correct. Everyone knew that US finance capital supported the Mussolini regime. Moreover, the fascist Mussolini regime and the invasion of Ethiopia were supported by many Euro-Amerikans of all classes. There was a certain love affair between Fascist Italy and White Amerika. They had a lot in common; two oppressor nations ruling large Afrikan colonial populations. That is why the New York correspondent for the *Corriere Della Sera*, Italy's most respected newspaper, wisely reassured the Italian public after Emperor Selassie fled that the Euro-Amerikan people would not really oppose the occupation: **"America knows the Negro well, and understands how to treat him."**[10]

While the Roosevelt Administration and the two capitalist parties issued token statements of opposition to the war, the US Empire was close to the Italian Empire. The Italian government had openly backed the election of then New York City Mayor Fiorello LaGuardia, with funds as well as words. Pleased that President Roosevelt's early New Deal cabinet included outspoken followers of Mussolini's theories, Mussolini himself sent off a message praising "the intensive cult of dictatorship to which President Roosevelt is dedicating himself."[11] This love-fest was even seen in popular culture—in 1934, as the invasion neared, Euro-Amerikans made a big hit of Cole Porter's new song, "You're the tops—You're Mus-so-li-ni."[12]

The US bourgeoisie, not needing to observe the hypocritical poses of capitalist statesmen, was upfront in backing the conquest of Ethiopia. *Business Week*'s editorial for February 23, 1935, was titled **"Abyssinia for the Italians."** It said that since Italy had fewer colonies than the other Powers, they deserved sympathy in "exploiting" the only Afrikan nation still available. After the conquest, Myron C. Taylor, Chairman of the US Steel Corporation, held a lavish banquet at the Waldorf-Astoria Hotel to honor the new Italian Ambassador. Taylor toasted the conquest, praising Dictator Mussolini for "disciplining" Ethiopia.[13]

Opposite page, background: Crowd celebrating conquest of Ethiopia by Mussolini's war machine jams 116th St. New York Italians staged an impromptu parade complete with banners. (Photo by NY Daily News Archive via Getty Images); Top Inset: About 300 Italian-American women in Syracuse received polished-steel replacement wedding rings on May 25, 1936, after donating theirs to Benito Mussolini; Bottom Inset: Effigy of Ethiopian Emperor Haile Selassie hanged in a mass symbolic lynching in Boston's Italian-American community.

NZA LA LEGA L'ETIOPIA E NOSTRA

DUCE

MOR

ITALY

Mussolini's Iron Rings Go to Syracusans

CARRYING EFFIGY OF SELASSIE THROUGH NO. END

While most Euro-Amerikans were primarily indifferent to events in Afrika, the Italian-Amerikan community was solidly behind Mussolini. The invasion aroused "Italian pride" making the mostly poor Italian immigrants happy that "their" homeland was conquering Third World nations just like the other European Powers. This anti-Afrikan, pro-imperialist sentiment of the Italian-Amerikan community was spontaneously strong, although also heavily reinforced—at neighborhood movie theaters the newsreels showed Italian Bishops using holy water to bless Mussolini's tanks going off to battle. The Vatican itself had said that Italian colonization was bringing "civilization" to Afrikans.[14]

One history of US–Italian relations recalls the hysterical fever of national chauvinism that was manifested by the Italian-Amerikan masses in 1935:

"For Italian-Amerikans the Ethiopian War was a sustained catharsis. Tens of thousands of them turned out for rallies in New York, Chicago, Philadelphia, Boston, and elsewhere. Here women contributed their gold wedding rings, receiving steel rings from Mussolini which were blessed by a parish priest. At a Brooklyn rally the Italian Red Cross passed trays to collect gold watches, cigarette lighters, crucifixes, and other metallic mementos needed to finance the war … At another Madison Square Garden rally, Generoso Pope told an audience of 20,000 that he was to send a check for $100,000 to Rome, and his

paper, *Il Progresso*, confidently announced that '5,000,000 Italian-Americans who live in the United States are ready to immolate themselves on the altar of the great motherland.'"[15]

Pope's *Il Progresso* was the most popular Italian-language newspaper in the US. Its special campaign to help finance the invasion raised $1,000,000, with Italian-Amerikan small businesses contributing to support the invasion. **Some of this money came directly from Harlem, extracted from New Afrikans themselves.** At that time the busy stores, bars, and

restaurants in Harlem were owned and managed by settlers, including many Italian-Amerikans. Each Italian store had a photograph of Mussolini prominently displayed. James R. Lawson relates: **"No Black man could, in good conscience, go into most Italian bars in Harlem. Mussolini's picture hung over almost every Italian cash register up there."**[16] Claude McKay wrote back then that: **"The Italians control over seventy-five percent of the saloons and cabarets in Harlem ... Their patronage was 95 percent Negro ..."**[17]

The anti-Afrikan sentiment in the Italian-Amerikan community was so overwhelming that the Communist Party USA decided to compromise with it. While the Party's Black cadres were sent out to convince their community about the need to unite with Italian-Amerikans, the Party's work in that latter community tacitly went along with the pro-imperialist majority. That is, the Party found ways to soft-peddle or back off from the issue.

A sore problem was Congressman Vito Marcantonio, the radical Italian-Amerikan politician from upper Manhattan. He was the Party's closest ally in bourgeois politics during the '30s and '40s; the Party managed his campaign, supplied his funds, and lent him hundreds of campaign workers. In return, Marcantonio verbally lambasted capitalism and colonialism on the floor of Congress. He was the main Washington voice attacking US colonial rule over Puerto Rico. But on this issue he was in trouble. While most Italian-Amerikans were indifferent to Puerto Rico, any strong supporter of Ethiopian independence would lose badly in the Italian wards on election day.

Marcantonio's solution was to still criticize Mussolini, but to find radical-sounding positions from which to come out against Ethiopia. So when New Afrikans here fought back against pro-fascist Italian-Amerikan street gangs, Marcantonio denounced them for "race riots." When he had to consider the League of Nation's sanctions banning sales of arms and war supplies to Italy, Marcantonio opposed it as supposedly not anti-imperialist enough, as just a plot favoring British interests against Italian interests.[18]

During a debate on the war in the House of Representatives, Texas liberal Maury Maverick stated: "We may as well agree that certain special groups have come into the picture. I refer to the letters of certain leaders of the Italo-American groups ... saying they are entitled to special consideration for Italy."

Marcantonio jumped to answer: "Mr. Speaker, my good friend, the gentleman from Texas, has referred to the so-called Italian-Americans requesting special consideration in the matter of neutrality legislation. I simply want to inform my colleagues of the House that these so-called Italian-Americans are Americans of Italian extraction, and that the Americans of Italian extraction are not requesting special consideration. They are interested only in the welfare of America ... It is their desire to keep our nation out of war. They want peace. They are opposed to any scheme which would make our nation the tool of either the international racketeerism of the League of Nations or the imperialistic interests of any foreign nation."[19]

In Congressman Marcantonio's "Left" rhetoric, not taking sides against Italy was labeled a "peace" measure. He even stretched things so far that Generoso Pope and the other bourgeois Italian-American community leaders (who were proud to be pro-imperialist) were defended by him as supposedly being anti-imperialist. Still, the CPUSA backed Congressman Marcantonio up. They were unwilling to give up their biggest ally in the mainstream of the Italian-Amerikan community.

When Marcantonio praised the Nationalist Party of Puerto Rico, few Italians cared and his pro-Independence posture won him thousands of votes in Spanish Harlem. But to support Afrikan liberation would have driven him out of Congress. His Italian neighbors would have turned on him as a traitor to white supremacy. The Communist Party USA was deservedly close to Marcantonio, both steering a course of cynical opportunism together. So when the CPUSA manipulated its Black cadres into attacking nationalism, that Party only meant to attack the nationalism of the oppressed; the nationalism of the imperialist oppressor nations was fine to them so long as it was draped in false internationalism.

For all these reasons the work of CPUSA members in the Ethiopian support movement went on the opposite path from that taken by the New Afrikan masses. The program of the masses leapt right over sending "every penny" to Ethiopia or picketing a downtown office building. They weren't opposed to these things, but first and foremost they wanted to fight. Afrika was going to war for national survival, and the grassroots wanted to do their part in the War. In the Summer of 1935 a spontaneous upsurge rocked New Afrika, as thousands reached to pick up the gun. Many World War I veterans itched to at last use their skills fighting for their own cause. The Baltimore *Afro-American* reported that within a week the nationalist drive to sign up fighters for Ethiopia had produced almost a thousand volunteers in Harlem, 8,000 in Chicago, 5,000 in Detroit, 2,000 in Kansas City, and 1,500 in Philadelphia.[20] Is it so difficult to read the meaning of this movement? Even the unfriendly James W. Ford of the CPUSA had to concede that the Volunteer Movement had **"wide support"** for its **"heroic sentiments."**

Just like the Chinese people, the New Afrikan colony was fed up with "the humiliation of defeat and impotence." The attitude on the streets was, "Let the white liberals send telegrams to the Italian Embassy, we're going to fight for the Race." And that, of course, was the other aspect of the mass upsurge. However few or many made it to Ethiopia, the battleground for New Afrikans could only be right here in the US Empire. Just like the Chinese people, the New Afrikan masses correctly read the lesson of the Ethiopian War as fighting for their own national liberation. But there was no independent New Afrikan communist vanguard to organize this raw sentiment into a spearhead.

The day after the Italian invasion spontaneous mass fighting with fists, rocks, and baseball bats, broke out between angry New Afrikans and pro-imperialist Italian-Amerikans in both Harlem and Brooklyn. Over a thousand police were needed to stop the violence. In Harlem, Italian stores and Italian street-vendors—who were in general pro-Mussolini—came under physical attack by nationalist crowds. At evening, coming home from "the slave," hundreds and sometimes thousands in Harlem would stop to listen to the nationalist street-corner orators. Soon crowds fighting with the police, throwing rocks at police cars, became a part of community life. Pointing out the contradiction of New Afrikans giving money to the Italian war effort by having to buy from Italian merchants, nationalists called for New Afrikans to take over the economic life of their community and solve their own survival problems as well.

On the political level, New Afrikans overwhelmingly wanted a mass united front to link their Nation up with the war for Ethiopia. While the degree of political consciousness in 1935 should not be overstated, an oppressed people who began to rise up, who wanted a national united front against imperialism, had chosen the path of liberation. That they had to do so without an independent New Afrikan communism was a contradiction within the National movement.

DIVIDING THE NATION AGAINST ITSELF

While always shouting about unity, false internationalism was applied to divide New Afrika against itself. **To begin with, the CPUSA's Black cadres split the Ethiopian solidarity movement so that it could be wiped out.** Euro-Amerikan revisionism always portrayed New Afrikan nationalism as "narrow," as promoting "racial exclusiveness." But in 1935 the various nationalist organizations led in building a national united front around anti-imperialism together with the Communist Party USA and the integrationist liberals such as the Rev. Adam Clayton Powell, Jr. That united front, which was at first named the Provisional Committee for the Defense of Ethiopia, held its first rally on March 7, 1935. On a rainy night over 3,000 people jammed Harlem's Abyssinian Baptist Church. Wall banners read "Africa for the Africans," while Ethiopian flags of green, gold, and red were waved by the crowd. Speaker after speaker, including the prominent Harlem educator Dr. Willis Huggins, saluted the national unity achieved.[21]

The nationalist leaders displayed an internationalist orientation to the struggle and were in no way sectarian or "racialist." J.A. Rodgers, who had returned from a fact-finding mission to Italy, told the crowd: **"The Italian people are not unfriendly to Negroes, as experiences during my travels prove. This threatened attack on Abyssinia is a result of other forces operating**

within Italy." Rodgers pointed out how the first Italian invasion of Ethiopia in 1896 had been opposed by Italian workers with a general strike. After CPUSA spokesman James W. Ford pledged their support to the united front, the largely nationalist audience cheered. Then Arthur Reid of the African Patriotic League, one of the most militant of the nationalist organizations, rose to point out the importance of bringing communists into the united front:

> "There was some fear that the communists would not come through with flying colors in this meeting, but the speech of Mr. Ford has stilled that fear. The Communists have proven that all of us can work together. They have come through."

Reid said that this anti-imperialist unity was fulfilling the dream of Marcus Garvey: "We must unite, and after we unite we must fight."[22]

The CPUSA had also portrayed itself as a force for unity. James W. Ford had told the Harlem rally: "If we would stop fighting among ourselves ... long enough to unify our forces against our enemy—we would advance. Unless we do this we perish. But I don't believe we are going to perish. We are going to stick together."[23] The very next day the CPUSA began its campaign to split the young Ethiopian support movement. They demanded that the movement become an integrated one, and that the committee surrender its specific national character. Ford promised the committee thousands of Euro-Amerikan supporters, lots of "respectable" liberal endorsements, and thousands of dollars—if the "extreme nationalists" were kicked out. So much for unity.

The CPUSA had redefined the Ethiopian war as a joint anti-fascist struggle of Italian workers and Ethiopian patriots, which should be supported in Amerika by a joint movement of "Negro and white." CPUSA spokesman Ford wrote:

> "Certain Negro leaders in the united front refused to vote on the participation of the Italian workers in the united front, stating that they were willing to work with Negro radicals and Communists but would have nothing to do with white radicals. By the small margin of one vote, the count being 8 to 7, their participation for the time being was overridden.

"In view of the activities among the Italian workers in Italy under the leadership of the Communist Party and the willingness of Italian workers in the USA to work together with Negro people for the defense of Ethiopia, it is now clear that the policies of the extreme nationalists among the Negroes work against the interests of the defense of Ethiopia. These petty-bourgeois nationalist tendencies must be overcome if the real interests of the exploited Negro masses and the Italian workers are to be defended against fascism and war.

...

"A great task lies before us. Let us not permit our forces to be divided. Let us unitedly give the Ethiopian people and the Italian toilers that help which we can and must give."[24]

In this false internationalist view, the closest allies and co-victims of the Ethiopian people were not other Afrikans, not the Chinese people, not other oppressed people—**but the Italians**. Likewise, this false internationalism pictured **New Afrikans' closest allies as Euro-Amerikans**. The CPUSA's Black members and supporters were led to believe that the closest ally of each oppressed nation was its oppressor nation.

By July 1935 the CPUSA had succeeded in dividing the New Afrikan united front. They convinced the leadership of the New York UNIA (the Universal Negro Improvement Association—the main organization of Garveyism) to join

them and the liberals in ousting the African Patriotic League and other militant activists. Then Ethiopia support work was actually merged into the work of the CPUSA's integrated front-group, the American League Against War and Fascism. The outward success of this transformation was seen in the giant August 3, 1935, Harlem joint march against Italian aggression. With the CPUSA in charge, the march had no trouble in getting support from Roy Wilkins of the NAACP, A. Philip Randolph of the AFL, and many settler churches and unions. The result was a dazzling 25,000-person integrated march through Harlem: Euro-Amerikan college students and Garveyite security guards in uniform with the white-clad religious cultists of Father Divine and red arm-banded Euro-Amerikan garment workers. Thousands of Euro-Amerikan radicals took part in the grand parade.

Many New Afrikan activists were blinded by this outward unity and quantitative success. J.A. Rodgers said: "When white workers march in such numbers in such cordiality through a Negro neighborhood, it is something for Negroes to think very deeply about." By the Fall the movement had gone "big-time" and had essentially moved its base out of the New Afrikan community. The grassroots were being abandoned. The next major event was at Madison Square Garden, where 9,000 people (mostly Euro-Amerikan) applauded Captain A.L. King of the UNIA when he said: "'This is a fight of the masses against the classes. We Black people will join you liberal whites all over the world not only to protect the rights of Negroes but in the interests of all mankind." Parades and glittering events had supplanted hard struggle at the grassroots.[25]

By September 1935 the CPUSA's newspaper, *Negro Liberator*, was writing: "We call upon the already aroused Negro people in America to join hands with the Italian people and the white toilers … The Italian workers are fighting Mussolini right in his own back yard. FOLLOW THEIR LEAD, American workers! DOWN WITH THE 'RACE RIOT' INSTIGATORS!"[26] In other words, New Afrikans were being told to oppose uprisings at home and instead "follow" Italians. Supposed solidarity with Afrika was turned into its opposite.

There was no active struggle—armed or otherwise—by Italian workers against the brutal occupation of Afrika. Because of the success of Italian fascism's repression there was no longer an active workers' opposition inside Italy by 1936. The CPUSA's newspapers, including the *Negro Liberator*, kept reporting various Italian anti-war strikes, demonstrations, etc. But these supposed underground reports were nothing but fiction. The Comintern and the leadership of the Italian Communist Party, isolated in exile in Paris, had put out these propaganda inventions to cover up for their shortcomings.

While the Italian Communist Party published statements expressing anti-imperialist solidarity with the Ethiopian people, these statements had no reality in deeds. If anything, the reverse poli-

tics were being practiced. The Italian Communist Party leaders had been reduced to trying to get in with the fascists. They were actually begging for a united front with fascism! **Nothing of this was revealed here to the New Afrikan community, of course.**

After months of discussion, the Comintern and the Central Committee of the Italian Communist Party in exile had issued a major call for Italian oppressor nation reconciliation in August 1936. Issued on the occasion of Italian dictator Mussolini's official proclamation of victory over Ethiopia, the Italian communist call was titled **"Reconciliation of the Italian People for the Salvation of Italy."** In it Mussolini and his colonial crimes in Afrika were tacitly accepted: the line was advanced that the Italian workers should

unite behind the fascist state in order to rid it of the "fistful of big capitalist parasites," "the sharks," who alone had kept fascism from bringing prosperity to all Italy:

> **"To the Workers and Peasants**
> **To the Soldiers, Sailors, Airmen and Militiamen**
> **To the ex-combatants and volunteers of the Abyssinian War …**
> **To the entire Italian People!**
> **Italians!**

> **"The announcement of the end of the African war was greeted by you with joy because in your heart hope has been kindled that you will finally see an improvement in your difficult living conditions.**

Opposite page: Graziani was branded as the "Butcher of Ethiopia" for the horrific executions he oversaw. This page: Italian Communist leader Palmiro Togliatti.

"It was repeated to us that the sacrifices of the war were necessary to insure the well-being of the Italian people, to guarantee bread and jobs for all our workers, to realize—as Mussolini said—'that highest social justice which from time immemorial is the longing of the multitudes in their bitter daily struggle for the most basic necessities of life,' to give land to our peasants, to create the conditions of peace.

"Several months have gone by since the end of the African war, and none of the promises which were made to us have been kept ... only the fraternal union of the Italian people, achieved by the reconciliation of fascists and non-fascists, will be able to smash the power of the sharks in our country, and force them to keep the unfulfilled promises made to the people for many years ...

"Italian people!
Fascists of the old guard!
Young fascists!

"We communists take for our own the fascist program of 1919, which is a program of peace, freedom, and the defense of the workers. We say to you: Let us unite and struggle together to make this fascist program come true...

"Let us grasp hands, sons of the Italian nation! Let us grasp hands, fascists and communists, catholics and socialists, men of all opinions. Let us grasp hands and march side by side to win the right to be citizens of the civilized country which ours is. We suffer the same hurts. We have the same ambition: that of making Italy strong, free and happy ..."[27]

Of course the fascists, already firmly in power, scorned this plea for a united front. While the Comintern had approved that opportunistic move, with its failure Moscow center washed its hands of the Italian Communist Party leaders. After six months the united front with fascism line was reversed. The Comintern started investigating the Italian communist leaders for Trotskyism and possible infiltration by fascist agents. In 1938 the entire Italian Central Committee was dissolved as unreliable.[28] The European leadership that New Afrikan people here in the US Empire were supposed to "follow" were at best unconscious traitors, both to their own people and to genuine internationalism.

The CPUSA's divide and conquer tactics had resulted in a large rise in its power within the Nation. For example, it became strong enough to stage a well-publicized slander campaign against Dr. Willis N. Huggins, the assistant principal of Harlem Evening High School. Huggins was the most prominent nationalist educator in the Ethiopian support movement. In the Summer of 1935 he had been sent by the Provisional Committee for the Defense of Ethiopia to Geneva, to use the League of Nations as a world forum for rallying Afrikan support for Ethiopia. With the aid of Amy Jacques Garvey and C.L.R. James, Huggins met with the Ethiopian Ambassador to London. Their meeting resulted in a public statement of recognition by the Ethiopian Government for New Afrikan support activities. Dr. Huggins was also the founder of Friends of Ethiopia, which with 106 local branches was the most widespread New Afrikan solidarity organization.

But when Huggins protested against the CPUSA's takeover of the united front, they staged a campaign vilifying him as a "fascist," and as a supposed enemy of Ethiopia. The CPUSA publicly demanded that the Board of Education fire him, and even started a mass letter-writing campaign to Huggins' employers.[29] Strange tactics for those who said that New Afrikans must unite or "perish."

Dr. Willis N. Huggins

When the CPUSA split the Ethiopian support movement, they also dismantled its foundation in the masses and moved the campaign downtown. The struggle for Ethiopia in Harlem intersected mass life around the questions of who ran the community's businesses and how could New Afrikans solve their economic problems? The nationalists had one program for these questions. For them the struggle of Ethiopia and the struggle of New Afrikans were sides of the same struggle.

In May 1935 the Afrikan Patriotic League began a boycott of Italian icemen, while calling for the total ouster of Italian business from the community.* In particular they called on New Afrikans to stop patronizing the Italian bars. This was linked to a program of encouraging New Afrikan small business and retailing, while also doing mass struggle to enlarge employment in the community.

The nationalist call was very popular on the streets, since the contradiction of spending your meager dollars every day to financially support

---

* Before World War II there were no mechanical refrigerators. Wooden ice-boxes kept food cool, but required a new block of ice every few days. So every house was serviced by one or another ice-man (who had regular delivery routes like fuel-oil trucks or milkmen). As a low-capital, high-labor small business it was dominated by European immigrants. In Harlem, Italians owned most routes.

the conquest of Ethiopia was galling. Particularly since these same Italian-Amerikan businesses that contributed to Mussolini's military also refused to give jobs to New Afrikans and then rubbed it in by proudly displaying pictures of their champion, the Italian Dictator. Small wonder that many people wanted to sweep them away. At the large Abyssinian Baptist Church rally on March 7, 1935, a woman had stood up at the end of the meeting to ask for a boycott of Italian business in Harlem. A nationalist speaker suggested that such a boycott would be premature: "We will have to wait and see how these people act and meet them halfway." So the militancy of the masses had been doubly sharpened by the fact that these oppressor nation petty-bourgeois had been given a chance to change their ways.[30]

The CPUSA hurriedly assembled a counterattack to protect their integrationist schemes. Under their leadership the Provisional Committee denounced the nationalist campaign, proposing instead a mass boycott of goods imported from Italy. They publicized supposed blows against Italian aggression when they got many Euro-Amerikan businesses in Harlem to sign pledges not to sell imported Italian products. All such merchants were certified by the CPUSA as "anti-fascist." So the ice vendors pledged to import no ice from Italy, the bars promised to import no whiskey, beer, or gin from Italy, and so on. This campaign was totally phony, since New Afrikans bought little in the way of imported Italian food, clothes, or other consumer products. It was also beside the point.

The CPUSA and the integrationist liberals kept insisting that any attacks on Italian-Amerikan business only divided the ranks of Ethiopia's supporters. **Not only was that a complete lie, but so was their claim that Italian workers were anti-fascist.** James W. Ford pointed out that: "the Italian Workers Club of New York by telegram and through a delegate offered to come into the united front with the Provisional League for the Defense of Ethiopia." **That sounded nice, but the Italian-Amerikan anti-fascists could only muster a few hundred people, a small radical exile community, for their events, while the Italian-Amerikan pro-fascists held regular community rallies of thousands.** Even in the giant 25,000 person Harlem march the Italian-Amerikan radicals could only bring a few hundred workers. Once again, the visible "friendship" of a few settler radicals was advanced as the reason for embracing a hostile nation of oppressors.

On the other hand, while Italian businesses in the ghetto were natural targets, political campaigns centering around control of small retail trade were not the center of the anti-colonial struggle. The nationalists spoke from the desires of the masses, but they themselves were unable to unite, unable to effectively mobilize the sentiment they represented, and unable to give scientific leadership to the whole Nation. While the nationalists expressed the community's anti-imperialist anger, it was the CPUSA and the Black liberal establishment that won the mainstream leadership.

In China during this same time patriotic students organized similar boycotts of Japanese imports. There were similar violent reprisals against retail business that served the Japanese invaders. But that patriotic activity was just one strand in China's larger tapestry, along with cultural struggles, women's liberation, class awareness, and the great front of armed resistance, all guided by communism. The contrast is significant.

Both the CPUSA and its Black petty-bourgeois allies shared a common attraction towards Euro-Amerikan society. This was masked by lofty speeches, full of not only false internationalism but claims on nationalism as well. The Rev. Adam Clayton Powell, Jr. attacked the militant nationalists while hiding behind the name of Marcus Garvey: "The cause of Ethiopia is not a lost cause, but it is lost if we look at it from a nationalist viewpoint ... The militancy of Garveyism must be retained, the solidification of Garveyism must be carried on, but we must move within a greater program ... the union of all races against the common enemy of fascism."[31] These oily words reveal how strong the nationalist sentiment persisted at the grassroots, how even opponents had to pretend to honor it.

One of the most remarkable figures of the war was Hubert Julian, known as the "Black Eagle of Harlem"; he trained a squadron of pilots to defend the last independent country of Africa, In 1935 he became an Ethiopian subject and, briefly, leader of the Ethopian air force. A passionate man and an able pilot, he caught the imagination of Ethiopian and American Blacks alike and became, for a time, their hero.

PROMOTING
DEFEATISM & BETRAYAL

This was not a question of which leaders would march at the head of the mass movement. Deprived of its national united front, deprived of its roots in the daily struggles of the masses, robbed of its fighting character, confused by a process of embracing the oppressors, the nationalist mass movement broke up. Particularly after the Italian army took Addis Ababa, the Ethiopian capital, in June 1936, a mood of defeatism in the community became dominant. The question of which line to follow proved to be an immediate question of life or death for the movement.

Interestingly enough, the same two-line struggle was going on in China. **There, too, the defeatism around Ethiopia was not abstract but was rooted in defeatism about their own revolution.** So much so that Mao had to confront this directly in his Yan'an lectures "On Protracted War." He noted: "Before the War of Resistance, there was a great deal of talk about national subjugation. Some said, 'China is inferior in arms and is bound to lose in a war.' Others said, 'If China offers armed resistance, she is sure to become another Abyssinia.' Since the beginning of the war, open talk of national subjugation has disappeared, but secret talk, and quite a lot of it too, still continues."[32]

The CPUSA and the Black petty-bourgeoisie in general were pushing a policy of defeatism.

Their view was that it was no use for New Afrikans to raise their arms to fight in Afrika, to fight anywhere. All hopeless, all doomed, according to that slavish line. Only by relying on Europeans and Euro-Amerikans could they receive a few crumbs. So CPUSA spokesman James W. Ford attacked the spontaneous upsurge of armed volunteers for Afrika as "thoroughly impractical." Even in his attack, Ford had to concede that going to war against imperialism represented a personal decision of tens of thousands:

"The outfitting and transportation of 50,000 American Negro soldiers to Ethiopia, besides requiring a tremendous financial outlay, would mean 50,000 more mouths to be fed by the Ethiopian people. That is, provided they could ever reach Ethiopia. Ethiopia, it must never be forgotten, is surrounded by the colonies and war bases of other imperialist powers … The expedition would be costly, to say the least; would never reach its destination, and would divert energy and funds from assisting the Ethiopian people in a more real and powerful way."[33]

Could anyone write a speech that was more dragged down with whining, with defeatism and contempt for their own people? We can see why James W. Ford and other such Black leaders were at best "unconscious traitors." Such a problem—50,000 volunteer New Afrikan fighters but with no war to fight in. How about their own war? If 50,000 New Afrikan fighters couldn't reach Ethiopia, what could stop them from fighting on the South Side, in Harlem, Alabama, and Mississippi? How can communists say that something is bad when 50,000 oppressed men and women reach for arms and ask for leadership against imperialism? And at that very moment the armed sharecroppers movement in Alabama, which involved thousands of New Afrikans, was fighting on in isolation. This is why we say that within the 1930s anti-imperialist movement there were two lines on how to unite with Afrika and what anti-imperialism meant—one line led to national liberation and armed struggle, the other line led to defeatism and submission to Empire.

After the fall of Addis Ababa the CPUSA did nothing to stop mass discouragement about Ethiopia's prospects. Quickly they moved to phase out Ethiopia as an issue. Only J.A. Rodgers, John Robinson, and nationalists around the Ethiopian World Federation still kept pointing out that the war was not over, that the Ethiopian people were still fighting.

Mao himself emphasized at the time: "Why was Abyssinia vanquished? ... Most important of all, there were mistakes in the direction of her war against Italy. Therefore Abyssinia was subjugated. But there is still quite extensive guerrilla warfare in Abyssinia, which, if persisted in, will enable the Abyssinians to recover their country when the world situation changes."[34] Mao's confidence in the Afrikan people's struggle against imperialism was quite correct. It was the calm judgement, unshaken by momentary setbacks, of

a Chinese revolution that had already found its own "center of gravity" in armed struggle.

In fact the imperialist media painted the Italian position as much more favorable than it was. Due to the dispersed nature of rural Ethiopian society, the mass war mobilization was just beginning when the Italian army struck. The Ethiopian mobilization reached its peak during the Italian occupation, just when the US press was saying that the war was over. Continued resistance and counterinsurgency were savage. When the Italian Viceroy Rodolfo Graziani was almost assassinated in February 1937, the Italians killed 30,000 Afrikans in random reprisals. One leading historian commented:

"Never was Ethiopia under firm control. A vast amount of propaganda about the glories of empire cannot conceal the fact that the Italian army remained encamped there amid a hostile population which was just biding its time to rebel."[35]

In June 1936, US Minister in Addis Ababa, Cornelius Van H. Engert, wrote Washington that the occupation was weak. Engert said that the imperialist forces didn't even claim to occupy more that 40% of Ethiopia. The vast rural areas west of Addis Ababa were totally commanded by Afrikan guerrillas. The Italian army had been hit so hard in ambushes, according to the US Minister, that they were afraid to move more than five miles beyond the capital without a force of at least one thousand troops.[36]

So the defeatism about Ethiopia (**which was really based on defeatism about *all* national liberation**) was incorrect. In fact, although the Italian occupation would have been swept out by the Ethiopian people alone, the changes in the world situation led to the defeat of Italian imperialism within five brief years.

While the duty of communists was to help the masses put down defeatism, under the leadership of the CPUSA they actually did the reverse. The CPUSA told people that it was useless to continue supporting Ethiopia. **They did this by saying that the only solution to Ethiopia's subjugation was to defeat fascism back in Europe.** In other words, once again Europe was raised as the supposed salvation of the colonial peoples.

In the Spring of 1937 the Spanish Civil War began. The young democratic Spanish Republic was threatened by a fascist revolt within the Spanish Army, aided by Nazi Germany and fascist Italy. All over the world communists raised material support for Spanish anti-fascists. The CPUSA began openly recruiting thousands of volunteers to fill out the Abraham Lincoln Brigade, which would be the all–US Empire unit fighting in the Spanish Republican Army. New Afrikans were told to forget Ethiopia; that only by overcoming fascism in Spain would the Italian occupation be lifted. This lie carried contempt and defeatism about the liberation war of the Ethiopian people, a war that at that moment was still rising. The CPUSA's Black cadres were ordered to spread the new slogan: **"Ethiopia's fate is at stake on the battlefields of Spain."**[37]

This slogan was wrong in many ways: First, it was factually untrue in its form—that is, while Ethiopia was never defeated and regained its independence in five years, Spain was easily conquered by fascism. Further, Spanish fascism remained in power for thirty years. Most importantly, the Ethiopian people had to depend primarily on themselves alone for victory; not on Spain, not on China, not on Russia or any other nation. The fate of Ethiopia never rested on any events in Spain.

Thousands of Blacks were mobilized to work for the Spanish Republic—**as opposed to supporting Afrikan liberation**. Medical supplies and funds collected for Ethiopia by CPUSA-controlled committees were instead sent to Spain. (No one in Afrika or Alabama apparently needed liberation aid.) Just the year before the CPUSA was saying how "impractical" it was to send armed volunteers to Ethiopia. Now the CPUSA was telling New Afrikans that it was their internationalist duty to go fight in Spain. Incidentally, Republican Spain no less than Ethiopia was surrounded by imperialism. New Afrikan fighters in Spain had to be smuggled through France, covering the last leg to the border by a march through the mountains. One hundred New Afrikans served with the Republicans in Spain. Two died in combat, giving their lives to the world revolution. That they fell in battle was not tragic; what was tragic was that their courage and internationalist dedication were cynically manipulated and misused by the CPUSA. Their picking up the gun in Europe was used to divert New Afrikans from their own national liberation, away from genuine internationalism with Afrika.

So in 1935–1937 the settleristic Communist Party USA, together with petty-bourgeois Black elements, manipulated Black CPUSA members and supporters to destroy the nationalist mass movement. Discouraged, betrayed, distrustful of these leaders, the masses dropped away from organized revolutionary activity. In fact, most of the CPUSA's Black members also quit, aware too late that they had been led into betrayal. This was a brilliant victory for pro-imperialist integrationism within the mainstream of New Afrikan politics. But at the grassroots the anger of the oppressed still held. The week that Italian troops began occupying Addis Ababa, angry crowds in Harlem drove many Italian vendors out of business. Italian bars were attacked. Inside the New York UNIA angry nationalists removed Captain A.L. King from the leadership because of his complicity in the betrayal of their movement. None of this represented any victories against imperialism. What they showed, however, is that the grassroots, although unable to stop their leaders from frustrating their desires, were at least determined to take care of business on their own ground.

Ethiopian soldiers before being sent to the front.

COMMUNISM
IS 20TH CENTURY AMERICANIS

IV. Settler "communism"

Opportunism and oppressor nation chauvinism spread within the Comintern. **This represented bourgeois ideology still living on within its opposite, the new world revolution.** Thus, the betrayal of New Afrikans during the 1930s within the US Empire was not their problem alone, but reflected a worldwide problem. The Comintern itself had an incorrect system of "brother" parties, in which oppressor nation communists would "assist" and even supervise the communists in "their" colonies. Similarly, in settler regimes the Comintern maintained the principle of all communists irregardless of nationality being forced into a single party; despite national/political differences, despite different theoretical lines and strategies, and despite the desires of the oppressed. **So that in New Afrika, Algeria, Palestine, and Azania, oppressed nation communists were a "minority" disciplined within communist parties that were majority European settlers.** That this led to abuses can well be understood today.

Opposite Page: A comrade reading the Sunday Worker newspaper in front of poster by artist David Siqueiros at NYC Communist HQ. Photo by Alfred Eisenstaedt.

"COMMUNISM" VS. LIBERATION

Algeria is the clearest example of this phenomenon, where a false communist party forced through a historic split between nationalist rebellion and communism.[1] The "Algerian Communist Party" (PCA) was created in 1936 out of the Algerian section of the French Communist Party (PCF). Despite its name this party was neither Algerian nor communist. It was a supervised puppet of the French Communist Party, a party that never broke with loyalty to "its" colonial empire. **Using arguments of false internationalism, the French Communist Party had supported the involuntary "unity and integrity of greater France from the Antillean Islands up to Madagascar, from Dakar and Casablanca up to Indochina and Oceania" (as its 1944 program for a liberated France said).**

This "Algerian Communist Party" (PCA) developed as an actual enemy of Algerian liberation, a primarily French settler party (there were one million French settlers living in Algeria until 1961) with a minority of captive Algerians. During these years an Algerian revolutionary who wanted to join the world communist movement had to submit to the orders of this false party. As late as the end of World War II this "Algerian Communist Party" was still denying that an Algerian nation even existed: "**The pseudo nationalist who twaddle about independence forget that the conditions of this independence do not exist. Algeria does not have an economic base, a military force, nor a national identity ... There does not exist an 'Arab Algeria' ...**"

Both this Party and its oppressor nation "brother" party in France proved where their loyalties were during the great Setif uprising of 1945. On May 8, 1945, the Algerian nationalists used the official parade in the city of Setif, celebrating Allied victory over Germany, to demonstrate for their own liberation. 8,000 Algerians marched down the main street carrying pro-independence posters and green-and-white Algerian flags.

When the French police started shooting at the peaceful march, an uprising broke out and quickly spread across the countryside.

For five days fighting continued. Since the Algerians were largely unarmed, French casualties were limited to 103 killed and 100 wounded. **But in the savage French suppression of the uprising some 45,000 Algerians were killed. In the cities French settler lynch mobs took Algerian prisoners out of the jails and killed them. French airforce terror bombing raids destroyed forty Algerian villages. Thousands of unarmed Algerians were shot down in reprisals as French troops restored the colonial order.**

In this repression the "Algerian Communist Party" not only backed up the colonial regime's crimes, but took an active part in them. PCA

victims of the Sétif massacre

Secretary-General Amar Ouzegane said: "**The organizers of these troubles must be swiftly and pitilessly punished, the instigators of the revolt put in front of the firing squad.**" At Guelma, where the settler lynch mobs reached their peak, "Algerian Communist Party" cadres led in the mass slaughter of 700 Arabs. In France *L'Humanité*, the French Communist Party newspaper, claimed that "only" one hundred Arabs had been killed in all of Algeria, that there had been no repression, and reported the uprising as: "Troublemakers, inspired by Hitler, have staged an armed attack against the population …" We must remember that the French Communist Party was then still part of the French coalition government—the Air Ministry that carried out terror bombings of Arab villages was headed by a French Communist Party leader.

ASIANS UNDER
U.S. COMMUNISM

These bitter experiences were not just far-off events, unrelated to the u.s.a. Within the US Empire the Comintern had placed Asian communists under the direct supervision of the settler Communist Party USA. The CPUSA turned Asian revolutionaries away from Asia, ordering them to think as loyal "Americans." Internationalism was misused to mean an all-embracing "unity" with Euro-Amerikans and

their Empire, under the old principle: "**All roads lead to Rome.**" Asians became isolated from all other anti-colonial struggles, and even from each other. The net effect in this regard of the Comintern's policies was not more internationalism, but far less.

In the US Philippine colony the CPUSA representatives educated a petty-bourgeois leadership for the new communist party, the PKP (Partido Komunista ng Pilipinas). The original "first-line" leadership of the PKP were trade union militants, most notably Crisanto Evangelista (leader of the printers' union and the most influential unionist in the country). But their orientation was towards open, legal organizing in the cities. Within two years of the PKP's founding on 7 November 1930, the party was banned, the "first-line" leadership in prison, and the young communist movement disorganized without central command.

In this condition party cadres were unable to resist when the CPUSA, backed by the full authority of the Communist International, moved to reorganize the PKP's leadership, membership, structure, and political line. Over the next five years the PKP was surgically ripped apart. CPUSA Secretary Earl Browder had been in close touch with Philippine communists since his visit in 1927, when he was head of the Comintern's Pan-Pacific Trade Union Secretariat. Browder and his lieutenants promoted the careerist, pro-Amerikan clique led by Dr. Vicente Lava to become the secret "second-line" leadership that would take over the party. This began "a singular phenomenon in the entire international communist movement." For the entire rest of the PKP's life, some thirty years, leadership was passed on as family property by the Lava brothers: first Vicente Lava, then Jose Lava, and finally Jesus Lava. The re-established Communist Party of the Philippines (CPP) that is now leading the revolution has written:

> **"It was around 1935, however, while the Party was still outlawed by its class enemies, when a considerable number of Party members of petty-bourgeois class status crept into a fluid underground party that was deprived of a definite central leadership and trying to carry on political work, bringing with them their unremolded petty-bourgeois and bourgeois ideas. At the helm of this petty-bourgeois element within the Party were those who were greatly influenced by the empiricist and Right opportunist current spread by Browder. At this time, the Communist Party of the Philippines, under the auspices of the Communist International, was assisted by the Communist Party of the USA by seeing to it that cadres like Vicente Lava, who became its leading representative, would carry on Party work."[2]**

In 1936 CPUSA leader James S. Allen came to the Philippines to meet with both puppet Philippine Commonwealth President Quezon and the imprisoned communist leaders. Allen nego-

tiated a conditional release for the PKP leaders. Quezon was a liberal politician, tied to President Roosevelt's New Deal administration in the US. He was glad to release these controversial political prisoners once James S. Allen assured him that the PKP would now be ordered to support the US colonial administration.[3]

This was even made public in 1938, after Allen had personally arranged the merger of the PKP with the peasant-based Socialist Party. The founding statement of the loose merger party "defends the Constitution" of the colonial administration, and explicitly **"opposes with all its power any clique, group, circle, faction or party which conspires or acts to subvert, undermine, weaken or overthrow any or all institutions of Philippine democracy."[4]** Once puppet Commonwealth President Quezon saw how well the PKP had betrayed the masses, he met with James S. Allen and granted the PKP leaders the full pardon that the CPUSA had publicly begged him for.

By turning their faces toward New York and Washington, by conducting politics as taught by the settler CPUSA, the Philippine communist leaders had turned their backs on their own people. The PKP became even more preoccupied with parliamentary elections, liberal alliances, and petty-bourgeois civil liberties committees in Manila and the other cities. **Although they lived in a desperately poor peasant country, the PKP played at the reform politics of the imperialist metropolis.** We can't overlook the fact that the CPUSA didn't create the petty-bourgeois Philippine misleaders. It simply found them, like water finds its own level. False internationalism once again is shown to be an **alliance** between petty-bourgeois elements in both the oppressor nation and the oppressed nation. And that early Philippine communism was vulnerable to it because of its own internal contradictions, its own lack of science in concretizing socialism to its particular national-historical situation.

Throughout those years of the 1920s and 1930s the peasant masses, suffering under the lash of feudalism and colonialism, simmered with revolution. Armed peasant rebellions broke out time after time. The Tayug uprising of 1931, which took place two weeks after the founding of the party, ran its course without the PKP even bothering to relate to it. So when World War II began the PKP was unprepared, attempting to carry out legal political life in the capital city under the conditions of Japanese invasion! Once again the "first-line" leadership were easily arrested. The imperialist war forced the reluctant PKP into armed struggle. Although in later years the PKP went on to try guerrilla warfare, it was never able to shake off the leadership and class orientation fostered during the years of Comintern-CPUSA intervention. It died in the 1950s.

When the communist movement went through rectification in the late 1960s to re-establish a new Party, these old betrayals were specifically condemned. And the new Party

has always firmly insisted that while their liberation struggle must be part of the international united front against imperialism, that only the Filipino people shall determine the destiny of the Philippine nation.

In the continental US Empire this intervention was partially masked by integrationism. Still it is only when we examine this factor that long unanswered questions can be finally dealt with. When Japanese-Amerikans were ordered to the US concentration camps in 1942, they were politically unprepared—and appeared to be alone and without allies. Chinese, Filipino, Chicano-Mexicano, Native Amerikan, Black, and Puerto Rican revolutionaries were all unable to unite in struggle with them. Many Japanese-Amerikans asked then what internationalism meant if no one would fight in their defense? No one could aid them, because they had no independent strategy of struggle to protect their community. They had nothing of their own for people to unite with.

Yet, Japanese revolutionaries had a long tradition of internationalism in the US. Even before the Russian Revolution, Japanese who learned about socialist ideas while laboring in the US and then returned to Japan to continue the struggle, tried to establish ties of friendship with US workers. Japanese militants worked and organized alongside Mexican and Filipino workers in the fields. While Sen Katayama is well known in communist history as the founder of Japanese communism, few remember that he was educated in the Black Nation here as a divinity student at Fisk College. In fact, when the nationalist poet Claude McKay was about to be barred from the 1922 Comintern 4th Congress in Moscow (due to the hostility of the official CPUSA delegation), he called on his old friend Katayama for help.

McKay had emigrated to Harlem from rural Jamaica, where he had grown up, seeking to become a writer. At first he wrote while working as a Pullman porter. Soon McKay became a well-known editor and writer for radical journals. His poem "If We Must Die" (**"If we must die—let it not be like hogs"**), written in fury during the 1919 "race riots," is still famous today. McKay and Katayama had met in New York City, and had spent many evenings discussing politics together. By 1922, when McKay had arrived in Moscow, Sen Katayama was in his sixties and perma-

nently working in Moscow as a member of the Presidium of the Communist International (and a colonel in the Red Army). Katayama quickly arranged with the Bolshevik leadership for McKay to become a special guest of the Soviet peoples. The Euro-Amerikan CPUSA leadership had been accusing the independent-minded McKay of being a spy in order to get rid of him. Those settlers couldn't understand how a nationalist poet could call on an Asian communist leader as a comrade and personal friend.[5]

During the 1930s Japanese and Japanese-Amerikan communists in the US tried to meet their internationalist duty, not only in the union drives in canneries and sugar cane fields, but in opposing Japanese imperialism's invasion of China. Yet in 1942 they were unprepared to defend themselves, and without allies.

Mr. McKay Speaking in the Throne Room of the Kremlin, December 1923

To see what happened we should understand that other Asians here also found themselves suddenly isolated when under attack by imperialism. In 1936–37 the CIO's National Maritime Union (NMU) found itself locked in a long, difficult strike that would decide the unionization of East Coast shipping. Euro-Amerikan unionists alone were not able to idle all the ships. So the NMU had to recruit colonial sailors as allies. Led by Ferdinand Smith, a Jamaican communist, some 20,000 New Afrikan workers (primarily in the South) agreed to join the strike if the NMU would finally end the traditional Jim Crow conditions in shipping.[6]

In the strike center, New York port, where the NMU had 10,000 strikers, the CPUSA approached the 3,000 Chinese seamen to support their struggle. They agreed to join the union on the same basis as New Afrikans, demanding equal rights. Chinese seamen on US ships were by custom only paid three quarters of "white man's pay," and limited to being waiters and cooks. Customarily half their pay was kept by the company until discharge, to guarantee "good behavior." With the victory of the strike Chinese seamen won the formal support of the CIO for equal jobs and pay. One key issue of theirs was the right of shore leave. Chinese seamen could labor on US cargo ships, but could not take shore leave in US ports. The Chinese Exclusion Laws forbid them from leaving their ships while docked in US territory.[7]

Paradoxically, the victory of the NMU union drive—which had been led by the Communist Party USA—left the Chinese seamen even more isolated. In 1936 Congress

Indonesian sailors who walked off ships in U.S. ports in 1945 because they refused to transport Dutch troops and arms to be used against their homeland.

passed a bill subsidizing the shipping industry, giving companies high subsidies to carry US mail. At the request of the Euro-Amerikan trade unions, the legislation carried with it the stipulation that no foreign seamen could be employed. This was directly aimed at the Chinese. So in 1937, when the new legislation took effect, US ships fired and abandoned Chinese seamen at ports all over the world. Often the seamen were left penniless, without passage back to China.

In New York Harbor Chinese sailors on the Presidents Line ships SS Taft and SS Polk began an onboard sit-down strike. They were demanding their jobs back, with six months severance pay and fare back to China if dismissed. The workers formed the Chinese Seamen's Patriotic Association. The Euro-Amerikan communist leaders of the NMU said that they sympathized with their one-time Chinese allies. The National Maritime Union did pressure the company to give the fired Chinese workers severance pay, so that they could buy passage out. This small concession was made.[8] But the Euro-Amerikan communists told their former Chinese allies that the victorious union, which was "American," couldn't help foreigners keep jobs in violation of the US laws. All Chinese seamen without US citizenship were purged from the industry.*

But the "Chinese Problem" could not be swept out of US ports so easily. Thousands of Chinese worked on the ships of other nations, particularly of the British Empire. On British ships the Chinese were worked almost as slaves, beaten, ill-fed and often not paid. In 1942 Chinese workers on British ships in the port of New York started jumping ship after a British captain shot down and killed one brother, who had declared that he refused to take any more beatings. At the urgent request of the British, the US Immigration Service terrorized NY Chinatown for weeks, raiding homes and restaurants to find the fugitive Chinese seamen. Four hundred Chinese seamen were recaptured by US authorities, and were handed over to the British on the docks. It was a slave hunt.[9]

Through it all the Euro-Amerikan communists in the NMU sympathized publicly, but said that **their "American" union could not handle the problems of "foreign" workers on "foreign" ships.** In a city where the National Maritime Union had over 10,000 members, this supposedly communist-led union stood by watching with folded hands as Chinese seamen were hunted down like animals. The anti-imperialist union on the British ships, the Chinese Seamen's Union, was smashed by repression. The last Chinese sailors' resistance was broken when the British Government announced that any Chinese worker who tried to quit a British ship would be arrested by the US government and sent to be captive military labor in India. Again, the CPUSA and

---

* Later, high maritime casualty rates in war zones during World War II reopened the door to some Chinese employment on US ships.

NMU said that as good "American" organizations they couldn't oppose this.[10]

There were thousands of New Afrikan seamen, with many militants among them, as well as Chinese-Amerikan seamen. There were active communist groups among the Chinese-Amerikans, among Japanese-Amerikans, among Puerto Ricans. Why were those desperate Chinese seamen without allies right in New York City? Because all the colonial communists here were disciplined "minorities" under the direction of the Euro-Amerikan Communist Party USA. The more organized everything became, the more unionized workers were, the more colonial revolutionaries became "united" within the settler CPUSA, the less freedom there was to make genuine alliances. Latino and Asian and New Afrikan only had a relationship through the settler CPUSA. Like separate spokes on a wheel, their "unity" consisted of each of them having a heavy relationship to Euro-Amerikan communists, who were at the center of everything. **"All roads lead to Rome."** But none of them had independent relationships to each other or, **even more importantly, to their own people. What looked on the surface like lots of internationalism, turned out to really be no internationalism at all.**

This was one reason why Japanese-Amerikans had no allies when the concentration camp round-ups began in 1942. Once the treacherous CPUSA decided to support their imprisonment, they naturally blocked other Third World communists from fighting against the concentration camps.

Does this mean that the settler CPUSA bears the main responsibility for the lack of internationalism? Absolutely not. The main responsibility was held by Japanese-Amerikan revolutionaries.

We say that internationalism begins in self-reliance. There is a widespread trend of thought that really believes the reverse, that international solidarity is needed to compensate for weakness. This is what Japanese-Amerikan communists (most of them youth with little political education) believed in the 1930s. They thought that their people would be protected by the broad alliances woven by the Communist Party USA; that their small numbers were compensated for by joining the masses of liberal and radical settlers. This illusion was deliberately encouraged by the CPUSA, to be sure. Japanese-Amerikan communists joined the picket lines protesting Japan's invasion of China, boycotting Japanese silk, and demanding an end to scrap iron sales to the Japanese war industry—"Silk Stockings Kill Chinese." Japanese-Amerikan communists were united with Filipino and Chinese brothers and sisters in building the CIO Cannery Workers Union on the West Coast in 1936–1938. On 11 July 1937 Jack Shirai, a New York restaurant worker, fell in the defense of Madrid.[11] A Japanese-Amerikan revolutionary gave his life to help the Spanish people fight fascism. In doing all this young Japanese-Amerikan communists thought that they were building internationalism. But as the troops herded them into the trains to the camps, they learned the hard way that nothing had been built. **Internationalism is not a**

crutch for beggars, as some US revolutionaries today think it is.

Others could not aid their resistance if it had never been built into a real campaign of struggle. Shamefully, Japanese-Amerikan communism had never prepared to lead any program in their own defense. For years and years, as the storm clouds of US–Japan imperialist war darkened over Asia, as anti-Japanese chauvinism was whipped up by the imperialists, Japanese-Amerikan communism refused to deal with the coming crisis. No plans were made. No organization of political self-defense prepared. Years of possible preparation for the storm had been wasted. Only their own self-reliance, only their own early campaign of resistance, could have provided the basis for real solidarity between them and other peoples.

And once they were attacked, the CPUSA ordered the remaining Japanese-Amerikan communists to become collaborators. So in the concentration camps CPUSA "communism" became the ideology of traitors. Those "aka" (radicals) who still followed the CPUSA, together with the pro-imperialist civil rights leaders of the Japanese American Citizens League (JACL), became open collaborators. In the Manzanar camp the CPUSA members formed the "Manzanar Citizens Federation," which urged inmates to "prove" their loyalty to the Empire by volunteering to serve in the military and by doing war production labor on camouflage nets and in picking crops. Some CPUSA and JACL collaborators

also began acting as informers for the US military police. The opposite tendency in Manzanar was led by the Blood Brothers Organization, an angry, anti-Amerikan youth group known by its "Black Dragon" symbol.

This all came to a showdown in December 1942. The head of the inmates' Kitchen Workers Union was arrested by GIs after he publicly exposed how the Assistant Warden was stealing meat and sugar rationed for the prisoners. His elected replacement was also arrested. That night a crowd of 1,000 angry, shouting Japanese-Amerikans confronted GIs at the administration building. The GIs began shooting, killing two and seriously wounding eight (those with light injuries were hidden out by the people). After they had escaped the GIs, some of the "Black Dragons" decided that it was intolerable to let the informers just walk about. So that night attempts were made to correct the leading CPUSA collaborators. Finally, the US Army had to take the collaborators and their families into protective custody and move them out of the camp, to save their lives.[12]

Those Japanese-American CPUSA members, who had the heaviest responsibility to lead their people, had failed international communism and themselves. This is the verdict of history. How could other communists aid them in their struggle, when their own communist leaders were supporting the oppressors? The absence of internationalism was their own responsibility first and foremost.

U.N.I.A. Women (Garvey's African Legion), 1923.
Photo by James Van Der Zee.

EARLY NEW AFRIKAN COMMUNISM

Oppressed nation communists had two unresolved problems in the 1920s and 1930s. **The first was the widespread belief, common until the period of Algeria and Vietnam, that a numerically small oppressed people could not overcome a large oppressor nation. The second was petty-bourgeois ideology, manifested in the stubborn belief that the goal of the struggle was to live a privileged European life**, that liberation meant joining imperialism as equals. This petty-bourgeois ideology was the primary problem, causing the inadequate theories of struggle that defeatism fed on. These two errors intertwined to trip up the liberation movements of the 1920s and 1930s in the US Empire. For that matter, they still remained to strongly influence the new revolutionary movements that arose in the 1960s.

The first wave of New Afrikan communists took shape as a tendency within the nationalist movement. Like Marcus Garvey (whom they all knew), many of those early communists were Pan-Afrikanists from the West Indies.

Cyril Briggs, the founder of the Afrikan Blood Brotherhood, was from the British colony of Nevis. His close associate, the brilliant agitator Richard Moore, came from Barbados. In the Harlem of 1918–1920 these first communists were active and respected in the community. Briggs had been the editor of Harlem's leading newspaper, the *Amsterdam News*, before resigning in 1918 over the publisher's interference with his anti-war editorials. Briggs' close friend, the socialist W.A. Domingo, was the first editor of Garvey's newspaper, the *Negro World*. Richard Moore was a local representative of the *African Times and Orient Review*, the ground-breaking Pan-Afrikanist journal published from London by Duse Mohammed (who had been Marcus Garvey's mentor). Like Mao Zedong and General Zhu De in China, these early New Afrikan communists came to political awareness within the broad nationalist movement. And they had all been internationalist in their outlook before they became communists.[13]

The nationalist movement as a whole, however, was convinced that New Afrikans were too outnumbered and too weak to fight the settler Empire. This belief led Marcus Garvey to react conservatively to the growing political repression of the 1920s. His movement hoped for a friendly or at least a neutral relationship with the US bourgeoisie. The UNIA attempted to buy time until their pioneers and resources from the Western Hemisphere could return to take over the nation of Liberia, giving them a sovereign land base from which to expand outward

across the Afrikan continent. Garvey vainly tried to forestall repression by appearing to go along with US imperialism, even to the point of trying to make peace with the resurgent Ku Klux Klan. While the New Afrikan masses remained nationalist in their sentiments, the inability of the giant Garvey Movement to resolve this primary question left nationalism without a practical program for liberation, and laid the basis for the splintering and political confusion that quickly overcame the broad movement.

New Afrikan communists, while they pushed the necessity for armed self-defense, shared with other nationalists the doubts that their oppressed nation could defeat US imperialism. In 1918 Cyril Briggs founded the *Crusader*, the militant newspaper that would become the voice of the ABB, representing: **"TEN MILLION colored people, a nation within a nation, a nationality oppressed and jim-crowed, yet worthy as any other people of a square deal or failing that, a separate political existence."**[14] Briggs as well as Garvey was soon saying that mass repatriation to Afrika was forced on their people by **"Necessity."** It was only in the new world upsurge in socialism that Briggs saw the changed conditions that might allow Black people to finally win a just place for themselves in North Amerika. By 1921, Briggs was urging:

"Every Negro in the United States should use his vote, and use it fearlessly and intelligently, to strengthen the radical movement, and thus create a deeper schism within the white race in America…"

In Cyril Briggs' view of 1921, socialist revolution in the US oppressor nation would be the only condition under which "the African question" could be settled here. This was the view that brought Briggs, Moore, and the rest of the African Blood Brotherhood into the Communist International. This is an important point. **The early New Afrikan communists did not necessarily see an internal force within US settler society capable of redeeming it.** Nor were they naive, trusting integrationists. They only united the ABB into the CPUSA because they believed that the revolutionary vision and power of the Bolsheviks would kick Euro-Amerikan leftists into line as allies. In a real sense, those New Afrikan communists felt that they weren't really joining the US white Left (which they didn't think too highly of) but the Communist International of Lenin and Stalin. There is a fine but definite line between internationalism, which upholds the necessity for the oppressed and forward-looking peoples of the world to unite, and the error of seeing liberation as coming from external forces and not from yourselves. The ABB leaned heavily on the USSR as the supposed answer for the national dilemma faced by New Afrikans. The results were devastating.

When Black radical Harry Haywood told his older brother, Otto Hall, in 1922 that he too wanted to join the CPUSA, Hall secretly enrolled him in the African Blood Brotherhood instead. That, Hall said, was a temporary measure decided upon by the Black comrades until the CPUSA straightened out the racism in the local Chicago South Side branch. Haywood asked his older brother: **"And if you don't get satisfaction there?" "Well, then there's the Communist International!"** Hall replied. Haywood recalls: "I was properly impressed by his sincerity and by the idea that we could appeal our case to the 'supreme court' of international communism, which included such luminaries as the great Lenin."[15]

The first wave of New Afrikan communists were so vulnerable to false internationalism because they viewed the Bolshevik Comintern as their main ally **against** the racism of the Euro-Amerikan radicals. Further, they believed that the resulting alliance with Euro-Amerikans was the indispensable precondition for the small Black Nation to fight the US Empire. The results of this political delusion were larger than was first realized. For ten years the full meaning of joining the Comintern was masked, since Briggs, Moore, and most of their comrades had little contact with the white Left. Typical was their work in the Harlem Educational Forum and similar socialist ventures in cooperation with other Black radicals. But two important things had happened. Communism was being taken out of the broad nationalist movement. The African Blood Brotherhood was stillborn, within two years of its founding being dissolved into the CPUSA. This meant that the New Afrikan Nation didn't have self-determination over its own revolutionary forces.

By the early 1930s the settler Communist Party USA was operating on Black commu-

nism, ripping out its national revolutionary orientation. Cyril Briggs and Richard Moore, for example, were purged to make way for synthetic Black leaders whose only lifeblood was settler revisionism (James W. Ford Jr. and Harry Haywood became the two best known examples of the latter). Briggs was removed in 1933 from editorship of the Party's Black newspaper, the *Liberator*, and shifted out of Harlem to do other Party work. Richard Moore was charged with "petty bourgeois nationalism" in 1934 and removed as national secretary of the League of Struggle for Negro Rights.

Just as in the Philippines, the oppressor nation CPUSA changed the leadership of colonial communists and even the party membership and structure. To suppress the nationalism that always simmered among their Black members, the CPUSA banned any all-Black gatherings. No Black community party unit, work committee, social gathering, or even mass organization could take place without Euro-Amerikan CPUSA members in watchful attendance. In 1933 Louis Sass, a Hungarian-Jewish chemist, was made chief administrator of the overall Harlem branch. Increasingly key inner administrative roles with-

James W. Ford & Earl Browder

in the Party's Black activities were held by settler intellectuals (just as the Jewish James S. Allen was its main theoretician on Black politics). The Party was worried about a nationalist revolt within its ranks, and crudely dismembered the nationality-based structure that had been built earlier by the first Black communists. Remaining Black CPUSA members became trapped by an "internationalism" in which they were constantly guarded as though they were inmates.

W.E.B. DuBois

Having tactically united with some of the most brilliant revolutionary nationalists of the period, having built a small political base in the community on the basis of supporting the Black Nation, the settler CPUSA then began to use its disciplined Black followers as puppet political agents to pacify the ghetto.

For by 1935, under the impact of the Depression and the threat of Italian invasion of Ethiopia, the New Afrikan community was alive with resurgent nationalism. Dr. W.E.B. DuBois, founder of the NAACP and the most prominent New Afrikan intellectual in the US, had stunned the liberal establishment by rapidly moving towards a nationalistic militancy. The violent 1935 uprising on the streets of Harlem was being mirrored in the political evolution of the man who had been the No. 1 symbol of liberal integrationism. In the June 1934 editorial in the *Crisis*, the NAACP's magazine, Dr. DuBois called for New Afrikan separatism in words not dissimilar from those of his old foe Marcus Garvey:

"Instead of sitting, sapped of all initiative and independence; instead of drowning our originality in imitation of mediocre white folks ... we have got to renounce a program that always involves humiliating self-stultifying scrambling to crawl somewhere we are not wanted; where we crouch panting like a whipped dog. We have to stop this and learn that on such a program one cannot build manhood. No, by God, stand erect in a mud-puddle and tell the

white world to go to Hell, rather than lick boots in a parlour ..."[16]

Within the next year DuBois had used his position with the NAACP to call for **"A Negro Nation Within the Nation."** All those forces that had pushed up Dr. DuBois—the Black liberal petty-bourgeoisie and their powerful patrons in the establishment—then rushed to cut Dr. DuBois down. He was ousted from the NAACP leadership, white-listed at the Black colleges, unable to find employment or a forum. This was nothing unusual or unexpected. What was interesting was the fact that the political attack on Dr. DuBois was joined in by the white radicals in and around the CPUSA.

The prominent *Nation* magazine featured a major article on DuBois in its May 15, 1935, issue. The author was a Euro-Amerikan radical labor journalist, Ben Stolberg. Stolberg quickly linked DuBois' new nationalist views up with the nationalist mood of the New Afrikan community as a whole; which he described as **"jobless, hungry, bewildered, and rapidly finding escape in racial chauvinism."** Stolberg spoke for settler radicalism when he flatly declared that there would be **"no Black economy or Black autonomy."** He ended by criticizing New Afrikan people in a threatening way as **"a counter-revolutionary force in the American class-struggle."**[17]

Letters supporting white supremacist Stolberg's position appeared in subsequent issues, particularly after the National NAACP issued a statement criticizing Stolberg as having the views of a "Southern white bourbon." Four of the most prestigious Black professors, led by E. Franklin Frazier and Ralph J. Bunche, wrote a letter applauding Stolberg for "a brilliant and sound analysis." The four closed their letter by saying: "We, Negro teachers at Howard University, subscribe to the same kind of Southern white bourbonism."[18] The most interesting letter came from the CPUSA, which for years had been denouncing DuBois as one of the "lap dogs at the table of imperialism." CPUSA representative James S. Allen, their leading theoretician on colonial matters, wrote to assure his fellow settlers that the CPUSA joined ranks against New Afrikan nationalism in the revolutionary crisis:

"Petty-bourgeois Negro leaders (now including Dr. DuBois) and organizations are attempting to divert this upsurge into channels of separatism and segregation. It is precisely against such petty-bourgeois nationalism that the Communist Party fights ..."[19]

Stolberg, as well as others, had to concede that nationalism was the growing sentiment of the New Afrikan grassroots. Even the CPUSA admitted this. When a reader wrote to the *Negro Liberator* asking: "What is meant by Negro Nationalism?," the printed answer was: "Negro Nationalism (or petty-bourgeois nationalism) is the theory that the solution to the Negro question lies in one race fighting another ... The Negro people cannot free themselves without fighting in unity with their white allies for full equality ... Among the outstanding leaders of nationalism are Marcus Garvey and W.E.B. DuBois. The tasks of the League of Struggle for Negro Rights are to expose these leaders and at the same time to win **the rank and file Negroes, who are under the influence of nationalism**, to a program of struggle with their white fellow toilers for complete equality."[20] (our emphasis)

The united front against Dr. DuBois showed a growing convergence between the Communist Party USA and the Black petty-bourgeoisie. This took full form after the 7th Congress of the Comintern inaugurated the Popular Front Against Fascism policy in August 1935. **The CPUSA, with Comintern approval, interpreted the Popular Front policy to mean that New Afrikan communists should build broad, "interracial" coalitions on a liberal basis, with the goal of full assimilation into White Amerika.**

In the Winter of 1935 what was left of the Party's activity for New Afrikan self-determination was stopped. The CPUSA Central Committee officially shelved the issue itself, meaning that the Party still professed to believe in New Afrikan self-determination but would no longer organize around it. Both the League of Struggle for Negro Rights and the newspaper *Negro Liberator* were ended. In the South the armed Alabama Sharecroppers Union, which had grown since 1931 to 10,000 members in rural Alabama with 2,500 more in Mississippi, Louisiana, Georgia, and North Carolina, was dissolved the next October. The CPUSA Central Committee decided that the sharecropper movement was leading toward widespread armed struggle on the National Territory (which was certainly correct), which they didn't want. A small committee of white men in New York City had the power to order an armed New Afrikan mass organization, fighting for the Land, to give up. The Sharecroppers' Union had been created by sharecroppers themselves, but was overcome by false internationalism.

Now we can return to the question of the mass Ethiopian solidarity movement that swept the New Afrikan Nation in 1935–36, and understand how the CPUSA's treacherous line could prevail within the movement despite the nationalist and militant sentiments at the grassroots.

The Party's Black membership was rapidly growing then, but also changing in class terms. There were still many working-class nationalist members like Audley Moore, the famous woman organizer who had come to Harlem radicalism from the Garvey Movement in New Orleans. Increasingly, however, many Black members were professionals, white collar workers or students who saw the CPUSA as the only organization that would help them get advancement into White Amerika. Many of those who felt otherwise about their own goals were quitting. The young novelist Richard Wright, unable to match his "individuality" to the Party's program, almost left the Party then (he finally quit later in 1942). Wright turned down the offer of a European trip and possible promotion made to him as a bribe by Harry Haywood, a Black Central Committee member. He had noticed that the Party's air of crude opportunism that so disgusted him attracted many others: "... as I was losing touch with the Party, many other young Negroes of the South Side were entering it for the first time. The expansion of the Party's activities under the People's Front policy offered many opportunities to young Negroes who, because of race and status, had led cramped lives. The invitation to go to Switzerland as a youth delegate, which I had refused, was accepted by a young Negro who had fought the Communist Party and all its ideas until he had seen a chance to take a trip to Europe."[21]

An academic study of the CPUSA in Harlem brings out how important that united front with settler radicals became to the Black petty-bourgeoisie:

"**Between 1936 and 1939, the Communist Party emerged as an important focal point of political and cultural activity by Harlem intellectuals. 'My memory and knowledge,' Party organizer Howard Johnson recalls, 'is that 75% of black cultural figures had Party membership or maintained regular meaningful contact with the Party.' Harlem critics of the Party spoke bitterly of Party dominance of the black intelligentsia and feared they would use this to 'capture the entire Negro group.' 'Most of the Negro intellectuals,' Claude McKay wrote, 'were directly or indirectly hypnotized by the propaganda of the Popular Front,' ...**

...

"**... The new Party strategy called for the incorporation of the entire black community into antifascist alliances with white liberals and radicals, and it viewed the black intelligentsia as a pivotal group in its quest for 'sustained and fraternal cooperation' with the most powerful groups in black life—the NAACP, the Urban League, and the black church.**

"**The Popular Front Party's success among Harlem intellectuals, however, whether measured in membership or political influence, proportionately far exceeded its impact on Harlem's working class. Abner Berry and Howard Johnson, important Party leaders in the period (Johnson was a leader of the Harlem Young Communists League), both recall that the Party had a very high percentage of middle-class members—perhaps half—in a community where the overwhelming majority of the population was working class and poor. Although articles in the Party press did not discuss the Harlem Communist Party's social composition, the one Party branch in Harlem consistently singled out for praise during the Popular Front era, the Milton Herndon branch, was located in 'Sugar Hill,' probably Harlem's wealthiest neighborhood. The set of symbols and affinities that marked Popular Front politics in Harlem—linking the cause of**

Ethiopia with that of China and Loyalist Spain; identifying the persecution of Jews in Germany with that of blacks in the United States; viewing the New Deal and the labor movement as harbingers of black progress—had more weight among black doctors than they did among black domestics, or among parishioners of St. Philip's than worshippers in storefront churches.

"... Between 1935 and 1937, white-collar employment opportunities for Harlem blacks expanded enormously, partly as a result of liberal policies of the LaGuardia and Roosevelt administrations, and partly as a result of protests against discrimination led by left-wing unions and Harlem community groups. In the Emergency Relief Bureau, a center of leftist agitation, more than 1,100 blacks found employment, most in skilled positions, and thousands more received jobs on WPA projects set up during 1935 and 1936. Although most WPA jobs were in blue-collar fields—e.g., sewing or construction—the WPA represented a special boon for educated Harlemites: more than 350 found employment on a theatre project as actors, directors, and designers; other found jobs as writers and researchers and teachers on adult education programs; musicians and artists found employment in their specialties; and WPA health centers hired black doctors and nurses. Many Negro WPA employees had 'the best jobs they've ever

had in their lives,' the *Amsterdam News* declared. Thousands of Negro clerks and other white collar relief workers found the kind of employment they are trained for.'

"This expansion of opportunities in government employment coming at a time of stagnation and decline in black business enterprise, tended to undermine the

Selam Burke, WPA Federal Art Project sculptress, beside her bust of Booker T. Washington.

prestige of strategies emphasizing black self-sufficiency and give credence to those emphasizing interracial alliances ...

"These positive experiences with the left along with a profusion of new opportunities, gave educated blacks something of a buffer against nationalist ideologies which had a hold among less privileged sectors of Harlem's population. As the economic crisis persisted, and Harlem's poor fell into nearly total dependency on the relief system, street speakers preaching variations on Garvey's message expanded their popular following. Embittered by their isolation from positions of power and near-exclusion from the Harlem media, they combined shrewd critiques of interracialism with raw agitation of prejudice against Italians and Jews. Admirers of Japan, the first 'colored nation' to become a world power, they bitterly rejected any internationalism which lacked a racial component and urged Harlemites to 'think black, talk black, act black, and see black.'

"The pessimism inherent in this vision had deep roots in Afro-American culture—as Garvey's appeal demonstrated—but it failed to strike a chord among an upwardly mobile black intelligentsia and white-collar group that saw its position in American life materially improving and perceived anti-fascism as a worldview which gave legitimacy to their aspirations."[22]

The Afrikan elite supported the CPUSA's take-over of the Ethiopian solidarity movement because it also expressed their own class views. After the *Pittsburgh Courier* reported from Addis Ababa that the Ethiopian military was open to New Afrikan volunteers, in particular those with technical skills, the newspaper's owner announced that the Volunteer Movement was illegal. The US Government ordered the Ethiopian Consul-General to stop all recruiting of volunteers. Robert L. Vann, the *Courier*'s owner, was also an Assistant to the US Attorney-General.[23] In an "international" coalition the "Black Cabinet" and settler radicals were standing together against the nationalist upsurge in the streets.

These were class contradictions **within** the oppressed nation. Liberal integrationist leaders such as the Rev. Adam Clayton Powell, Jr. and the NAACP's Roy Wilkins had, after all, spent years in bitter conflict with the nationalists. After Powell had used the pulpit of his powerful Abyssinian Baptist Church in 1933 to criticize the illegal tactics of the nationalist "Jobs For Negroes Movement," nationalist Sufi Abdul Hammid set up his soapbox right outside the church. Crowds would gather as he damned the Rev. Powell as a degenerate taken up with alcoholism and sex. The nationalists were attempting to follow Marcus Garvey's vision in using Afrikan buying power and small retail trade as building blocks toward a future separate Afrikan economy. To them the boycott and displacement of Italian merchants was important—even a pushcart "business" can be a step upward to someone who has nothing. There was a nationalist ideological commitment to the creation of a commercial New Afrikan petty-bourgeoisie, and they had close ties to the independent New Afrikan merchants who shared their hostility to both white business and white unions.[24]

Black intellectuals openly scorned these limited ghetto ambitions. Rev. Adam Clayton Powell, Jr. sneered at them in his column in the *Amsterdam News*: **"Give the Italian haters Antonio's fish cart, Tony's ice business, and Patsy's fruit stand and they'll forget all about Haile Selassie."** To the college-educated Black professionals running a cramped food stand or a little shoe shop would only be a come-down. They as a class could have far different social goals than self-educated street organizers. Black professionals wanted to get their "rightful place" in the mainstream of the settler Empire's institutions—in government agencies, medical centers, the big corporations. The CPUSA's liberal integrationism backed with mass protests fit their class politics. So when the Black white-collar petty-bourgeoisie got a chance to help liquidate Afrikan solidarity into a fashionable Euro-Amerikan cause, they became intoxicated with this false internationalism. One history recounts this strange episode of Black professionals pretending to be European:

"Because this perspective was widely shared among educated blacks, Communists had little difficulty in developing an enthusiastic support network in Harlem for the Spanish Loyalist cause. In the spring of 1937, Communists, using the slogan 'Ethiopia's fate is at stake on the battlefields of Spain,' worked to make the Spanish Civil War the preeminent cause for internationally-minded blacks. They encouraged blacks to serve in the International Brigades as soldiers and medical workers and to contribute money and medical supplies which they had collected for Ethiopia to the Spanish government. 'The material aid which they could not give to the Land of the Ethiopians,' William Patterson wrote, 'separated as they were thousands of miles and innumerable difficulties imposed by ... capitalist governments, can be given through Spain.'

"Nationalist leaders bitterly attacked this initiative, but many black intellectuals adopted the Spanish cause with great fervor. Several nurses and doctors active in United Aid for Ethiopia (including Dr. Arnold Donawa, the former head of Howard University dental school) volunteered for the Abraham Lincoln Brigade; Harlem churches and professional organizations sponsored rallies for the Loyalist cause; and black relief workers and doctors raised enough funds to send a fully equipped ambulance for Spain. Two blacks who died in Spain—Alonzo Watson and Milton Herndon—were honored with memorial services at leading Harlem churches (St. James Presbyterian and

United and Integrated

Integrated and united against fascism in the A.L.B. Front left to right: Mexican, Afro-American, Philipino, Cuban, Japanese-American.

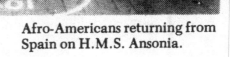

Afro-Americans returning from Spain on H.M.S. Ansonia.

Comrades-in-arms on their return from the battlefields.

Abyssinian Baptist) and torchlight parades through the community. A Carnegie Hall Concert for Spain, sponsored by a Harlem and Musicians' Committee for Spanish Democracy, featured people like Cab Calloway, Fats Waller, and Count Basie, and a dinner in honor of Salaria Kee, a black nurse who served in Spain, drew virtually the entire black nursing staff from Harlem and Lincoln Hospitals.

"By 1938, support for Spain had assumed an almost fashionable air, becoming a symbol of sophistication and political awareness among Harlem's intelligentsia. 'There was much speech making, singing, and dancing for Spain,' George Streator recalled. 'Spanish freedom and Negro freedom were made to be synonymous.'"[25]

This class contradiction took place within the larger framework of Empire and neo-colonialism. Popular Front strategy by the CPUSA was very effective at not only splitting a New Afrikan united front, but at playing off nationalists against each other. Captain A.L. King of the UNIA was persuaded to join the CPUSA's joint campaign against other nationalists. Communists got a suspicious UNIA leader to address a meeting of their Italian Workers Club in 1935. Instead of the open animosity he expected, the nationalist leader was greeted by the Italian communist audience with warm applause and donations of money. Touched by this unexpected show of respect, the UNIA leader was won over to being a CPUSA

ally. Even within the nationalist movement there were those who didn't reject Babylon as a thing, but only opposed it tactically because they themselves were not accepted by the oppressor society. Many nationalists were successfully reached by the CPUSA.

Essentially the New Afrikan National Movement, which had made great strides, was hijacked by a coalition of petty-bourgeois Euro-Amerikans and petty-bourgeois Blacks, who "recognized" each other as the joint leadership. The New Afrikan masses were frozen out, allowed no voice in their destiny. At a time when the New Afrikan proletariat was growing politically, the effect was to force them as a class out of the movement. There was a movement program mainly for Black intellectuals, white-collar workers, and professionals, which advanced their narrow class interests. There was an AFL-CIO industrial trade union program, of a purely economic nature, for that small percentage of New Afrikan urban workers who worked with settlers in major industry—steel, auto, chemical, rubber, etc. In those sectors the CPUSA was attempting to convert the New Afrikan workers into a relatively better-paid, settler-led, labor aristocracy split off from the rest of the New Afrikan proletariat.

But for the majority of the New Afrikan proletariat, unemployed, casual labor, domestics, etc., the movement literally had no program. Nor did it have one for the millions of New Afrikan sharecroppers and farm

laborers it had so casually abandoned. The movement simply left the vast majority of its oppressed Nation on the side. Black radicals co-opted by the CPUSA had come to represent a petty-bourgeois program. The same was true of the nationalist movement, however much it shared the anger of the colonial oppressed.

Claude McKay wrote with bitter rage at that insolent class viewpoint of Black CPUSA official-dom in the '30s:

"Once I mentioned to Mr. Manning Johnson the fact of hundreds of Negroes working in the innumerable coffee shops, sandwich shops, fish-and-potato shops, Southern-cooking restaurants, etc. in Harlem. Mr. Johnson is a college graduate, an efficient organizer of the Cafeteria Union and prominent in the Communist hierarchy. I said I thought it would help the community if those workers were welded together in a General Union of Negroes or some such organization. But at the places I mentioned Mr. Johnson sneered as stink-pots.

"He was right. These Harlem places cannot be compared to cafeterias downtown. But after all, the whites whom we envy—beating our brains out against the walls of their preju-dice—they too began at the bottom."[26]

The result of pushing the New Afrikan prole-tariat out of their own national movement, of turning would-be communists into oppressor nation puppets, was easy to see. Blacks started leaving the Communist Party USA and its influ-ence. Even the Black professionals discovered that the settleristic CPUSA was hard to live in. In 1936–1938 the Party recruited 2,320 new Black members in New York, but at the same time lost 1,518 Black members. In 1946 Black Party leader Doxy Wilkerson admitted: "Tens of thousands of Negroes who instinctively rejected our illu-sions remained entirely without our influence. And many thousands of those who entered our ranks failed to find the answers they sought …"[27] **The collapse of the New Afrikan Liberation Movement at the end of the '30s reflected not lack of mass consciousness but the failure of their leadership.**

Right: Rosa Lee Ingram and sons Sammie Lee and Wallace in Albany, Georgia, jail cell, 1948. Their sentence to die in the electric chair for having defended themselves against settler violence was handed down by an all-white, all male jury on February 7, 1948. When their executions were scheduled for February 27, 1948, less than three weeks later, protests erupted against the trial and sentences, which had been conducted in haste and secrecy. Their sentences were commuted to life in April 1948, and they were paroled in 1959 Photo: Associated Press.

From One Generation to the Next!

Ours is a struggle with continuity, unbroken except occasionally in our own minds. We have, and must continue to struggle from one generation to the next; evolving in time and space, a people in motion, regaining independence and making history.

Ours is a mass struggle, a people's struggle, a struggle involving the participation of the young and the old, the female and the male. Ours is the struggle of an entire people, a whole nation oppressed and moving toward a new way of life on a planet made mad by greed and fear.

Our struggle involves our elders, the refugees who were forced to abandon the National Territory, head north and northwest, during the "migrations."

They were REFUGEES, those who "migrated" from the National Territory during the WWI and WWII years. Our elders were REFUGEES during the years of the "Black Codes" when they fled the National Territory.

The cities of amerikkka are full of New Afrikan refugees who entered them during the '30s, the '40s, escaping the klan and the southern prison. One step ahead of the hounds, a few minutes ahead of the lynch mob is how many New Afrikans came north. Refugees, from the National Territory.

New Afrikans now living in Peoria, Brooklyn, Oakland and Des Moines, were born in Clarksdale, Mississippi, and Greensboro, North Carolina. Twelve-year-old bloods boarded trains in New Orleans, Mobile and Atlanta, loaded with stained brown paper bags of cold chicken, cardboard suitcases, and dreams of big cities where work was available and where white folks weren't so mean.

We became refugees from the National Territory; We came with dreams and We wanted "to forget the past," to forget the oppression and terror, to forget the snarls of red necks and the strange fruit of poplar trees. Far too many of us forgot that the struggle goes on, from one generation to the next. We forgot that We were simply refugees, and not yet free.

The '40s, '50s and even the early '60s were years which saw New Afrikan faces rubbed with Royal Crown so they wouldn't be "ashy"; saw our heads plastered with Murry's, saw noses and lips as repulsive objects in the thin-shaped beauty standards of amerikkka.

These same years saw us move gradually farther from our first stops upon leaving the trains and buses; they saw the families that came north move farther "out south" and into dwellings just abandoned by whites; they saw us move further from each other and the strength which allowed us to survive and maintain the consciousness of ourselves as one people, struggling from one generation to the next, until We are free.

Being colonial subjects situated so near the seat of empire has blurred our vision. Slaves in "the richest country in the world"—while still slaves—are "better off" than slaves elsewhere. Amerikkka is the "big house" of the plantation it has made of a good part of the world. It is more difficult now than in the past, for us to feel acutely the chains that bind us—enough so that We begin again to pass on the history, to begin again to socialize the children and hand down the awareness that comes with being taught the survival/resistance techniques needed to overcome the obstacles to our independence presented by the settlers who rule.

From one generation to the next is how We must move, until the nation is sovereign.

Atiba Shanna
New Afrikan POW Journal Book Three

Organize the Unorganized New Afrikan Masses

Marchers with SCLC sign for the Savannah Freedom Now Movement, during the March on Washington, 1963. Photo by Marion S. Trikosko.

V. Freedom Now!

"Well, if the Blacks, and the Puerto Ricans, and the Chicanos and the Indians all get what they want, then there won't be any United States …"

Oregon high school student
questioning a Cherokee speaker from the
American Indian Movement

So the reawakening of anti-colonial struggles here within the continental Empire in the 1960s was still ideologically unaware. It was a situation in which oppressed peoples went through rapid changes, trying and growing beyond different approaches and organizations, as cities burned and US imperialism was thrown on the defensive. The oppressed started rediscovering their true situation, their own heritage, and the reality of their Nationhood. There were four main characteristics to those '60s movements:

1. They rapidly evolved towards armed struggle, with self-defense leading to armed organizations. Anti-government violence had mass approval and participation.

2. Awareness of separate nationhood grew— of not being part of the US oppressor nation. This was seen in the reexamination of culture, in language, religion, dress, and the arts. Sovereignty over the land became a key concept.

3. National liberation struggles here were not seen as isolated to themselves, but as parts of a world revolution of the oppressed. People were influenced by India, Ghana, Algeria, Cuba, Vietnam, and many other peoples' struggles. Crazy Horse and Ho were both seen as heroic teachers. Socialism was introduced as an alternative to "the American Way."

4. The urban movements were in most cases under the class leadership of the petty bourgeoisie and the lumpen. Which meant that their political programs embodied an ambivalent, "love-hate" relationship towards imperialism. Even the most militant organizations were amalgamations of those who were fighting for liberation and those who, whatever they thought they were doing, were fighting for a share of Babylon.

The national movements did not reach a proletarian viewpoint. This limitation undermined the great advances of the '60s movements. Even among those who picked up the gun, driven by anger and need for change, even within revolutionary organizations, this covered-over ambivalence helped create setback after setback. Recently, for example, arrests after an abortive NY expropriation were followed by the defection to the Government of a number of fighters and supporters of the RATF (Revolutionary Armed Task Force), most notably supposed "BLA" members Peter Middleton and Tyrone Rison. Both have been publicly denounced as traitors. But to see them just as unexplained betrayals of no known origin is less than useful. They have roots within the movement's unresolved character. Folks should see that a Tyrone Rison and a Peter Middleton are legitimate descendants of the class confusion of Huey Newton and Eldridge Cleaver..

1. THE CIVIL RIGHTS STAGE OF ANTI-COLONIAL STRUGGLE

From the start the 1960s Black movement had a dual character, of being both rebellious and loyalist, of both arousing the New Afrikan masses and trying to restrain them, of being an anti-colonial movement with neo-colonial views. The Southern Civil Rights Movement that opened up the 1960s was a clear example of this dual character. It was a movement, largely led by ministers and other New Afrikan community leaders, committed to nonviolence and with a moderate program of desegregation. It was explicitly Christian and pro-Amerikan in its outlook. Liberal whites were seen not merely as allies but as "brothers" and "sisters." Yet the student sit-ins that began on February 1, 1960, in Greensboro, NC, rocked the US Empire.

The Southern Civil Rights struggle was a movement that defied and exposed the colonial power. The women and men of that young movement were consciously part of the world anti-colonial rising. To see this fully we have to deal with the class nature of the movement. While the Southern Civil Rights movement drew support from all classes of the Nation, its young leaders and activists were primarily from the petty-bourgeoisie. Most were college students. Theirs was a class and a generation that was profoundly influenced by the world anti-colonial transformation.

Throughout the 1950s national liberation movements had risen against the European colonial powers. Red China and the Democratic Republic of Vietnam were successful. India in 1950, Ghana in 1957, and Algeria in 1962 had won self-government. Rev. Martin Luther King, Jr. and Coretta Scott King were guests of Prime Minister Kwame Nkrumah at Ghana's independence ceremony on March 6, 1957. Rev. King was a world figure because of the Montgomery, Ala. Bus Boycott of 1956. Their visit provided a striking contrast: in Ghana, Western-educated Afrikans ran their own government, while in Alabama the Rev. Martin Luther King, Jr. was unable to vote, hold public office, attend the state university, or eat at a downtown restaurant. Young ministers, professionals, and students sought out the new ideas from abroad, in particular the nonviolent civil disobedience philosophy of Gandhi in India. As they watched anti-colonialism sweep the Third World, New Afrikan communities came to the decision that Rev. King was himself echoing in every speech: **"We have a determination to be free in this day and age. This is an idea whose time has come."**[1]

The Southern movement took form around the strategy of nonviolent direct action. We should emphasize that this was, at that time and place, a strategy of illegality, of danger, of arousing people to direct confrontations with the colonial oppressor. Whether it was sitting-in at a segregated lunch counter or bus station, or defying court orders to march on a county courthouse, the movement deliberately broke the colonial law. If the institutionalized fear of settler violence had kept many from protesting their oppression before, now the Sit-In movement promised to fill the jails. Young and old pushed toward police lines, no longer willing to be stopped by settler terrorism. The illegal sit-ins spread from Greensboro to cities throughout the South, with some 3,600 arrests within the year.

Inevitably the anti-colonial struggle moved to a higher level, growing beyond this initial stage of nonviolent civil rights protests. Nonviolent civil rights strategy was tried and then discarded by the New Afrikan masses, who found that it was a failure, incapable of forcing an entrenched settler-colonial regime to change. Albany, Georgia in

Ronald Martin, Robert Patterson, and Mark Martin sit-down strike at F.W. Woolworth, Greensboro, NC, Feb. 2, 1960. Photo: UPI.

1961–1962 was the decisive test. Despite nine months of illegal sit-ins and marches with over 1,500 arrests locally, national publicity, statements of support by a bipartisan collection of US Senators and Governors, together with the presence of settler ministers, rabbis, and students from all over the North, the Civil Rights movement was unable to win anything, not even token desegregation of public facilities. Lerone Bennet has written that **"Albany, by any standard, was a staggering defeat for King and the freedom movement."** King was finally forced to leave the city by the angry local movement leadership.

The Southern movement strategy of nonviolent mass pressure, of filling the courts and jails, disrupting the normal business of public places, completely failed. The liberal *New Republic* commented: "Once the goal was to fill the jails. But the Albany City Jail, which had working agreements with fortresses in neighboring counties, proved a bottomless pit. Not since Albany has anyone taken Rev. King literally when he has talked of filling the jails of the South."[2] Over thirty Southern police departments sent officers to Albany to be trained in smothering Black protests. A suddenly famous Albany Police Chief Pritchett was flown North by the Ford Foundation to address a top-level seminar for police chiefs. And in Harlem, Minister Malcolm X was pointing out the true meaning of the Albany defeat.

Albany represented the surfacing of a political crisis. The Freedom Movement had started millions of New Afrikans moving towards liberation, and yet its widely proclaimed strategy of nonviolent protest was unworkable. The creative result of this contradiction was already being born among the people themselves, as in the Albany struggle. When Rev. King led 250 singing marchers towards the Albany City Hall on December 17, 1961, the arrests were watched by a curious crowd on the sidelines. Hidden within that crowd were the members of two youth gangs, who had secretly come on their own initiative to jump out and defend the marchers if the arresting police got violent.[3] By the next July, militant youth had left the sidelines and taken the center stage. After a woman was badly beaten by a sheriff's deputy while attempting to deliver food to activists in a rural prison camp, two thousand New Afrikan youth took over streets and whole blocks in a night-long uprising on July 24, 1962. Police cars were stoned, and eventually pulled out of the ghetto. The stage of protests was leading to the stage of rebellion.

2. THE BULLET & THE BALLOT

The impending failure of the nonviolent Civil Rights movement was primarily a crisis for two classes—for the US bourgeoisie and the Black petty-bourgeoisie. In response to the threat of liberation war, the US Empire drew the colonial petty-bourgeoisie closer to itself as a shield while enacting a revamped neo-colonial program to pacify the masses. Civil Rights became the US Government's official pacification program, while the hollow shell of the dying Civil Rights movement was itself taken over by US imperialism to be used against the deeper anti-colonial rebellion.

By the time of President Kennedy's assassination on November 22, 1963, the imperialist State had mobilized behind its new counterinsurgency program—the Ballot and the Bullet. That strategy was a watered-down replica of the original Black Reconstruction of the 1860s and 1870s. It reminds us of Marx's comment that all great events in history happen not once but twice—"the first as tragedy and the second as farce." Under its new strategy imperialism stepped up its search and destroy missions in the New Afrikan communities. Not only to violently neutralize militant leaders and organizations as a danger per se, but to clear the way for the Empire's hand-picked Civil Rights leadership to command the struggle.

This loyalist leadership directed the protest movement back around towards neo-colonialism as a goal, towards begging to be accepted into Babylon as citizens. Instead of mass struggle—which shoots off in rebellious directions—the Empire wanted its loyalist Civil Rights leaders to convince New Afrikans that voting in US elections should be their main weapon. And that their basic philosophy should be to look up to the Federal Government as New Afrikan people's special protector and economic provider. To the extent that such a loyalist Civil Rights movement influenced them, New Afrikans would be disarmed in all senses of the word. So in the US Empire's 1960s strategy, persuading New Afrikans to get tied up in US bourgeois politics and shooting down those who still dissented were joint parts of the same counterinsurgency plan—the ballot and the bullet.

At Albany, for example, where the nonviolent movement had taken on a mass character that might lead to rebellion, and where the embattled local organizers had thrown off the restraining national Civil Rights leadership, the Kennedy Administration struck at the grassroots. President John F. Kennedy told the press that he thought that the city government should work out a negotiated agreement. His brother, US Attorney-General Robert Kennedy, held a late-night meeting on Albany with NAACP President Roy Wilkins, Mel Wulf of the ACLU (American Civil Liberties Union), Walter Fauntroy of SCLC (Southern Christian Leadership Conference), and other Civil Rights leaders. They were told that for the first time in the South, teams of FBI agents had been sent into Albany to set up Federal criminal indictments. Front-page newspaper articles in early August 1962 portrayed the Government as sympathetic to the Albany Freedom Movement. This was just a deception.[4]

Meanwhile in Albany itself, thirty-five FBI agents had interviewed naively cooperative Civil Rights activists. Fifty-eight New Afrikans were then subpoenaed to appear before a Federal grand jury in Macon, the first Southwestern Georgia grand jury called over Civil Rights activity. But to their surprise they found that they and not the racists were the target. The imperialist strategy called for little visible police violence on the main streets of Albany itself, where the international media might publicize it. Everywhere outside city limits, however, in the surrounding towns and rural areas, police suppression of the movement intensified.

In nearby Americus, Georgia, on August 8, 1961, three SNCC (Student Nonviolent Coordinating Committee) field workers watching a demonstration were attacked by Americus police. After being tortured, the three were charged with intent to murder and insurrection (death penalty offenses) and held without bail for three months. A protest demonstration the next day was violently smashed by a posse made up of Americus police, deputized Klansmen, county police, and state troopers. New Afrikan elderly and teenagers alike were severely clubbed and burned with electric cattle prods. On that same day, US Attorney-General Robert Kennedy was personally holding a Washington press conference to announce that his Macon, Georgia grand jury had indicted nine Albany Civil Rights workers for organizing a boycott of a settler grocery store. A US Justice Department spokesman, in answer to questions from surprised newsmen, said: **"There is no evidence of police brutality in Americus."**

Eight of the nine Civil Rights workers were convicted after a token trial in which the US

Attorney struck off every potential New Afrikan juror, resulting in an all-settler jury. Sentences ranged from five years suspended up to two years in prison.[5] In coordination with the FBI operation, the local Klan blew up four Albany New Afrikan churches. The US counterinsurgency strategy on the one hand allied with the "moderate" national Civil Rights leadership and portrayed the Government as supporting democratic change, while on the other was using unofficial terrorism to intimidate the New Afrikan community, and was repressing the Movement infrastructure with direct police violence and FBI frame-ups. While everyone thought of the national Civil Rights leadership and the Klan as total opposites, both were coordinated arms of the sophisticated, US counterinsurgency campaign. In his speech to the 1963 March on Washington, SNCC Chairman John Lewis was going to charge: **"It seems to me that the Albany indictment is part of a conspiracy on the part of the Federal Government ..."** That line was censored out of his speech at the united insistence of the rest of the Civil Rights leadership.[6]

Even before Albany, at the beginning of the Sit-In movement, the development of Civil Rights politics was being influenced by counterinsurgency strategy. At the June 1961 SNCC Conference in Louisville, Kentucky, Tim Jenkins made a proposal that the movement turn away from militant confrontations and illegal protests—and instead focus its energies on voter registration. This proposal actually originated with the Government. Burke Marshall,

Assistant Attorney-General for Civil Rights, and Presidential "minorities" advisor Harris Wofford, together with Stephen Currier of the Taconic Foundation and the representatives of the Field Foundation, had worked out the proposal in secret meetings with Jenkins. The latter was then the Black Vice-President of the liberal National Student Association (NSA), the federation of college student governments. While Jenkins has always denied working for the CIA within the Civil Rights Movement, at that time the CIA was using the NSA as its main front for international student work. Some NSA officers have admitted covertly cooperating with the CIA, which was supplying a good part of the National Student Association budget.

The Jenkins proposal shocked many young activists, and created a sharp political struggle. Some called it a sell-out of the movement. At the SNCC meeting the Rev. Martin Luther King, Jr. intervened as a moderator, listening sympathetically to the militants for hours, finally getting a compromise proposal passed in which SNCC would approve both government-sponsored voter registration and militant direct action. King sincerely spoke for the importance of working with the US Government. What the students (and the New Afrikan community) didn't know was that the first secret deal was already being made to pull away from mass struggle.

In May 1961 the Congress of Racial Equality (CORE) had launched the Freedom Rides, a national attack on segregated interstate transpor-

tation. Integrated teams took Greyhound and Trailways buses through the Deep South, refusing to sit in the back of the bus or limit themselves to "colored" waiting rooms. A frenzy of hatred gripped the settler South as an amazed world watched. The first Greyhound bus was stopped and burned by a settler mob outside Anniston, Alabama. The second reached Birmingham, where a KKK assault organized by the FBI sent two Freedom Riders to the hospital.

Throughout the South mobs of settlers, coordinated by police and the FBI, violently attacked Freedom Riders. In Montgomery, after a mob of one thousand settlers injured Euro-Amerikan reporters and John Siegenthaler, a White House aide, seven hundred US Marshals were flown into town to maintain order. The Kennedy White House was concerned that this orgy of settler violence, front-page news around the world, would undercut their plans to pacify the ghetto. SCLC and Rev. Martin Luther King, Jr. also called the high-risk Freedom Rides "unfortunate." King surprised his public by refusing to go himself. Robert F. Williams telegrammed Rev. King in anger: **"You're a phony. Gandhi was always in the forefront, suffering with his people. If you are the leader of this nonviolent movement, lead the way by example."**

So after US Attorney-General Robert F. Kennedy was turned away when he appealed for a "cooling-off period," the Rev. Martin Luther King, Jr. proposed a "temporary lull" in Freedom Rides instead. Which was the same thing. Robert F. Kennedy had convened a secret meeting with the Civil Rights leadership. There the President's brother had explained why the Administration needed an end to the violent confrontations. He said that the Government and the Civil Rights leaders really wanted the same things. Both their interests would be satisfied not by militant struggles but by registering millions of New Afrikan voters in the South. New Afrikan voting would integrate local Southern government, prevent "riots," and give the liberal Democrats extra votes to help the White House.

If the Civil Rights leadership would quietly phase out the freedom rides in favor of Government-sponsored voter registration campaigns, Kennedy promised, he would give their organizations an initial $250,000, and get the Interstate Commerce Commission to rule in the Fall that segregation of bus, train, and airline travel was forbidden. Of course, Kennedy couldn't give them money directly. He arranged for the Taconic Foundation, whose settler President Stephen Currier became a part of the Civil Rights leadership, and the Field Foundation to divide the money up between the NAACP, SCLC, SNCC, and CORE. Kennedy promised them as much money as they needed to fight Robert Williams, Malcolm X, and the other nationalists.[7] The Civil Rights leadership accepted the imperialist program. At that same time Andrew Young was to be added to King's SCLC staff. Young was working directly for Field Foundation, in charge of spending $100,000 in the South persuading the movement to concentrate on voter registration projects.

Two blood-splattered Freedom Riders, John Lewis and James Zwerg stand together after being attacked and beaten by pro-segregationists in Montgomery, Alabama.

3. THE YEAR OF COUNTERINSURGENCY

The decisive year for imperialism's new policy was 1963, when the Empire moved into a stepped-up neo-colonial campaign. New Afrikans were reluctantly, over the bitter protests of the settler masses, conceded some bourgeois democratic rights in the South. These rights were in the form of second-class ("minority") Empire citizenship. Even so the change was considerable. Within the space of a few years New Afrikans could both shop and work at downtown department stores, be policemen and sheriffs, shift from Black colleges to major universities, elect Black officials to local government, and for a while play at being real citizens of Great Babylon. This was the final step in a process: the change that had earlier forced paper US citizenship on the Indian nations in 1924, and Hawaiians and Puerto Ricans as well.

In the 1960s the Black petty-bourgeoisie emerged in a key role, as an intermediary class between the US bourgeoisie and the New Afrikan masses. The petty-bourgeoisie as a world class has a vacillating and intermediary character, neither owning the means of production as does the bourgeoisie nor supporting society through its labor as does the proletariat. But in an oppressed nation the petty-bourgeoisie is, as a whole, an intermediary class between the people of its own nation and the occupying imperialist bourgeoisie. This is a relationship involving both conflict and accommodation.

One reason that imperialism's counterinsurgency offensive was so effective was that it used a vulnerability in the ideological armor of the New Afrikan movement. Because of their role as an intermediary class, oriented to imperialism, the petty-bourgeois leadership of the struggle were fixed on the idea that the Federal Government was the answer to New Afrikan people's problems. Not the enemy, but the reluctant savior. Despite all the publicly professed faith in the "decent majority" of settlers finally waking up to justice, no one in the Civil Rights leadership (or on the streets) actually believed this nonsense. Rev. King himself, after the 1962 KKK-FBI bombings of Albany churches, wrote white Southerners off: "**The Negro stands little chance, if any, of securing the approval, consent, or tolerance of the segregationist white South.**" It was the Federal government that was seen as the big power which, when finally cajoled or pressured into action, would give equality to New Afrikan people—if necessary over the objections of white people. In Albany the students marched towards jail invoking President Kennedy in song:

"Oh, Mr. Kennedy, take me out of misery.
Freedom's coming and it won't be long.
Look at segregation, look at what it's done
**   to me.**
Freedom's coming and it won't be long."

Martin Luther King himself exemplified this contradiction. King rejected political violence not only on philosophical grounds, but because he felt it impractical for his struggle. Like many others of his class, King was so convinced of the superiority of White Amerika that he didn't believe that armed struggle against it could ever win: **"... internal revolution has never succeeded in overthrowing a government by violence unless the government had already lost the allegiance and effective control of its armed forces. Anyone in his right mind knows that this will not happen in the United States."** Again and again he emphasized his view that Black revolt could not win against settlers: **"We have neither the techniques, the numbers, nor the weapons to win a violent campaign."** This has been the fundamental viewpoint of the Black movement on their relationship to the oppressor nation.

King struggled to build close ties to the White House, and to persuade the government to support the freedom movement. In return he felt himself bound to support the US Government in many ways. While Rev. King regularly disregarded the state court injunctions and rulings against demonstrations, he thought it wrong to disobey a Federal court order even if it was unjust. Not once in his political career would he ever break a Federal law or court order, a position that he admitted to his associates but tried to conceal from the public.[8]

King honestly could not comprehend the thinking of Malcolm X and other militant nationalists. On several occasions Malcolm had

tried to bridge the gap; in both 1957 and 1960 he had invited King to speak at Muslim events. On the latter occasion King had been invited to address the 1960 Muslim Education Rally in a large armory in New York City. King always declined. He told a friend: '"**They have some kind of a strange dream of a Black nation within the larger nation. At times the public expressions of this group have bordered on a new kind of race hatred and an unconscious advocacy of violence.**" King at that time could not understand anyone not wanting to be part of the "American Dream."

At the same time Rev. King was launching new Civil Rights campaigns and criticizing the Kennedy Administration, which was clearly hoping to stall off the unpopular Civil Rights reforms indefinitely. He wrote: **"If tokenism were our goal, this administration has adroitly moved us toward its accomplishment. But tokenism can now be seen not only as a useless goal, but as a genuine menace."** In the Spring of 1963 SCLC began its major Birmingham, Alabama campaign, designed to prove that King's nonviolent direct action strategy could still win.

It was there that the alliance between the US bourgeoisie and the Black petty-bourgeoisie protest leadership was firmly cemented. For Birmingham—a steel and coal industrial center that was a terroristic fortress of segregation—

Residents gather on a street corner, Birmingham, Alabama, 1963. Photo by Colin Jones/The Observer.

was the Albany struggle all over again. The local settler-colonial regime stood fast, while police clubs, dogs, and high-pressure water hoses battered the crowds of marchers. Birmingham held the world's attention, and its rabid Police Commissioner "Bull" Connor became a world symbol of Americanism. On "Project C Day," May 2, 1963, six thousand New Afrikan children from age six up marched, singing in wave after wave, on City Hall. 950 of them were arrested as the settler police ran out of paddy wagons, and crowds of seven- and eight-year-old girls chanted "Freedom!," "Freedom!" Still there was no softening, no concessions by the local settler government. By May 7, 1963, over two thousand demonstrators were in jail, with no resolution in sight.

It was on that afternoon that the situation started turning. New Afrikan demonstrators, attacked by police, began fighting back. Three thousand New Afrikans fought police with barrages of rocks and bottles up and down Birmingham's business district, while the settler Chamber of Commerce watched from their windows high above in shock. What nonviolent marches couldn't accomplish, the first spectre of

rebellion did. The White House was galvanized into action. President Kennedy had his Cabinet members call their Birmingham corporate friends and push for a negotiated settlement. Ford Motor Company, Royal Crown Cola, Birmingham Trust National Bank, US Steel, Tennessee Coal & Iron, and other big corporations started demanding an immediate settlement.

Within two days the city and the protest movement had reached a milestone agreement, desegregating department stores in downtown Birmingham. Hoping that the breakout of the masses could be smothered in the publicity over the desegregation pact, President Kennedy praised the settlement in a speech and offered Federal guarantees on its implementation. The US bourgeoisie had finally intervened to give the nonviolent Civil Rights movement a boost, to save it from another Albany-type failure, and to short-circuit mass confrontations which were leading to rebellion.

But on the night of May 10, 1963, new fighting broke out in Birmingham, on a far larger scale. Late that evening the home of Martin's

Over 450 Negro Children Arrested in Birmingham

Teachers Shout Encouragement as Pupils March On City Hall, Parade, Picket Stores in Massive Demonstration; No Violence Reported

BIRMINGHAM, Ala. — Police from behind hastily set up police

brother, A.D. King, was bombed. An hour later the New Afrikan–owned Gaston Motel was also dynamited. As news spread a rebellion broke out, with thousands of New Afrikans seizing a nine block area until 5 a.m. Police cars were trashed, an officer stabbed and others injured by stoning. Birmingham newspapers the next morning ran a front-page photo of Police Chief Inspector Haley, his face bloody and dazed. Settler-owned stores were burned while angry crowds drove off firemen. SCLC leaders were onlookers, powerless to stop the rebellion.

The Birmingham rebellion absolutely convinced the government that even larger reforms were needed to dampen the fires of revolt. As King said: **"The sound of the explosion in Birmingham reached all the way to Washington."** On June 11, 1963, President Kennedy, addressing the Empire, called for Congress to pass the now-historic Civil Rights Act. The failure of the nonviolent Civil Rights movement and the spreading breakout of anti-colonial struggle by the New Afrikan masses, forced the imperialist government and the Black petty-bourgeois protest leaders to wake up and admit how much they needed each other, to back each other up. This was the true meaning of the March on Washington, which on August 28, 1963, brought 250,000 persons to Washington as a pacified backdrop for King's "I Have A Dream" speech.

Children sift through the wreckage of homes destroyed during the rioting that erupted following the racially motivated bombing of the nearby home of Reverend A.D. King, brother of Martin Luther King, and the Gaston Motel, where King and others organising the protests had stayed. Photo by Colin Jones/The Observer.

The March on Washington was a pro-Government propaganda exercise, marking imperialism's takeover of the Civil Rights movement. While the New Afrikan masses were angry and moving into violent rebellion, their organized leaders were trying to pacify them into inactivity. It was Malcolm X who first exposed the March on Washington, echoing the questioning that was also growing at the grassroots of the Freedom Movement:

"When Martin Luther King failed to desegregate Albany, Georgia, the civil-rights struggle in America reached its low point. King became bankrupt almost, as a leader. The Southern Christian Leadership Conference was in financial trouble; and it was in trouble, period, with the people when they failed to desegregate Albany, Georgia. Other Negro civil-rights leaders of so-called national status became fallen idols. As they became fallen idols, began to lose their prestige and influence, local Negro leaders began to stir up the masses. In Cambridge, Maryland, Gloria Richardson; in Danville, Virginia, and other parts of the country, local leaders began to stir up our people at the grassroots level. This was never done by these Negroes of national stature. They control you, but they have never incited you or excited you. They control you, they contain you, they have kept you on the plantation.

...

"... This is what they did with the March on Washington. They joined it. They didn't integrate it, they infiltrated it ... And as they took it over it ceased to be hot, it ceased to be uncompromising. Why, it even ceased to be a march. It became a picnic, a circus ... They controlled it so tight, they told those Negroes what time to hit town, how to come, where to step, what signs to carry, what song to sing, what speech they could make, and what speech they couldn't make; and then told them to get out of town by sundown. And every one of those Toms was out of town by sundown."[9]

The No. 1 purpose of the March was to tie up militant activity in the communities, to defuse youth by misdirection, getting local organizers all wrapped up during the promised "hot summer" in organizing busloads for the super-event in Washington. The other main purpose of the March was to publicly applaud the Kennedy Administration, and to picture settler liberalism as the ideology of justice for New Afrikans. On June 22, 1963, Stephen Currier of the Taconic Foundation, who was now the man who controlled Black protest funds, led the "Big Six" Black leaders in to meet with President Kennedy and his associates at the White House. When Kennedy worried about the March because of the risk of some real struggle breaking out, Pullman Union leader A. Philip Randolph answered: **"The Negroes are already in the streets. It is very likely impossible to get them off. If they are bound to be in the streets in any case, is it not**

Robert Kennedy, Martin Luther King Jr., Roy Wilikins, A. Philip Randolph

better that they be led by organizations dedicated to civil rights and disciplined ... rather than to leave them to other leaders who care neither about civil rights nor nonviolence?" Currier, Lyndon Johnson, and Robert Kennedy agreed, and President Kennedy said that the Government would support the March.

Less than a month afterwards, Stephen Currier united all the bickering Civil Rights organizations into one Council for United Civil Rights Leadership, which he became the co-chairman of. Currier promised the Black petty-bourgeois leaders $1.5 million, with $800,000 handed out at the meeting. Militant SNCC got the smallest share by far—only $15,000—with the agreement that their money would be "sharply upgraded" later if they became more obedient.

The March itself had no struggle or even protest about it. Confused marchers were handed pre-printed picket signs (mostly made by the United Auto Workers Union) with only Government-approved slogans. No militancy, attacks on the Government, or spontaneous activity was tolerated. The speech by SNCC Chairman John Lewis was ordered censored and rewritten, from initially saying **"we cannot support the Administration's civil rights bill"** to the reverse: **"True, we support the Administration's civil rights bill."** Stricken out were SNCC's threats of armed struggle: **"The next time we march, we won't march on Washington, but we will march through the South, through the heart of Dixie, the way Sherman did."** After being reduced to polite spectators just listening for hours to pro-imperialist speeches, the crowds were ordered to leave town as soon as possible. The contempt that the March leaders had for the New Afrikan people—and how much they wanted to break them of all spirit and self-respect—can be seen in the confession of Bayard Rustin, the March's chief organizer:

"You start to organize a mass march by making an ugly assumption. You assume that everyone who is coming has the mentality of a three-year-old. You have to tell them every little detail of what they should do ... even how to leave when the March ended."[10]

Before the March the Black protest leaders were scared, and had to tell President Kennedy that the masses were out of control, in the streets.

After the March the leaders thought they could safely laugh at their own people as having "the mentality of a three-year-old." But while the new counterinsurgency campaign took over the movement, the anti-colonial rebellion continued to deepen and spread. The bourgeoisie, understanding this, continued to support harmless protest activity, publicizing the chosen leaders and lavishly funding their activities. Martin Luther King tried to get the settler public to understand how civil rights protests were actually helping to restrain the Black Revolution, and were thus in settler interests:

"It is not a threat but a fact of history that if an oppressed people's pent-up emotions are not nonviolently released, they will be

violently released. So let the Negro march. Let him make pilgrimages to city hall. Let him go on Freedom Rides. And above all, make an effort to understand why he must do this. For if his frustrations and despair are allowed to continue piling up, millions of Negroes will seek solace and security in Black nationalist ideologies."

The US bourgeoisie had learned that New Afrikan Revolution was much closer than they had thought, and that drastic neo-colonial reforms were needed to undercut the mass rising until it had run its course. Further, that the Empire needed to take over and sponsor the unsuccessful nonviolent protest movement, needed to make it look more successful for New Afrikan

people. The Civil Rights leadership and their organizations were put on imperialism's payroll; pushed every day by the imperialist media just like breakfast cereal or deodorants.

The dual role of the New Afrikan pettybourgeoisie as a vacillating and intermediary class was also being played out, as they ran back and forth allying with both sides. They called for mass protests against oppression, but only so that they could negotiate with the Government to end the protests. Many perceptive people had seen after Birmingham that nonviolent protest politics could not even pressure the Empire. Only the threat of rebellion had the power to force concessions from imperialism. This was to become important as the movement developed.

4. MALCOLM AND REBELLION

The years 1964–1966 were ones of rapid transition, as the New Afrikan Nation moved towards the stage of revolution. Ghetto rebellions spread, becoming common for the first time. The anti-colonial struggle was taken up by the masses and ignited across the continent. In the rising ideological debate over what path New Afrikans should take, Malcolm X became the central figure leading the Nation towards liberation. His political lessons were a guide for starting the New Afrikan revolution.

These developments were due to an internal dynamic, which was itself part of the larger dialectic of oppressed and oppressor nations within the framework of the settler Empire. Major differences exist within the settler Empire over imperialism's neo-colonial program. Most settlers have always believed that neo-colonialism is too good for New Afrikans. While the US Big Bourgeoisie and the liberal intelligentsia backed President Kennedy's Civil Rights Act, reactionary elements of the local bourgeoisie wanted to simply repress the anti-colonial rising without reforms or concessions. In this the reactionaries had overwhelming support from the settler masses. This was true not just in the Deep South, but in all regions—as true in Chicago as it was in Jackson.

Much of the state apparatus, including the FBI, was openly allied to the reactionary elements. So in Birmingham and elsewhere, the FBI worked with the KKK to answer the March on Washington with continued terroristic bombings and assassinations. The timing of these attacks only further angered the New Afrikan masses and exposed the futility of Civil Rights politics. Even before his neo-colonial legislation could get enacted by Congress, on November 22, 1963, President Kennedy himself was removed by his imperialist opponents. Malcolm X penetrated the neo-colonial crisis:

"Now that the show is over, the Black masses are still without land, without jobs, and without homes ... their Christian churches are being bombed, their innocent little girls murdered. So what did the March on Washington accomplish? Nothing!"[11]

Unable to get over with the awakening New Afrikan masses, caught in the fire between settler reaction and the liberation struggle, the existing Civil Rights leadership broke down. While nonviolent demonstrations were still the predominant form of organized activity, nonviolence was finally admitted to be only a tactic of weakness. Armed self-defense became an integral part of Southern Civil Rights work. In 1965 the Deacons for Defense, an armed defense guard for Civil Rights activity, was formed in Louisiana and soon spread to other Southern states. The historic Meredith March through rural Mississippi during June 1966 showed the contradictions: during the day the March stressed the standard nonviolent protests, complete with prayer rallies, while at night the March defense guard had to drive Klan snipers off in exchanges of gunfire.

That Mississippi March was also notable for its display of the Civil Rights leadership's fragmentation and flailing about. James Meredith, the first New Afrikan student at the University of Mississippi, was conducting a one-person March to Jackson, the state capital, to symbolically establish the right to free movement without fear. That was a direct challenge to the settler power. On June 6, 1966, as Meredith was crossing the Tennessee border into Mississippi, he was wounded by a shotgun attack in broad daylight. There was national outrage over the casual brazenness of the attack.

James H. Meredith, who in 1962 became the first African American to attend the University of Mississippi, is shot by a sniper shortly after beginning a lone civil rights march through the South.
Photo by Jack Thornell.

The next day Civil Rights leaders and activists flew in from all over the US, as the movement publicly vowed to continue Meredith's March through Mississippi to its conclusion. Martin Luther King, SNCC's Stokely Carmichael, CORE National Director Floyd McKissick, and Mississippi NAACP Director Charles Evers, led the hundreds of defiant marchers into Mississippi. But at the starting rally in Memphis, Stokely Carmichael roused the crowd with his militant version of Civil Rights politics: **"I'm not going to beg the white man for anything I deserve. I'm going to take it."** Not to be outdone in rhetoric, CORE's McKissick said that since America's symbol was the Statue of Liberty, **"They ought to break that young lady's legs and throw her into the Mississippi."**

As the marchers slowly crossed Mississippi the physical harassment, police pressure, and danger grew. SNCC's Willie Ricks and Carmichael began popularizing the slogan Black Power. SCLC people were still shouting **"Freedom Now"** as a chant, while SNCC people started chanting **"Black Power"** instead. More and more marchers refused to sing the line **"Black and White Together"** in the movement song **"We Shall Overcome."** The militant mood was so strong that even King's associate Rev. Hosea Williams, at the Greenwood rally, got carried away and shouted to the crowd: **"Whip that policeman across the head!"** Trying to rescue SCLC from Williams' rhetoric, King rose to say diplomatically, **"He means with the vote."** Carmichael yelled: **"They know what he means."** In Yazoo, King was booed as he tried to lecture the marchers on nonviolence.

In Philadelphia and Canton, Mississippi the March was met with violence. Rev. King tried to hold a memorial service in Philadelphia for the three slain 1964 Mississippi Summer workers—Goodman, Chaney, and Schwerner—but it was broken up by a Klan mob. The settlers threw fireworks into the assembled marchers, and then started physically assaulting people. New Afrikan youth fought back, which temporarily cooled the violence. But that night the camped marchers were again attacked, this time by KKK snipers. There were four Klan attacks with gunfire that night. The Deacons for Defense, the Louisiana armed self-defense organization that had come along but had so far abided by the agreement on nonviolence, began firing back. In Mississippi even pro-US Civil Rights needed a military component.

Maneuvering to avoid the confrontation, King wired President Johnson pleading for Federal marshals to be sent in to protect them. The President didn't answer. The White House was displeased at King associating with the militant Civil Rights forces. Washington agreed with the local power structure that the trouble-makers should be discouraged. At Canton, Mississippi, Stokely Carmichael demanded that the March show how militant it was by pitching their tents against police orders. Firing their tear gas ahead of them, State troopers and Canton police routed the two thousand marchers as they were making camp. Police ran through the clouds of tear gas into the panicked marchers, clubbing and whipping at will. The militant leaders could only tell people to make for the nearest church. The next day the US Attorney General said that he deplored police overreaction, but that the marchers had provoked the police.

Neither SNCC, CORE, nor SCLC could tell people what to do about these problems. By 1966 all factions of the Civil Rights leadership, from Whitney Young to Stokely Carmichael, were desperate over their growing irrelevance as far as the masses were concerned. Andy Young of SCLC warned: **"We have got to deliver results—nonviolent results in a Northern city—to protect the nonviolent movement."** Their problem was that the New Afrikan masses by the hundreds of thousands were voting against the Empire with Molotov cocktails, in festive uprisings that the Civil Rights leaders could not head off, control, or even pretend to influence.

From 1963 to 1966 the mass ghetto rebellions, which at first so shocked White Amerika, gathered momentum. In Chicago, high school student leaders aided by local civil rights leaders led 225,000 New Afrikan students out of school in October 1963. Their total mass boycott, which showed the depth of anti-colonial unity in the larger community, demanded the ouster of segregationist School Superintendant Ben Willis. The school boycotts jumped to New York, where over 400,000 New Afrikan students joined. In Jacksonville, Florida fighting resulted in the Spring of 1964 after Klansmen shot down a New Afrikan woman in random terrorism. Jacksonville High School students evacuating from a KKK bomb threat attacked settler police and reporters. According to Federal authorities it marked the first use by New Afrikans of Molotov cocktails.[12]

Rebellions in Harlem, Brooklyn, Rochester, Elizabeth, Patterson, Jersey City, Chicago, and Philadelphia in 1964, set the stage for the great Watts uprising of 1965 in Los Angeles. The Molotov cocktail was now common. In Watts the struggle lasted for days, only ending after National Guardsmen with heavy automatic weapons occupied the community. The death toll was 34, with hundreds wounded and 4,000 arrested.[13] As King, Young, and Bayard Rustin toured

the burnt-out area, a group of youths shouted at them, **"We won!"** One rebellion participant joyfully told a minister: **"Every day of the riots was worth a year of Civil Rights demonstrations."** The next Summer, in 1966, there were 43 urban rebellions. Police and Guardsmen in both Chicago and Cleveland encountered sniper fire.

Throughout this period there were both spontaneous mass outbreaks and also mass actions led or initiated by small cadre groups against the police. Revolutionary nationalists and fighters of various political views, many of whom had never been in the Civil Rights movement, were making their presence known.

When the New Afrikan ghettoes rose in rebellion, Malcolm X was the only major figure whose leadership was actually acknowledged by the people in the streets. A 1964 *NY Times* report on US Government concern over Malcolm said: **"Malcolm is regarded as an implacable leader with deep roots in the Negro submerged classes. At one point in the Harlem riots, the same people who booed Bayard Rustin and James Farmer of CORE shouted, 'We want Malcolm.'"**

Unlike most of the various Civil Rights leaders, whether militant or puppet, Malcolm X was not a creation of foundation grants, liberal churches, the imperialist media, or the Black establishment. Nor was Malcolm X someone who had soared meteor-like into prominence because of his oratory, although he himself was unsurpassed as a public speaker. Malcolm X was a true leader of the New Afrikan people because he had put his life in their service, teaching and organizing the masses. What so many have overlooked is that Malcolm was a leader in fact not just in name; a builder, recruiter, strategist who actually started masses of people moving on the path of national liberation. When Malcolm came out of prison to the Nation of Islam in 1952 there were only four temples and less than 2,000 members. Malcolm spent years recruiting and building the NOI until it had over 50 mosques and approximately 200,000 members. It was Malcolm X's leadership that was the political rock upon which the revolutionary period was begun.

Malcolm X was the first New Afrikan leader in this century to speak primarily to the oppressed masses, and to tell the masses the complete truth as he knew it. That's why he was a great teacher; because he believed in his people and knew that they could change the world. The electricity he created was based on that—unlike Roy Wilkins or Stokely Carmichael or Martin Luther King, Malcolm was going to tell you what was really going on, was going to "pull the cover off" the oppressor and his flunkies. As part of this, Malcolm told the masses the truth about their own movements, about the false leaders who were created by and served the colonizer. When he learned about the corruption of his own teacher, Elijah Muhammad, Malcolm unflinchingly told New Afrika about the real situation: **"Muhammad is the man, with his house in Phoenix, his $200 suits, and his harem. He didn't believe in the Black state or in getting anything for the people. That's why I got out."**[14] That was unpopular, but he did it.

Whether it was reminding New Afrikans that they were not "Americans," or organizing trained security units, Malcolm X was the bearer of advanced ideas. Again, not just as talk but in deeds. By the '60s, Malcolm's weekly rallies at 125th St. and Lenox Ave. in Harlem were drawing so many people—many thousands—that the police had to close the streets to automobile traffic. One day Malcolm calmly told the crowd: **"If you look at the rooftops you'll find that the white boys have the CIA and all those people with their guns on the rooftops, but next to every white man there's a Black Muslim, so we have the situation well in hand."**[15] And near every imperialist security man there was an armed Muslim. That's the kind of advanced leadership that Malcolm gave people. This was at a time, we should recall, when the Civil Rights leaders were always asking the police or the FBI or the US Justice Department for "protection."

Malcolm fought to get New Afrikans out of the trap of thinking that they were "minority" citizens in Amerika. Malcolm never wanted to become part of the US oppressor nation, with or without Civil Rights. He thought and did his political work as an Afrikan, and as part of the oppressed world majority. His international stature was so great that Civil Rights leaders began to get the picture that they had to start talking more like him or get left out in the cold. In December 1964 two SNCC representatives visited Afrika to build international support. A written report to SNCC by them shows the surprise that Malcolm's influence had on them:

"Among the first days we were in Accra, someone said, 'Look, you guys might really be doing something—I don't know, but if you are to the Right of Malcolm, you might as well start packing right now 'cause no one'll listen to you!' Among the first questions we were continually asked was, 'What's your organization's relationship with Malcolm?' We ultimately found that this situation was not peculiar to Ghana; the pattern repeated itself in every country ... Malcolm's impact on Africa is fantastic. In every country he was known and served as the main criteria for categorizing other Afro-Americans and their political views."[16]

Malcolm's political thought was not, as we all know, a finished product. Standing head and shoulders above his contemporaries, his work was still a journey cut down in midstream. He had yet to come to grips with communism, with proletarian class ideology, although he was consciously anti-capitalistic. Malcolm's break with Elijah Muhammad's doctrine was a new beginning. He was not above his Nation, but was a part of the fertile questioning and reexamining that characterized his times and his movement. Shortly before his death he told an interviewer: **"But I still would be hard pressed to give a specific definition of the over-all philosophy which I think is necessary for the liberation of the Black people in this country."**[17] Still left unanswered at his death were the practical questions of program: How New Afrikans will overcome oppression, what specific society they need to build, and who should lead them?

VI. Vietnam Catalyst

Vietnam was a catalyst in the generalized political crisis that overtook the US Empire starting in 1967. US imperialism had willfully picked Southeast Asia as the battleground for a decisive test of strength, an arrogant showdown with world socialism and national liberation. But their unsuccessful invasion brought to light all of US imperialism's weaknesses and contradictions. **The War awakened tens of millions of people to political life.** It was a turning point, proving that a small and undeveloped nation could defeat a large Empire, that an oppressed people guided by socialism could throw out the strongest imperialist power. People's War in Vietnam was a model to revolutionary-minded people throughout the world. That was even true for some Euro-Amerikan youth, who were part of a generation of dissent. For the first time in settler history revolutionary tendencies were created that looked to the leadership of the oppressed Third World.

The issue of the war had an important impact on mass politics. As the Government was morally discredited and its criminal violence against the Vietnamese people understood, political violence against the Empire was legitimized. The draft suddenly connected Main Street USA to land mines, ambushed patrols, and the Tet offensive. Everyone was pushed to choose sides, to be for or against the Government, as protesters burned draft cards and US flags, fought police in the streets, and bombed ROTC buildings. And for the oppressed, the experience of the War accelerated their understanding of colony and Empire.

From 1965 on US imperialism jolted the Empire with the rapid escalation of its War. College students, feeling threatened by the draft, began holding mass Teach-Ins to debate Government policy. SDS (Students for a Democratic Society), which had been a small, social-democratic college group that was very anti-Marxist, began to take on a mass character and become more militant. One social scientist notes how dramatic the US military buildup was: "In 1965, at the time of the first national Teach-In, the US had approximately 30,000 troops stationed in that forlorn nation and a total casualty rate of 2,283 killed and injured. In 1967, by the time of the May anti-war rallies, we had approximately 375,000 troops under arms in Vietnam, a considerable number of additional troops in Thailand, and a total casualty rate of 60,000. And by 1969, two years later yet, the United States had approximately 500,000 troops under arms ..."[1]

The Vietnam War posed a new crisis for the Black petty-bourgeoisie, many of whom were anticipating the fruits of Federal Civil

Rights patronage. Traditionally the Black petty-bourgeoisie had welcomed the US Empire's foreign wars. Wartime was viewed as an exceptional opportunity to "advance the race." During wartime the need for New Afrikan labor and men at arms gave the Black leadership a chance to demonstrate their useful loyalty to the Empire—and ask for concessions in return. W.E.B. DuBois and the NAACP supported the US war effort during World War I (a position DuBois soon regretted). In World War II A. Philip Randolph, Paul Robeson, Adam Clayton Powell, and the NAACP gave all-out support for US conquests in Europe and Asia.

It was only in 1948, after waiting years for integration and "equal opportunity" in the armed forces, that the Black petty-bourgeoisie began to balk at supporting the war machine. After a fruitless meeting with President Truman, A. Philip Randolph issued a call for New Afrikan college students to resist the draft. A League for Non-Violent Civil Disobedience Against Military Segregation was formed: "I personally pledge myself to openly counsel, aid, and abet youth, both white and colored, to quarantine any Jim Crow conscription system ... I shall call upon all colored veterans to join this Civil Disobedience movement and to recruit their younger brothers in an organized refusal to register." Response was positive: polls in 1948 showed that 70% of New Afrikan college students favored the anti-draft campaign. Youth began refusing to register and refusing to serve in the Army.[2]

Randolph was hastily recalled to Washington, where a deal was struck to end the struggle before it could politically develop. President Truman signed the famous 1948 Executive Order No. 9981, ordering the military to practice "equality ... without regard to race, color, religion, or national origin." The Black petty-bourgeoisie had won their second major legal concession in this century from the Government. In return, Randolph had promised the imperialists that he would totally disband the League, suppress the talk that had already begun of forming a New Afrikan anti-imperialist movement, and isolate those New Afrikan anti-war resisters who had already gone to prison. The Black petty-bourgeois protest leadership, having called their people into action as a bargaining chip for neo-colonial deals, once again abandoned their followers. From then through the Korean War in the 1950s and into the early Vietnam period, the Civil Rights leadership was a supporter of US imperialism's far-flung military adventures.

At first the 1960s saw merely the continuation of this slavish practice. In July 1964 the mainstream Civil Rights leadership—SCLC's King, Bayard Rustin, and A. Philip Randolph, Whitney Young of the Urban League, and the NAACP's Roy Wilkins—issued a call for a halt on all New Afrikan demonstrations until the national elections were over in November.[3] President Johnson had wanted to ensure settler votes by proving how his programs were controlling the New Afrikan movement. In December 1964, when Martin Luther King went to Sweden to receive the Nobel Peace Prize, he still refused to criticize US foreign policy. When pressed by European reporters, King said that he couldn't oppose US military operations then going on in the Congo against the Patrice Lumumba government.[4] The position of the Black petty-bourgeois leadership in 1965–66 on the Vietnam War was clear. The Urban League, NAACP, the SCLC Board of Directors, National CORE, Rustin and Randolph, all went on record that New Afrikans should only concern themselves with Civil Rights issues. As King was to admit unhappily, his own class felt that a "Negro ought not speak out on such matters." Many of them, King remarked angrily, hoped to get ahead through the War.[5]

Anti-war sentiment was very strong, on the other hand, among New Afrikan youth, particularly on the streets. Nationalists had been denouncing the US invasion since it began, and had been agitating for resistance to the imperialist draft. In 1964 Charles "Mao" Johnson, one of the leaders of the UHURU nationalist formation in Detroit, sent a public statement of resistance to his draft board: **"THERE AIN'T NO WAY IN HELL that I'm going out like a fool and fight my non-white Brothers in Asia, Africa and Latin America for 'White Devils' ... I support everything you oppose and oppose everything you support."**[6] Propaganda campaigns took place around the 1965 draft refusals of General Gordon Baker in Detroit and Ernie Allen in California. When boxing champion Muhammad Ali popularized resistance as well as the slogan "No Vietcong Ever Called Me Nigger,"

the New Afrikan opposition to the Vietnam War could not be hidden.

Anti-imperialist sentiment began breaking through the crust of the pro-government Civil Rights Movement in July 1965. Martin Luther King himself had been bothered about the moral inconsistency of urging pacifistic nonviolence on New Afrikans while totally condoning napalming Vietnamese villages. He had been under heavy pressure from SCLC staff, his Euro-Amerikan socialist advisors, and even his father not to speak out. Finally, at a rally in Petersburg, Virginia, King broke step with the rest of the mainstream leadership: **"I'm not going to sit by and see the war escalated without saying anything about it ... The war in Vietnam must be stopped.**

There must be a negotiated settlement even with the Viet Cong." That act marked the beginning of King's divergence from the Government. At CORE's National Convention in Durham, NC the rank-and-file passed a resolution condemning the war. While CORE Director James Farmer (and Marvin Rich, the Euro-Amerikan liberal who really ran National CORE) managed to get the motion rescinded, the sentiment of the membership was evident. And on July 28th, SNCC passed out an angry leaflet in McComb County, Mississippi over the death in Vietnam of McComb resident John D. Shaw—starting down the path already blazed by revolutionary nationalists.[7]

The US Government tried to hold back the tide. All of a sudden Rev. King's telephone calls to the White House went unanswered. Word went out that Blacks who wanted Civil Rights reforms and patronage jobs should be loyal to the Johnson Administration. At the April 1965 SCLC Board of Directors meeting, the Board had voted that King could not criticize the war while speaking for SCLC.[8] In October of that year UN Undersecretary Ralph Bunche, the first Black to win a Nobel Peace Prize, said that if Martin Luther King refused to stop criticizing the War he "should positively and publicly give up" his leadership of the Civil Rights Movement. The Urban League's Whitney Young said at the White House that Blacks were "more concerned about the rat at night and the job in the morning" than about Vietnam. Even Bayard Rustin, Rev. King's long-time advisor and key strategist,

publicly argued that King was wrong. Anti-war politics were controversial in the middle-class New Afrikan community back then.[9]

When SNCC became the first Civil Rights organization to formally come out against the US invasion, on January 6, 1966, it was greeted by "patriotic" hysteria from the Black Establishment. Political struggle intensified when Rev. King himself came out in support of Julian Bond, SNCC Communications Director, who had been barred from his seat in the Georgia State Legislature because of SNCC's stand. But the motion and sentiment of the New Afrikan masses was clear. SCLC's annual convention in April 1966 reversed the Board of Directors, endorsing Rev. King's anti-war position.

On April 15, 1967, Martin Luther King, together with Harry Belafonte, helped headline the massive 125,000-person Spring Mobilization anti-war march to the UN. That march was coordinated by SCLC's James Bevel; 200 Euro-Amerikan draft resisters publicly burned their draft cards before Stokely Carmichael took the microphone to accuse the US of genocide in Vietnam.[10] Part of the Civil Rights Movement had broken with the Johnson Administration to re-join other liberal settler allies in the new anti-war movement. While the petty-bourgeois Civil Rights leaders who did break with the Government chose to express their anti-war position in one way, characteristic of their class, anti-war sentiment took a very different form among the New Afrikan masses.

•।ய।• •।ய।• •।ய।•

In the US oppressor nation dissent over the Vietnam War finally grew to the point that it forced the Johnson Administration out of office in 1968, and certainly played a part in limiting imperialism's military options in Southeast Asia. Major contradictions came to light. Robert Williams had noted: "The American mind has been conditioned to think of great calamities, wars and revolutionary upheavals as taking place on distant soil. Because of the vast upper and middle classes in the USA, that have grown accustomed to comfortable living, the nation is not prepared for massive violence ... The soft society is highly susceptible to panic."[11]

Just at a time when Euro-Amerikan youth, with the security of the '60s boom years, were trying to reform settler society, the Government was ordering them to fight in a "dirty" war that was meaningless to them, in remote Asian jungles. To youth searching for justice, nothing seemed less just. The outrage sprang in part from their privileged lives, but was nonetheless socially explosive. 1965 saw 9,741 appeals of draft status to state appeals boards; 1966 saw 49,718 appeals; 1967 it jumped even higher to 119,167 appeals of draft status. Many thousands of youths were moving to Canada or becoming resisters, while millions were evading the draft on technicalities.[12]

The anti-war movement was the "Civil Rights Movement" of settler college youth. It was their movement, using all that they'd learned from watching the Sit-Ins and the Civil Rights protests. White students gained the intoxicating feeling that what they did was world news, was making world history. Campuses became centers of feverish protest activity. The Vietnam War struggle was a framework that helped foster alternative culture, dissent in all ways from attitudes toward police to language to consumerism. Revelations over imperialism's immorality changed the way both Government and the major corporations were viewed. When the Harris Poll interviewed college students in June 1970, after the Spring protests over Nixon's invasion of Cambodia, the social shock wave of the '60s could be seen: 67% of the students advocated basic changes in "the system"; 11% said that they were "far left" (19% on the West Coast); 10% said that violence was the only way to change society.[13]

Imperialism's use of violence as an answer, particularly when settler college students themselves began getting beaten up and teargassed, gave legitimacy in their eyes to anti-Establishment violence. In particular, any form of disruption or illegal violence against property associated with the military or war industry was applauded. Anti-war ministers assured people that "human rights are more important that property rights." The role of political violence in the student movement was far greater than is now usually admitted. A history of SDS proves how true this was, and in particular outlines how the dimensions of anti-war violence reached a peak in May 1970, after Euro-Amerikan college students were shot down at Kent State:

"In the spring of 1968, when bombs were first used by the white left, there were ten bombing instances on campuses; that fall, forty-one; the next spring, eighty-four on campus and ten more off campus; and in the 1969–70 school year (September through May), by an extremely conservative estimate, there were no fewer than 174 major bombings and attempts on campus and at least seventy more off-campus incidents associated with the white left—a rate of roughly one a day.

"The targets, as always, were proprietary and symbolic: ROTC buildings (subject to 197 acts of violence, from bombings to window breakings, including the destruction of at least nineteen buildings, all of which represented an eight-fold increase over 1968–69), government buildings (at least 232 bombings and attempts from January 1969 to June 1970, chiefly at Selective Service offices, induction centers, and federal office buildings), and corporate offices (now under fire for the first

Captain Ron Snyder and members of Charlie Company at the body of Jeffrey Miller. Kent State, May 4, 1970.

time, chiefly those clearly connected with American imperialism, such as the Bank of America, Chase Manhattan Bank, General Motors, IBM, Mobil, Standard Oil, and the United Fruit Company).

"But the violence wasn't all bombings and burnings. On the campuses this year there were more than 9,408 protest incidents, according to the American Council on Education, another increase over the year before, and they involved police and arrests on no fewer than 731 occasions, with damage to property at 410 demonstrations, and physical violence in 230 instances—sharp evidence that the ante of student protest was being upped. Major outbreaks of violence occurred in November in Washington, when 5,000 people charged the Justice Department and had to be dispelled by massive doses of CN gas (this was the demonstration which Attorney General Mitchell and Weatherleader Bill Ayers both agreed, in totally separate statements with totally different meanings, "looked like the Russian Revolution"); at Buffalo in March when police clashed with students and twelve students were shot and fifty-seven others injured; at Santa Barbara in February, when students kept up a four-day rampage against the university, the National Guard, local police, and the Bank of America, more than 150 were arrested, two people were shot, and one student was killed; at Berkeley in April, when 4,000 people stormed the ROTC building, went up against the police,

and kept up an hours-long assault with tear gas, bottles, rocks; at Harvard in April, when several thousand people took over Harvard Square, fought police, burned three police cars, trashed banks and local merchants; at Kansas in April, where students and street people caused $2 million worth of damage during several nights of trashing and demonstrations, forcing the calling out of the National Guard; and finally the massive confrontation of May.

"... And for the first time in recent American history, actual guerrilla groups were established, operating in secrecy and for the most part underground, each dedicated to the revolution and each committed to using violent means.

...

"It is important to realize the full extent of the political violence of these years—especially so since the media tended to play up only the most spectacular instances, to treat them as isolated and essentially apolitical gestures, and to miss entirely the enormity of what was happening across the country. It is true that the bombings and burnings and violent demonstrations ultimately did not wreak serious damage upon the state, in spite of the various estimates which indicate that perhaps as much as $100 million was lost in the calendar years 1969 and 1970 in outright damages, time lost through building evacuations, and added expenses for police and National Guardsmen. It is also true that they did not create any significant terror or mass disaffiliation from the established system … in part because Americans generally cannot conceive of violence as a political weapon and tend to dismiss actions outside the normal scope of present politics as so unnecessary and inexplicable as to seem almost lunatic. Nonetheless, the scope of this violence was quite extraordinary. It took place on a larger scale—in terms of the number of incidents, their geographical spread, and the damage caused—than anything seen before in this century. It was initiated by a sizable segment of the population—perhaps numbering close to a million, judging by those who counted themselves revolutionaries and those known to be involved in such acts of public violence as rioting, trashing, assaults upon buildings, and confrontations with the police—and it was supported by maybe as much as a fifth of the population, or an additional 40 million people—judging by surveys of those who approve of violent means or justify it in certain circumstances. And, above all, the violence was directed, in a consciously revolutionary process, against the state itself …

"The culmination of campus violence occurred in May, without doubt one of the most explosive periods in the nation's history and easily the most cataclysmic period in the history of higher education since the founding of the Republic.

"On April 30, Richard Nixon announced that American troops, in contravention of interna-

tional law and the President's own stated policy, were in the process of invading Cambodia, and within the hour demonstrations began to be mounted on college campuses. Three days later a call for a national student strike was issued from a mass gathering at Yale, and in the next two days students at sixty institutions declared themselves on strike, with demonstrations, sometimes violent, on more than three dozen campuses. That was remarkable enough, especially for a weekend, but what happened the following day proved the real trigger.

"On May 4, at twenty-five minutes after noon, twenty-eight members of a National Guard contingent at Kent State University, armed with rifles, pistols, and a shotgun, without provocation or warning, fired sixty-one shots at random into a group of perhaps two hundred unarmed and defenseless students, part of a crowd protesting the war, ROTC, and the authoritarianism of the university, killing four instantly, the nearest of whom was a football field away, and wounding nine others, one of whom was paralyzed for life from the waist down. It took only thirteen seconds, but that stark display of governmental repression sent shock waves reverberating through the country for days, and weeks, and months to come …

"The impact is only barely suggested by the statistics, but they are impressive enough. In the next four days, from May 5 to May 8, there were major campus demonstrations at the rate of more than a hundred a day, students at a total of at least 350 institutions went out on strike and 536 schools were shut down completely for some period of time, 51 of them for the entire year. More than half the colleges and universities in the country (1,350) were ultimately touched by protest demonstrations, involving nearly 60 percent of the student population—some 4,350,000 people—in every kind of institution and in every state of the Union.* Violent demonstrations occurred on at least 73 campuses (that was only 4 percent of all institutions but included roughly a third of the country's largest and most prestigious schools), and at 26 schools the demonstrations were serious, prolonged, and marked by brutal clashes between students and police, with tear gas, broken windows, fires, clubbings, injuries and multiple arrests; altogether, more than 1,800 people were arrested between May 1 and May 15. The nation witnessed the spectacle of the government forced to occupy its own campuses with military troops, bayonets at the ready and live ammunition in the breeches, to control the insurrection of its youth; the governors of Michigan, Ohio, Kentucky, and South Carolina declared all campuses in a state of emergency, and the National Guard was activated twenty-four times at 21 universities in sixteen states, the first time such a massive response had ever been used in a nonracial crisis. Capping all this, there were this month no fewer than 169 incidents of bombings and arson, 95 of them associated with college campuses and another 36 at government and corporate buildings, the most for any single month in all the time government records have been kept; in the first week of May, 30 ROTC buildings on college campuses were burned or bombed, at the rate of more than four every single day. And at the end of that first week, 100,000 people went to Washington for a demonstration that apparently was so frustrating in its avowed nonviolence that many participants took to the streets after nightfall, breaking windows, blocking traffic, overturning trash cans, and challenging the police.

...

* "Protests took place at institutions of every type, secular and religious, large and small, state and private, coeducational and single-sexed, old and new. Eighty-nine percent of the very selective institutions were involved, 91 percent of the state universities, 96 percent of the top fifty most prestigious and renowned universities, and 97 percent of the private universities; but there were also demonstrations with a 'significant impact' reported at 55 percent of the Catholic institutions, 52 percent of the Protestant-run schools, and 44 percent of the two-year colleges, all generally strict and conservative schools which had never before figured in student protest in any noticeable way. Full details can be found in a study by the Carnegie Commission on Higher Education, 'May 1970: The Campus Aftermath of Cambodia and Kent State.'"

144

"... Despite Hoover's claim on November 19, 1970, that 'we have no special agents assigned to college campuses and have had none,' documents liberated from the FBI office in Media, Pennsylvania, four months later indicate that every single college in the country was assigned an agent and most of them had elaborate informer systems as well. Even as tiny a bureau as the Media one engaged in full-time surveillance and information gathering on every campus in its area, sixty-eight in all, ranging from Penn State with its thirty-three thousand students down to places like the Moravian Theological Seminary with thirty-five students and the Evangelical Congregational School with forty-one, and it used as its regular campus informers such people as the vice-president, secretary to the registrar, and chief switchboard operator at Swarthmore, a monk at Villanova Monastery, campus police at Rutgers, the recorder at Bryn Mawr, and the chancellor at Maryland State College. As if that was not enough, the FBI added twelve hundred new agents in 1970, mostly for campus work, established a 'New Left desk' (plus an internal information bulletin called, without irony, 'New Left Notes'), and its agents were directed to step up campus operations ..."[14]

It is hard for those who didn't experience those years to grasp how the moral imperative of ending the War sanctioned anti-imperialist violence to millions of Euro-Amerikans. On the night of August 24, 1970, the Army Math Research Center at the University of Wisconsin at Madison was totally blown up by the anti-war student New Year's Gang. Four years later Karl Armstrong was arrested in Canada for the bombing. At his Toronto extradition hearing, not only professors and businessmen and Vietnam vets turned out to testify for Armstrong, but even former US Senator Ernest Gruening of Alaska. Gruening, who committed many colonial crimes in his own career, told the court: **"We should have supported the Viet Cong and the NLF ... Resistance to this war is not only an obligation but a solemn duty of the citizens of this country... All acts of resistance are fully justified, whatever form they may take."**[15]

Karl Armstrong worked in the 1964 election campaign of Lyndon Johnson. But as he said, the War forced his personal evolution: "In the space of 2–3 years after 1966, I would get flashes of what was happening in Vietnam. At a certain point I really grasped what was going on there, and I wondered what had really happened to me, why I didn't feel that before. I began to really question my own values, my own humanity, what I had become to that point. The revelations in Indochina made me question everything in this country ... I knew it was going to be a very destructive act. I thought that if the bombing of the AMRC would save the life of one Indochinese ... to me that would be worth it. Property doesn't mean anything next to life."[16]

The Vietnam War struggle awakened millions of settler youth to political activism and com-

mitment, whether to electoral reform politics or to women's liberation or to socialism. The New Left was born out of this movement. Both armed revolutionary organizations and solidarity with national liberation movements, although numerically small trends, appeared for the first time in US oppressor nation history in the 1960s. The tragedy is that while there have always been individual Euro-Amerikan revolutionaries—and even small groups—that supported national liberation, the settler Left parties and trade unions had kept them ineffectually isolated and under control. Until the 1960s.

The New Left that grew out of the anti-war movement only laughed at such old-fashioned backwardness. They had been awed by the power of guerrilla warfare in Vietnam; impressed by the humanism and personal integrity of Che Guevara in a way that they never were by their own Government leaders. Heroic Vietnamese women were an example of women's liberation. By 1967 it was quite common for student activists to talk about armed revolution as the only way to "change the system," as the popularly vague expression went. This generation of settler radicals related to Third World revolutions as novices and students. This was a healthy corrective, necessary for the development of genuinely revolutionary Euro-Amerikan politics.

Revolutionary sentiments became so popular, although undeveloped, that even student leaders who were completely liberal in their outlook began to speak about armed struggle. In July 1967 Tom Hayden of SDS declared: **"urban guerrillas** are the only realistic alternative at this time to electoral politics or mass armed resistance." At the June 1967 SDS Convention at Ann Arbor, National Secretary Greg Calvert said: **"We are working to build a guerrilla force in an urban environment ... Che sure lives in our hearts."** Assistant National Secretary Dee Jacobson agreed: **"We are getting ready for the revolu-** tion."[17] SDS had grown to over 6,000 members (it was to grow much larger in the next year) and linked up anti-war activists on hundreds of campuses. While there was no political leadership, experience, party, or strategy, there certainly was an unprecedented current of pro-revolutionary sentiment among Euro-Amerikan youth.

Revolutionary Contingent marches towards Pentagon, October 21, 1967. Walter Teague center. Photo: CANLF.

Within the broader Anti-War movement the idea of revolutionary solidarity, of internationalism, began to grow. When Walter Teague and the US Committee to Aid the National Liberation Front of South Vietnam first began showing up at East Coast peace demonstrations with a large Vietnamese flag, they were called "crazies" by the liberal and pacifist leaders. At first, anti-war marches were supposed to be "American" and "patriotic," politely respectable dissent. The sight of fifteen or twenty youth with an "enemy" flag was shocking.

By early 1967, Teague had joined with John Gerassi, Frank Gillette, and other New Yorkers to organize the Revolutionary Contingent. The RC tried to jack up the militancy of the giant April 15, 1967, anti-war march to the UN (the rally that both King and Carmichael spoke at). Their "contingent" raised the slogan "Support the Vietnamese Revolution" as opposed to the official march slogan of "Stop the War Now." Carrying Vietnamese and other national liberation banners, the small contingent broke away from the official march route to physically assault the Army recruiting booth in Times Square. The US flag was burned. What was thought extreme in early 1967, a militancy few would take part in, was just foreshadowing what many thousands would be doing within a year.

Revolutionary Contingent's political program, which was heavily influenced by Guevarism, explicitly urged US protesters to join guerrilla movements in the oppressed world:

"The Revolutionary Contingent is calling for two things from the dissenters all over the USA. One is the use of creative energy in designing and carrying out dramatic, radical, peace demonstrations, which will be 'escalated' ... Guerrilla action means fast, destructive actions, from which the perpetrators escape ... This leads to the second call: for persons to join the struggle against US imperialism in other countries. The Revolutionary Contingent has been in contact with representatives of the national liberation movements active on the American continent, and they have consented to call for citizens of the USA to join them (see Che Guevara's 'Message to the Tricontinental'); of course, only those with skills of use to guerrillas—medical and/or technical—and who are willing to fight are wanted ... We can no longer talk—we must fight!"[18]

Obvious problems existed with the RC, from police agent provocateurs using "militant" actions to start fights with other anti-war activists to the RC's inability to work within the broader anti-war movement. And on a larger scale, a program that had no revolutionary answers for here ("The purpose of the Revolutionary Contingent is to enable those American radicals who have found the struggle in the United States itself useless at this time, to go abroad and fight in liberation movements in other countries.") could not play a role in all the new political forces being born in the US oppressor nation. But like other young collectives and revolutionary groupings at that moment, the short-lived RC manifested the new trend of anti-imperialist internationalism.

•ıﻟﻟı• •ıﻟﻟı• •ıﻟﻟı•

For New Afrikans opposition to the War was not a separate struggle; it enriched their own liberation movement. Some organizations, such as SNCC and SCLC, united with the activities of the Euro-Amerikan anti-war movement. Others such as National Black Draft Counselors worked to build resistance in their own communities. On the mass level, the simmering rebellion among New Afrikan GIs did much more than just protest the war, it played a large part in ending it.

As everyone knows, New Afrikans were present in the US forces in Vietnam far above their percentage of the US Empire population. Colonial cannon-fodder, New Afrikans would often comprise 50% or more of the actual infantry platoons that were seeking out the Vietnamese liberation forces. In 1970, New Afrikans accounted for 22% of the US casualties. This was no accident. One soldier, Ron Brown, told a *Boston Globe* reporter: **"In my mind Vietnam has killed a lot of young Blacks in this country, eliminating them, as if the war was a plan to do so."**

While New Afrikan youth had far less chance of escaping the draft than Euro-Amerikans, there

was also a conscious imperialist program to pacify the ghetto by draining off street youth to 'Nam. The idea was to take unemployed young men—who were identified as the main force in ghetto "riots"—into the Army regardless of supposed literacy, medical, or arrest standards. This program, started in 1966, was called "Project 100,000" (although in the end many times that number were taken). It was the brainchild of White House advisor Daniel Patrick Moynihan. He cleverly put it forward not as an "anti-riot" program, but as a social welfare measure. Moynihan had hypothesized that these unemployed men were allegedly maladjusted because they had been dominated by New Afrikan women ("disorganized and matrifocal family life"). The best way to help them, Moynihan said, would be to send them to fight in Vietnam, which was in his words a **"world away from women."** Col. William Cole, in command of the Army's 6th Recruiting District in San Francisco, was more to the point when he said: **"President Johnson wanted those guys off the street."**[19] The Vietnam free-fire zone was to be a pacification program for New Afrikans as well as Asians—or as many said, **"using the nigger against the gook."**

President Johnson's plan backfired on US imperialism, spreading the Black Revolution to Army bases and Navy carriers around the world.

And in Vietnam, to be sure. That there was heavy white supremacy in the imperialist military needs no explaining. New Afrikan resistance took many forms. In August 1968, elements of the 1st and 2nd Armored Divisions at Fort Hood, Texas went on alert for possible "riot control duty" (counterinsurgency) in Chicago. The White House was worried that anti-war protests at the Democratic Party Convention might also trigger mass rebellion in the ghetto. After several hundred New Afrikan GIs gathered at a spontaneous base protest rally that night, saying that they would not bear arms against their own people, forty-three were arrested and court martialed (the "Ft. Hood 43").

These protests and embryonic organization took place throughout the imperialist military. 139 New Afrikans, half of whom were women, were arrested after demonstrations at Ft. McClellan, Alabama in November 1971. In West Germany, Gen. Michael Davidson of the US 7th Army admitted that **"Black dissident organizations could turn out 1,500 soldiers for a demonstration."** He admitted it because they were in fact doing it. In the Navy, shipboard rebellions, in which New Afrikans were joined by small numbers of anti-racist Euro-Amerikan sailors, became common. Self-defense actions against oppressive officers and seamen led to outbreaks of mass fighting. On the aircraft carrier US Kitty Hawk the mass fighting on October 11, 1972, lasted for 15 hours, ending up with the hospitalization of forty settler officers and men. On the carrier US Constellation, New Afrikan

self-defense struggles forced the captain to cancel a 1972 training cruise and race for port to get police reinforcements.[20]

The spearhead of the struggles—which were not "anti-war" struggles in the narrow sense, but anti–oppressor nation struggles—took place in 'Nam, where the war brought everything to a head. Under intense danger and oppression, New Afrikan GIs began to focus their energy on their common identity and resisting the settler military. Afro hairstyles, Afrikan jewelry, music, political study, and setting up their own territory were universal. Sabotage by noncompliance was widespread.

A report on the Vietnam base situation by the 1970s from the Lawyers Military Defense Committee stated: **"Thus, the power gained by Blacks was subtle. They simply did not go along with the program, go to the field, or, in many units, work. The cost of this was that about 10 percent of their number would be in jail, under charges or pending administrative discharge, at any one time. As one Black said: 'If I don't go to the field, what are they going to do? Put me in jail?' Laughter followed."** One out of every ten New Afrikan GIs in 'Nam was in jail or on charges on any given day. Sixty percent of the prisoners at the main stockade at Long Binh (known everywhere as "the LBJ"—Long Binh Jail) were New Afrikans. Almost all the maximum security prisoners were there for being "militants," New Afrikan or other Third World. Small wonder that when New Afrikan GIs at the

Long Binh base commemorated Rev. Martin Luther King, Jr.'s birthday in 1971 with a march, the column was headed by the liberation flag and the GIs chanted: **"Free the Brothers in the LBJ!"**[21] and **"Free Angela Davis!"** The New Afrikan Revolution was starting to take place in 'Nam.

The level of armed resistance with settlers was high and reaching the take-off point. Fistfights, shootings, and armed standoffs between New Afrikan GIs and white supremacists were common, at times immobilizing major Army bases (such as Danang in early 1971). Individual incidents fall into familiar patterns. One night in January 1971 two settler majors, returning from drinking at the officers club, passed a hootch where loud soul music was being played. The two majors went in and ordered the brothers to turn it off, yanking the electric cord out when the men refused. In the ensuing argument both settler officers were shot to death. One soldier, Alfred "Brother Slim" Flint, was sentenced to 30 years at hard labor.

The same month conditions reached an intolerable level at a small fire base outside Khe Sanh, due to a white supremacist lieutenant and sergeant leading their settler GIs in an upfront manner: the Confederate flag flew over the fire base, and New Afrikans were openly called "nigras." When a New Afrikan GI tried to explain to the new settler company commander why New Afrikans were refusing to go out on patrol under those circumstances, the John Wayne-ish officer

grabbed for his .45 pistol. Pvt. James "Brother Smiley" Moyler was then forced to blow him away with his M-16.

Assassinations of officers was a rapidly growing phenomenon, particularly since many settler GIs also found it necessary to eliminate or intimidate piggish officers. Fraggings—the anonymous grenade rolled into an officer's tent or room as he slept—became a permanent part of 'Nam folklore. The Lawyers Committee said: **"Fraggings became so common that the 'lifers'** [career military men, usually officers and noncoms—ed.] **were in perpetual fear of their men. (Fragging was not an all-Black phenomenon, though.) One company commander told an LMDC lawyer that he jumped every time he heard a clap of thunder. Officers and NCO's played what was called 'musical beds'— they moved every night. Some commanders would take an enlisted 'hostage' to sleep in their hootches at night."**[22] In 1969 there were 96 officially documented fraggings in units in Vietnam. That number jumped to 209 in 1970, and then jumped again to 154 for just the first six months of 1971. One Army brigade had 45 fraggings, assassinations, or attempted shootings of officers in just eleven months.[23] And these were just the officially documented cases. Many settler officers conveniently got "missing in action" or died during patrols.

Nixon and Kissinger, diehard warmongers if ever there were any, didn't pull the troops out of Vietnam because they wanted to. US imperialism was forced to pull its occupation force out of Vietnam because the military was literally starting to come apart, at the brink of mass mutinies and armed rebellions. Drug use and anti-war sentiment were demoralizing and eroding settler GIs at the same time that the Vietnamese liberation armies had blocked "the light at the end of the tunnel." US Marine Corps historian Col. Robert D. Heinl, Jr. reported in 1971: "… our Army that now remains in Vietnam is in a state approaching collapse, with individual units avoiding or having refused combat, murdering their officers … dispirited where not near mutinous."[24]

Imperialism was losing control of its own military, which was potentially a much bigger crisis than Indochina itself. Washington officials visiting Army bases were freaked out at the development of "Black militant" culture—in West Germany and in some units in 'Nam, New Afrikans had often replaced the regulation salute with the "Power" sign (raised fist). Astonished brass would watch as local settler officers would be forced to return salutes to New Afrikans giving them the "Power" sign. Fear of New Afrikan mutinies was ever-present in command levels. Nixon had to get the troops out of Vietnam quick or risk losing his army.

•|ய|• •|ய|• •|ய|•

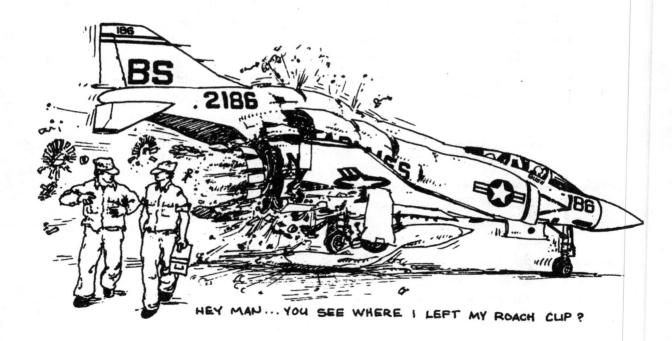

HEY MAN … YOU SEE WHERE I LEFT MY ROACH CLIP?

The anti-war struggles also serve us as a textbook on internationalism. To begin with, internationalism was not a one-sided, spontaneous development in the US, but was due in large measure to the correct leadership of our Vietnamese comrades. For many years they had studied US political affairs, and had carefully planned and organized ties with progressive-minded Amerikans. Conferences abroad to deepen personal ties with anti-war activists, special literature, coordination between the US anti-war leadership and their own political offensives, all characterized the detailed work Vietnamese comrades put into the development of close relations.

Secondly, US solidarity was never seen by the Vietnamese as a substitute for educating and mobilizing their own people to military victory. Even at the height of the US anti-war storm, the Vietnamese comrades never even suggested that liberation would come any other way than through People's War. It was their own strategic understanding of self-reliance as primary that became the foundation for successful internationalism. International solidarity not only requires correct leadership, but cannot be a substitute for self-reliance on both sides. This is in distinct contrast to the prevailing attitude within the US Empire now.

International solidarity was built by the Vietnamese on a principled basis. They never intervened within the US movements, despite their considerable prestige, to boost some factions or leaders as opposed to others. Neither did

they ever countenance the slightest suggestion that their foreign friends could determine the policies of the Vietnamese liberation struggle.

During the complex course of the war, at several points organizations influenced by Trotskyism attempted to put themselves forward as more advanced than the Vietnamese Communist Party on how Vietnam's liberation struggle should be conducted. Around the Paris Peace Accords, for example, groups such as the Socialist Workers Party and the Progressive Labor Party accused the Vietnamese comrades of "selling out" to US imperialism. The Vietnamese sharply reproved such positions (which in any case were soon proved to be confused at best) while stressing as still primary the solidarity between their Revolution and progressive-minded peoples within the Empire.

The Vietnamese consciously developed alliances with a broad spectrum of Euro-Amerikans—from peace leaders like Rev. A.J. Muste to the Weatherman-SDS to liberal opportunists such as Ramsey Clark and Tom Hayden. These relationships were built on two levels: on a primary level they tried to make common cause with **everyone** who recognized their national sovereignty and the justice of their liberation struggle. This included the large and respectable National Mobilization Committee as well as the small, widely-disliked Workers World Party. On a broader level the Vietnamese tried to encourage every constructive contradiction around the War within US society. Every proponent of either negotiations or US troop withdrawal was encouraged. Even though the Vietnamese knew that US Senator George McGovern was no more their friend than Lyndon Johnson or Richard Nixon, they publicly encouraged his 1968 Presidential campaign in order to further the disunity within the imperialist camp. In no case did the Vietnamese narrow or limit their international alliances to suit the desires of one or another ally. No one was the "chosen" ally or owned the Vietnamese solidarity "franchise."

Within the US Anti-War movement the rapid progress of internationalism was, of course, also uneven and with its own contradictions. Euro-Amerikan anti-war activists tended to view the anti-war struggle as theirs, as wholly Euro-Amerikan. And today, in the 1980s, the imperialists and their media tend to portray the settler anti-war movement as the decisive factor in the US defeat. While the opposition to the war within White Amerika was massive, its point of unity was opposition to the "senseless" losses of US troops. Most settlers who opposed the War on that basis were politically pro-imperialist overall.

So after the Nixon Administration was forced to withdraw US troops in 1971–1972, organized settler opposition to the War totally collapsed seemingly overnight. Some of the anti-war radical bombing was done out of a disbelief that the movement could end the War. Which was in fact true. The New Afrikan Revolution, as we have seen, continued to play a much more important role in destroying the US war effort that the Euro-Amerikan peace activists have ever understood.

The mass Chicano Moratorium Movement in the Southwest, which led to the January 31, 1971, East Los Angeles Massacre in which sheriff's deputies shot down 35 unarmed Chicano demonstrators, showed how the solidarity between two national liberation movements had a special significance. The Chicano Moratorium began in 1970, grew just as the white Anti-War movement was declining, and became a rallying point to unite the Chicano Movement. The chairperson of the Chicano Moratorium Committee was Rosalio Muñoz, a draft resister and former UCLA student leader. On February 28, 1970, the new Moratorium group in Los Angeles held a 6,000-person march in pouring rain. A film of the march was shown around the Southwest, leading to a decision to hold a National Chicano anti-war rally in Los Angeles at the end of the Summer. In the Spring and Summer there were local Chicano anti-war demonstrations all over Colorado, Texas, California.

On August 29, 1970, the great National Chicano Moratorium took place in the East Los Angeles barrio. 20,000 Chicanos, together with Asian, Indian, New Afrikan, Puerto Rican, and Euro-Amerikan allies, marched down Whittier Boulevard to Laguna Park. Many thousands lined the streets, cheering and joining in. Families with children came to the Laguna Park rally. Wedding parties joined the march, with bridal gowns and tuxedos and all. It was a festive day. **The Moratorium was far more than an anti-war action. It was a mass statement against oppression, in which anti-imperialist slogans and consciousness were very evident.** Using the pretext of a disturbance at a nearby liquor store, sheriff's deputies and riot police began moving against the rally, driving the thousands out of the park with tear gas, clubs, and bullets. The crowds resisted the police and there were fist-fights, barrages of bottles, and police cars torched. Afterwards Laguna Park was littered with lost shoes and lost children. Three people were killed. One, KMEX news director Ruben Salazar, was shot by police in the Silver Dollar Cafe, where he had stopped after the melee. Salazar was the most vocal critic in the Los Angeles media of police brutality. That night there were "riots" and burning of stores in the barrios in the area. Four policemen were shot.

After that anti-police violence spontaneously erupted at barrio marches and demonstrations. The customary community parade on Mexican Independence Day, September 16th, ended in mass fighting between rock-throwing youths and the police. Chants of "Chicano Power'" and "Raza si, guerra no" against the Vietnam War, grew during the parade. At the parade's end, fighting began. 64 deputies and police were injured, one deputy and two Chicanos wounded by gunfire. On January 9, 1971, the Moratorium brought 1,000 demonstrators to a rally against police brutality in front of LA police headquarters. Again fighting broke out. Finally, on January 31, 1971, the Moratorium held a rally of 10,000 Chicanos. Afterwards a thousand Chicano youth attacked the sheriff's police station, setting it afire. As the militant crowd attempted to move up Whittier Boulevard, the deputies opened fire. Suddenly people were falling. At least 35 Chicanos were shot (some with lighter wounds stayed away from hospitals and police), one of whom died. 22 more than were shot at Kent State.[25]

Days of Rage, Chicago 1969. Photo by David Fenton/Getty Images.

VII. The Birth of Euro-Amerikan Anti-Imperialism

"It is not defeatist to acknowledge that we have lost a battle. How else can we 'regroup' and even think of carrying on the fight? At the center of the revolution is realism."

Comrade George Jackson

There are two opposing political lines today on what is responsible for the setback of the 1960s revolutionary movements within the US Empire. One line, the most popular and prevailing opinion, doesn't wish to recognize that the '60s movements were truly defeated. And to the extent that it admits this fact, places the blame on **external** factors, primarily the "savage imperialist repression" of the FBI's COINTELPRO. The other line, today just beginning to be articulated, believes that the defeats were very profound and primarily due to **internal** factors, to our own political weakness and the unresolved contradictions within our various national movements. We can see this in the '60s Euro-Amerikan revolutionary movement, a movement which suffered defeat despite the fact that it wasn't even scratched by imperialist repression.

The US oppressor nation revolutionary movement that began forming in the late 1960s in and around SDS (the college Students for a Democratic Society) had a definite class character and a definite political program. Its ranks were composed of petty-bourgeois youth, with a leadership that tended to come from elite universities and from the most privileged classes and strata. Its program was and still is centered on solidarity work with the national liberation movements. With no proletarian class in its own society, that young movement was drawn to the struggles of oppressed nations. It was an important beginning that for the first time white people were not automatically seen as the center of everything, that young Euro-Amerikans understood that they were not only more privileged, but were politically backward compared to the revolutions of the Third World. The revolutionary idea of taking leadership from the oppressed began to take root.

In late 1969 SDS, the mass national organization of student radicalism and protest, split into two political tendencies. The first was the Anti-Imperialist tendency, most visibly led by the Weather Underground Organization. Many of their leading personalities had been among the most-publicized student radicals. They viewed the struggle as primarily an anti-imperialist one, and advocated armed propaganda actions to spark off the spontaneous cultural/political uprising of settler youth. Comradely ties were established with both the Vietnamese and Cubans. The second, opposing school of thought was the "Marxist-Leninist party-building" tendency, initially led by the Progressive Labor Party's "Worker-Student Alliance" and the Revolutionary Youth Movement 2 student bloc (whose elements became the October League, Revolutionary Communist Party, etc.). This tendency viewed the struggle as a classic, European-style worker vs. capitalist workplace conflict, and advocated using trade union reform campaigns to build a party like the 1930s Old Left. China was seen as the only world vanguard by them. And so some thousands of radical settler youth began the search for revolutionary answers to the future of the US Empire.

Fifteen years of practice have brought both tendencies to defeat. Their common situation is that neither tendency was able to put its program into successful practice, although initially each was leading thousands of activists and supporters. The "M-L party-building" tendency was never able to build a party and has no following among white workers. The Anti-Imperialist tendency does not lead any mass struggle against US imperialism, and has never been able to build either an army or revolutionary organization worthy of the name. **We do not wish to belittle the efforts of many comrades, but we find it necessary—a question of life and death—to now be painstaking about what is real.** We are not going to discuss the "M-L Party-Building"

tendency, since it was always a rightward trend of Bourgeois Marxism imitating the old CPUSA. To us the development of revolutionary forces within the US oppressor nation rested with the efforts and decisions of the overall Anti-Imperialist tendency.

The new Anti-Imperialist tendency that had come together in 1968–70 out of the student anti-war movement was on an organizational level both large and decentralized, without any overall coordination of organization. Its people were active on many fronts, in university anti-war groups, community organizing projects, local defense committees for the Black Panthers or other Third World militants, prison support groups, small clandestine collectives or other embryonic revolutionary groupings (actually, many were in two, three, or all of the above simultaneously or in quick serial order). While the Weather Underground (WUO) was doubtlessly the most publicized organization of this tendency, it actually had organized and directly led only a small percentage of the whole political current.

On the political level, the Anti-Imperialist tendency struggled from the beginning with a major contradiction around its settlerism. **That it even had this struggle was important progress.** And uneven political development was inevitable for a brand-new revolutionary movement—the first ever in its nation. It was also true that this was a student leadership, created in a few short years on college campuses. When they had to confront the larger society—the "real world"—the Anti-Imperialist leadership had little idea of what to do. The principal problem was that even those Euro-Amerikans who looked to the national liberation wars as the vanguard, who viewed themselves as following the Vietnamese, Mao and Che, and the New Afrikan Liberation Movement, did so in a settleristic way. **That is, the new settler revolutionaries were relying on the oppressed nations—New Afrikans in particular—to solve their problems for them.** Privilege and parasitism, the hallmarks of White Amerika, extended even to revolution, which the revolutionary settler elite would supposedly get simply by sticking close to the Third World struggles. **"Hitching a ride on the BLM."** Or as Bernardine Dohrn exclaimed: **"There's going to be a revolution, and Blacks are going to lead it."** That was a very popular concept then among US revolutionaries as a whole (encouraged by the Black Panthers, SNCC, the League of Revolutionary Black Workers, and others).

The movement's inability to overcome its settlerism was decisive in the end. This can be seen, for example, in the development of two different organizations, in opposing wings of the Anti-Imperialist tendency and with different history, program, and tactics. Despite the real political contributions of both, they were at first crippled and then led into defeat by their settleristic thinking.

Liberation Support Movement

The Canadian-based LSM (Liberation Support Movement) was best-known for its pioneering role in Afrikan liberation support work. It was a relatively small staff organization, with educational centers in British Columbia, the Bay Area, Seattle, and New York City, rather than a mass membership organization. Its founder and chairperson was Don Barnett. A radical anthropologist, Barnett had spent years working in Afrika and had developed relationships with many revolutionaries there. His books *Mau Mau From Within* and *The Revolution in Angola: MPLA* became basic reference works on Afrikan liberation. LSM actually started as the "African Support Committee" in the late 1960s, at a time when few here knew who Amilcar Cabral or Agostinho Neto were—or even where Mozambique was on the map!

LSM's political line was a radical departure from the customary perspectives of the settler left. It correctly opposed Eurocentrism, of seeing Europe and the US as the center of political events. And LSM faced the fact that the level of imperialist social bribery was so high here that the Euro-Amerikan masses were pro-imperialist. Their conclusion was to make proletarian internationalism a reality by merging with the vanguards in the Third World: "... we in LSM view the revolutions of the countryside as the vanguard forces of a single revolutionary process ... The central component of our strategy has been the development of proletarian internationalist links with national liberation movements."[1]

Don Barnett, in laying out LSM's program, saw himself and his comrades as full participants in the revolutions of the Third World. While he recognized the important difference between oppressor ("city") and oppressed ("countryside") nations economically, Barnett's version of internationalism wiped out these distinctions in politics. LSM's undeveloped internationalism didn't really grasp the right of self-determination of oppressed nations or the reality of nations and national differences at this stage of history:

"... I would suggest that what we need is a dual 'urban-rural' strategy. On the 'rural' or neo-colonial front this will involve United States revolutionaries, together with militants of other metropolitan centers, in both direct and indirect participation in revolutionary anti-imperialist struggles ... there are literally thousands of young militants in the capitalist centers who would be willing to serve in the anti-imperialist struggles in the imperial 'countryside' ... In fact, as the revolution spreads to increasing numbers of colonies and neocolonies within the United States–dominated international capitalist system, the whole notion and reality of exclusive 'national' boundaries may begin to fade into relative insignificance. It is surely time for the United States Left to realize—and act accordingly—that there will not be an isolated 'American' revolution."[2]

Although LSM in 1968 pictured a future in which many thousands of Euro-Amerikan, French, German, Japanese, and other oppressor nation youth would play a significant role in the revolutions of Afrika, the reality was quite different. LSM did accomplish a number of positive things. While some cadre like Carroll Ishee (who recently died in combat with rebel forces in El Salvador) patiently sought technical education so that they could usefully participate in a liberation army, LSM's real work was as a basic US-Canadian support group. Funds were raised, medical supplies sent, literature printed, speaking tours sponsored. The first North Amerikan lecture tour by an MPLA representative was

Don Barnett and MPLA member in Angola

arranged by LSM in 1970. In 1975 LSM bought and set up a printshop for MPLA in Angola. LSM literature and slideshows were the main sources of information here for some time on the movements in Angola, Mozambique, Guinea-Bissau, and Zimbabwe. At a time when attention was focused on Southeast Asia or Latin Amerika, LSM's educational work about Afrika was an important contribution.

The central error lay in these Euro-Amerikans and Europeans falsely assigning their work a revolutionary status, and falsely locating their work as within the movements of other nations. In LSM's subjective thinking the Afrikan guerrillas fighting in the forests and the Euro-Amerikans operating a printing press in Oakland, California were both parts of the **same** revolutionary movement. Showing a slideshow **about** Afrikan revolution was made equal to actually **doing** the Afrikan revolution. In reality, LSM was strictly an organization of those who sympathized with and supported the revolutions of **others**—and by this we mean **other nations**. Not content with this modest contribution to internationalism, LSM tried to blow its significance up into a whole different thing. There is an old saying that "the road to Hell is paved with good intentions." In this case solidarity and good intentions became a cover for advancing the parasitism so deeply rooted in settler culture.

What is key here is not whether one is showing a slide show or shooting a rifle (although that too is an issue), but whether people take up their true political responsibilities as revolutionaries. LSM refused to deal with the complex problems and duties of making revolution in the US oppressor nation by pretending to themselves that they were too busy making long-distance revolution for Angola and Mozambique. While this is an example of petty-bourgeois subjectivism in political strategy, LSM was only more open and above-board than others in how they viewed matters. It is common in the US Left for "revolutionaries" to think that supporting the revolutions of others is all that is required. Revolution is reduced to a spectator sport.

LSM's unwillingness to confront their own reality as European settlers, as privileged citizens of the settler Empire, inevitably left them open first to subjectivism and then to negating their original anti-imperialist intentions. LSM shied away from directly supporting in deeds those who were fighting "their" Empire, such as the BLA or AIM or the FALN. This is the first duty of any oppressor nation communist, as we know. Conveniently, it was thought more important to directly support those who were fighting in far-off Afrika against Portuguese or British imperialism. "Solidarity" became a cover for its opposite. Communist words but **liberal** deeds.

Even more, the Euro-Amerikans in LSM assigned themselves as the main comrades (and de facto representatives) here of the Afrikan liberation movements. This meant several things. First, LSM exaggerated its potential role (which was very limited) and downplayed the historic relationship between New Afrikans and the continental Afrikan struggle. Insofar as possible, LSM tried to keep Afrikan liberation solidarity a "white" issue under settler control (a familiar story to be sure).

Then too, LSM's aid was not of the "no strings" variety. As supposed equal participants in Afrikan liberation wars, LSM demanded that it be allowed to inspect how its aid was used. That is, LSM policy held that it was their right and duty to inspect guerrilla bases and visit liberated zones, interviewing Afrikan cadres and fighters in depth. And they regularly did so, particularly in Angola. This arrogant interventionism became characteristic. For years LSM conducted a running feud with ZANU (Zimbabwe African National Union), maintaining that ZANU was not a legitimate liberation party and wasn't conducting a guerrilla war.

Finally, in 1974 LSM had to admit that **"today ZANU is carrying the major burden of armed struggle in Zimbabwe"** and tried to establish friendly relations with ZANU; LSM continued criticizing ZANU for not letting LSM observers into their guerrilla camps and into their rural underground. *LSM News* not only still said in print about ZANU that **"we have to remain somewhat sceptical regarding their claims to 'liberated' areas and population,"** but said that **"ZANU claims"** could be **"substantiated"** by LSM observers. Why should a liberation army of 20,000 fighters, with popular bases of support, need validation by visitors from an oppressor

nation? This is the kind of "equality" that colonial missionaries or intelligence agents aspire to. It should be no surprise that by 1975 many people, including some Afrikan revolutionaries, questioned if LSM had been infiltrated or taken over by the CIA as an intelligence-gathering project.[3]

Like the tip of an iceberg, to grasp that LSM was practicing false internationalism only leads us deeper. After all, it takes two sides to make a relationship. Why did some national liberation parties go along with and encourage LSM? There is no doubt that LSM consciously or unconsciously targeted its efforts on less politically developed and more internally divided liberation movements. LSM would never have been able to practice its arrogant interventionism on the Vietnamese communists, for example. LSM's strongest connection was to the Angolan struggle and specifically to MPLA, but at a time not so coincidentally when the Angolan liberation movement was divided into three warring parties and MPLA itself was split into three openly hostile factions (complete with assassination attempts and coups). There was a strong neo-colonial current there. **Confused and opportunistic alliances are rarely one-way streets.**

LSM's false internationalism led it into a blind alley. As the Afrikan liberation movements— once almost unknown here—got close to seizing state power, they became very attractive to liberal imperialism. Church groups, liberal foundations, international bodies such as UNESCO, Oxfam, World Council of Churches, etc. all got interested in them. Other (and larger) settler left groups suddenly discovered where Guinea-Bissau, Angola, Mozambique, and Zimbabwe were on the map, and got involved in solidarity activity. LSM rapidly became a smaller and smaller factor in the overall aid situation. In May 1974, MPLA President Neto led a delegation on a Canadian solidarity tour. But the tour was sponsored indirectly by the Canadian Government, and LSM was cut out. What really said it to LSM was that MPLA didn't even bother to tell them about the tour.[4] LSM's opportunistic program met its end when its former allies found bigger opportunities elsewhere. The chickens always do come home to roost. Increasingly unimportant and cut off from Afrika, with a program that plainly didn't work, LSM went out of existence.

While LSM bears responsibility for its own politics, it is important to see their problems as general within the Euro-Amerikan New Left and not completely unique. Intervening in the affairs of oppressed nations is an old liberal settler habit. Trying to get over on revolution by fastening yourself parasitically to one or another national liberation movement became popular in the '60s. LSM was just more politically explicit, a clearer example. Again, the LSM cadre began with revolutionary intent and concern for meeting internationalist obligations. And their effort led to real contributions. But when petty-bourgeois settlerism prevailed and finally became primary, LSM's positive aspects were negated and could not be used toward building a new revolutionary movement.

LSM group photo, Richmond, BC, early 1970s.

The Weather Underground

The Weather Underground (WUO) was at the other end of the Anti-Imperialist tendency from LSM. While LSM's program called for joining the revolution taking place in the Afrikan "countryside," WUO called on settler youth to make revolution in the "city" of the US metropolis. Instead of just **supporting** revolutionary guerrillas in other countries, WUO called on settler youth to **be** guerrillas in their nation. While other organizations of the Anti-Imperialist tendency, such as Venceremos or the George Jackson Brigade, were making the same breakthrough, the WUO became famous as **the** example of Euro-Amerikan armed activity.

Like LSM, "Weather" correctly understood that imperialist social bribery had corrupted the society as a whole. And in their first statement—"You Don't Need a Weatherman to Know Which Way the Wind Blows"—of June 1969, they began with that point:

"We are within the heartland of a world-wide monster, a country so rich from its worldwide plunder that even the crumbs doled out to the enslaved masses within its borders provide for material existence very much above the conditions of the masses of people of the world … All of the United Airlines Astrojets, all of the Holiday Inns, all of Hertz's automobiles, your television set, car and wardrobe already belong, to a large degree to the people of the rest of the world."[5]

This was a political understanding that developed apace with the Sixties youth culture, out of people first made aware by the biting criticism of the New Afrikan Liberation Movement. It was a significant break with the revisionist settler Left which always tried to win mass support by promising to outbribe imperialism, to provide even more for the Euro-Amerikan masses.

"Weather" went further, taking this analysis into practice. In one of the key WUO speeches made at the SDS Cleveland Conference in August 1969, Billy Ayers took up the accusation often hurled at WUO that "You guys aren't into serving the people, you're into fighting the people." He pointed out:

"We thought that you don't serve people by opening a restaurant, or by fighting for a dollar more; you serve the people, that means **all** the people—the Vietnamese, everybody, by making a revolution, by bringing the war home, by opening up a front. But the more I thought about that thing 'Fight the people,' it's not that it's a great mass slogan or anything, but there's something to it … There's a lot in white Americans that we do have to fight, and beat out of them, and beat out of ourselves."[6]

The identification of Babylon and the initial refusal to gloss over the corruption that Euro-Amerikans have internalized, was one of the political contributions of the WUO. In these and other political strengths the WUO was representing a new consciousness by the Anti-Imperialist tendency as a whole. WUO had a large current of sympathy, although the organization itself began small and stayed that way. Their communiqués were widely reprinted. Supporters existed in local defense committees, food co-ops, drug abuse programs, "counter-culture" newspapers, rural communes, and throughout the university subculture. Other small clandestine collectives, usually involved in bombings against government and corporate buildings, were encouraged to form by WUO's example and call to action. In particular many were moved by WUO's argument that Euro-Amerikan revolutionaries could not just lay back and let the Third World do the fighting and dying. As Bernardine Dohrn said in "Communiqué No. 1": **"Black people have been fighting almost alone for years. We've known that our job is to lead white kids into armed revolution."**[7]

To understand what happened to the WUO, which chose the terrain of armed struggle, we must analyze them from a political-military standpoint. The first obstacle to understanding "Weather" is its fame, which cast misleading images around it. WUO leaders were headline celebrities, while their organization was discussed and denounced from every political corner of White Amerika. From the beginning the FBI publicly labeled WUO as a terrorist menace. FBI Director J. Edgar Hoover called WUO **"The most violent, persistent and pernicious of revolutionary groups."** In his testimony before Congress in March 1971, Hoover said: **"Investigation has identified over 1,544 individuals who adhere to the extremist strategy**

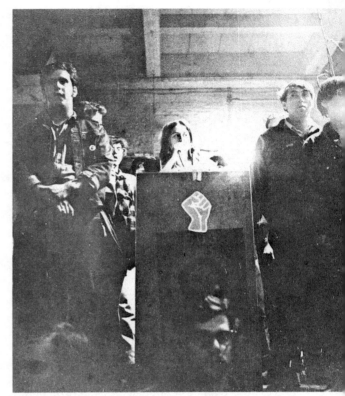

Bernardine Dohrn addresses the SDS convention in Chicago in 1969.

of the Weatherman." Two months later Irvin Recer, Supervisor of FBI Domestic Intelligence, said in a lecture at the Army War College that the WUO were "fanatical revolutionaries." And Hoover himself raised the WUO to the threat level of the Black Panther Party in his March 2, 1972, testimony before Congress:

"Urban guerrilla warfare by black extremist organizations such as the Black Panther Party, by white radical groups, such as the Weathermen, and by other organized terrorists, is a serious threat to law enforcement and the entire nation."[8]

The FBI had put WUO in the "big time" category. In May 1970 it announced **"one of the most intensive manhunts in FBI history"** had begun for nine WUO leaders. Bernardine Dohrn made the FBI's Ten Most Wanted list. A number of WUO cadre went underground on indictments for explosives or conspiracy to start "riots." By 1972, over 20 WUO cadre were officially listed by the FBI as fugitives.[9]

On their part, most of the revisionist opponents of armed struggle also attacked the WUO as terrorists. As late as November 1981, after the Nyack Brinks arrests, we find the newspaper of Amiri Baraka's League of Revolutionary Struggle (ML), *Unity*, still trying to explain WUO as terrorist: "… their terrorist line and isolation from the masses … Groups like the Weather Underground have existed throughout modern history. In Lenin's time, small groups of educated intellectuals threw bombs and engaged in terrorist activities to 'excite' the masses."[10] This is fairly typical for the Bourgeois Marxist organizations. Similar things were said about the George Jackson Brigade, SLA, Sam Melville-Jonathan Jackson Brigade, and so on.

The very first thing to understand about "Weather" is that they never were a terrorist organization. This is merely a clinical fact, neither praise nor condemnation. The original Russian terrorists, for example, were called that because they erroneously believed that the fear of assas-

sination could cause the Czarist regime of the 1870s to literally fall apart, to stop governing. They were terrorists because they planned to create real terror—and did, by killing high officials from the Czar himself to the Minister of Justice, police, and cabinet officers. This was usually done by throwing powerful, home-made bombs by hand from point-blank range. The courage and revolutionary idealism of these terrorists—among whom was Lenin's older brother—was legendary, and most of them gave their lives. Or to take an example on the Right, the imperialist death squads in El Salvador are considered terrorist for obvious reasons. Terrorism is a specific type of political-military activity. Nor is it always incorrect. Lenin in his day noted the importance of terrorism and select terrorist units in specific circumstances (although not as the general strategic line of the struggle).

The Weather Underground never tried to kill anyone, never tried to create terror, and never did. Bourgeois Marxists and the FBI misuse such political-military terms for their own reasons. We need to be precise. In the imperialist media the WUO was portrayed as "drug-crazed hippie bombers." It was an error that the WUO, like the SLA after them, was seduced by its bourgeois media image, playing into and along with it. Its actual military program was the opposite of terrorism. WUO had definite military tactics: carefully selected minor property bombings of government and corporate buildings. Great care was taken that no imperialist police, soldiers, or officers were killed. No extensive damage or disruption of overall settler life was done. The WUO bombings were symbolic military actions, deliberately having neither military nor economic effect. They were media propaganda actions, each one selected to both hopefully radicalize the mass movement and to show the WUO's leading role.

Certainly its most famous single action was the bombing of a washroom in the US Capitol Building on March 1, 1971, in protest of President Nixon's escalation of the war in Laos. Again, on January 29, 1975, WUO placed a bomb in

the third floor washroom, next to the Agency for International Development offices, in the US State Department building, to protest President Ford's request for increased military aid for the Cambodian and Saigon puppet regimes. These were well-planned media actions, intended (in the WUO's words about the bombing of the Capitol washroom) **"to bring a smile and a wink to the kids and people here who hate this Government, to spread joy."**[11]

So while the FBI and the revisionists have always pictured the WUO as very "extreme," ex-

US Capitol damaged by WUO bombing

ceptionally militaristic, it is much more accurate to say that WUO was a typical part of the militant protest movement. Small bombing and sabotage conspiracies, martial arts classes, firearms training, and assorted illegal activities were common in the Movement by that point. The military actions of the WUO, far from being either terrorism or bloody armed adventures, were militant protest activities in step with the sharpening mood of the student New Left.

The contradiction lies in the fact that protest actions, even illegal and violent ones, do not in themselves necessarily constitute a war. What the WUO was doing was not war, despite what it may have thought. While there were continuing wars between the US Empire and rebellious elements within its colonies and neo-colonies, there was not yet revolutionary war between the settler Left and "their" Empire. This is simply a matter of fact. **We can see it in the de facto agreement by the WUO and the imperialist security forces not to shoot or harm each other.**

We can see it in the levels of combat. In 1972 the FBI's official summation for the year on urban guerrilla actions (everything from ambushing police to expropriations, bombings, and setting up weapons caches) places the total at 195 actions, with eleven police killed in action and forty-three wounded by guerrillas. Of the 195 actions **only 14** were attributed to Euro-Amerikan revolutionaries (including the WUO). The BLA alone accounted for 25 actions, with the PG-RNA and other similar nationalists credited with 20. More to the point, almost all the combat with security forces was by the New Afrikan Liberation Movement. While they were fighting a very uneven, almost one-sided, war, sustaining heavy casualties and losing ground to multi-leveled counterinsurgency, the WUO was doing periodic protest bombings while carefully neither giving nor taking casualties. This is a reflection of the **general** stage of consciousness and struggle in the US oppressor nation.* It is just important now, long after those events, to be clear that the US New Left was not engaged in revolutionary war—no matter how much they sympathized with or supported the national liberation wars that others, the Vietnamese or New Afrikans, were locked in.

Like LSM, the Weather Underground took up proletarian internationalism but in a subjective way. These were new concepts to the settler nation, and the 1960s protest movement as a whole took up solidarity with national liberation struggles with great enthusiasm, but in faddish, one-sided, and undeveloped ways. WUO's uncertainties about revolutionary war had their

---

* Those small collectives that did attempt military-political activities beyond the protest level—such as the George Jackson Brigade and Sam Melville-Jonathan Jackson Brigade—found themselves abandoned by the Movement. The WUO itself was none too enthusiastic about embracing Euro-Amerikans who were actually trying to do combat.

roots in **political confusion about interna-tionalism** as it actually applied to the here and now of the continental Empire. What does it mean to "follow Third World leadership"? Can anti-imperialism, which is international, have **national** form? How can European settlers over-throw privilege and parasitism?

In a settler Empire, one that is both a "prison house" of Third World nations and peoples as well as the No. 1 imperialist power, for young revolu-tionaries to be uncertain about proletarian inter-nationalism inescapably means being **in practice uncertain about parasitism, uncertain about solidarity**, and so on. WUO, LSM, and the whole rest of the New Left envisioned that there would be only one united revolution in the US. Even in separate movements, they believed that New Afrikans, Euro-Amerikans, other Third World peoples (in that order of importance) would achieve de facto unity in overthrowing the only enemy—the US ruling class. This not only had a reasonable logic to it, this was what the "heaviest" Black revolutionaries they were allied to were saying. Huey Newton and the BPP explicitly said that everyone was united under BPP leadership in one revolution "against Fascism." John Watson of the Detroit League of Revolutionary Black Workers also told them that they were united in one revolution, albeit unequally since the Black vanguard would **"do the chopping"** while the Euro-Amerikan supporters would meekly follow behind and **"do the whittling."** Malcolm and nation-building had been left behind. And wasn't this "following Third World leadership"?

The effects of this confusion on the WUO's political-military development were drastic. WUO believed that it was fighting an inevitably victorious revolutionary war—although as an organization they themselves were not doing any such thing—because they looked to the Black Liberation Movement to do it for them. As the initial "You Don't Need a Weatherman ..." doc-ument makes plain, even the projected revolu-tionizing of White Amerika would be accom-plished **with or without settler effort** by the Black Revolution overthrowing US imperialism as a whole. In their view, the main task of settler radicals was only to try and keep up enough with the New Afrikan Liberation Movement so that Euro-Amerikans kept some role in the united revolution. So while LSM saw themselves being carried to revolution by Afrikans in Angola and Mozambique, **WUO saw themselves being carried to revolution by Afrikans in the US Empire.** "Hitching a ride on the BLM." WUO's "You Don't Need a Weatherman ..." said:

"... if necessary, black people could win self-determination, abolishing the whole impe-rialist system and seizing state power to do it, without this white movement ... Blacks could do it alone if necessary because of their centralness to the system, economically and geo-militarily, and because of the level of unity, commitment, and initiative which will be developed in waging people's war for sur-vival and national liberation ... Already, the black liberation movement has carried with it an upsurge of revolutionary consciousness among white youth ... It is necessary to defeat both racist tendencies: 1) that blacks shouldn't go ahead with making the revolution, and 2) that blacks should go ahead alone with it. The only third path is to build a white movement which will support the blacks in moving as fast as they have to and are able to, and still itself keep up with that black movement enough so that white revolutionaries share the cost and the blacks don't have to do the whole thing alone."[12]

Again like LSM, the WUO looked to external forces **outside themselves** and outside their nation to make **their** revolution. This view was an Achilles heel, which turned internationalist recognition of the leading world role of national liberation struggles into a revolutionary parasitism. From there further sliding, into opportunism and survivalism, could not be resisted. It became easy to let others do the fighting and dying, so long as the WUO's media reputation was maintained. Neither solidarity against the

INTERSTATE FLIGHT - MOB ACTION; RIOT; CONSPIRACY
WANTED BY FBI

The persons shown here are active members of the militant Weatherman faction of the Students for a Democratic Society - SDS.

Federal warrants have been issued at Chicago, Illinois, concerning these individuals, charging them with a variety of Federal violations including interstate flight to avoid prosecution, mob action, Antiriot Laws and conspiracy. Some of these individuals were also charged in an indictment returned 7/23/70, at Detroit, Michigan, with conspiracy to violate Federal Bombing and Gun Control Laws.

These individuals should be considered dangerous because of their known advocacy and use of explosives, reported acquisition of firearms and incendiary devices, and known propensity for violence.

If you have information concerning these persons please contact your local FBI Office.

William Charles Ayers

Kathie Boudin

Judith Alice Clark

Bernardine Rae Dohrn

US Empire nor a Euro-Amerikan revolutionary movement could be built on that quicksand.

The issues are not tactical military ones, of more or less shooting. For example, the WUO's central justification was that they were leading white youth to finally unite on the world battleground with the Vietnamese, Cubans, Afrikans, and all the oppressed fighters combatting imperialism. This was to be the first real solidarity. As Bernardine Dohrn said in "Communiqué No. 1":

> "**Hello. This is Bernardine Dohrn.** I'm going to read A DECLARATION OF A STATE OF WAR … We celebrate the example of Eldridge Cleaver and H. Rap Brown and all Black revolutionaries who first inspired us by their fight behind enemy lines for the liberation of their people.

> "Never again will they fight alone."[13]

Now, in the first place, the New Afrikan Revolution wasn't "alone," since it represented 35 million people and was tied to other revolutionary struggles and nations on every continent. **While the sentiment is perhaps progressive, it isn't true that if Euro-Amerikans aren't with you then you are "alone."** Perhaps the reverse would be closer to what the WUO really meant—without the Black Revolution then WUO felt "alone." While the WUO maintained a public facade of armed solidarity, this was practically impossible since the national liberation struggles were at war and the WUO and the settler New Left were not. Symbolic bombing actions were done to protest killer cops in New York, to protest the assassination of George Jackson, and so on. Individually these actions might seem to have merit. But as a whole they were only used as cover for false internationalism, for lack of solidarity.

WUO consistently refused to aid the BLA or other guerrillas in practice, refused to help hide fugitives, and eventually refused to even aid imprisoned fighters. All of this was done secretly, while the public media show of "bold revolutionary action" and solidarity was kept up. In other words, the difference in practice between the revisionists and WUO was that the revisionists didn't offer solidarity while the WUO pretended to. The WUO leadership was only carrying out the logic of its real situation, since if the organization—which was not at war—would have been dragged into the "free-fire zone" it would have been in a very different situation. In a classic case of survivalism, the WUO leadership placed their own personal safety as the highest priority, equating it with the survival of the Revolution.

Bernardine Dohrn herself, in her political self-criticism, details this:

> "This is Bernadine Dohrn. I am making this tape to acknowledge, repudiate and denounce the counter-revolutionary politics and direction of the Weather Underground…

> …

> "We denied Black and Third World organizations aid and support they requested and rejected offers of meetings and joint work

unless they were completely on our terms. That is, our security and our safety were placed above that of Third World and Black organizations. This was especially true of struggles under heavy attack by the state, under severe and murderous repression. I characterized these groups as left-sectarian, dangerous and threatening to us. By placing our protection and resources above the revolutionary principles of proletarian internationalism, we in fact operated to control Third World movements by making support and resources available only on our terms ...

"Meanwhile, this organization refused to seek out or recruit revolutionary women fugitives. We characterized these women as anti-men, anti-communist, anti-Marxist-Leninist. Actually, the central committee feared their effect on women in the organization ... We attacked and defeated a tentative proposal for a women's underground, to carry out anti-imperialist and revolutionary feminist armed struggle.

"While denying support of Third World liberation, to revolutionary armed struggle forces and to revolutionary women fugitives, we used resources and cadre's efforts to support opportunist and bourgeois men fugitives. The most glaring example of this is our support in the form of time, money, cadres, of Abby

Hoffman, a relationship which produced media attention for us, through the articles in *New Times* and his TV program.

...

"By the summer of 1975, the attack on the women's movement and feminist politics was naked and bitter ... This attack on women and the women's movement was carried out in a very personal way against women most identified with the women's movement. The consequences were the collapse of several women's organizations, and the withdrawal of anti-imperialist women from women's political work. It resulted in taking women out of anti-rape work and the defense of Third World women like Joann Little, Inez Garcia, and Yvonne Wanrow.* It meant an end to women's health care projects, abortion and anti-sterilization work, and work with women prisoners."[14]

WUO's inability to go forward into armed struggle was directly related to two problems: 1. There was no ready-made proletarian base in the US oppressor nation. There was, in fact, no social base at all for revolutionary war except for a small sector of radicalized petty-bourgeois youth. At the December 1969 Flint "War Council," one WUO spokesperson said that Euro-Amerikan involvement in Revolution was so irrelevant that after the Revolution they would be under a Third

---

* These were women—Black, Chicano, and Indian respectively—who had been imprisoned for armed self-defense.

World dictatorship from abroad, **"an agency of the people of the world," But to go to war with no idea of where the mass social base was to root the struggle in, was daunting.** Would-be Euro-Amerikan guerrillas could not base themselves in the Chicano community, for example. **And WUO never really understood that no revolutionaries find conveniently ready-made, pre-packaged social bases but must develop and build the masses and themselves in the same process.**

2. WUO took pleasure in speaking of itself as white shock troops, as "vandals" and "crazy motherfuckers." But in reality they never accepted the position of being soldiers (communists). The small organization considered itself the only true leadership over the entire settler movement. Not soldiers at all, but a privileged elite of petty-bourgeois leaders and headquarters staff. As an organization WUO was unwilling to face death, unwilling to accept the possibility/probability of being physically wiped out. This had roots not only in WUO's petty-bourgeois character (which was unavoidable) but in the yet unanswered problems of making revolution in a non-proletarian oppressor society. These difficulties were hardly unique to WUO or to any organization or faction in the New Left.

FDNY responds to Weatherman townhouse explosion.

For those reasons WUO never seriously approached armed struggle. And indeed, soon began backing further away from it. This was particularly true after Townhouse, the March 1970 incident in which three Weathercadre were killed in a dynamite accident. A pattern emerged: periodic property bombings would be done. WUO communiqués threatening major blows would be issued—everything from **"attacks will be carried out on pigs"** to promised raids on prisons to free H. Rap Brown and the Soledad Brothers. Which, of course, never happened. All this was to give the impression of a "heavy" revolutionary force. Meanwhile, the WUO Central Committee was trying various other strategies to get out of their dilemma and win a popular base of support among Euro-Amerikans. This dishonest and ambivalent situation finally led to the WUO abandoning clandestinity, which was useless to them except as a publicity gimmick, and taking up the program of legal reformism. WUO had exploited the prestige of armed struggle without ever entering it strategically. Its token bombings were used as a tactic to cover up for this.

At the beginning, in 1969, WUO saw revolution as a free gift from the New Afrikan Liberation Movement. As its contribution WUO hoped to command a small army of white drop-outs—"greasers," motorcycle gangs, dopers, high school rebels—irresistibly drawn into the chaos created as New Afrikans overthrew the US Government. They initially saw armed struggle just as violent disruption, creating havoc. Anything that disrupted society was revolutionary. The slogan was

"The bigger the mess the better." Weatherleaders still considered themselves as imperialism's bad children, thumbing their noses at society by shocking behavior. The mood of that period can be recaptured in Bernardine Dohrn's speech to the last public SDS-Weather gathering, the December 1969 "War Council":

> "Since October 11 we've been wimpy on armed struggle ... We're about being a fighting force alongside the Blacks, but a lot of us are still honkies and we're scared of fighting. We have to get into armed struggle ... We were in an airplane, and we went up and down the aisle 'borrowing' food from people's plates. They didn't know we were Weathermen; they just knew we were crazy. That's what we're about, being crazy motherfuckers and scaring the shit out of honky Amerika."[15]

Within six months of going underground in 1970 there was a clearer grasp of their difficult situation. A definite strategy emerged: to find a base of popularity in the petty-bourgeois drug subculture. While WUO opposed truly rebellious cultural forces being born—most notably Women's Liberation—it glorified drug use (and implicitly the petty-bourgeois drug traffic and subculture) as revolutionary. Hard words like socialism and communism faded out of political statements, replaced by vague hymns to drug use. This also began their practice of opportunistic deals with various drug celebrities.

On September 13, 1970, the WUO assisted LSD "guru" Dr. Timothy Leary's escape from a minimum security prison in California. Their ties to Leary were put forward as revolutionary armed struggle.* In *Communiqué No. 4,* WUO glorified Leary as a supposed "political prisoner, captured for the work he did in helping all of us begin the task of creating a new culture ..." The communiqué went on to say: "LSD and grass, like the herbs and cactus and mushrooms of the American Indians and countless civilizations that have existed on this planet, will help us make a future world where it will be possible to live in peace."[16] There was no mention of socialism or communism.

Not only was the model of a drugged society laid off on Indians, but the communiqué dragged in the names of the NLF, Al Fatah, PFLP, etc. as groups the WUO was "with." That was a cover-up, to fend off questions as to why an organization supposedly started to give armed solidarity to the oppressed should free a petty-bourgeois drug "guru" as its first major action. The communiqué dishonestly ends:

"With Rap Brown, Angela Davis, with all Black and brown revolutionaries, the Soledad Brothers ... Our organization commits itself to the task of freeing these prisoners of war.

"We are outlaws, we are free!

"Bernardine Dohrn"

Already the "solidarity" with oppressed nation revolutionaries was a conscious lie, part of the cover-up. WUO had no plans to or intentions of sacrificing itself freeing POWs. A revolutionary underground supposedly set up to do armed struggle in solidarity with national liberation, had within months turned into its opposite. Not solidarity, but rip-off. Settlerism not overcome, but still dominant even in an armed underground group.

The trend of the Leary action was solidified in the pivotal *New Morning—Changing Weather* document of December 1970. *New Morning* conspicuously downplayed armed struggle and support for national liberation. Instead, the petty-bourgeois drug subculture was appealed to as the supposed base of a "revolutionary culture," a youth nation:

"This communiqué does not accompany a bombing or a specific action. We want to express ourselves to the mass movement **not as military leaders** [our emphasis—ed.] **but as tribes at council.** It has been 9 months since the townhouse explosion. In that time, the future of our revolution has been changed decisively."

New Morning said: "But the townhouse forever destroyed our belief that armed struggle is the only real revolutionary struggle ... The deaths of three friends ended our military conception

---

* Leary went into exile in Algeria with the Cleaver wing of the BPP. He and Eldridge Cleaver held many "revolutionary" press conferences together. That was the period of the WUO-Cleaver media alliance.

of what we are doing." Instead, WUO praised the vanguard role of the alternative culture: "They've moved to the country and found ways to bring up free wild children. People have purified themselves with organic food, fought for sexual liberation, grown long hair. People have reached out to each other and learned that grass and organic consciousness expanding drugs are weapons of the revolution."[17]

The Panther 21, leading cadres of the NY BPP who were imprisoned in a major COINTELPRO operation, answered *New Morning* in an open letter. "We, of the Panther 21, take this opportunity to greet you with a spirit of revolutionary love and solidarity ... This letter is to acknowledge your actions—and like how we have watched your growth—and to relate to you how we have felt revolutionary joy on both accounts. This letter is also a response to your latest communiqué— 'New Morning—Changing Weather.' In it we can sense and feel your frustration and sense of isolation. We know the feeling well, having felt it ourselves for the last 21 months. We also very keenly feel the loss of direction, the confusion and chaos that is running rampant out there ... So from our experiences, we are responding to your communiqué because although we can fully understand where you are coming from—we sensed a certain mood and saw certain statements in your communiqué that sent chills up our spine ... We can also see that you feel—and rightfully so—the need for more support from the mother country youth. But we feel that most of the mother country youth culture communes smack heavily with

escapism—a danger you must be aware of and guard yourselves against."[18]

The Panther 21 urged WUO not to give up, to continue armed struggle. WUO refused to answer or discuss the criticism, since their whole strategy was to back away from armed struggle while still claiming its prestige.

The *New Morning—Changing Weather* line helped cover for the retreat to the sidelines, but it was not a guide to base-building. Between 1970 and 1973 the mass movement collapsed still further, while the alternative youth culture developed in a patriarchal, hip-capitalist manner, cynical to struggle and withdrawn into their own individualized concerns. The obvious irrelevance

Weather Underground Communique

of *New Morning* led the WUO to jump to another strategy in 1973–74, centered on the publication of the book *Prairie Fire*. The book was met with great interest in the Movement. Thousands of people eagerly read it. And not only because a political book from the most celebrated radical bombers in Amerika had curiosity value. While *Prairie Fire* was ideologically outdated for the time, it nevertheless had important strengths. We must remember that in 1974 the settler protest Movement had essentially evaporated. The New Left itself was self-destructing in the sterile, shrinking "party-building" debates of would-be Maoists. Everything good from the '60s seemed to be dying. For some, *Prairie Fire* seemed to be a reaffirmation of the vital links between armed struggle and popular mass movements, settler counter-culture and the rebellious Third World.

Prairie Fire was subtitled *The Politics of Revolutionary Anti-Imperialism*, and covered everything from a capsule history of settler reform movements to sections on the Palestinians, PAIGC, BLM, Native Amerikans, Women's Liberation, and so on. An entire chapter was devoted to the Vietnamese, as the most important struggle for Euro-Amerikans (**"All for Vietnam"**). The book sharply broke with the *New Morning* line. Armed struggle was verbally affirmed: "We are a guerrilla organization. We are communist women and men, underground in the United States for over four years ... Our intention is to engage the enemy ... to wear away at him, to harass him, to isolate him, to expose every weakness, to pounce, to reveal his vulnerability."[19]

PRAIRIE FIRE

THE POLITICS OF REVOLUTIONARY ANTI-IMPERIALISM

POLITICAL STATEMENT OF THE WEATHER UNDERGROUND

The petty-bourgeois drug subculture was no longer uncritically praised. In a sharp turn-about, Prairie Fire criticized people with **"a flippant attitude toward consciousness-expanding drugs"** (although WUO carefully stopped short of opposing drug use by settler youth). The book evaluates WUO's chosen social base in sober terms. Noting that a once-positive development of **"nomads, communal semi-hustlers, sharing a certain sense of being alien to and in opposition to the imperial way of life,"** had by 1973 **"withdrawn to rest on its privileges, dissociating itself from active opposition to racism ..."**[20]

Early in *Prairie Fire* the WUO explicitly repudiated its *New Morning* line, admitting that they had retreated from struggle:

"We have to learn from our mistakes …

"Reaffirming the importance of mass movement and political as well as military struggle, we wrote New Morning in December 1970. But New Morning gave uncritical support to youth culture and came to represent a repudiation of revolutionary violence. The Panther 21 wrote a generous and fighting criticism of New Morning from prison, which warned us against putting down our weapons. They correctly pointed to the necessity to continue to fight and our need to teach our people to fight. By failing to answer, we lost an opportunity to engage in dialogue with these brave and dedicated comrades."[21]

Often on target in its anti-imperialism, the book summed up many of the weaknesses but also the political gains of the young settler Movement:

"Our movement must discard the baggage of the oppressor society and become new women and new men, as Che taught. All forms of racism, class prejudice, and male chauvinism must be torn out by the roots. For us, proletarianization means recognizing the urgency of revolution as the only solution to our problems and the survival of all oppressed people. It means commitment, casting our lot with the collective interest and discarding the privileges of empire. It means recognizing that revolution is a lifetime of fighting and transformation, a risky business and ultimately a decisive struggle against the forces of death."[22]

Prairie Fire's impact temporarily strengthened the WUO, rallying supporters and winning new friends. WUO tried to be a real presence at the first national Socialist Feminist Conference in 1975. A public organization, the Prairie Fire Organizing Committee, was formed to gather supporters and be the legal, aboveground arm of WUO. *Prairie Fire* had sent out a call: "At this time, the unity and consolidation of anti-imperialist forces around a revolutionary program is an urgent and pressing necessity."

Yet, three years after the publication of *Prairie Fire* the WUO broke up, discredited as a leadership organization. Their crisis was precipitated by the new "revolutionary program." On the surface it appeared as a more developed synthesis of Anti-Imperialist themes—solidarity with national liberation, armed struggle, revolutionary culture. **Underneath that deliberate surface impression, the Prairie Fire line totally reversed the original direction of the Weather Underground.** Where at first the WUO leadership played with being **"guerrillas,"** and then played at being **"outlaws,"** by 1974 they had decided to rejoin the reformist left and play at being **"Marxist-Leninists."**

Part of *Prairie Fire's* popularity was that it subtly catered to the settler nationalism that US Bourgeois Marxism had always been infected with. The FBI commented in a report for other security agencies: "The Weather Underground has adopted, to a degree, more of an 'old-left' Marxist line in recent months and has gained considerable support in the process." We can easily trace the surfacing of these reformist politics from *Prairie Fire*'s class analysis, to its solidarity program, to its strategy for the Movement.

1. In *Prairie Fire*, the WUO leadership put forward the new strategy of representing the whole settler population (except for a small imperialist class), as their base of support. They sharply criticized their own earlier periods in which they did not identify with the white majority:

"We were wrong in failing to realize the possibility and strategic necessity of involving masses of people in anti-imperialist action and organization. We fixed our vision only on white people's complicity with empire, with the silence in the face of escalating terror and blatant murder of Black revolutionaries. We let go of our identification with the people— the promise, the yearnings, the defeats."[23]

In its discussion of "The Changing Nature of the Working Class," *Prairie Fire* identified itself with WUO's supposed working-class base for revolution: **"The great mass of the white collar workers, clericals, service people, teachers and professionals are underpaid, exploited ... They comprise the majority of the US workforce not at home."** It is specifically noted that these settlers were not middle class, but working class.[24]

Once "Weather" saw the settler white-collar, suburban masses as corrupted and highly privileged, oppressors themselves comprising a loyal base for imperialism. That view was too radical, and was unpopular with settlers. Now WUO had reversed itself. This same settler white-collar majority were supposedly **"underpaid, exploited"** workers. That view was much more popular with settlers. And that was the usual Bourgeois Marxist narcotic to help **"identification"** with those who were indifferent to genocide and lived lives of **"complicity with empire."**

•|山|• •|山|• •|山|•

2. *Prairie Fire* revealed a problem for WUO. It had two conflicting sets of friends to identify with. On the one hand, it had been called into being by the New Afrikan Liberation struggle, and its members had always pointed to the leading and heroic role of Black fighters. On the other hand, its would-be social base included the settler majority that supported **"escalating terror, and blatant murder of Black revolutionaries."** WUO found itself identifying with both sides of the liberation war. They found their solution in the deepest traditions of their people. If President Johnson had tried "using the nigger against the gook," then WUO could also do the same (only in reverse). Or **"All for Vietnam."** Just as today the white Left declares that internationalism means solidarity with Central Amerikan struggles, while paying only lip-service to liberation struggles within the "u.s.a."

This was a very heavy matter. Bernardine Dohrn said in her 1976 self-criticism: **"We pitted other national liberation struggles against the Black movement. For a long time it was Vietnam."** "Weather" members and supporters had always been proud to stand beside the Vietnamese people. Theirs was genuine pride that their organization had never abandoned Vietnam as so many had. The new '70s fad of pseudo-Maoism was eating away at solidarity with heroic Vietnam, and the Movement needed the WUO to help strengthen Anti-Imperialism. Weather Underground leadership cynically exploited that love and respect that its people had for Vietnam. Not just to promote themselves. But to slyly oppose the most dangerous and unpopular path of solidarity with Black Liberation—**"using the gook against the nigger."**

WUO pointed out: "The Vietnamese struggle is the most significant political event of our generation. Understanding the history of the Vietnam War is a key to understand the present world situation, the present governmental crisis, the present possibilities for the revolutionary movement here, and a correct anti-imperialist perspective. This is the era of national liberation, and for most of the past fifteen years, Vietnam has been the leading force in this struggle."

But this general analysis was twisted in being applied to the particular situation here, in being brought home:

"The seriousness of our threat was growing. The killings of students at Jackson State and Kent State had a significant effect on the youth movement. The war was brought home ... During that time, the anti-war movement reached its greatest strength and the largest and most militant demonstrations took place. Inspired by the Black Panthers and other Black fighters, many whites such as Sam Melville, Cameron Bishop, the New Year's Gang in Madison, and ourselves began building armed struggle ...

...

"ALL FOR VIETNAM

"The vanguard nature of Vietnamese liberation in the past decade means that we can approach the difficult question of class analysis, consciousness and potential, by looking at how various groups within society were affected by anti-war struggle. This way we avoid an idealist or opportunist class analysis, and begin with our understanding, based on practice, of the leading anti-imperialist forces in society. Black and Third World people, and young people—especially students and members of the armed forces—responded to the Vietnam War in the most consistently principled way ... Support for the leading force in the fight against the enemy is the essential and necessary content of proletarian internationalism here and now.

"Many organizations pay lip-service to the anti-imperialist struggle. But those movement organizations who, in practice, did not come to give **full support to the Vietnamese as the main priority of class struggle** made a serious error [our emphasis—ed.]. This was especially true during the 1972 Final Offensive, when—between the launching of the offensive on March 31, 1972 and the signing of the Cease-Fire Agreement on January 27, 1973—the slogan of the movement should have been: 'All for Vietnam!' By this measure we criticize our own practice during the final offensive, when we organized under the slogan, but were not successful in carrying out our full program."[25]

We quote this passage because it helps us to understand what oppressor nation anti-imperialism is and is not. *Prairie Fire* deliberately blurred and tried to erase the distinction between anti-war and anti-imperialist. Between the broad Anti-War Movement and the small Anti-Imperialist tendency. This trick made it sound as though there were a mass, anti-imperialist struggle of millions of settlers, which was not true. The US Anti-War Movement brought together many widely diverse political points of view, united only by the common demand that US combat troops be withdrawn from Indochina. Which is why the larger Movement came to an end once US troops were finally withdrawn. Most settler critics of the War were still overall **pro-imperialist**, opposed to national liberation and socialism particularly inside "their" Empire.

The WUO slogan **"All for Vietnam"** as **"the main priority of class struggle"** falsely defined

internationalism solely in terms of the Anti-War Movement. That slogan for the period 1971–73 ignored a concrete analysis of the actual struggle going on here within the continental Empire. It actually opposed national liberation.

BRING THE WAR HOME!

SDS

As we know, the main aspect of that period here was the attempt by the oppressed nations within the continental Empire to break through to a higher level of struggle, to move from spontaneous rebellion and resistance to national liberation. The particular feature of that period was the attempt, by movements being decimated in the Amerikkkan free-fire zone, to move from Civil Rights and self-defense to armed guerrilla action and self-government, even initial liberation of some National Territory. These attempted breakthroughs were turned back by US Imperialism with qualitative losses for the anti-colonial insurgents. Anti-Imperialism **within** the continental Empire was defeated. This period was pivotal, then, the deciding round in the anti-colonial rising of the 1960s.

■ By 1972 the Provisional Government of the Republic of New Afrika, representing the revolutionary nationalism of the Black Nation, had been crushed in its attempt to set up a temporary capital on New Afrikan–owned land in Mississippi, symbolizing their intention to **Free the Land**. On August 18, 1971, Jackson Police and FBI captured two RNA residences in Jackson, taking three casualties in the process. The defense case of the RNA-11 began. Almost thirty of the most dedicated RNA cadre were in the state prisons of Louisiana and Mississippi. In response to the RNA-11 arrests, the largest New Afrikan demonstration in the history of Jackson took place. The settler Anti-War Movement and New Left did not defend or support the PG-RNA in any way. Many felt that since the PG-RNA were separat-

ists they "deserved" no support. **WUO refused to recognize the Provisional Government; refused to oppose the counterinsurgency campaign against it; refused to give political or material support to the defense case.**

■ By 1973 the attempt to launch the New Afrikan guerrilla struggle, using the "autonomous and decentralized" ex-BPP units known as the Black Liberation Army, had received serious setbacks. The struggle did not end, however. In 1973 BLA units had twelve engagements with police, inflicting nineteen casualties. Looking back, the BLA-CC wrote:

"... The spark we hoped would start the fire that would burn Babylon down was extinguished by State propaganda organs and special anti-guerrilla squads. Many comrades moved to the South hoping to establish a southern base; this too failed because we lacked knowledge of terrain and people, so again we moved back to the cities, this time as fugitives with little popular support among the masses. Our primary activity at that period was hiding out and carrying out expropriations. With the deaths of Woody and Kimu we launched assaults against the police that set them on edge; their counter-attack saw us at the end of 1973 with four dead, over twenty comrades imprisoned in New York alone. In New Orleans, Los Angeles, and Georgia, BLA members were taken prisoner by Federal agents working with local police to crush the BLA."

In private communication the BLA had asked WUO for political-military support: assistance for fugitives such as Assata Shakur, other forms of practical cooperation, political campaigns to help impede the FBI counterinsurgency campaign. WUO refused totally. WUO leadership adopted their position that New Afrikan guerrillas were **"dangerous and threatening to us."** This position was kept secret so as not to discredit WUO.

■ The US reconquest of liberated Wounded Knee on May 9, 1973, was another nodal point. AIM fighters from many Indian nations had helped Oglala Sioux patriots assert armed self-government under US military siege. Despite much public sympathy, imperialism not only

crushed nation-building, but launched a Phoenix program to assassinate or otherwise "neutralize" grassroots AIM cadre and supporters. Hundreds fell. A wave of terrorism swept the Plains, as Indian patriots kept being found dead in "accidents," "suicides," or unexplained shootings. A news white-out by imperialism, in which the New Left cooperated, shielded their Phoenix program in silence.

When Anti-Imperialism was defeated, thrown back within the oppressed nations, it signified a **general reversal** for all revolutionary forces within the continental Empire. The settler Anti-Imperialist tendency suffered a profound defeat

as well. It was not Vietnam that was ultimately decisive here. As we can see from the fact that the Vietnamese victory coincided with the collapse of the New Left. The settler New Left tended to picture anti-imperialism as a "Solidarity Supermarket," where each season well-meaning Euro-Amerikans could stroll the aisles picking and choosing from among the many liberation movements of the world which ones they wanted to "support," depending on the latest fads. So-called internationalism was trivialized to resemble a recreation or a hobby. Rather than **being** guerrillas, **being** revolutionaries in deeds as WUO had once set out to do.

There were concrete reasons for the failure of the Anti-Imperialist tendency to join the struggle in the decisive period. First and foremost, the national liberation movements were themselves still ill-organized, and politically unable to give correct leadership to their alliances. US oppressor nation anti-imperialists were stunned at the disappearance of the mass Anti-War Movement, unorganized to carry out revolutionary tasks in the face of the imperialist counter-offensive.

So as decisive Anti-Imperialist battles were being fought here, settler Anti-Imperialism found itself standing safely on the sidelines as spectators. And there with everyone else was the WUO, covering up by shouting **"All for Vietnam."** Could there be a more profound defeat? While the mass Anti-War Movement was the sheltering "sea," the rich political current in which Anti-Imperialism grew, settler Anti-Imperialism was born out of the challenge and example of the New Afrikan Liberation Movement. Vietnam was indeed the pivotal **world** confrontation between socialism and imperialism, but it was not a **substitute** for the

specific revolutionary tasks of every nation and people.

Babylon was the battleground for Euro-Amerikans as well, on one side or the other. Settler anti-imperialists had rightfully aspired to fight side-by-side with the oppressed. To have, at the decisive moment, politically abandoned anti-colonial risings was to lose their own heart and soul. **What function did settler Anti-Imperialism have if it could not raise a hand against the raging imperialist counter-insurgency?** What was left was a stillborn movement, a hollow shell of verbal anti-imperialism.

•ILJI• •ILJI• •ILJI•

3. WUO's final strategy for the Movement was to give up the last remaining vestiges of Anti-Imperialism, and to regain settler popularity by leading a mass, legal reform movement. WUO planned to coopt all the dissident causes within the continental Empire into one gigantic public movement, whose unifying focus would be broad economic demands. Prairie Fire urged its readers to unite everyone **"Against The Common Enemy"**:

"We can foresee a time of food riots, unemployment councils, tenants anti-eviction associations, neighborhood groups, anti-war organizations. The left must organize itself to understand the continuing crisis of our times and mobilize the discontent into a force for freedom.

"Organize poor and working class people. Go to the neighborhoods, the schools, the social institutions, the work places. Agitate. Create Struggle ..."[26]

Settler trade-unionists, welfare mothers, disabled persons, Asians, New Afrikans, Chicano-Mexicanos, Puerto Ricans, Native Amerikans, lesbian and gay activists, drug dealers, university professors, prisoners, doctors and nurses, settler community organizers, civil libertarians, PTA leaders, the BLA, lawyers, anti-war activists, would all hopefully combine into one public reform movement under the supreme leadership of the WUO. Since it would serve no purpose any longer, clandestinity and even token military actions would be abandoned. That was the final strategy of the WUO, that guided their activity from 1974–1977.

To promote this reformist strategy, *Prairie Fire* was written to falsely picture the Euro-Amerikan people as not only **"underpaid"** and **"exploited"** but as being **anti-imperialist**. Confusing the difference between the mass Anti-War Movement and the small Anti-Imperialist tendency did that. It was also necessary to disguise how much settlers hated Black Liberation ("dangerous and threatening to us") and were indifferent to genocide. To do this *Prairie Fire*, while paying lip-service to the Black Nation, downplayed and even whited-out the New Afrikan liberation struggle. For example, in the passage about bringing the war home WUO lists the two major campus repressions of 1970 as important events in the development of the settler Anti-War Movement:

"The seriousness of our threat was growing. The killings of students at Jackson State and Kent State had a significant effect on the youth movement. The war was brought home ..."[27]

That was an amazing lie, even for the WUO. It was also a revealing lie. We can compare the Euro-Amerikan response to the two separate repressions, at the very peak of student Anti-War militancy.

The Vietnam wasn't "brought home," as *Prairie Fire* said, to Jackson State. The fourteen New Afrikan students were shot down because of their own war, their own liberation struggle. That is why revolutionary nationalism popularized the slogan: "Amerikkka is the Blackman's Battleground." WUO was trying to slide around the uncomfortable truth that there was also a battleground right here, on which everybody had to choose their role. They arrogantly sought to erase the difficult lessons of the Black Revolution. And their own founding (**"We're about being a fighting force alongside the Blacks ..."**)

Publication of *Prairie Fire* was followed by more military actions. In 1975 there were four WUO property bombings: January 29th at the State Department in Washington (and a bomb

---

KENT STATE (OHIO)

May 4, 1970: National Guards fire on anti-war demonstration, shooting down thirteen settler youth (killing four).

Major political issue, front-page news. *New York Times* gave it a 4-column wide headline and 51 inches of copy.

Settler youth outraged. Storm of protest both spontaneous and organized by Movement. Demonstrations held at 1,350 schools. 536 schools closed by student strikes. Violent demonstrations at 73 schools. 169 bombings and arson attacks on government and war-related buildings.

JACKSON STATE (MISSISSIPPI)

May 14, 1970: State and local police machine-gun a dormitory at Black college, shooting down fourteen Black students (killing two).

Treated as a minor event. *New York Times* had short, 6-inch story only.

Settler youth indifferent. Movement opposed, but unable to organize protests. Only 53 school demonstrations, most of them at Black colleges.

WUO bombs National Guard office in Washington, DC to protest both Kent and Jackson State repressions.[28]

that didn't go off in Oakland); June 16th at the New York City branch of Banco de Ponce, in support of Puerto Rican cement workers' strike; September 5th in Salt Lake City at Kennecott Copper Corp., in protest of the overthrow of the Allende regime in Chile. At the same time a new WUO political-military document supposedly giving guidelines for protracted war was put out.

Not only was this renewed military activity put on after the WUO's 1973–1974 decision to adopt building a legal reform movement as the main revolutionary strategy, but while it was going on the WUO Central Committee decided to give up and surface as soon as possible. **In other words, irregardless of what the WUO military cadre thought they were doing, their bombings were only used to oppose armed struggle.**

When we think about it, this is not so hard to comprehend. The Weatherleaders had few credentials, other than personal fame, now that the '60s campus revolt had ended. They had no record of organizing new settlers, of providing communist leadership, of any accomplishments other than their fame as "white guerrillas." So they needed a military show to give themselves a renewed media fix, to get enough leverage within the Movement to pull off their new schemes.

WUO's strategy was named "inversion." Under "inversion" lawyers were found to prepare for possible trials after surfacing. Led by Leonard Boudin, radical lawyers issued a public call for amnesty for the Weather fugitives. An anti-leadership critique by the "Revolutionary Committee WUO" charged: "Overtures were made to the Democratic Party in connection with break-ins against family and associates of the WUO. This provided the possibility of deals in return for the trials being a lever for purging Nixon people from the Justice Department and the FBI."

A full-length documentary film, "Underground," was done of the Central Committee to promote their new image as peaceful-minded middle-class settlers loyal to their people. Yippie celebrity Abbie Hoffman, arrested while selling cocaine, was given aid as a fugitive in return for his giving the WUO a media endorsement on a network television interview. Soon the "Weather" leaders hoped to end their underground and resume fully legal settler political life.[29]

In the Spring of 1975 WUO published *Politics in Command*, their new political-military doctrine. Its outer appearance of armed struggle was just a thin coating, designed to get people to swallow its poisonous ideas. On the one hand it smoothly quoted or paraphrased lessons of revolutionary war plucked from Chile, Uruguay, Vietnam, and Cuba. It said: "We are at an early stage of protracted revolutionary war. We need a strategy to last, to grow and to organize for many years to come …" Yet it never said what that strategy was.

Instead, WUO planted poisonous little barbs like: "… a comparatively small sector of the population actively supports armed struggle … the

NAT'L HARD TIMES CONFERENCE CHICAGO JAN 30-FEB 1

HARD TIMES ARE FIGHTING TIMES

When It Flood Times Here Cultural Collective

THESE ARE HARD TIMES AND EVERYWHERE PEOPLE ARE STRUGGLING TO SURVIVE. ACROSS THE NATION THERE ARE CUTBACKS IN SOCIAL SERVICES, WHILE THE LARGEST PART OF OUR TAX DOLLAR GOES TO THE PENTAGON. IN NEW ENGLAND WE FACE ANOTHER WINTER'S SOARING FUEL PRICES, WHILE THE OIL COMPANIES TAKE IN RECORD PROFITS FROM AN "ENERGY CRISIS" THEY CREATED.

THE U.S. GOVERNMENT AND THE BUSINESSES THAT CONTROL IT HOPE TO KEEP THEIR PROFITS UP BY KEEPING US DIVIDED AND POWERLESS. WHEN A BOSS WON'T HIRE SOMEONE BECAUSE OF THE COLOR OF THEIR SKIN, OR PAYS WOMEN LESS THAN MEN FOR THE SAME WORK, WE ARE SET BACK. WHEN WHITE PEOPLE PUT THEIR FRUSTRATION INTO KEEPING BLACK PEOPLE OUT OF 'THEIR' SCHOOLS INSTEAD OF JOINING IN THE FIGHT

FOR EQUAL, QUALITY EDUCATION FOR ALL WORKING CLASS KIDS, IT'S A DEFEAT FOR US ALL. WHEN WE MAKE OUR UNIONS FIGHT FOR US, THEY ARE ATTACKED. THE LONG STRUGGLES FOR NON-DISCRIMINATORY HIRING ARE BEING SET BACK THROUGH DISCRIMINATORY LAYOFFS.

STILL, PEOPLE ARE RESPONDING WITH RALLIES, SIT-INS, AND WORK STOPPAGES. IN NEW HAMPSHIRE THERE WILL BE SEVERE CUTS IN MEDICAID THIS FEBRUARY, BUT WOMEN ON WELFARE ARE ORGANIZING STATEWIDE. IN THE JAMAICA PLAIN SECTION OF BOSTON, WHERE RENTS WERE "LEGALLY" RAISED THIS YEAR, BLACK, LATINO, AND WHITE NEIGHBORS RECENTLY BLOCKED THE EVICTION OF A PUERTO RICAN GRANDMOTHER. EACH COMMUNITY AND WORKPLACE HAS ITS OWN STORY TO TELL.

HUNDREDS OF GROUPS ARE SPONSORING A NATIONAL HARD TIMES CONFERENCE. BY TALKING WITH EACH OTHER ABOUT OUR COMMON PROBLEMS WE CAN FIND OUT JUST HOW STRONG PEOPLE'S RESISTANCE IS, AND WE CAN JOIN TOGETHER IN A NATIONAL CAMPAIGN TO FIGHT BACK.

MANY OF US REMEMBER THE DEPRESSION OF THE THIRTIES AND UNDERSTAND HOW IMPORTANT ORGANIZATION AND UNITY WERE IN WINNING SOCIAL SECURITY, UNEMPLOYMENT INSURANCE AND IN BUILDING THE UNIONS. THE MOVEMENT OF THE SIXTIES FOR CIVIL RIGHTS AND AGAINST THE INDOCHINA WAR TEACH THE SAME LESSON. U.S. POWER HAS BEEN WEAKENED BY PEOPLE ALL AROUND THE WORLD. THE DEMANDS WE ARE MAKING CAN BE WON... OUR LONG HISTORY OF STRUGGLE PROVES IT...

STOP THE CUTBACKS • ROLL BACK PRICES • JOBS & INCOME FOR ALL

PLEASE SHARE YOUR IDEAS WITH US! THIS CONFERENCE IS BEING SPONSORED BY A BROAD-BASED COALITION OF GROUPS NEW ENGLAND REGIONAL OFFICE FOR THE NATIONAL HARD TIMES CONFERENCE - 32 RUTLAND ST. BOSTON MASS. 02118 617-267-6557 test of actions is primarily the ability to win people." The implications led in an obvious direction. The best armed strategy was no armed strategy. If armed actions should be judged "primarily" on the basis of their popularity, and if they are unpopular … In the same vein, *Politics in Command* finished by stressing the need for an "open," "legal," and "peaceful" revolutionary movement—supposedly working hand-in-hand with the armed struggle! It isn't hard to catch the drift. *Politics in Command* tried to use WUO's prestige as supposed fighters to undermine political confidence in armed struggle, to soften up people into surrendering along with the WUO leadership.[30]

The next-to-final step in "inversion" was the attempted launching of the WUO's grand reform coalition, representing the settler Left, assorted Third World activists and groups, and people from the various protest movements (ecology, union reform, women's rights, prison support, etc.) Led by the WUO's Prairie Fire Organizing Committee, this coalition promised to help everybody fight "Hard Times" by winning new government reforms. Not so incidentally, the Hard Times coalition would have also incorporated the Third World movements under WUO leadership and have given the Weatherleaders a mass defense organization if they were charged with heavy offenses after surrendering.

The political collapse of anti-imperialism can be seen in the fact that WUO saw the continental national liberation movements as just

"**minority**'" component parts of a single, US Empire–wide reform movement under their settler command. Third World radical figures were involved to give cover to the WUO's attempted co-optation of the Third World movements. An alliance was made between PFOC and Juan Mari Bras' Puerto Rican Socialist Party (PSP). Left settler critics of the Hard Times line were rebuked for "racism," and reminded that they were implicitly criticizing Third World leaders who were involved. WUO said that they were "following Third World leadership."

The WUO Central Committee issued a political attack on its settler critics in September 1975. Titled "Our Class Stand," it strongly pushed for co-optive relationships with Third World people: "White revolutionaries have largely cut themselves off from these relationships. Great opportunities exist at this time, waiting to be seized. But too often white revolutionaries shrink from these openings, sometimes using 'support for self-determination' as an excuse."

In January 1976 almost 3,000 people from all over the continent met in Chicago to attend the founding Hard Times Conference. While it initially appeared impressive, the conference rapidly began self-destructing. Activists from autonomous movements began criticizing the lack of content or any visible purpose other than setting up WUO's hegemony. Women's movement criticism was particularly sharp. The main blow came when the Black caucus denounced the Hard Times leadership for racism. Irreconcilable differences appeared, even though most revolutionary New Afrikan organizations had been too opposed or indifferent to the conference to attend.

WUO's inability to even anticipate the shark-filled waters it was opportunistically jumping off into was illustrated by its disaster with the Black Caucus. Naively, WUO leaders thought that as long as they had a few hand-picked Black and Puerto Rican allies the conference could be controlled. **It never occurred to WUO that what they had done, other rival settler opportunists could do as well.** One of the main crowd-stirring denunciations of the PFOC-Hard Times leaders came from a Black woman with grassroots credentials. Secretly, however, she was being paid full-time by a rival settler radical group, and was under their leadership. Another major Black figure attacking PFOC was a Midwestern factory organizer, who had been secretly recruited by the rival October League M-L, and had come to the conference to help torpedo it. A settler organization arranged for one of the historic RNA leaders to come. When WUO clumsily tried to ice him (by limiting his speaking time to 5 minutes) they set off a hornet's nest of righteous anger. And on and on. WUO never knew what hit it.

After several days it was evident that the Hard Times strategy couldn't be implemented successfully. Even strong intervention to prop up PFOC by their Puerto Rican Socialist Party allies (and the proposed July 4, 1976 People's Bicentennial rally) couldn't build a "new movement" out of shallow politics, unclear and opportunistic alliances, and a stale program of no struggle.[31]

The public disaster area of the Hard Times line precipitated a final factional upheaval within the Weather Underground. Jeff Jones, Bernardine Dohrn, Billy Ayers, Celia Sojourn, and Joe Reed were purged and left the organization. Both WUO and PFOC were swept into a bitter and public "rectification" campaign. WUO quietly died, transferring its political and military roles to the aboveground PFOC (already much stronger than its parent organization). Remnants held out in clandestinity, but most underground WUO cadre surfaced by ones and twos and dealt with their largely minimal legal situation.

Those who gave up are today professionals, teachers, and social workers. They have returned home to the embrace of their class and nation. A British writer, telling of a charming, Thanksgiving turkey-and-wine lunch at the home of the editor of the *New York Times Book Review*, remarks that his table-mate was "a woman who'd achieved notoriety a decade earlier by blowing up her father's house in Greenwich Village ..."[32] The WUO leadership became what they once rebelled against. Their young children go to private settler schools and elite "public" schools. Respectable social reform activity occupies their spare evenings. Theirs is the life of the "comfortable left."

•।ய।• •।ய।• •।ய।•

It is hard to envision a defeat so complete as that suffered by 1960s Euro-Amerikan Anti-Imperialism. Not even repressed, but tripped up by their own inner weaknesses. Why? People didn't risk themselves in bombings and illegal actions because they weren't for armed struggle. And they didn't go through so many struggles with their own white supremacy just because they wanted to betray internationalism.

With hindsight it is clear that there was no way that the 1960s New Left could have successfully leapt into armed struggle. As we know armed struggle is the highest and most decisive form of struggle, but therefore the most difficult. The period of revolutionary civil wars in China took one hundred years. And even after the Chinese finally established a communist party they still had to grow through periods of great offensives and equally great setbacks before they worked out how to conduct armed struggle. For a US student movement without any communist party or understanding, with no prior revolutionary experience or tradition, to master those challenges in several years would have been a miracle. Particularly in the heart of Babylon, with all its distorted culture.

We should see that WUO's contribution—like that of the entire Movement—was to begin a process, to have joined in first raising a revolutionary opposition within the settler nation. In like fashion their errors were so important because they were general to the Anti-Imperialist tendency. Otherwise others would have forged past them and shown everyone a better way in practice.

The WUO itself, even during its public "rectification" factional struggle in 1976, was essentially a blank as to why they reversed direction. In her self-criticism Bernardine Dohrn woodenly said: "Why did we do this? I really don't know. We followed the classic path of white so-called revolutionaries who sold out the revolution." The line of the winning faction, the short-lived Revolutionary Committee, said little more. They limited their analysis to praising the general line of the book *Prairie Fire*, claiming that the WUO followed "a principled political line" of armed solidarity from 1970–1974, and placing the blame for only "two years" of "wrong direction" on the old Central Committee.[33] The Central Committee was denounced by them as opportunist, male chauvinist, elitist, white supremacist, and so on. All true, but frankly just as true of the Revolutionary Committee. The easy addiction of "explaining" setbacks in a facile manner, even by trashing a few leaders, can no longer be afforded. Communists must get to the root of things, to the inner contradictions.

To understand what happened to the WUO we have to examine the moment of their crisis, during the period in 1970 beginning with Townhouse. On March 6, 1970, a large dynamite explosion in the Wilkerson family townhouse in Greenwich Village, NYC, killed Diana Oughton, Ted Gold, and Terry Robbins. The young WUO

was shaken by their first and only loss. While the immediate cause was thought to be technical carelessness (constructing bomb circuits without test lights and safety switches), WUO leadership placed the primary error on militarism by that collective and the organization as a whole. *New Morning*, ten months later, summed up why the WUO felt it had to reverse direction away from Townhouse:

"Diana, Teddy and Terry had been in SDS for years; Diana and Teddy had been teachers and spent weeks with the Vietnamese in Cuba. Terry had been a community organizer in Cleveland and at Kent; Diana had worked in Guatemala. They fought in the Days of Rage in Chicago. Everyone was angered by the

Smoke billows out of 18 W. 11th St. following fire and explosion.

Explosions & Fire Destroy Village Townhouse; 1 Dead

By JOSEPH MODZELEWSKI

The body of a redhaired youth was found beneath the charred ruins of an expensive Greenwich Village townhouse after three violent xplosions demolished the building shortly before noon yesterday.

Two young women barely escaped death and another person was feared dead in the blast that triggered a six-hour fire at 18 W. 11th St.

The body was discovered six hours after the first explosion by firemen who had been forced from the charred building earlier when beams and bricks fell on them.

Search of the building was stopped shortly after 6 p.m. because of danger to men searching the debris. Con Ed brought in a crane to knock down the remaining shell at the request of the Fire Department. The search for other possible victims will continue this morning.

Fire Chief John O'Hagan said the victim's body was badly mangled under the rubble of the collapsed four-story structure.

The building is owned by a former ad executive, Joseph P. Wilkerson, who is now on vacation on the Caribbean island of St. Kitts. It is believed that his daughter, Kathy, 20, was one of the girls who fled the townhouse.

The explosions—believed triggered by a gas leak—also damaged two adjoining brownstone buildings, one the home of Academy Award-nominee Dustin Hoffman and his wife, Ann. Mrs. Hoffman had just left her

second-floor apartment at 16 W. 11th St. and was halfway down the block when the blasts ripped through the townhouse.

Norman Seeley, sexton of the Church of Ascension at the corner of Fifth Ave. and 11th St., rushed from his church to the burning building.

"There was a nude girl standing in the basement window frame, screaming and pointing to others trapped in the explosion," Seeley said.

As 18 pieces of fire-fighting equipment responded to the blaze, the nude girl and her companion, both covered with soot, emerged onto the street where they were met by Mrs. Susan Wager of 50 W. 11th St.

They Take Baths

Mrs. Wager took the distraught girls to her home, where they took baths and borrowed clothes.

"I don't know where they went after that," said the housewife. "They said they were going to the drugstore for medicine, but they never came back.

"I kept asking them if anyone else was in the building, and I think they said two more persons. They were too upset to talk."

The identity and the where-

abouts of the two young girls, whom Mrs. Wager described as between 15 and 18 years old, remained a mystery.

A Red Cross emergency team offered shelter to the victims left homeless by the explosions—including Hoffman and his wife—but the residents of the affluent, tree-lined street all declined temporary shelter.

Ann Hoffman was shaken by the disaster, biting her lip and looking glassy-eyed after she rushed back into her home to rescue her dog. The couple's 4-year-old son was in nursery school at the time of the explosions.

Hoffman rushed down from his W. 55th St. offices to the scene and carried several paintings out of his damaged home. The paintings, he explained, were gifts of an artist friend.

The blast came with such force that it blew out several third floor windows of an apartment across the street at 15 W. 11th St.

An off-duty housing patrolman, Vincent Calderone, who aided in efforts to rescue the two girls, was taken to nearby St. Vincent's Hospital, where he was treated for a cut hand.

At 4 p.m., police began broadcasting a citywide bulletin for the two missing girls who escaped the building.

death of Fred Hampton. Because their collective began to define armed struggle as the only legitimate form of revolutionary action, they did not believe that there was any revolutionary motion among white youth. It seemed like Black and Third World people were going up against Amerikan imperialism alone.

"Two weeks before the townhouse explosion, four members of this group had firebombed Judge Murtagh's house in New York as an action of support for the Panther 21, whose trial was just beginning. To many people this was a very good action. Within the group, however, the feeling developed that because this action had not done anything to hurt the pigs materially it wasn't very important. So within two weeks time, this group had moved from fire-bombing to anti-personnel bombs. Many people in the collective did not want to be involved in the large scale, almost random bombing offensive that was planned. But they struggled day and night and eventually, everyone agreed to do their part.

"At the end, they believed and acted as if only those who die are proven revolutionaries. Many people had been argued into doing something they did not believe in, many had not slept for days. Personal relationships were full of guilt and fear. The group had spent so much time willing themselves to act that they had not dealt with the basic technological considerations of safety. They had not considered the future: either what to do with the bombs if it had not been possible to reach their targets, or what to do in the following days.

"This tendency to consider only bombings or picking up the gun as revolutionary, with the glorification of the heavier the better, we've called the military error.

"After the explosion, we called off all armed actions until such time as we felt the causes had been understood and acted upon. We found that the alternative already existed among us and had been developed within other collectives. We became aware that a group of outlaws who are isolated from the youth communities do not have a sense of what is going on, cannot develop strategies that grow to include large numbers of people, have become 'us' and 'them.'

"It was a question of revolutionary culture ... People are forming new families. Collectives have sprung up ... Many of these changes have been pushed forward by women both in collectives with men and in all-women collectives. The enormous energy of sisters working together has not only transformed the movement internally, but when it moves out it is a movement that confuses and terrifies Amerika ... we have seen the potential strength of thousands of women marching, it is now up to revolutionary women to take the lead to call militant demonstrations, to organize young women to carry the Vietcong flag, to make it hard for Nixon and Ky to travel around the country ..."[34]

We can feel their fear and indecision. New Afrikan revolutionaries were being targeted by the Empire. The BPP was being destroyed. So some in WUO wanted to take the step of counter-terror, of starting to kill their fellow settlers. Despite all the years of heavy rhetoric, bringing matters to that knife's edge produced heavy internal disagreements, "guilt and fear," dismay at having to cross the line. People felt estranged both from each other and from the Movement. Most neither wanted to take lives nor to give up their settler way of life. And it was glaringly obvious that if New Afrikan revolutionaries, with much more organization and base, were being decimated, then WUO's **"group of outlaws who are isolated"** faced even quicker defeat. Doing the promised right thing, "fighting alongside the Blacks," only seemed a counter-productive death trap.

WUO's isolation problem was not imaginary but very real. It was also self-imposed. Only five months before, in mobilizing for the October 1969 Days of Rage street fighting demonstrations, WUO had planned for several thousand youth. These would have left Chicago "toughened psychologically, militarily, and politically" as a cadre to in turn mobilize a projected youth army of 20,000 within the next few months. Instead, less than 300 youths took part in the Chicago demonstrations. Faced with indictments and trials for conspiring to create riots, the leading Weatherpeople had to go underground without any army or organized mass base at all. How then to stay alive and prosper politically? As we know,

the organization decided to put lots of distance between itself and the New Afrikan liberation struggle, preserve themselves, and appeal for support from the petty-bourgeois drug subculture.

Feelings within WUO of being weak, isolated and desperate, on the brink of armed struggle, were not objective in the larger sense. While the mass Anti-War Movement was ebbing, the same emerging contradictions within settler society that had created WUO were still at work. WUO was not exceptional. That same year and season there were hundreds of bombing, arson, and other militant assaults on "pig" institutions by settler students. Not guerrilla actions, but the angry, radicalized edge of the declining mass movement. Thousands of settlers marched, went to public rallies, and contributed funds to protest the repression of the Black Panthers. Not decisive and only an unorganized, small minority, but to anti-imperialism very important. And the oldest and newest liberation movement of all, Women's Liberation, was starting to break out. Rebelliousness and attempts to build a revolutionary culture were in the air then, although chaotic and searching for new understanding. But WUO saw themselves as the only people doing really revolutionary things. They never wanted to work with others, learn from others, but only to command support.

While WUO came to believe that the practical carelessness of Townhouse meant that a less "heavy" military emphasis was needed, that too was petty-bourgeois subjectivism (and vacillation). Objectively, their supposed carelessness and lack of planning only showed the necessity of taking military aspects more seriously, not less. The political error of Townhouse, if WUO's facts are true, was not an overly "military" emphasis, but a lack of attention to military matters, together with the error of seeing armed struggle as a "macho," patriarchal, and individualistic exercise. This has unfortunately become very familiar to all of us.

WUO never saw the organic interrelationship between armed struggle and the building

Clockwise from top: Terry Robbins, Diana Oughton, Ted Gold.

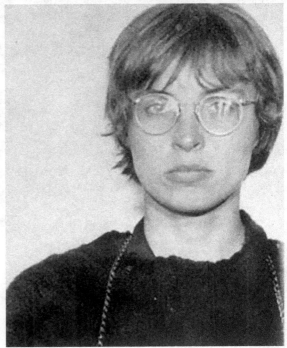

of new social forces. Armed struggle was seen by them in a bourgeois way, as purely "military" violence or alternatively as a symbolic media event. Throughout its history, from *New Morning* to *Prairie Fire*, and from Hard Times to the Revolutionary Committee, WUO consistently didn't understand what anti-imperialism was. It made anti-imperialism into a false internationalist abstraction. For example: WUO always explicitly posed armed struggle as an **alternative** to revolutionary culture. **Either** you emphasized armed struggle and mass clandestinity **or** you emphasized revolutionary culture. This is the kind of shallow thinking that visualized Yan'an as only a big military barracks. And revolutionary culture only as a big dope party.

Even more importantly, WUO always pitted anti-imperialism vs. women's liberation. In practice they always bitterly fought against Women's Liberation while paying minimal lip service to it. WUO looked to the potential of the young revolutionary culture—which was as important as they said—but they appealed to and promoted its **most backward elements**. WUO's vision of the revolutionary culture was a male-dominated, macho, parasitic one—as they said, **"nomads, communal semi-hustlers."** That's why male drug dealers looked so good to WUO but rebel-

Photo by Paul Sequeira

lious women didn't. So just as their armed struggle was only symbolic, their revolutionary culture only parasitic, their anti-imperialism was false internationalism, increasingly divorced from the genuine rebelliousness within their own nation.

WUO didn't understand the crisis in the Movement. While *New Morning* gushed about "the enormous energy of sisters working together has ... transformed the movement internally," the exact reverse was happening. The New Left was dying because of its inability to become truly anti-imperialist. While the New Left spoke of revolution, it was addicted to a capitalistic way of life—petty-bourgeois male-dominated elites, puffed up with individualistic self-importance, making busy on the sidelines.

One direct reason for the collapse of the New Left was that thousands of radical women were leaving it, forced out by their need to be free to fight their own oppression. WUO and the rest of the male-dominated New Left tried to play on women's feelings of solidarity, to guilt-trip them with Vietnam or the Black Panthers into being passive. It was false internationalism to use Madame Binh's name as a club **against** women's anti-rape work, or to use Vietnam **against** the need for autonomous women's community. Just like the rest of the male-dominated New Left, WUO saw the rising of women as something to rip off ("the enormous energy") and to suppress.

WUO never understood the need for socialist nation-building of their own. Another nation or an imperialist conflict may topple your own nation's government or ruling class—but only your own people can defeat capitalism amongst themselves by building socialism. Imperial Japan was smashed by external forces in World War II, but without socialism from within Japanese imperialism was quickly restored. **Revolution for us means socialism. As Mao pointed out, construction and destruction are linked. To build we must destroy. But it is equally true that to destroy (imperialism) we must build (socialism among the people).** Only Euro-Amerikans could do this for their nation, even though other nation's revolutions may chop down the US Empire in size and power. Just as settlers cannot build the Black Nation, so the Black Nation cannot rebuild Euro-Amerikan society. Internationalism is built on the foundation of self-reliance.

So that the WUO's undermining of women's liberation, their supporting the parasitic "alternative culture" of Abby Hoffman and drugs (as opposed to a revolutionary culture), meant that it was opposing the very social forces that carried the first seeds of a non-oppressive future for White Amerika.

VIII. Black Power and New Afrikan Revolution

"You and I were born at this turning point in history; we are witnessing the fulfillment of prophecy. Our present generation is witnessing the end of colonialism, European-ism, or 'white-ism' … How can Amerika atone for her crimes? … A desegregated theater or lunch counter won't solve our problems. Better jobs won't solve our problems. An integrated cup of coffee isn't sufficient pay for four hundred years of slave labor, and a better job in the white man's factory or position in his business is, at best, only a temporary solution. The only lasting or permanent solution is complete separation on some land that we can call our own."

Malcolm X

What shook the Empire in the 1960s was that New Afrikans—and in particular the New Afrikan proletariat—began to assert themselves as a people. This new awareness was manifested in every sphere of life. Welfare mothers asserted that they had rights, and were going to invade welfare offices until the system got off their backs. Olympic athletes used their sports to dramatize the demand for Black Power. Jazz and popular music began to express rebellion. In auto plants New Afrikan workers created revolutionary nationalist alternatives to bourgeois unionism. Emerging national consciousness moved student boycotters in high schools as well as dissenting sailors on aircraft carriers. In the New Afrikan urban rebellions of 1963–1968, millions of people, primarily proletarians, took part in mass anti-colonial outbreaks. And on March 31, 1968, a convention of five hundred nationalists in Detroit, Michigan founded the Provisional Government of the Republic of New Afrika (PG-RNA).

These political changes did not overcome neo-colonial contradictions within the oppressed nation because the petty-bourgeoisie was still in charge. While the New Afrikan proletariat, the grassroots, had gained awareness of itself as the leading class, it had only begun developing revolutionary science. The masses could not control their own movement. Even the liberation movement remained in the class domination of a sector of the Black petty-bourgeoisie. **Relations with the Euro-Amerikan Left were still characterized by false internationalism. This false internationalism, even amidst a national revolutionary advance, betrayed uncertainty not only about the means of liberation but uncertainty about the goal.**

The Black radical petty-bourgeoisie was in general half-hearted about independence, and consistently tried to use alliances with the Euro-Amerikan petty-bourgeoisie to substitute for the New Afrikan proletariat. Many petty-bourgeois radicals and "cultural nationalists" turned to phony "Marxism-Leninism" in the early 1970s as a cover to merge themselves back into class unity with the petty-bourgeois Euro-Amerikan Left. And Euro-Amerikan radicals continued their intervention and meddling within the New Afrikan nation, although better cosmetized as "solidarity." **With the Movement dominated by the Black petty-bourgeoisie, the point of unity of Black united fronts continued to be the demand for US Government reforms.**

So the political course of the 1960s New Afrikan liberation Movement became knotted in an apparent paradox: between the growth of anti-colonial consciousness among the masses, on the one hand, and the stalled development of the first New Afrikan guerrillas on the other hand. In 1969–1971, New Afrikan urban guerrillas took to the offensive, attacking the hated police. But despite the general mood of anti-colonialism within the Nation, the first wave of urban guerrillas soon found themselves abandoned by the movement and politically isolated.

This paradox goes to the heart of the two-line struggle, between socialism and neo-colonialism, within the Movement and indeed within the New Afrikan Nation. This two-line struggle is a form of the world-historic two-line struggle between the proletariat (and its ideology) and capitalism (and its ideology).

A PERIOD OF CRISIS

By 1968 the New Afrikan Nation was in the grip of political transformation, which took the specific form of a generalized uprising against the US colonial oppressor. Between 1963 and 1967–68 mass urban rebellions spread across the continent, growing in number and intensity. From the 1963 outbreaks in Birmingham, Chicago, Philadelphia, Savannah, and Cambridge, Maryland to the one hundred and twenty-five rebellions that erupted after the assassination of the Rev. Martin Luther King, Jr. in April 1968.

In the transformation within the New Afrikan colony in the late 1960s millions upon millions were awakened to political life and political issues. It was widely agreed that New Afrikan people were not free, and everything was intensely debated and judged on the basis of how it related to aiding liberation—history, sports, religion, criminality, philosophy, war and peace, economic systems, everything.

Masses of people rejected loyalty to the US Empire. To talk revolution against the US Government became common and accepted. In the wake of the 1967 rebellions, even US Government interviewers found that 52.8% of Newark "rioters" told them that they opposed any support of the US in foreign wars, irregardless of who the US was fighting. People came to identify more with other Third World oppressed nations than with the US Empire. Increasing political unrest and even outbreaks of rebellion by New Afrikan GIs told Washington that their own colonial military was becoming politically unreliable.

Aftermath of DC riots, April 8, 1968.
Library of Congress. Photo by Warren K. Leffler.
Opposite page, photo by Marion S. Trikosko.

The urban rebellions marked both the popular acceptance of anti-colonial violence and the breakdown of the old colonial mechanism of control.

Imperialism had discovered that the old way no longer held. New Afrikan people were "out of control." Pigs could no longer intimidate folks. The "thin blue line" that had patrolled the ghetto had been smashed. To regain control in many areas, the US Empire was forced to re-occupy the ghetto with US Army and National Guard troops, with tanks and jeep-mounted heavy machine guns. **Imperialist order could only be reestablished over the hostile population by outright military invasion. Just as in Saigon or the Dominican Republic.**

The old system of puppet misleaders had broken down as well. Token government officials, conservative reverends, and Civil Rights spokesmen had been thoroughly exposed and brushed aside. **The masses had found new unity and self-respect by throwing aside Uncle Toms and by using violence against the oppressor.** The old way no longer worked for imperialism.

The crisis was only put down by the Empire's emergency counterinsurgency campaign. Not only by destroying centers of revolutionary organization, but in restructuring their colony through co-opted Black Power politics, breaking up national communities on a physical level, gutting the People's culture, and maneuvering the growing street force into mercenary warlordism.

The last is an important indicator of irreversible change.

Imperialism would rather that its colonial subjects stay unarmed and passive. But this can no longer be. **The New Afrikan Nation is armed and will never be disarmed.** And, just as in old, pre-revolutionary China, the heightened imperialist social dislocation is forcing many into the streets, futureless and desperate. Rather than have New Afrikans turn to combining in revolutionary violence, the authorities have encouraged the growth of warlord gangs. These gangs spread drug pacification, disorganize the community, absorb angry and desperate youth in killing each other, and act as police informers and mercenary agents. Just as in the old China of the 1920s, New Afrika is increasingly a chaotic, armed camp of warlordism. We must see this as a dialectical process. Imperialism is brutally creating the raw human material of revolution or reaction.

Back in 1964, Malcolm stood on the front lines and pointed ahead to where the struggle was going:

"… A couple of weeks ago in Jacksonville, Florida, a young teen-age Negro was throwing Molotov cocktails. Well, Negroes didn't do this ten years ago. But what you should learn from this is that they are waking up. It was stones yesterday, Molotov cocktails today; it will be hand grenades tomorrow and whatever else is available the next day … There are 22 million African-Americans who are ready to fight for independence right here."[1]

Newark, 1967

1. THE REBELLIONS
OF 1967–1968

The Empire has tried to cover up the political character and meaning of the New Afrikan urban rebellions by calling them "riots," and associating them with short tempers in hot summer weather. In no cases did the rebellions show random violence. **They were "festivals of the oppressed."** Everything of the colonial oppressor was attacked by spontaneous group action, from police cars to rip-off stores. Property of the exploiter was liberated, while property of New Afrikan households was untouched. Crowds armed only with rocks and bottles burned police cars and tried to force the occupying colonial army out of New Afrikan areas.

The political character of the confrontation was unintentionally confirmed by President Johnson's emergency National Advisory Commission on Civil Disorders. Their report, for example, related how the July 1967 Newark, NJ rebellion began with spontaneous efforts to rescue a taxi cab driver who was being tortured by the police.[2] After people in the Hayes Housing Project witnessed the man being dragged, unable to walk, into the 4th Precinct Station, the spark was lit. Within minutes telephone calls went out to community organizations from the Projects. Cab radios spread the word to New Afrikan workers around the city. Within 30 minutes a large and angry crowd gathered across the street from the station, while a caravan of New Afrikan taxis gathered at City Hall in protest. Civil

Rights "leaders" tried to pacify the crowd as police moved the wounded cab driver to a hospital. When Molotov cocktails were thrown at the station, a police charge with nightsticks dispersed the crowd for that night.

The next day anger in the community mounted as word spread. That evening a protest rally was called at the police station. Nationalist leaflets and word of mouth had brought out folks. When the city Human Rights Commission Director tried to cool things by announcing that the Mayor would appoint a committee to "study" the incident and also promote a Black police-man to Captain, booing and shouting began. To shouts of "Black Power" the Uncle Tom was driven away with rocks. The police station was attacked while burning and expropriation of settler businesses began. Thousands of people, too many to be stopped or arrested by greatly-outnumbered police, started taking the groceries, TVs, furniture, medicines, and clothing that the oppressed had already paid for a million times over.

Newark was placed under martial law in the early hours, with nervous State troopers and National Guard reoccupying the New Afrikan

REPORT FROM BLACK AMERICA

Whites in a 1969 *Newsweek* poll rejected even the basic premise that the ghetto's slum housing and recession unemployment were due to discrimination and not some failing of the Negroes themselves; they were therefore inclined to doubt that most of black America's complaints were justified. And suddenly even the most circumspect Negro leaders had the uneasy feeling that it was 1877 all over again ... that the Second Reconstruction had come like the first to the verge of collapse.

Perhaps so. But this time, in contrast to the last, Negroes will not go quietly; they have come too far in their struggle to stop now. Ten to twenty percent of them do despair of their future in America—are persuaded, that is, that the nation is not worth defending in a world war; that Negroes should withdraw into a separate black nation...

THE BLACK MOOD I: THE YOUNG

THE PERCENTAGE WHO:	Northern Under 30	Negroes Over 30
Approve the idea of black power	68	43
Think violence will be necessary	36	20
Believe the riots have helped	50	32
Would like a separate black nation	27	18

Newsweek 1969 // Editors' note: "Northern Under 30" is sic, but probably supposed to say "Negroes."

areas. Snipers bedeviled the soldiers and police. Afterwards the Newark Police told the Presidential Commission that it had officially confirmed 79 sniping incidents, although only one settler police lieutenant and one fireman had been killed by gunfire. In response the invading forces shot up the New Afrikan areas at will. The housing projects were hosed with heavy machine-gun fire. Washington, DC Urban League Assistant Director Horace Morris, who was about to drive away from a visit with his family, saw both his younger brother and his 73-year-old stepfather shot down, the latter fatally. Police had opened fire on folks just standing in front of their apartment building. In total twenty-one New Afrikans were killed in Newark. At night, after curfew had been imposed, National Guard jeeps would cruise around shooting out the windows of stores that had been left alone because they had "Soul Brother" signs on them. The rebellions were simple, oppressed against oppressor.

In interviews and studies of arrest records, the Commission found that those who took an active part in rebellion were typical of the community. In Detroit their interviewers found that 11% of the residents age 15 and older in rebellious neighborhoods admitted to having taken part, with another 20–25% as admitting to having been on the scene. As a whole, the Commission was forced to describe the typical "rioter" as having: **"great pride in his race ... He is extremely hostile to whites ... He is almost equally hostile toward middle-class Negroes. He is substantially better informed about pol-itics than Negroes who were not involved in the riots."** In other words, the Government's own study was forced to portray the oppressed people who rocked the Empire as politically motivated and aware.[3]

It is revealing how the Commission contrasted them with their opposite, the Uncle Tom "counter-rioter," who the Government frankly admitted was un-typical of the colonial masses in both class and feelings about the Empire:

"The typical counter-rioter, who risked injury and arrest to walk the streets urging rioters to 'cool it,' was an active supporter of existing social institutions. He was, for example, far more likely than either the rioter or the noninvolved to feel that this country is worth defending in a major war. His actions and attitudes reflected his substantially greater stake in the social system; he was considerably better educated and more affluent ..."[4]

The oppressed nation character of the rebellions was shown by the events around the April 1968 assassination of the Rev. Martin Luther King, Jr. In many ways this was a nodal point, a point where mounting quantitative changes finally result in a qualitative change in the basic nature of the thing. It was no longer a matter of policing demonstrations, of turning off fire hydrants and breaking up angry crowds in one community or another. It was a matter of using crack US Army divisions, National Guard troops and all available police to regain control against a simultaneous mass rebellion that ran from coast to coast. King had moved from being one of the chief props in imperialist-sponsored Civil Rights to becoming a major thorn in the Empire's side. Still a Christian minister, still an apostle of nonviolence and integration, King had grown and evolved with the struggle. He was attacking the US war effort; the luster of his name was helping raise world opposition to the US invasion of Vietnam. Even more explosive, his work threatened to link up the New Afrikan struggle with Vietnam.

The failure of Civil Rights had pushed him to reach for new plans. In Memphis, where he gathered national attention for the New Afrikan sanitation workers' strike, King gave notice that he intended to support the New Afrikan proletariat, and not just college students, in their political struggles.

In fact, he planned to unify the oppressed into one new movement—and aim it at direct confrontation with the US Government. His planned Poor People's Campaign was going to recruit tens of thousands of poor people—of all nationalities—and bring them to Washington, DC for a mass Gandhian campaign of nonviolent civil disruption. King planned to send thousands of the oppressed in human waves to surround and occupy key US Government offices, including the US Capitol. The masses would camp in downtown DC and not leave Washington until their demands were met. As

we can well imagine, the Empire was not going to let that happen.

The prospect of having to either openly repress masses of militant demonstrators or let their seat of government be overrun was not an acceptable choice to the imperialists. And what if mass, anti-Government battles spilled over into the Washington ghetto, already smoking with recent rebellion? No, King had to be neutralized. The threat by the Empire had been communicated in various ways.

In Memphis, King had announced that for the first time he was going to defy a Federal court order and lead a march in support of the New Afrikan workers' strike. The Memphis City Attorney said in court on April 3rd that if the march took place **"someone may even harm Dr. King's life ..."**[5] King refused to back down, and that night gave his famous sermon foreseeing his death: "I may not get there with you, but I want you to know tonight that we as a people will get to the promised land. So I'm happy tonight. I'm not worried about anything. I'm not fearing any man." The next afternoon, April 4, 1968, he was assassinated, as Malcolm X had been before him.

His assassination was a nodal point, brutally cutting off any remaining life in the old Movement. After Rev. King, there was no other major Civil Rights leader willing to lead the masses against the center of oppression, the US Government. For that matter, the soft-nosed bullet from a Remington 30.06 rifle also blew away illusions about nonviolent integration, about "redeeming" White Amerika, about New Afrikans and settlers healing their differences and freely mingling together in a reformed amerikkka. The assassination had also underlined the fact that imperialism would not willingly tolerate anyone organizing and leading the New Afrikan Nation. No unprotected national leadership or organization that was dangerous to the Empire would be permitted to survive.

Within hours the rebellions broke out anew in some 125 cities across the Empire. Again buildings burned and police were attacked. 65,000 US Army troops and National Guardsmen were needed to reinforce state and local police in containing the outbreaks. Fires burned within sight of the US Capitol building; smoke hung over the city. The White House was so worried that US Marine machine-gun teams were posted on the Capitol steps and select military units were placed on alert, ready to rush to Washington to defend the Empire's headquarters.

Even within these select military units the anti-colonial crisis had a political effect. The 6th Cavalry Regiment (Mechanized) at Ft. Meade, Maryland, which spent that year on-and-off alert for "riot control" intervention in Washington, was polarized along national lines. Settler officers had secret orders to watch for conspiracies among their New Afrikan troops. By the Summer hand-picked MP units patrolled the fort after 11:30 p.m. with orders to detain any New Afrikan GIs on the streets in groups of more than two.

New Afrikan soldiers were discussing refusing to follow orders. On the other side, many settler officers and men were eager to go to war against the New Afrikan colony. One lieutenant openly said: "If I can't get to 'Nam and kill some gooks then maybe I'll at least be lucky enough to get a couple coons."

At Ft. Campbell, Kentucky, New Afrikan GIs staged a rebellion of their own on the nights of April 10–11th, as soon as the base stood down from being on 24-hour "riot control" alert after King's death. Fighting took place with known racists all over the post, an MP jeep was destroyed, and the entire base had to be placed under curfew.[6] In Vietnam, New Afrikan GIs staged memorials and political meetings as the word raced around: "They killed Martin!" Again, we can see that the fundamental political contradictions between the New Afrikan oppressed nation and the US Empire took on many forms, and did pervade every sphere of life.

New Afrikan high schools and even grammar schools emptied. Countless local marches and demonstrations took place. In Washington, for example, one hundred high school students led by SNCC's Black Antiwar Antidraft Union marched out to Howard University, picking up two hundred more youth on the way. There they joined 1,000 Howard students in an angry rally. The US flag was torn down from the University flagpole, and the New Afrikan green, black, and red flag run up in its place to cheering.[7] There were confrontations everywhere. In Oakland the police raided the Black Panther Party. After surrendering to the police young Bobby Hutton, surrounded and blind from tear-gas, was shot down in cold blood.

Those April 1968 rebellions were completely political, and could hardly be explained away as bad tempers due to hot weather. They were a united mass response of the New Afrikan grassroots to a political assassination. Martin Luther King, Jr. was not the only or even the main political leader, but he was both a leader and a symbol to the world of the New Afrikan anti-colonial struggle. His death was taken to heart by millions. His assassination was understood as a calculated blow aimed at the entire liberation struggle. And the masses laid the primary blame not on a "lone gunman," not even on a Government conspiracy, but on the US oppressor nation as a whole. "They killed Martin!" the word ran.

2. BLACK POWER MOVEMENT: REVOLUTION OR "PIECE OF THE ACTION"

When the shout "Black Power" first came to white attention across that Mississippi summer of 1966, an incredulous White Amerika took it like a life-threatening blow to the body. Black Power represented to the masses an attitude of bitterness, separatism, and uncompromising militancy. It spoke the language of the masses. Black Power leaders sneered at Civil Rights integrationism. They urged New Afrikans to arm themselves. Yet, only two years later US imperialism was financing some Black Power organizing, leading petty-bourgeois Black Power figures were collaborating with the police, and President Richard Nixon had promoted himself as the big boss of a co-opted Black Power Movement.

This underlined the ongoing two-line struggle within the New Afrikan Movement, and how Black Power contained two political trends: one anti-imperialist and one pro-imperialist. The first trend, which was reflected in the mass approval for the slogan, interpreted Black Power to stand for self-determination, for militant separation from the oppressor society and its culture. The second trend denied that Black Power had anything to do with that. That second trend believed that revolution by the masses should be merely a threat, to be exploited by the colonial petty-bourgeoisie to get more concessions from the US bourgeoisie. In their class view the goal of Black Power was to finally integrate into the US oppressor nation, finally getting "a piece of the action."

There were two Black Powers—one grassroots and one petty-bourgeois, one revolutionary nationalist and one neo-colonial. It is important to remember that the second, petty-bourgeois trend tried to blur the political differences, to sound as militant and nationalistic as possible. The grassroots trend of Black Power led into the revolutionary nationalist movement. This was the political heritage carried on by Malcolm X, who had helped create Black Power with his program in the 1950s of self-pride, self-reliance, self-defense, and independence from the US oppressor nation. This trend helped create the Black Panther Party, the Provisional Government of the Republic of New Afrika, the League of Black Revolutionary Workers, and the Black Liberation Army. It led folks from armed self-defense to the concept of revolutionary armed struggle. The second, petty-bourgeois trend led to foundation grants, government poverty pimps, the dead-end of electing Black bourgeois politicians, and to the liquidation of mass struggle.

The grassroots wanted revolutionary nationalist leadership. This was proven not only by Malcolm's towering reputation, but by their positive response to organizing efforts. There has always been a revolutionary current, sometimes on the surface and sometimes hidden, within the New Afrikan Nation. Even while the 1955–56 Montgomery Bus Boycott was bringing the non-violent Civil Rights Movement into the world's eye, the armed self-defense movement led by Robert Williams in the small town of Monroe, North Carolina, was stirring up the New Afrikan masses.

Rob Williams was discharged from the Marines in 1955, and returned to his hometown of Monroe, NC in Union County. **Within three years both he and the New Afrikan struggle in that small town would be internationally known as heralding a new season of struggle.** The local Klan had threatened the small Union County NAACP chapter, which was the only local civil rights group. So the petty-bourgeois NAACP leaders wanted to dissolve the chapter

in order to save themselves. When Williams, a new member, objected, they voted him in as President and then they resigned. Only Dr. Albert Perry, an older physician, agreed with Williams. Together they rebuilt the chapter by going to the grassroots, always stressing the need for armed self-defense.[8]

At first, as Williams said, **"when I started talking about self-defense, I would walk through the streets and many of my Black neighbors would walk away to avoid me."** With two years of patient organizing, oriented towards the proletariat instead of the "elite," they had recruited an impressive number of New Afrikan working people—domestics, day laborers, grandmothers, and teen gang-bangers. To get inexpensive US Army surplus rifles Williams formed a branch of the National Rifle Association. Veterans were recruited. By 1957 the Monroe self-defense guard got its baptism of fire, driving off a Klan assault on Dr. Perry's house. Day and night New Afrikans kept an eye out for settler intruders, phoning reports into a self-defense headquarters which would alert armed units into full readiness.

While the Union County NAACP fought with lawsuits and picket lines, and tried to open swimming pools, the library, and other public facilities to New Afrikans, it always made the official Civil Rights movement uneasy. People recognized that the Monroe organization was politically different, the start of a more militant movement. Williams, Dr. Perry, Mae Mallory, and the other Monroe activists were forced to fight for support within the Civil Rights Movement, but increasingly had to operate on their own. In advance of the times, the small Monroe Movement pursued propaganda campaigns and alliances on an international scale. Although most of the known Monroe activists had been fired from their jobs, the national Civil Rights leadership saw to it that no aid was given to the Monroe Movement. The besieged New Afrikan community there was literally going hungry. We can see the emerging two-line struggle, in which the Monroe Movement had to hold out under attacks not only from the Klan and State Police, but also from the NAACP and SCLC. Williams and his coworkers had to be their own movement—to raise funds in the North, publish their own political journal, make their own secret arrangements to truck in arms,

David Simpson (l.) and James Thompson lose freedom as their mothers (r.) leave Wadesboro courtroom in tears.

N. C. NAACP To Appeal 'Kissing Kids' Case

A Superior Court judge's refusal to free two Negro boys, who were jailed six days then sent to a reform school because one of them was kissed by a five-year-old white girl, will be appealed, the Monroe (N. C.) NAACP announced. Claiming that the boys were held because they were juvenile delinquents, the state charged David (Fuzzy) Simpson, 8, and James Hanover Thompson, 10, forced the unidentified girl to kiss Thompson. But the boys said the girl kissed one of them while they were playing cowboy with two other white boys and girls. The NAACP also relocated the boys' mothers, after they were fired from their jobs as domestics and threatened.

food, and medicine at night, and make their own alliances with sympathizers from other nations.

In late 1958 the Monroe Movement became world-famous, partly because of the so-called "Kissing Case." It began when a young Euro-Amerikan girl kissed a nine-year-old New Afrikan boy on the cheek as a greeting. When the girl's parents found out about it, they went to the Monroe police. The nine-year-old boy and a companion were arrested and eventually sentenced to 14 years in prison for rape. Unable at first to free the children, the Monroe Movement struggled to wake people up about the case. Newspapers in Europe and then Afrika started writing about it. Soon it became an international scandal exposing US colonial injustice. Enraged crowds stoned US Embassies. Finally the White House had to intervene to release the young children and end the publicity.

Williams and the Monroe Movement had to fight the "Kissing Case" without any support from the National NAACP, which was trying to isolate or silence militants any way they could. Finally, in 1959, the National NAACP announced that it had suspended Williams for six months for publicly stating that New Afrikan men in Monroe would defend women against settler attacks. This only made Williams an even greater hero to the grassroots. During one visit to New York City, local youth gangs took over an NAACP rally in Harlem, shouting and refusing to let the Uncle Toms speak unless they first gave the microphone to Rob Williams.

Left: FBI wanted poster for Robert F. Williams.

Opposite page: Mao Zedong meets with Williams, October 1, 1966.

The Monroe Movement had friends and supporters throughout the Nation, and overseas as well. Even though it was only one small town, the militants in Monroe lit a spark that burned more brightly than the entire Black petty-bourgeois officialdom. Their influence came not from numbers, but from the power of applying righteous ideas—of raising armed struggle as against the official doctrines of nonviolent liberalism. Williams and his family were finally forced into a long exile in 1961. At first from Cuba and then from Beijing, Williams worked to educate the movement back in the US Empire about revolutionary nationalism.

What is significant is how the two-line struggle emerged within the early Southern Civil Rights Movement, even in the 1950s. Turning to the New Afrikan proletariat with a correct line of armed struggle produced lessons that from a small beginning spread throughout the New Afrikan Nation. This prepared the way for the new stage of revolutionary consciousness that made up one trend within Black Power.

In exile Robert Williams was to become International Chairman of RAM, the Revolutionary Action Movement, the first of the three major New Afrikan revolutionary organizations of the 1960s.[9] Although seldom mentioned today, RAM was labeled as the most dangerous New Afrikan folks in Amerika back in the mid-1960s. Congressional investigations were held about RAM, and police denounced RAM in press conferences. Nothing, the public was told by authorities, was too murderous for RAM to attempt. RAM members were arrested for an alleged plot to blow up the Statue of Liberty. RAM members were charged in an alleged plot to correct the No. 1 and No. 2 Uncle Toms, Roy Wilkins of the NAACP and Whitney Young of the Urban League. RAM was even charged with a conspiracy to wipe out thousands of Philadelphia police and city officials, by feeding them cyanide-poisoned coffee and sandwiches from a street canteen after luring them to a staged "ghetto riot." As we know, when the imperialists put out lots of smoke there's usually some fire involved.

RAM was a serious attempt that failed to build an armed national revolutionary organization, a New Afrikan version of the Algerian FLN or the July 26th Movement of Cuba that didn't sustain itself or survive. It never was "legal"; it never was a Civil Rights organization. It was the result of the new message of Williams and Malcolm X, trying to put their insights into practice. From the start they aimed at armed socialist revolution. RAM developed into a broad network of revolutionary nationalists, a semi-public

organization with clandestine cells and full-time traveling organizers. No one could have any doubts about what RAM was trying to do. As their journal, *Black America*, said in 1964:

"... The Revolution will 'strike by night and spare none.' Mass riots will occur in the day with the Afro Americans blocking traffic, burning buildings, etc. Thousands of Afro Americans will be in the street fighting; for they will know that this is it. The cry will be 'It's On!' This will be the Afro American's battle for human survival. Thousands of our people will get shot down, but thousands more will be there to fight on. The Black revolution will use sabotage in the cities—knocking out the electrical power first, then transportation, and guerrilla warfare in the countryside in the South. With the cities powerless, the oppressor will be helpless."[10]

RAM had its beginnings among New Afrikan college students in Ohio. The news in 1961 of Robert Williams' flight into exile had been a catalyst, bringing a small group together to discuss how a Black revolutionary movement could be built. These students already had varied political experiences between them—of student sit-ins in the South, fighting for activist student government at Black colleges, going to SDS Conferences, studying with white Trotskyist groups, being in the Nation of Islam, and so on. By the Summer of 1962 those still struggling together had decided to try starting such a New Afrikan revolutionary movement in one city, Philadelphia, as

a test. Don Freeman, Wanda Marshall, and Max Stanford were leading activists in the student network that would become RAM.

Like Williams, the young revolutionaries began by working within the local NAACP. They soon discovered that hundreds and sometimes thousands of street youth could be attracted to militant direct action. By 1963 street demonstrations in North Philadelphia, blocking construction sites where New Afrikans had been denied jobs, turned into violent confrontations between police and crowds of militant New Afrikans. RAM had developed a definite perspective which it spread to other cities. RAM cadre worked within the existing civil rights organizations, pushing militant actions and raising the need for armed self-defense, as part of a strategy of turning the Civil Rights Movement into a Black Revolutionary Movement. The street force or lumpenproletariat were considered the main revolutionary force, with teenage men (as young as age 14 years) seen as the fighters and older working-class nationalists seen as the cadre.

RAM organizers used direct agitation, leafletting, and talking with the street force in schoolyards, pool halls, and street corners. Revolutionary nationalist classes were set up, teaching Afrikan history and the organization's line. The national RAM organization that eventually emerged was based on clandestine local cells, with the central leadership forming coalitions with existing Black organizations to prepare for a national liberation front.

RAM worked with and through many different mass organizations in trying to develop revolutionary consciousness. There is certainly much evidence that their work found a ready response at the grassroots. The Afroamerican Student Associations that led the fight for New Afrikan history in the public schools of Philadelphia, Cleveland, Chicago, New York, and other cities, were guided by RAM. In Chicago, for example, RAM cadre, working behind-the-scenes at their 39th St. UMOJA Black Student Center, coordinated the October 1968 high school strike that brought out half the city's New Afrikan high school students. There the city Afroamerican Student Association united recognized student leaders from over twenty New Afrikan high schools. RAM classes discussed guerrilla warfare and socialism with young activists.[11]

By 1966 RAM was trying to build mass New Afrikan political parties in cooperation with SNCC and other radical or nationalist groups. At that time SNCC had formed the Lowndes County Freedom Organization (LCFO) in rural Alabama, as a Black Power organizing project. Using the black panther as its symbol, the organization was an all–New Afrikan electoral alternative to the regular Democratic Party, doing voter registration gun in hand and running candidates for county offices.

The concept of a militant New Afrikan political party had stirred up much interest across the country. So RAM got SNCC's permission to use the black panther symbol and start Black Panther Parties in the Northern New Afrikan ghettoes. Local Black Panther Party organizations were set up in New York, Cleveland, Philadelphia, San Francisco, and other cities. RAM wanted to use these parties as New Afrikan united fronts, eventually so commanding the day-to-day politics of the community that the oppressor Democratic and Republican Parties would be forced out of the New Afrikan areas.

There were at one time three militant Black parties which used the black panther symbol, with two of them also both using the name "Black Panther Party." For in 1966 two nationalist students at Oakland, California's Merritt College—Huey Newton and Bobby Seale—had formed the paramilitary "Black Panther Party for Self-Defense." It is this party, with its now-famous uniform of black beret and leather jacket, that is best known today.

The three parties were not only separate organizations, but were very different. SNCC's Lowndes County Freedom Organization (LCFO) was primarily a Civil Rights electoral party, whose thrust was to elect Black officials in county government offices such as clerk and sheriff. In rural Alabama its base was primarily radicalized New Afrikan workers and students. The Oakland, California Newton-Seale Black Panther Party for Self-Defense was a public, paramilitary vanguard, which sought to mobilize the New

Afrikan lumpen under their leadership around armed self-defense of the community. Despite the identical name, RAM's party was different in program, leadership, and class composition. It was intended as a multi-class front. Different militant groups with different leaders would hopefully work together within the party. The aim was to unite the New Afrikan nation around one political voice, which would be so strong that it could dictate which Black candidates got elected to local offices. Armed activity under RAM's perspective could not be public, and would be kept separate from the public formation. In any case, RAM's ambitious party did not survive, which permitted Newton and Seale to drop the tag phrase "for Self-Defense" from their name, and become known simply as the Black Panther Party.

While RAM's Black Panther Parties did not take root in some cities, in New York the party quickly developed into real unity. Not only RAM cadre and SNCC organizers, but Amiri Baraka's Harlem Freedom School, Jesse Gray's tenants' anti-slum movement, New Afrikan socialists such as Bill Epton (famed for his role in the 1964 Harlem rebellion), and many other nationalists joined in. The NY Black Panther Party as a militant united front led marches against police brutality, organized youth to help take over and fix up slum buildings, ran classes on Afrikan history and other political topics, and was forming groups within each ghetto public school. Asian-American activist Yuri Kochiyama, who was part of the Harlem Freedom School at the time, recalls:

"The Party had a broad outreach; it was still growing. At the time there was only this one, large, militant, grassroots organization. They were trying to get Black principals in Harlem and in Bedford-Stuyvesant. There had been demonstrations at quite a few schools."[12]

But RAM organizing was smashed by US counterinsurgency. On June 21, 1967, the NYPD's Bureau of Special Services (BOSS—the political police) arrested seventeen RAM members for an alleged conspiracy to assassinate NAACP Director Roy Wilkins and Urban League Director Whitney Young. The police claimed that their raids had found illegal weapons, plastic cans full of gasoline, and 275 packets of heroin. This was the Queens 17 defense case, a forerunner of the Panther 21 case. Main FBI-NYPD targets were Adekouya Akinwole (sn Herman Ferguson), a nationalist assistant principal of a Brooklyn public school, and Muhammad Ahmad (sn Max Stanford), the Field Chairman of RAM. Three months later, on September 27, 1967, Philadelphia police arrested more RAM cadre for another alleged conspiracy, this time to supposedly kill thousands of police and city officials with poisoned coffee and sandwiches. That was just the tip of the iceberg, as many RAM members were arrested during rebellions and in other confrontations.

The suppression of RAM became a textbook case for the FBI. RAM cadre were taken out of action that Summer. George C. Moore, head of the FBI Racial Intelligence Section, cited the RAM case in his February 29, 1968, internal memo on COINTELPRO strategy against the BPP: "The Philadelphia office [of the FBI] alerted local police who then put RAM members under close scrutiny. They were arrested on every possible charge until they could no longer make bail. As a result, RAM leaders spent most of the Summer in jail ..."[13]

With many leading cadre in jail or tied up in trials, and others fugitives, with paranoia over police infiltrators mounting, RAM floundered. Like Malcolm's OAAU, like Robert Williams' Union County, NC NAACP chapter, RAM had not solved the task of revolutionary infrastructure, of spreading a network of organizing among the masses even while the imperialist counter-

Herman Ferguson at court. February 27, 1968. Photo by Vic DeLucia/New York Post Archives.

insurgency was raging. Or as Atiba Shanna has put it, organizing "in the free-fire zone."

RAM was advanced in its time precisely because from the beginning it was oriented toward leading a national liberation war. It was also not fully developed since it was a pioneer, the first wave. It was a serious attempt that failed, unable to advance its practical work beyond a certain point because its basic politics had not yet developed past that point. Its Field Chairman and main theoretician, A. Muhammad Ahmad (sn Max Stanford) has written: "RAM was plagued with the problem of translating theory into practice, that is, developing a day-to-day style of work (mass line) related to the objective materialist reality in the United States. Like most

The Los Angeles War Cry

'Burn, Baby, Burn'

Black revolutionary organizations, RAM was not able to deal successfully with protracted struggle." We recall that Malcolm, the most important strategist of the 1960s, had been assassinated in 1965. Many other OAAU (Organization of Afro-American Unity) members had been assassinated or imprisoned, and the organization itself died before it had a chance to put its planned mass programs into effect.

There can be no doubt that the first wave of New Afrikan revolutionaries in the 1960s accomplished a historic task and started the movement in the right direction. But due to the incomplete political development of the new movement, New Afrikan revolutionaries were unable to build organizations that could withstand the political police.

So despite the hunger for revolutionary nationalist answers down in the grassroots, among the proletariat, there was a profound leadership vacuum during the anti-colonial crisis in the New Afrikan Nation. The masses had exposed and **pushed aside** the traditional puppet mis-leaders—conservative reverends, token Black Government officials, etc. The nonviolent Civil Rights integrationists had been made **irrelevant** by the mass anti-colonial rebellions. And the new revolutionary current had been **neutralized** before it had developed by their own political weaknesses and the imperialist counterinsurgency which took full advantage of them.

THE 12-POINT PROGRAM OF RAM

PROJECTS AND PROBLEMS OF THE REVOLUTIONARY MOVEMENT

1. DEVELOPMENT OF A NATIONAL BLACK STUDENT ORGANIZATION MOVEMENT. *ASM, the Afro-American Student Movement, the student branch of RAM was formed to organize black students into a strong, well-organized student movement that can fight against injustices against Afro-American students and black people in general. PURPOSES: 1. To educate the Afro-American to the economic, political, and cultural basis of the racial situation in the United States and the world. 2. To develop unity with Africans in the United States and the world. 3. To unite and organize Afro-American students to become active in the Afro-American Liberation Struggle. These purposes would develop revolutionary cadres in the high schools, junior high and colleges. The climax of such a program would be the development of a nationwide black student school strike which would repudiate the educational system. This strike would be over what black students are and are not taught. ASM's purpose is to show black students that the only way to succeed in life is to cause a revolution in this country. ASM would develop groups around black history, students rights, and also over conditions under which Afro-American students must operate. This all-black national student organization would build to establish total social dislocation. With students demonstrating the guerrilla force will have a base for mass support. It should be noted that this support is coming from youth. This will eventually rally young black workers and the unemployed. ASM will politicalize the black student community and will serve as the vanguard in the struggle. When the Afro-American student strike is initiated it will be left to RAM to have other segments of the black community to strike in sympathy. If guerrilla warfare is being waged, this strike would be in support of the guerrillas. ASM on campus would develop political parties to take over student government. The objective is to obtain power in black colleges.*

2. DEVELOPMENT OF IDEOLOGY (FREEDOM) SCHOOLS. *The purpose of the "Freedom" schools would be to develop cadres, with the revolutionary theory and doctrine of RAM. These schools will teach the history of the movement, current events, political theory, methods of social action, methods of self-defense, basic principles of guerrilla warfare, techniques of social dislocation, propaganda techniques and indoctrination, black history, etc. Essentially the schools will be political.*

3. DEVELOPMENT OF RIFLE CLUBS. *The rifle clubs will be made up of local veterans and other people from community. The purpose of the rifle club is to develop a black militia capable of protecting the black community. This militia would work with the liberation army and would serve as a base for the establishment of a community government.*

4. DEVELOPMENT OF LIBERATION ARMY (GUERRILLA YOUTH FORCE). *The purpose of the Liberation Army is to carry out political, economic, physical overthrow of this system. The Liberation Army's role is to take over cities, cause complete social dislocation of communications, etc. "Our countryside is the cities all over the country". Therefore, the major part of guerrilla warfare in the U.S.A. will take place in the cities. The cities are the pockets of power and heart of the economy.*

5. DEVELOPMENT OF PROPAGANDA, TRAINING CENTERS AND NATIONAL ORGAN. *The purpose of this center is to train cadre in techniques and methods of propaganda and also to act as a center for the movement. Classes in intelligence, etc., will be taught. The two most important things are a press and a publishing company.* <u>Black America</u> *is RAM's national organ. It will act as an organizer and coordinator for the movement. It will be a journal of ideas and direction.*

6. DEVELOPMENT OF UNDERGROUND VANGUARD. *RAM can be classified as an underground vanguard. All RAM members will be working to spread the vanguard as far as possible. The purpose is to develop a revolutionary machine that is capable of continuing the revolution if the leader or leaders are wiped out.*

7. DEVELOPMENT OF BLACK WORKERS "LIBERATION" UNIONS. *The purpose of the liberation movements are to fight for better conditions on jobs, to organize Afro-American to spy, etc., for the purpose of a national strike, etc. Women's leagues will also play an important role in the national strike. The purpose of Women's leagues is to organize black women who work in whitie's homes.*

8. DEVELOPMENT OF BLOCK ORGANIZATION (CELL). *Our plan is to have black community organized by blocks. A person's job, once becoming a member of RAM, is to organize his or her block. This can be done by telling friends about RAM, having informal meetings or parties discussing issues, etc., and/or having a RAM field organizer on the scene to make new contacts. Once two or more RAM members are in one block they become a cell which works in the neighborhood to make the cell larger and to make more cells. Once a group of cells are developed they make a section. This will be left to the judgment of local cadre.*

9. DEVELOPMENT OF NATION WITHIN NATION CONCEPT, GOVERNMENT IN EXILE, ROBERT WILLIAMS IN EXILE. *RAM's position is that the Afro-American is not a citizen of the U.S.A., denied his rights, but rather he is a colonial subject enslaved. This position says that the black people in the U.S.A. are a captive nation suppressed and that their fight is not for integration into the white community but one of national liberation. RAM's program is one of overthrow meaning simply the overthrow of white rule, capitalist rule, in other words, white America by black America. Stated even simpler, it means the black man taking over this country. To do this we will have our government already in exile, of which Robert Williams is leader. Also RAM's job is to educate the black community to who Robert Williams is and what he stands for. The program will build up for Robert Williams for President in '68 in the black community, signifying a complete repudiation of the existing political system.*

10. DEVELOPMENT OF WAR FUND (POLITICAL ECONOMY). *The political economy and war fund was developed to build our war machine. The political economy works as follows: each person capable makes a weekly pledge. From this pledge comes a weekly sum to keep the war fund going, thus we have a political economy. Also fund raising activities and methods will be used to develop the war fund.*

11. DEVELOPMENT OF BLACK FARMER COOPS. *In the delta area (black belt) in the South, especially Mississippi, this is necessary. This can keep a community and guerrilla forces going for a while.*

12. DEVELOPMENT OF ARMY OF BLACK UNEMPLOYED. *The brothers and sisters who are unemployed are an army to be organized. The struggle should put continued pressure on the Federal government by demonstrating North and South against racial discrimination on Federal backed industry. Also in the North, the struggle against union discrimination will bring things to a head.*

3. THE CO-OPTATION OF BLACK POWER

It was only in such a leadership vacuum that the Black Power Movement could have been co-opted so easily by settler imperialism and its Black allies. As a slogan "Black Power" spread like wildfire among the masses, who wanted something more militant than Civil Rights. But its vagueness (unlike slogans such as "Free the Land") concealed within it the fact that there were two very different meanings to Black Power. **To the young militants, to the angry people in the streets, Black Power meant rejecting White Amerika, seizing some kind of Black independence from the oppressor.** But to the leading petty-bourgeois forces of the Black Power Movement the goal was only equality with all other US citizens.

Separation from the oppressor was not seen as a step in moving toward national independence, but only as a tactical regroupment so that Blacks as a supposed "ethnic group" could bargain for their "piece of the action" just like the Irish, the Jews, the WASPs, and other US "ethnic groups." The Empire tries to define oppressed nations as "ethnic groups" so as to deny their existence as nations. This blurs New Afrikans, Puerto Ricans, etc. in with Italian-Amerikans, Irish-Amerikans, etc., just as earlier the oppressed were only categorized as "races" in order to hide their national status.

The stated goal of neo-colonial Black Power ideologists was actually integration with White Amerika, only repackaged in a nationalist-sounding way in order to appease the anger of the grassroots. Thus, as an organized movement, Black Power became reactionary very quickly. As early as 1969, *The Black Panther*, newspaper of the Oakland-based BPP, warned about this:

"Black Power has come a long way since that night in 1966 when Stokely Carmichael made it the battle cry of the Mississippi March Against Fear. For a time it was a slogan that struck dread into the heart of white America— an indication that the ante of the Black man's demands had been raised to a point where the whole society would have to be reoriented if they were to be met. But Black Power hardly seems a revolutionary slogan today. It has been refined and domesticated ... by Richard Nixon, seemingly the most unlikely of men ... The President has indicated since assuming office that he sees nothing dangerous in the upsurge of a Black militancy, provided that it seeks a traditional kind of ethnic mobility as its end, even if it wears Afro costumes and preaches a fiery race pride while it sets up businesses and replaces white capitalists as our society's most visible contact with the ghetto ...

"He has made a surprising alliance with certain forces of Black militancy. This may seem audacious, even dangerous, like playing with the fires of a revolutionary Black consciousness.

But it is actually a time-tested technique. The Nixon Administration's encouragement of cultural nationalism and its paternal interest in Black capitalism are little more than an updating and transposition into a domestic setting of a pattern established years before by US power abroad. Although the State Department, the US Information Agency, the Ford Foundation and hosts of other organizations were involved, it was primarily the Central Intelligence Agency which discovered the way to deal with militant Blackness ..."[14]

It is important to see that petty-bourgeois Black Power as a philosophy and a program was a desperate effort to make integration work for the Black petty-bourgeoisie. Even some radical initiators of Black Power made that plain. In his historic September 1966 article "What We Want," Stokely Carmichael of SNCC said that the main strategy was uniting the Black community to elect Black politicians into office. This, Carmichael claimed, would make Blacks so "equal" to whites that integration would become real:

"... Politically, Black Power means what it has always meant to SNCC: the coming-together of Black people to elect representatives and to force those representatives to speak to their needs. It does not mean merely putting Black faces in office ... Integration, moreover, speaks to the problem of Blackness in a despicable way. As a goal, it has been based on complete acceptance of the fact that in order to have a decent house or education, Blacks must move into a white neighborhood or send their children to a white school. This reinforces, among both Black and white, the idea that 'white' is automatically better and 'Black' is by definition inferior ... Such situations will not change until Black people have power—to control their own school boards, in this case. Then Negroes become equal in a way that means something, and integration ceases to be a one-way street. Then integration doesn't mean draining skills and energies from the ghetto into white neighborhoods; then it can mean white people moving from Beverly Hills into Watts, white people joining the Lowndes County Freedom Organization. Then integration becomes relevant."[15]

Carmichael's unreal and misleading vision of "relevant" integration was not just naive. These views were put together, we must remember, a year after Malcolm X was assassinated, four years after Robert Williams was forced to flee into exile, years after the call for national liberation had been raised within the movement. While some militants who raised the slogan were trying to push the struggle forward, the neo-colonial political framework was in conflict with their own desires. **The Stokely Carmichaels and Ron Karengas and Amiri Barakas saw the US oppressor nation as the only "real," legitimate nation.** They didn't see New Afrikan people as an oppressed Nation, but only as an "ethnic minority" inside the US oppressor nation. Ron Karenga was a former graduate student at the University of California. After the Watts Rebellion in 1964 he formed "US" (United Slaves), the most influential "cultural nationalist" organization of the 1960s. His protégé was Amiri Baraka (sn Leroi Jones), the Black poet and playwright. Baraka became the leader of the Black Power Movement in Newark, NJ and the Congress of African People (CAP). Both men made the journey to pseudo-nationalism and then back to liberal integrationism/assimilationism via the cover of phony "Marxism-Leninism." As someone remarked: **"Every year they got a new philosophy, but they always got a foundation grant."**

For that reason the petty-bourgeois Black Power theorists all saw peaceful integration into White Amerika as the final goal. Among the most explicit was Rev. Nathan Wright, chairman of the 1967 Newark Black Power Conference (which was the first one) and later head of the Black Studies Dept. at San Francisco State University: **"Black Power in terms of self-development means we want to fish as all Americans should do together in the main stream of American life."**[16]

Navy Recruiting Poster, 1972

In their 1967 book on Black Power, Carmichael and Charles V. Hamilton said that Black separatism was only a tactic to gain bargaining power for integration into Amerika: **"The concept of Black Power rests on a fundamental premise: Before a group can enter the open society, it must first close ranks. By this we mean that group solidarity is necessary before a group can operate effectively from a bargaining position of strength in a pluralistic society."**[17] It's revealing that SNCC's Stokely Carmichael, who at that point was a self-proclaimed "socialist" and a partisan of Third World liberation wars, would explain the US oppressor nation as **"open"** and **"pluralistic."** David Rockefeller and Richard Nixon would have agreed with that. The obvious confusion existed between roundly denouncing the US as evil, imperialist, oppressor, colonialist, and so forth—and then putting out a strategy based on the assumption that this oppressor society was **"open"** for you. This confusion had its roots in the class role of the New Afrikan colonial petty-bourgeoisie.

Pseudo-nationalism was the sudden rage. Audiences at Black Power conferences would be treated to the full spectacle when Ron Karenga spoke. Karenga had been written up in *Life* and other bourgeois media as the most extreme and dangerous. The sight of the Simbas, US's paramilitary guards, drilling with arms for news photographers, thrilled White Amerika. Karenga would be preceded on stage by an aide and his guards, all in US "uniform" (shaved head for the leaders, mustache, shades, dashiki-like shirt of his design). His aide would order the audience to rise and chant "All Power to the Black Man" over and over. Karenga himself would then denounce integration while dropping hints about their main "weapon" for liberation—at the end of the rap he would reveal that the main "weapon" was only voting for Black candidates in elections! So while even veteran Black journalists referred to Karenga as an "extremist Black nationalist," only the outer packaging was in any way different.[18] "Cultural nationalism" was a phony nationalism that opposed the independence of the New Afrikan Nation. Instead, it argued that militant talk, different clothing, and getting involved in US elections would allow New Afrikans to find a satisfactory place for themselves within White Amerika.

Ron Karenga stands outside courtroom in Los Angeles

Co-opted Black Power made possible an improved relationship between the colonial petty-bourgeoisie and their masters. **This was not immediately apparent to the grassroots.** The New Afrikan families in Alabama who turned out to picket at courthouses, proudly carrying Black Power signs ("Move on over, or we'll move on over you!") were charged up by the air of defiant assertiveness and "race pride." Washington street youth attending early "Black history" courses and organizing their friends took Black Power to mean nationalist opposition to the oppressor.

But it was precisely this seemingly militant, seemingly nationalist tone of voice, that made Black Power so useful to the Empire. When Black Power leaders spoke of the vision of Black people controlling all institutions of their own communities, it seemed to give voice to the anti-colonial urban rebellions. Black Power's angry image allowed the colonial petty-bourgeoisie, temporarily shaken up and out by the growing mass consciousness, to reassert its leadership over the New Afrikan Nation. And therefore to have something to sell their colonial masters in return for a few pieces of silver. What they had to sell was their own people.

Many petty-bourgeois Black Power leaders began working with the police. In Newark, Amiri Baraka had formed the United Brothers, a united front to elect more Black politicians to city government. Their goal was to elect a Black mayor. Baraka understood bourgeois politics well enough to understand that he had to make

deals with the local settlers and the police. In April 1968 the United Brothers worked with the Newark police to "cool" the rebellion which broke out after Martin Luther King's assassination. Baraka publicly disassociated himself from the rebellion. On April 12, 1968, he held a joint press conference with Newark Police Captain Charles Kinney and Anthony Imperiale, the leader of the local armed white racist organization.[19] Baraka denounced the rebellions as just confused New Afrikans being manipulated by unnamed white radicals. He also made it clear that his Newark Black Power Movement and the armed white supremacists were cooperating. Pig captain Kinney jumped in to add that New Afrikan rebellion was only a conspiracy led by white SDS students. That was how the most prominent petty-bourgeois Black Power leader reacted to the assassination of Martin Luther King, Jr.

Meanwhile, in Los Angeles, Baraka's close associate Ron Karenga had his "US" organization also out on the streets with the police, using their influence to try and stop the rebellion there. Karenga had a secret planning meeting with Los Angeles Police Chief Thomas Reddin. No wonder that the *Wall Street Journal* praised Karenga as: **"typical of many militants who talk looting and burning but actually are eager to gather influence for quiet bargaining with the predominantly white power structure."**[20]

We can see how very useful that kind of co-opted Black Power was to the colonial authorities.

Imperialism had quickly realized that. The CIA had previously arranged for the prestigious Ford Foundation to be their main instrument for penetrating and subverting Afrikan liberation movements. There have always been both public and secret links between the CIA and the Ford Foundation. Richard Bissell was a public staff member of the foundation and less publicly CIA Deputy Director for Plans, for instance. Ford Foundation grants were used to fund "social science research" (i.e. intelligence operations), buy off opportunistic Afrikans, and cover up for US subversion of popular movements.[21] As *The Black Panther* said, this operation was simply expanded in 1966 to include the domestic New Afrikan communities. This new effort was overseen by none other than Ford Foundation President McGeorge Bundy, who as former National Security Advisor to Presidents Kennedy and Johnson had run the National Security Council and had helped plan the US invasion of Vietnam. "Charity begins at home."

The Ford Foundation singled out Cleveland as their test case in pacification. In 1966 New Afrikan rebellion there shook the city. Ford Foundation President Bundy told the press in 1967 that "it was predictions of new violence in the city that led to our first staff visits in March." In May 1967 the Foundation gave Dr. Kenneth Clark, Black psychologist and former head of all Harlem poverty programs, $500,000 to rehabilitate the Civil Rights leadership. In June 1967, after chairing several secret Civil Rights leadership meetings, Dr. Clark announced that all the top leaders would cooperate in calming ghetto unrest in Cleveland. **"Underlying causes of unrest,"** Clark said, **"are found in classic form in Cleveland."**

On July 14, 1967, the Ford Foundation announced that it was giving $175,000 to the Cleveland chapter of CORE (Congress of Racial Equality) for organizing. This was on the surface amazing. CORE had been started in 1942 by a coalition of Euro-Amerikan radical pacifists, mostly religious, and a handful of Black followers. Of all the historic Civil Rights organizations it was most known for its dedication to pacifist civil disobedience and social integration. But by 1967 it had undergone drastic change. At the 1966 Convention CORE voted to embrace Black Power politics. Civil disobedience and settler leaders were tossed overboard. CORE's founding National Director, James Farmer, was replaced by the more militant-sounding Floyd McKissick from North Carolina. Special Ford Foundation training programs prepared new "nationalist" CORE leaders such as Roy Innis (the very first trainee). It was noteworthy when the Ford Foundation began lavishly funding a supposedly Black militant group. A Cleveland CORE leader said: **"Our job as an organization is to prepare people to make a decision on revolution or not. The choice is whether to take land and resources and redistribute them."**

Cleveland CORE used the money to organize and pay New Afrikan youth for a Summer voter registration drive, and for setting up a

Ann Arbor Sun, May 17, 1974.

HOW the FBI ATTACKED the BPP

Alprentice "Bunchy" Carter

What follows is continued from last issue's article on how the FBI's Cointel-pro activities were directed against the Black Panther Party throughout the United States. This article originally appeared in Boston's The Real Paper.

LOS ANGELES, 1969

In Los Angeles, William Hynes, a former undercover agent in the IWW, participant in the Palmer Raids of 1919-1920 and a coordinator of police infiltration and disruption of the effort to form industrial unions in the Thirties, was named Hoover's man on the scene. Hynes set up a liaison between the LAPD and the FBI devoted to ferreting out subversives in the area. The local Red Squad was superseded in 1942 by the Metropolitan Division of the LAPD (Metro), a more modern, sophisticated vehicle for cooperating with the G-Men in conducting the war against the enemy within.

After the Watts riots of 1965, one of the first urban conflagrations of the Sixties, Metro was expanded from 90 agents to over 200. The LAPD also established a new intelligence unit, the Criminal Conspiracy Section (CCS), that would almost exclusively deal with the new black militant organizations. The previous links were maintained between the FBI and the local intelligence forces, with the FBI supplying information on radicals and encouraging suggestions on how to eliminate them. More often than not, local police departments served as the operational wing of the FBI program. They, too, wasted no time.

On January 17, 1969 a meeting took place on the UCLA campus to determine who the Black Student Union would appoint as its director. There was considerable acrimony between the competing factions, one led by Black Panthers John Huggins and Alprentice "Bunchy" Carter and the other headed by Ron Karenga of US (United Slaves), a group that saw the revival of African culture as the salvation of American blacks. When the Karenga-sponsored nominee for the BSU post was turned down by a majority vote, garnered by the effective leadership of Huggins and Carter, US activists pulled out guns and killed the Panthers. Five US members were indicted for murder and conspiracy and three of the five were ultimately apprehended and convicted of second degree murder.

But the basis of the feud was not as apparent as it seemed. By all outward appearances the origin of the conflict seemed to be ideological: "cultural nationalists" arrayed against "revolutionary nationalists." But Ron Karenga's shaved head, dashiki dress and Swahili incantations were an external mask; Karenga was a voodoo witchdoctor for the secret police.

The Wall Street Journal reported, "A few weeks after the assassination of Martin Luther King...Mr. Karenga slipped into Sacramento for a private chat with Governor Reagan, at the governor's request. The black nationalist also met clandestinely with Los Angeles Police Chief Thomas Reddin after Mr. King was killed."

According to a former undercover agent for LAPD's Criminal Conspiracy Division, Louis Tackwood, Karenga was financed, armed and encouraged in the attack on the Panthers by the police. Tackwood claims that he acted as the liaison between CCS and Karenga's United Slaves. "I contacted Ron Karenga and gave him orders to the effect that was given to me," Tackwood states in a book based on his confessions, "The Glass House Tapes," "that he was to curtail the Panther Party's growth no matter what it cost." Tackwood's alle-

gations were confirmed in a lie detector test conducted by Chris Gugas, a past president of the American Polygraph Association, who prominently displays an autographed picture of J. Edgar Hoover in his office.

(Karenga lost whatever support he had built up after the murder of the UCLA Panther leaders. He was recently arrested for torturing two black women who he said were trying to poison him, convicted and sentenced to one to ten years in prison.)

The deaths of Huggins and Carter did not stop Panther organizing in Los Angeles. Various community programs were started in Watts despite the intense level of police harassment. But then the level of harassment grew even more intense.

Four days after the raid on Fred Hampton's apartment, on December 8, 1969, at 3 am, the Special Weapons and Tactics Squad (SWAT) stationed themselves outside of the Central Avenue Panther headquarters in Watts. The SWAT squad, armed with AR-15 automatic rifles, was supported by one hundred policemen, snipers squads carefully perched on nearby buildings and an armored personnel carrier.

At 5:30 in the morning the assault began. The Panthers who were sleeping in their offices, returned the fire of the police and a four-hour battle ensued. The police dumped dynamite on the roof of the headquarters, lobbed in tear gas and kept up a steady stream of gunfire. At 9:45 am the Panthers poked a white flag

When the Karenga-sponsored nominee for the BSU post was turned down by a majority vote...US (United Slaves) activists pulled out guns and killed the Panthers...Ron Karenga's shaved head, dashiki dress and Swahili incantations were an external mask; Karenga was a voodoo witchdoctor for the secret police.

out of a window and surrendered; six of the thirteen who emerged from the battered building were wounded. Among those arrested was a 42-year-old ex-convict, Melvin "Cotton" Smith, number three in command of the Panther chapter, resident weapons expert and keeper of the arsenal. Cotton Smith was a CCS agent. Like William O'Neal, Smith had been placed in a sensitive position of security within the organization.

The web of undercover police activity was also extended in Los Angeles to entrap supporters of the Panther defense effort in alleged criminal activity. Two leaders of the Friends of the Panthers in Los Angeles, Donald Freed, playwright and author ("Executive Action"), and Shirley Sutherland, actress and then wife of movie actor Donald Sutherland, were arrested in 1969 for allegedly illegal possession of hand grenades.

The hand grenades had been delivered in a wooden box to Freed's house by a member of Friends of the Panthers, James Jarrett, who had introduced himself to the group as a Vietnam veteran disaffected with the war and racism. Later disclosures in the case substantiated Jarrett's claim but not his motive. In Vietnam he had been a CIA operative, leading political assassination teams into the countryside to dispose of National Liberation Front cadres. Jarrett had also plied his trade in neighboring Cambodia and Laos. Upon returning from Indochina, he served as a trainer of the LAPD SWAT squad, the shock troops in the assault on Panther headquarters.

The case against Freed and Sutherland was eventually dropped after two years of convoluted legal wrangling. By then Jarrett had faded back into the intelligence netherworld and the LA Panthers had been fragmented into bitterly contesting and dispirited Cleaver and Newton factions.

The time from the LA raid to the LA Panther trial (almost two years) was a period of constant FBI and police action against the Panthers throughout the country. A selective chronology illustrates all too well the relentless nature of the government program.

SEATTLE, 1970

The first major raid of 1970 against the Panthers was aborted by Mayor Wesley Uhlman of Seattle. On February 8, Mayor Uhlman stated that the Alcohol, Tobacco and Firearms Tax Unit of the Internal Revenue Service had requested Seattle police participation in a raid on local Panther headquarters. Uhlman denied the request, because, he said, it "smacked of Gestapo type tactics." IRS Commissioner Randolph W. Thrower verified Mayor Uhlman's statement.

In the spring of 1970, Seattle became the scene of one of Cointelpro's more bizarre outings. According to The Los Angeles Times, Alfred Burnett, a man charged with felonious violation of his parole, was inducted into the FBI inner sanctum as an informer. Burnett served inside the Seattle Panthers until the FBI and the local police apparently decided that in order to show that they could solve a wave of bombings, they would set off a bomb themselves and catch a patsy. Burnett placed a bomb in a real estate office, notified the police, but forgot exactly where he had put the explosive. He swore in an affidavit that he then offered $75 to Larry Ward, a black veteran only two weeks back from Vietnam with no previous political record, to find the bomb. Ward agreed and Burnett deposited him at the real estate office. The police closed in on Ward, who started to run; they opened fire with shotguns, killing him. The majority of a grand jury ruled that the killing of the unarmed Ward was unjustified homicide, but the authorities refused to prosecute. To do so would have unveiled the intricate Cointelpro program.

BALTIMORE, 1970

On May Day, 1970, in Baltimore, 150 police descended on the local Panther headquarters and arrested 10 people. Baltimore Police Commissioner Pomerleau publicly declared that the raid was undertaken because he had received important data from the FBI.

J. Edgar Hoover, in one of his periodic papal bulls, stated on May 9th that the bleeding hearts were wrongly accusing the police of harassment, particularly insofar as the raids on the Black Panthers were concerned. The Director's judgment was rendered: the Panthers were ranked somewhere below Dr. Martin Luther King in his pantheon of anti-Christs.

SAN FRANCISCO, 1970

Meanwhile, the FBI was drafting a scheme to plant a phony double agent in the Panthers. A Cointelpro document discloses that the FBI had approached the San Francisco police department to arrange for black policemen to befriend top Panther leaders. The policemen were to appear enraged with this police experience and offer to supply the Panthers with important inside information and plans. In fact, the supposedly dissatisfied cops would be agents feeding the Panthers false information that would sow division within the organization and give the police that much more of a jump on the situation. The ingenuity of the FBI lay in its disengenuous methods.

PHILADELPHIA, 1971

The National Committee to Combat Fascism (NCCF) was a group set up by the Panthers specifically to raise the issue of the police raids and arrests. The NCCF was to attract all of the assorted groups and tendencies on the left and coalesce them around the single most vital issue for the Panthers. The Panthers were planning a gathering of these diverse groups under their aegis for

McGeorge Bundy with JFK, 1962. Abbie Rowe—
National Park Service/JFK Presidential Library.

voter mobilization drive for the November 1967 city elections. Ford Foundation funds paid for Cleveland CORE to set up rallies for the Black candidate for Mayor, Carl Stokes. And in the elections, Stokes became the first New Afrikan mayor of a major US city (in the 20th Century). While both rebellions and savage police repression took place in 1968, Stokes' election was the beginning of a new pacification maneuver. Cleveland CORE hailed this election as a Black Power victory. A Ford Foundation representative praised the redirecting of mass energy into elections **"as a flowering of what Black Power could be."**[22]

Foundation President McGeorge Bundy came out for independent Black community school boards, which was one of Stokely Carmichael's main Black Power demands in 1966. Co-opted Black Power had become a golden alliance between the colonial petty-bourgeoisie and the Empire's ruling class. Just as the early, militant, direct-confrontation Southern student movement had been increasingly sidetracked into voter registration and bourgeois elections in the early '60s, the Northern New Afrikan rebellions were in part pacified by the same tactic put over under the nationalist-sounding cover of co-opted Black Power.

The manipulation of the Black Power Movement by the CIA, using many different covers, was made public policy by the Nixon Administration. All three present and past National Directors of CORE, for example, were personally bought up: James Farmer, who had always claimed to be a pacifist-socialist, became a sub-Cabinet official in the Nixon Administration; Floyd McKissick became a loud Government supporter in return for the promise of millions of dollars in Federal loans for his ambitious "Soul City" housing development; Roy Innis made CORE an organization for hire, unashamed at working for the CIA, the Zionists, the South African Boers, and any other reactionaries willing to pay for a Black Power endorsement. President Nixon personally pushed the neo-colonialized concept of Black Power, saying in his historic national broadcast on April 25, 1968:

"For too long white America has sought to buy off the Negro—and to buy off its own sense of guilt—with ever more programs of welfare, of public housing, of payments to the poor, but not for anything except keeping out of sight … much of the Black militant talk these days is actually in terms closer to the doctrines of free enterprise than to those of the welfarist thirties—terms of 'pride,' 'ownership' … What most of the militants are asking is not separation, but to be included in—not as supplicants, but as owners, as entrepreneurs—to have … a piece of the action.

"And this is precisely what the Federal central target of the new approach ought to be. It ought to be oriented toward more Black ownership, for from this can flow the rest—Black pride, Black jobs, Black opportunity and yes, Black power …"[23]

When Republic of New Afrika-Provisional Government Co-President Imari Abubakari Obadele was finally released from Federal prison he was shocked at all the regressive cultural changes in the New Afrikan community. Imari had spent years in Federal prison during the 1970s. As President of the PG-RNA, Imari had led the move to establish a nation-building center in Mississippi and Louisiana. This move was crushed by US counterinsurgency, ending in the August 1971 FBI-COINTELPRO raids in Jackson, Mississippi. Like other POWs, Imari noted the changes that the defeats had made in the Nation's life. Most shocking in his eyes was seeing young women with processed hair—and finding out that this was because so many boyfriends were demanding it of them. To Imari it seemed as though they were in ignorance putting symbolic slave chains back on themselves.[24] These cultural regressions are not disconnected from the pseudo-nationalist "cultural nationalism" of co-opted Black Power, which had a tremendous effect in the late '60s and 1970s on the daily lives of millions.

The Black Power Movement spoke in angry, militant-sounding language amplified by the imperialist media; it absorbed the energies of many honest and self-sacrificing New Afrikans. But like every political movement that assumes capitalist social relations and capitalist economic production, **its inner cultural content was not about liberation but about enslavement.** To note that the Black Power Movement was explicitly anti-Communist is just one part of it. Black Power explicitly preached the inferior position of New Afrikan women to New Afrikan men, for example. On the grounds that the kind of male-chauvinist, patriarchal nuclear family advocated by Carmichael, Karenga, and others (Daniel Patrick Moynihan) was somehow authentically "African revolutionary" or "communist"—while it was actually only their slavish imitation of the European capitalist family. Carmichael swaggered around saying: **"The only position for women in SNCC is prone!"** Ron Karenga said: **"What makes a woman appealing is femininity, but she can't be feminine without being submissive."** "Black Power" as capitalistic "Super-

Fly." And so the popularization of so-called Black Power only helped put the mental chains of slavishness and cultural regression back on folks.

The persistent effects of the co-opted Black Power counterinsurgency strategy can be seen in the lingering belief that electing Black politicians is a step toward freedom. In particular, the election of Black mayors is seen as the same thing as New Afrikan control of their nation. Not only bourgeois politicians, but "nationalists," militant reverends, and the settler Left regularly turn out to tell the New Afrikan Nation this lie.

There are three things we have to understand about this. The first is that Black bourgeois politicians have no power at all. Richard Hatcher of Gary, clearly the most progressive of the Black mayors, said: "There is much talk about Black control of the ghetto. What does that mean? I am mayor of a city of roughly 90,000 Black people, but we do not control the possibilities of jobs for them, of money for their schools, or state-funded social services ... Will the poor in Gary's worst slums be helped because the pawn-shop owner is Black, not white?"[25]

The second thing is to see Black Power's vision of community control for what it is. Since there is no way, under imperialism, for New Afrikan people to **communally** control the established institutions that determine their lives, to speak of "Black control" without socialism and national liberation only means the promotion of Black petty-bourgeois into supposed positions of institutional authority. That is why so much

activity centers around electing Black mayors, having Black police commanders, Black school officials, Black corporate managers, Black office supervisors, Black professors, and so on. In other words, co-opted Black Power involved no power at all for the New Afrikan grassroots, but meant plenty of promotions and new opportunities for the neo-colonial petty-bourgeoisie.

And lastly, we should see that the neo-colonial city ghetto is a puppet state. **Co-opted Black Power was the CIA's forerunner for the less successful South Afrikan "bantustans" or "tribal homelands."** As we know, the settler-colonial regime of "South Africa" has set up within it little Afrikan pseudo-states. These fraudulent, dummy tribal governments placed in barren areas are used to pretend that the settler regime respects the democratic rights of Afrikans. Each of these little tribal pseudo-states is complete with an Afrikan "President" and "Cabinet," Afrikan officials, flag, and a little police force in snappy uniform. The "tribal homeland" has no real Land, no economic base, no independent relation to the world, no practical power or real sovereignty. But it has highly-paid Afrikan officials. Mayor Kenneth Gibson would be right at home there. Newark is a "tribal homeland" or "bantustan," if you understand the dialectical relationship between Black Power "democracy" and Indian reservations and "South African" apartheid.

This time, vote like Homer Pitts' whole world depended on it.

He'll get his degree. Then what?...laborer, factory job...or his own business? A vote for Richard Nixon for President is a vote for a man who wants Homer to have the chance to own his own business. Richard Nixon believes strongly in black capitalism. Because black capitalism is black power in the best sense of the word. It's the road that leads to black economic influence and black pride. It's the key to the black man's fight for equality—for a piece of the action. And that's what the free enterprise system is all about.

THIS TIME... NIXON

AUTHORIZED AND PAID FOR BY THE NIXON-AGNEW CAMPAIGN COMMITTEE. MAURICE H. STANS, FINANCE CHAIRMAN; PETER FLANIGAN, DEPUTY CAMPAIGN MANAGER.

4. FALSE INTERNATIONALISM & REVOLUTIONARY SETBACKS

The repression of the first wave of New Afrikan revolutionaries seemed but a momentary setback at the time. Robert Williams and the Monroe Movement in the 1950s, RAM and Malcolm's Organization of Afro-American Unity in the 1960s started a revolutionary movement which promised to become even stronger. The late 1960s were a tumultuous time when the whole world was on the move pushing imperialism back. In Vietnam the stakes kept getting higher, US casualties kept growing, while the liberation army was kicking ass. Che had left his cabinet minister's office in Havana and become a guerrilla again. People's War was starting all over Afrika. And in China the Great Proletarian Cultural Revolution was rising against capitalist road bureaucracy within socialism. It was a revolutionary high-tide in the world. A heady time. Revolution here seemed to be not only likely but inevitable—and soon, too.

A second wave of New Afrikan revolutionary organizations came right on the heels of the first. These were sons and daughters of the urban rebellions, part of the grassroots trend of Black Power. The Black Panther Party for Self-Defense in 1968, the League of Revolutionary Black Workers also in 1968, the Afrikan Liberation Support Committee and other new groupings quickly gained a mass following. New revolutionary organizations and bold new tactics grew side-by-side with the neo-colonial trend, challenging it for hegemony over Black Power.

The subsequent victory of the neo-colonial petty-bourgeoisie in co-opting the Black Power Movement was therefore not a simple thing. It involved certain imperialist-sponsored activities and propaganda. It also involved clearing the revolutionary alternative away with repression. Like the first wave of New Afrikan revolutionary organizations, the second wave was also unable to survive combat with the political police. The national revolutionary movement had severe internal contradictions, was incompletely developed, and was not able to seize the political leadership of the Nation away from the neo-colonial petty-bourgeoisie.

We need to apply dialectical and historical materialism to the development of the armed struggle beginning in the 1960s. Dialectics holds that all things develop through the working out of their own internal contradictions, not through conspiratorial maneuvering of outside forces. The beginning of modern New Afrikan armed struggle met defeat. Not because of FBI-COINTELPRO or the Klan, but because its own confusion over class and national goals and their relationship to armed struggle left it unable to combat the political police.

The Black Panther Party for Self-Defense, founded by Huey Newton and Bobby Seale in 1966, becomes for us a window to see deep into some of these contradictions within the armed struggle. While the BPP for Self-Defense was not necessarily the largest or the most advanced of the New Afrikan revolutionary organizations exploring armed struggle, it was certainly the most public. The Party self-consciously projected itself into the public eye, and its collision course with police gunfire made its development a matter of public record.

Armed struggle, as the highest form of struggle, inescapably imposes the need for the clearest political consciousness while at the same time being the necessary condition for such advanced consciousness. The Party was from its birth in 1966 an armed formation, in which **every** member was committed to fight the oppressor and if need be die in combat. Many, many 'rads did die, and still today the kamps of Babylon hold former Panthers as well as other revolutionaries of the 1960s and 1970s. Of revolutionary audacity and courage the membership of the Party lacked nothing. But this Party came together at a time when political consciousness was young, raw and undeveloped, and when necessarily petty-bourgeois/lumpen class views dominated. **For that matter, the BPP explicitly based itself on the lumpenproletariat, and tried to advance using petty-bourgeois/lumpen military concepts.**

The Black Panther Party's political-military strategy had come under considerable criticism at the time from forces within the revolutionary nationalist movement, who unfavorably contrasted it to People's War. RAM criticized **"Huey's open display of guns, brandishing**

them into the police's faces …" and the related BPP lack of underground structure or any long-term planning for mass organization. The RNA-PG said that **"Black Panther pronouncements and actions CREATE pretexts for US military action, by the police …"**[26] But there are no accidental strategies.

The BPP was born out of the nationalist movement on the West Coast. For some five years Huey Newton and Bobby Seale were part-time students at Oakland's Merritt College, while increasingly taken up with political discussions, street corner nationalist rallies, activity in the New Afrikan college student organization at their school, and study of Fanon, Mao, and other political writers. For most of those years they had been members of a "cultural nationalist" organization, the Afro-American Association. Both, however, had grown disillusioned with it. Huey had gotten into a fight at a party, knifed a brother, and spent eight months in jail. Bobby had briefly related to RAM, but split under disputed circumstances. He says that he quit because RAM wasn't into action. RAM leadership insisted that he was purged for drinking and misappropriating funds. In any case, by 1966 both Huey Newton and Bobby Seale were still part of the loose San Francisco Bay Area nationalist scene, and were looking for something new to do politically.[27]

In the Spring of 1966 Huey, Bobby, and another brother were strolling up Berkeley's Telegraph Ave., the center of student recreation off the University of California-Berkeley

October 1966
Black Panther Party
Platform and Program

What We Want
What We Believe

**Huey P. Newton Minister of Defense
Black Panther Party**

1. We want freedom. We want power to determine the destiny of our Black Community.

We believe that black people will not be free until we are able to determine our destiny.

2. We want full employment for our people.

We believe that the federal government is responsible and obligated to give every man employment or a guaranteed income. We believe that if the white American businessmen will not give full employment, then the means of production should be taken from the businessmen and placed in the community so that the people of the community can organize and employ all of its people and give a high standard of living.

3. We want an end to the robbery by the CAPITALIST of our Black Community.

We believe that this racist government has robbed us and now we are demanding the overdue debt of forty acres and two mules. Forty acres and two mules was promised 100 years ago as restitution for slave labor and mass murder of black people. We will accept the payment in currency which will be distributed to our many communities. The Germans are now aiding the Jews in Israel for the genocide of the Jewish people. The Germans murdered six million Jews. The American racist has taken part in the slaughter of over fifty million black people; therefore, we feel that this is a modest demand that we make.

4. We want decent housing, fit for shelter of human beings.

We believe that if the white landlords will not give decent housing to our black community, then the housing and the land should be made into cooperatives so that our community, with government aid, can build and make decent housing for its people.

5. We want education for our people that exposes the true nature of this decadent American society. We want education that teaches us our true history and our role in the present-day society.

We believe in an educational system that will give to our people a knowledge of self. If a man does not have knowledge of himself and his position in society and the world, then he has little chance to relate to anything else.

6. We want all black men to be exempt from military service.

We believe that Black people should not be forced to fight in the military service to defend a racist government that does not protect us. We will not fight and kill other people of color in the world who, like black people, are being victimized by the white racist government of America. We will protect ourselves from the force and violence of the racist police and the racist military, by whatever means necessary.

7. We want an immediate end to POLICE BRUTALITY and MURDER of black people.

We believe we can end police brutality in our black community by organizing black self-defense groups that are dedicated to defending our black community from racist police oppression and brutality. The Second Amendment to the Constitution of the United States gives a right to bear arms. We therefore believe that all black people should arm themselves for self-defense.

8. We want freedom for all black men held in federal, state, county and city prisons and jails.

We believe that all black people should be released from the many jails and prisons because they have not received a fair and impartial trial.

9. We want all black people when brought to trial to be tried in court by a jury of their peer group or people from their black communities, as defined by the Constitution of the United States.

We believe that the courts should follow the United States Constitution so that black people will receive fair trials. The 14th Amendment of the U.S. Constitution gives a man a right to be tried by his peer group. A peer is a person from a similar economic, social, religious, geographical, environmental, historical and racial background. To do this the court will be forced to select a jury from the black community from which the black defendant came. We have been, and are being tried by all-white juries that have no understanding of the "average reasoning man" of the black community.

10. We want land, bread, housing, education, clothing, justice and peace. And as our major political objective, a United Nations-supervised plebiscite to be held throughout the black colony in which only black colonial subjects will be allowed to participate, for the purpose of determining the will of black people as to their national destiny.

When, in the course of human events, it becomes necessary for one people to dissolve the political bands which have connected them with another, and to assume, among the powers of the earth, the separate and equal station to which the laws of nature and nature's God entitle them, a decent respect to the opinions of mankind requires that they should declare the causes which impel them to the separation.

We hold these truths to be self-evident, that all men are created equal; that they are endowed by their Creator with certain unalienable rights; that among these are life, liberty, and the pursuit of happiness. That, to secure these rights, governments are instituted among men, deriving their just powers from the consent of the governed; that, whenever any form of government becomes destructive of these ends, it is the right of the people to alter or to abolish it, and to institute a new government, laying its foundation on such principles, and organizing its powers in such form, as to them shall seem most likely to effect their safety and happiness. Prudence, indeed, will dictate that governments long established should not be changed for light and transient causes; and, accordingly, all experience hath shown, that mankind are more disposed to suffer, while evils are sufferable, than to right themselves by abolishing the forms to which they are accustomed. But, when a long train of abuses and usurpations, pursuing invariably the same object, evinces a design to reduce them under absolute despotism, it is their right, it is their duty, to throw off such government, and to provide new guards for their future security.

campus. Telegraph Ave. was a crowded "hippy" street scene, sidewalks busy with vendors and hustlers. As they passed an outdoor cafe, Bobby impulsively decided to jump up on a chair and recite his latest poem to the white student crowd. Police showed up, Seale was dragged down, and both Newton and Seale ended up in jail for getting into a fistfight with the pigs. Huey decided that they had to form a revolutionary organization that stood up to the pigs. They named it the Black Panther Party for Self-Defense.

With the help of Huey's brother Melvin, they drafted the Party's ten-point program, that began with "**1. We want freedom. We want power to determine the destiny of our Black community.**" And ends with: "**10. We want land, bread, housing, education, clothing, justice and peace. And as our major political objective, a United Nations–supervised plebiscite to be held throughout the Black colony in which only Black colonial subjects will be allowed to participate, for the purpose of determining the will of Black people as to their national destiny.**" The BPP ten-point program reflected the growing influence of revolutionary nationalism, of recognizing the distinction between the oppressor nation and the oppressed nation.

Their start is almost folklore now. Newton, a pre-law student, had carefully researched California's legal code as it related to guns and the police. At that time the state law allowed people to carry loaded pistols, rifles, and shotguns so long as they were not concealed. Newton and some others decided that this loophole in the law could be exploited. The first task was getting weapons. One day they were reading the newspaper about how the famous "little red book," *Quotations From Chairman Mao Tse-Tung*, had just been published in English. Huey got an idea. They went across the Bay to China Books, where the "little red book" had just gone on sale, bought a bunch, and drove back to Berkeley. Within an hour, hawking the "little red book" at the gate to the University of California campus, they sold all the books they had. With that money they drove back to China Books, bought the store's whole stock of "little red books," and sold them all to curious Berkeley students. They made enough money to buy two shotguns.

By that Fall of 1966 the BPP had recruited its first members, mostly from Huey's neighborhood in Oakland, and had set up a storefront office. It says something about the popular mood that folks could be recruited to join a tiny political group whose members had to publicly face off with the police, while carrying guns. In public face-offs, Panthers refused to hand over their guns to the pigs, insisted loudly that "**If you shoot at me, or if you try to take this gun, I'm going to shoot back,**" and all the while lecturing the gathering New Afrikan crowd about their rights. The first time that happened, in front of the BPP's Grove St. storefront office, a dozen men who had been watching immediately joined up.

In the next year the Party became a presence on the New Afrikan political scene. Not only was it growing rapidly but its aggressive armed stance had electrified folks. In April 1967 the BPP was asked by the family of Denzil Dowell, a 22 year-old youth who although unarmed had been shot six times in cold blood by Richmond police, to help them investigate the killing. Panthers interviewed witnesses and proved that the official police account was a fabrication. Guarded by twenty armed Panthers, Newton and Seale spoke to a street rally of 150 persons in the Dowell family's Richmond neighborhood. Panthers accompanied the family and other New Afrikan residents to meet with the County Sheriff and District Attorney. Three hundred New Afrikans, some as young as twelve years old, applied to join the BPP that month in Richmond.

Another person who had joined the Party in early 1967 was Eldridge Cleaver, fresh out of Soledad Prison. Cleaver had become the New

WHY WAS DENZIL DOWELL KILLED

The BLACK PANTHER
VOLUME 1 · APRIL 25, 1967 · NUMBER 1
P.O. BOX 8641 OAK. CALIF. EMERYVILLE BRANCH
BLACK COMMUNITY NEWS SERVICE
PUBLISHED BY THE BLACK PANTHER PARTY FOR SELF DEFENSE

APRIL FIRST 3:50 a.m.

"I BELIEVE THE POLICE MURDERED MY SON" SAYS THE MOTHER OF DENZIL DOWELL.

Brothers and Sisters of the Richmond community, here is the view of the family's side of the death of Denzil Dowell as compiled by the Black Panther Party for Self Defense, concerned citizens, and the Dowell family. As you know, April 1st, 1967, Denzel Dowell (age 22), was shot and killed by an "officer of the Martinez Sheriff's Department", so read the newspaper.

But there are too many unanswered questions that have been raised by the Dowell family and other neighbors in the North Richmond community. Questions that don't meet the satisfaction of the killing of Denzil. The Richmond Police, the Martinez Sheriff's Department, and the Richmond Independent would have us black people believe something contrary to Mrs. Dowell's accusation. That is, her son was "unjustifiably" murdered by a racist cop.

There are too many questionable facts supporting the Dowell family's point of view.

These questionable facts are as follows:

1. Denzil Dowell was unarmed so how can six bullet holes and shot gun blasts be considered "justifiable homicide"? (Con't Page 2)

WE BLACK PEOPLE ARE MEETING SATURDAY 1:30 AT 1717 SECOND STREET LET US SUPPORT THE DOWELL FAIMLY EVERY BLACK BROTHER AND SISTER MUST UNITE FOR REAL POLITICAL ACTION

Page 3 · THE BLACK PANTHER—April 25, 1967

in September, 1966;

—The beating of a 14 year old girl in East Oakland in October, 1966.

These are only a few of the murders and brutal beatings by racist cops that have happened and been reported in the newspaper and are known about in the black community.

BROTHERS AND SISTERS THESE RACIST MURDERS ARE HAPPENING EVERY DAY; THEY COULD HAPPEN TO ANY ONE OF US.

BROTHERS AND SISTERS WE MUST UNITE. MANY OTHER MURDERS AND BRUTAL BEATINGS HAVE TAKEN PLACE WITHOUT US DOING MUCH OF ANYTHING

BUT LET'S STOP IT NOW!

WITH SOME REAL NITTY GRITTY POLITICAL ACTION

ARMED BLACK BROTHERS IN RICHMOND COMMUNITY

15 Black Brothers, most of them armed; with Magnum 12 gauge shot guns, M-1 rifles, and side arms, held a street rally at the corner of Third and Chesley in North Richmond last Saturday afternoon about 5 P.M. The nice thing about these Bloods is that they had their arms to defend themselves and their Black Brothers and Sisters while they exercised their Constitutional Rights: Freedom of Speech, and the right to Peacefully Assemble. And while they exercised another Constitutional right: the right to bear arms to defend themselves.

The racist cops could only look on. The Dog Cops made no attempt to break up the meeting like they generally do when Black people get together to sound out their greviances against the white power structure. The point to get firmly into your mind is that both the Black Brothers and the racist cops had "POWER". They had righteous "GUN POWER", but the significant thing is that the Black Brothers had some of this POWER. In the (con't page 4)

MEETING APRIL 29TH EVERYBODY THIS COMMING SATURDAY SO WE'LL KNOW WHAT TO DO AND HOW TO DO IT NOW! 1717 SECOND STREET NORTH RICHMOND AT 1:30 P.M.

Left's most promoted prisoner-writer, an object of settler "radical chic." Already he was the Black staff member for the glossy New Left magazine *Ramparts*. Eldridge was a lumpen superstar. In February 1968 his book about himself, *Soul On Ice*, was published to rave reviews in the bourgeois media. Within weeks it was on the top ten bestsellers list. His entry into the Party leadership gave them a celebrity who was a brilliant propagandist. New Afrikans who had never heard of Robert Williams or Ella Collins were given Eldridge as the theoretician of revolution.

By 1968 new Party chapters were springing up from coast to coast. In grammar schools New Afrikan children would sport black berets and play at being Panthers. There were many chapters in California: Oakland-Berkeley, San Francisco, Richmond, East Palo Alto, Los Angeles, San Diego, Sacramento. Speaking tours by Bobby Seale and Eldridge had set up new chapters in Chicago, Cleveland, New York, Philadelphia, and other major cities. In January 1969 the BPP was claiming 45 chapters, although some of these were just on paper. Members came from all classes: from the street force and from the children of the "Black Bourgeoisie," from SNCC and from the US Army, from factory laborers and college intellectuals. Internal FBI studies concluded that 43% of New Afrikans under the age of 21 **"had great respect for the BPP."**

Many 'rads were drawn to the Party because they were searching for advanced ideas. Bourgeois accounts of the BPP stress the drama of its gun display, while downplaying the fact that it was a political party. As a revolutionary party the BPP emerged as harsh, no-fooling-around critics of both bourgeois nationalism ("Green Power") and the "cultural nationalism" trend. They said that people who went around in dashikis, who gave themselves Afrikan names and who sprinkled Swahili words in their vocabulary, but who refused to pick up the gun against the oppressor, were "buffoons" and "pork chop nationalists." The Party formally pointed out that nationalism was not itself a social program, and that only socialism could liberate the oppressed. These words had weight coming from a party which was talking about land and a popular vote to decide New Afrikans' "national destiny."

However, these advanced-sounding words expressed but a part of the Party's reality. The two-line struggle is an expression of fundamental contradictions. As such it is present in all spheres of life, within all political phenomena. So the two-line struggle was not just between the old Civil Rights Movement and the revolutionary nationalism of Williams and Malcolm, for instance. It was also within the Civil Rights Movement, as we saw when the militant wing of the nonviolent movement, led by SNCC, broke with the old concepts of integration and became more nationalistic. The two-line struggle continued within that as well. We saw how the move for Black Power, which was at first primarily a more grassroots and nationalist trend, contained within it its own opposite—i.e. a disguised form of neo-colonialism.

The Oakland BPP leadership was in reality much less advanced than Malcolm and Williams. In significant ways they were less advanced than RAM. What sounded advanced was in part borrowed rhetoric. The BPP for Self-Defense was influenced by the petty-bourgeois student "counter-culture" of the San Francisco Bay Area. Just like their settler counterparts, Huey and Bobby were putting on instant political line by borrowing rhetoric from the Chinese Red Army, from Mao, from Malcolm, from RAM, and so on.

We can see what this meant in the Sacramento Action, which first launched the BPP for Self-Defense into national fame. On May 2, 1967, a delegation of Panthers arrived at the California Capitol Building, ostensibly as "lobbyists" to oppose a bill then being passed which took away the right to carry arms in public. Twenty of the male Panthers openly carried rifles, shotguns, and pistols (six women and three men on parole were unarmed). Governor Ronald Reagan, who was outside on the lawn when the Panthers arrived, was hastily hustled back into his office by security guards. Seale read a statement by Huey Newton on the right of self-defense, as reporters and TV cameras surrounded the Panthers. Obviously, the "lobbying" was a media publicity action. The small delegation ended up on the Assembly floor, with the state legislators, and were ejected by police. All were peacefully disarmed, arrested on various minor charges, and released on bail.

The action was extremely successful. There was a storm of national publicity, establishing the Oakland BPP as very militant, the "baddest" revs around. Morale shot up inside the group. One Panther said: "I felt great … I hope it won't come to bloodshed but if it does and if I die, I'll know I did my part. That's a good feeling because up till now there haven't been too many men or women that could say that." Many folks got interested in the Party, as Huey seemed to be making his favorite slogan, "Political power comes out of the barrel of a gun," work in practice.

The only problem was that Mao (who was the author of Huey's favorite slogan) meant something completely different by it than the Oakland BPP did. In Sacramento the Panthers cleverly exploited a temporary loophole in the state firearms laws, which allowed them to give their legal, peaceful demonstration the threatening atmosphere of gunplay and militancy. It was successful "guerrilla theater." But Mao was talking about **being** guerrillas, not just threatening to be guerrillas. He was talking about People's War for liberation by the masses. "The real thing."

In raising the gun, for whatever strategy, the Oakland BPP became a lightning rod, a target and conductor of energy. Many folks felt, as that Panther said after Sacramento: "If I die, I'll know I did my part." There was a surge of grassroots militancy toward and into the Party. Even if the New Afrikan liberation movement didn't have all the right answers then, young 'rads refused to be slowed down. They wanted to join the struggle, help push it to new heights, and the BPP was what was most ready and accessible. And they were willing to put their lives on the line. That was the revolutionary spirit that gave the Party a role much greater than its leadership. The two-line struggle helped create the BPP, and existed within the Party as a growing contradiction between those who wanted to push on to revolutionary war vs. those who wanted to return to White Amerika, only on better terms of servitude. The two-line struggle was eventually to split the BPP, in the process creating a new revolutionary advance—the Black Liberation Army.

The BPP as originally conceived lasted less than three years, collapsing under the first counter-attack from the security forces. At first the security forces had been surprised by the Panthers, and had taken the time to plant agents and informers, make plans, and put out propaganda preparing public opinion.

The Oakland leadership was neutralized. On the night of October 28, 1967, Oakland police stopped a car driven by Huey Newton. In the ensuing conflict Pig John Frey was killed and another policeman wounded four times. A badly wounded Huey Newton was arrested for murder, and later convicted on September 8, 1968. The entire program of the Party was shifted to "Free Huey!" defense work. On April 6, 1968, Eldridge Cleaver was arrested in the police raid in which Lil' Bobby Hutton was killed. Hutton was the BPP treasurer, and at age 15 had been the first 'rad recruited off the block by Huey and Bobby. Faced with revocation of parole and return to prison, Eldridge Cleaver went into Algerian exile

in November 1968. Bobby Seale himself was arrested in New Haven, Conn. on a conspiracy murder charge. At first David Hilliard, National Chief of Staff, and finally Elaine Brown ended up running the Oakland headquarters.

Everywhere the same scenario was being played out. Panthers in various cities tried to carry out "legal" Serve the People programs, such as Free Breakfast Programs for schoolchildren and Free Health Clinics, but collided with well-prepared police. Known Panther automobiles were stopped. Shootouts and frame-ups spread as the FBI's COINTELPRO campaign took effect. On January 17, 1968, Los Angeles Panthers Bunchy Carter and John Huggins were killed. On April 2, 1969, the NY Panther 21 were arrested in a bombing conspiracy frame-up. Three weeks later the Des Moines, Iowa BPP office was bombed. On December 4, 1969, the FBI and Chicago police assassinated Panthers Fred Hampton and Mark Clark. These were only a few incidents out of a floodtide of counterinsurgency. There were over 1,000 arrests of BPP members, raids on offices in 11 states, over 400 confrontations with the police, and over 30 Panthers shot down.[28]

These blows completely disoriented and turned around the Black Panther Party. **The original program of self-defense of the New Afrikan communities was abandoned in practice, since the BPP was unable even to defend itself.** Instead of mass organizing projects and armed self-defense against the police, the BPP's main activities degenerated into selling the newspaper

on street corners, doing fundraising with liberal Euro-Amerikans, publicizing the "Free Huey!" campaign, running in US elections, and sending off money to Oakland. The BPP had, in effect, turned into a legal defense committee primarily oriented to begging for settler support. It was in this political rout that the Party split, between the so-called Oakland and East Coast factions.

To understand these problems we have to go back to the interwoven questions of the Party's class character, its military concepts, and its fundamental relationship to the US oppressor nation. The two-line struggle between socialism and neo-colonialism was always manifested in all areas of the Party's life. We can see it not only in the political-military program, but in the Party's false internationalism with the Euro-Amerikan Left.

Even when new things come into being they carry with them the old, and until and unless these old ideas and class views are consciously struggled out through study and practice the old still retains its grip. This interpenetration of opposites characterized the political-military strategy of the Black Revolution. Some people did new things in the old ways and other folks pursued old objectives in new ways. Adventurism and flightism marked the subjectivity characteristic of petty-bourgeois/lumpen operations.

There was a temporary unity in the Party around the strategy of public, "legal" armed organization. But this unity mixed together two different points of view. Many of the young revs involved genuinely wanted revolution, but were still so indoctrinated as to believe that they had political rights as "US citizens." These rights would protect them, they thought, during a building period while they openly prepared for revolution. That is, they still had incorrect ideas about bourgeois democracy. For example: the NY Panther 21 related how, after having heard rumors that a big bust was coming down, they discussed their situation; they decided that since they were not violating the written laws they had nothing to fear from the police. When doors were pushed in and folks arrested at gunpoint, some of the Panther 21 laughed at the faked-up police charges. They soon stopped laughing.[29] This first point of view was politically uneducated, but honest.

The other point of view within the Party never really intended to make revolution. Their plan, whether conscious or unconscious, was that the mere display of guns and a willingness to individually shoot it out if vamped on, would frighten White Amerika into making concessions, reforms. These successes would then make the "Vanguard" national political figures, going in a few years from being poor college students to becoming the equivalents of Jomo Kenyatta or Adam Clayton Powell, Jr. That was the petty-bourgeois/lumpen view of Newton, Seale, Cleaver, and some others. **These people**

did have angry and nationalistic sentiments, as oppressed colonial subjects, but were not committed to national liberation.

In his lumpen theorizing about nation-building, Eldridge Cleaver expressed his admiration for "Israel" and tried to convince New Afrikans that imitating Zionist settler-colonialism was the road to liberation: **"The Jews did it. It worked. Now Afro-Americans must do the same thing."** Not surprisingly, that was the same Eldridge who flipped around and ran to embrace the White Right when his personal situation got tough.[30]

The Huey who threatened individual public shootouts without involving the masses in protracted war became the person who left the struggle for private commerce. Petty-bourgeois/lumpen ideas stand in contradiction to proletarian ideas of class solidarity, class ideology, and a class base for all political-military operations to free the Nation.

All this was harshly exposed in the free-fire zone, where the Party perished—its military strategy failing while the pressure of struggle forced contradictions to a decisive point. Many of the best cadre died or disappeared into prisons. The top petty-bourgeois/lumpen spokesmen—Huey, Bobby, and Eldridge—sold out in various ways. Left in an impossible military situation, a revolutionary current pushed ahead to seize the initiative back from the imperialists. Offensive operations were begun by the first "autonomous and de-centralized" units of the Black Liberation

Army. The split was a split around not only armed struggle, but about the **goals** of picking up the gun.

The Black Panther Party was nationalist, but in fact never committed itself to a strategy for freeing the Land, to winning independence over the National Territory. The October 1968 BPP Platform and Program says under its point number ten that **"we want … as our major political objective, a United Nations–supervised plebiscite to be held throughout the Black colony … for the purpose of determining the will of Black people as to their national destiny."** While clearly recognizing the New Afrikan Nation's right of independence, the platform also left the door open for thinking of staying with the US if settlers made concessions. To say that you are for something—such as liberation—but to have no strategy for ever getting it, can only raise questions.

The Party's false internationalism originated in its class viewpoint. Folks had a confused view of the New Afrikan proletariat. We say "confused" because many Panthers, when they praised the lumpen as the main revolutionary class, were really talking about the most oppressed layers of the proletariat. That is clear in revolutionary statements such as "Message to the Lumpen," published by the revolutionary wing of the Party in NY. Other elements in the Party really did hold the proletariat in contempt. The BPP's heavy propaganda about "the People," "Serve the People," praising Newton as the "Supreme Servant of the People," etc. only expressed this confusion,

in which neither nation nor class was clearly dealt with.

While many individual Panthers were modest and correct in their work and in their relationship to the masses, the Oakland leadership was not. They believed that "Vanguarding the action" gave them license for limitless arrogance and contempt for all others. To mention that Bobby Seale used to have his bodyguards pull shotguns and pistols on other Movement activists, and threaten to kill them if his whims weren't followed, is just a small example of how the Oakland HQ related to other New Afrikans and Third World people.

When the US Empire vamped on the BPP and they were, despite their intentions, unable to defend themselves, the Party strategy had failed. A new strategy was adopted. The Oakland BPP leadership turned to their natural ally, the Euro-Amerikan petty-bourgeoisie. The Party leadership didn't turn to the New Afrikan proletariat because they neither knew how to organize the Nation nor did they really trust their own people. Their neo-colonial class unity with the white petty-bourgeoisie came to the front in the crisis. This was justified as some kind of internationalism, of supposedly winning needed "allies" to the liberation movement.

The new strategy of becoming a legal, "Black and White united" defense campaign was initially centered on an electoral alliance with the Peace and Freedom Party (PFP). In this alliance the BPP used its members and supporters to get enough New Afrikan voters' signatures to put the new PFP on the California ballot. In return, the liberal and radical settlers involved in this anti-war protest party publicly supported the BPP defense campaign, and Eldridge Cleaver himself became the PFP Presidential candidate. The alliance was quietly worked out with PFPer Bob Avakian, a well-to-do student activist who had been with Eldridge on the *Ramparts* magazine staff. The *Ramparts* magazine clique, which included Eldridge and Bobby, was central to the BPP for a while. Folks who had called themselves urban guerrillas, who had promised to defend the New Afrikan community with arms, were instead campaigning for US President for a white protest party. It was a sad clown show.

The alliance was first justified as necessary to save Huey's life, as though the program of the Black Panther Party was primarily to take care of its leaders. *The Black Panther* newspaper explained: "At the inception of the Black Power reaction, Stokely Carmichael told white people that Blacks would be willing to work with them, on a coalition basis ... When Minister of Defense Huey P. Newton got arrested, we began a frantic search for ways of building a broad base of support to set him free. We were not of a frame of mind to be playing petty games or to indulge our egos. We were down to the nitty-gritty of serious business ..."

Soon Eldridge Cleaver was picturing the Party's shift to "Black-White" election campaigns as part of a wonderful change. He told the press that the new alliance had already produced "a very noticeable decrease in this pervasive, undirected hostility and racial tension" by New Afrikans against Euro-Amerikans. Now, he said, Blacks and whites in areas of PFP organizing "find it much easier to circulate and work together." Cleaver was desperately courting the white liberals.

It was clear that this was not a temporary expedient, but a shift to the right after "legal" armed self-defense had failed. Revolutionary nationalism was given up. In a key political address to the founding convention of the California Peace and Freedom Party, on March 16, 1968, Cleaver stunned the audience by declaring that the "era" of Black Power was over: "So that we say that we're at the end of an era ... we see no reason for continuing this stance of isolation one from the other ... Let's get together and move in a common fashion against a common enemy." The BPP was developing the new concept that by taking control over and leading the radicalized settler petty-bourgeoisie they would have a white counter-balance to shield themselves against state repression. In other words, that white people were once again the answer to the problems of the New Afrikan Nation.

The Oakland leadership became committed to uniting with the settler petty-bourgeoisie, if necessary (and it was) against their own National Movement and against their former comrades. We note that so long as Eldridge thought that this policy might personally promote and protect him he took a leading role in pushing it. False internationalism had

been used to abandon the national struggle. Opportunism had been masked as "solidarity."

This new line was called "The United Front Against Fascism," imitating the 1935 campaign of the same name initiated in Europe by the Communist International. *The Black Panther* repeatedly printed full-page extracts of an old speech by Comintern leader Georgi Dimitrov, in which he urged Americans to create "a Workers and Farmers Party" to safeguard US bourgeois democracy.[31] In July 1969 a mass radical conference was assembled in Oakland by the Party. This "National Revolutionary Conference For A United Front Against Fascism" tried to unite the Euro-Amerikan New Left under Oakland BPP leadership.

While Eldridge, Bobby, and Huey were trying to build a liberal united front with the petty-bourgeois settler Left, they refused to participate in building a revolutionary united front for armed struggle **within** the New Afrikan Nation. False internationalism was a cover for dis-uniting the oppressed nation. Nor was there any fascism as such taking place. The thousand settler radicals at the Oakland conference were in no danger from police raids in the night. What was going on was imperialist counterinsurgency to crush the New Afrikan national revolutionary movement. And only the New Afrikan masses could deal with that.

Consciously or unconsciously, the Panther leadership had initially counted on lots of visibility, lots of media publicity, white support and white lawyers to protect them. This false

internationalism left the Party burning in the "free-fire zone" with no viable political-military strategy. Their military failure directly stemmed from unclarity about what the goal was, and about what class could make revolution possible.

To sum up: In part the successful co-optation of Black Power was due to the fact that misleading elements of the period broke away from the national movement to partially base themselves in the radicalized Euro-Amerikan petty-bourgeoisie. As military setbacks grew, the incorrect idea was

promoted that white "allies" would be the answer to the problem. In a class alliance, the settler petty-bourgeoisie reached into the anti-colonial struggle to boost up like-minded New Afrikans as a false leadership. The New Afrikan proletariat, which had been stirred up and drawn into struggle by leaders such as Robert Williams and Malcolm X, found itself politically abandoned in favor of petty-bourgeois white "allies." And the Euro-Amerikan Left used "solidarity" and being "allies" to promote the Hueys and Eldridges, like-minded leaders to its taste, rather than recognize the Provisional Government of the Republic of New Afrika or stand up for the Black Liberation Army.

This false internationalism was not limited to the Panthers alone. Both SNCC and the League of Revolutionary Black Workers, to name two important revolutionary organizations of the period, were hamstrung because of their inability to overcome petty-bourgeois/lumpen class leadership and its supporting alliances. When James Forman was Secretary of SNCC he appeared to have an individual alliance with the settler Communist Party USA (CPUSA). Of course, Forman had individual relations and alliances with many settler liberal and radical petty-bourgeois groupings. And the CPUSA had always related to SNCC, and had always tried to influence it as "friends." That is, there was nothing exclusive on either side. In this particular case, we can see how such a private alliance worked to the mutual benefit of both petty-bourgeois parties, but betrayed the struggle.

CPUSA fundraising in the North raised tens of thousands of dollars annually for SNCC, channeled through Forman. This helped Forman's power-base within SNCC, since he was able to furnish some activists with cars, money, and other necessities. Forman, in return, publicly related to the CPUSA as "friends." **But more than that, the CPUSA privately obtained a veto-power over some SNCC activity.**

The 1965 Chicago struggle against the House Un-American Activities Committee (HUAC) was one such case.[32] In the Spring of 1965 the reactionary Congressional committee announced that it would spend the Summer "investigating Communist subversion within the Civil Rights Movement." Public HUAC hearings as a right-wing propaganda forum, prison sentences for Movement activists who refused to testify against their 'rads, were all anticipated. HUAC's first stop was to be Chicago, where the FBI had prepared a tired handful of Black flippers to testify that the movement was a conspiracy run by Moscow. But the big publicity was planned to come from exposing "Communists" within Mayor Daley's administration. The Southern cracker Congressmen running HUAC wanted big headlines for themselves, and had named Dr. Jeremiah Stamler, a Chicago Board of Health official, as a supposed long-time secret Communist. Once launched to media fanfare, the HUAC investigation would then leave Chicago to tour the South, attacking local New Afrikan activists at each stop.

James Forman had sent a call to action, asking SNCC and CORE militants in Chicago to derail this right-wing campaign before it got to the South. A campaign of disrupting the Congressional hearings with Sit-Ins and mass demonstrations was planned. Rev. Fred Shuttlesworth of the Birmingham Movement spoke at a large Chicago rally to raise expected bail and defense funds, and some $3,000 was gathered. The CPUSA played a major role in these preparations. Forman himself was to arrive in time to lead the fight the day of the Sit-Ins.

On that morning Forman was there, accompanied by his assistant (a Euro-Amerikan leader of the local "Friends of SNCC"). The HUAC hearings were held in the former Federal Court Building, which was right on Lake Michigan in the exclusive "Gold Coast" neighborhood. Forman led the SNCC and CORE activists into the hearing room. Reporters, TV cameras, and lots of Chicago police, FBI, and Federal marshals crowded the lobby and sidewalk. The word was, to wait for Forman to give the signal. The morning passed. As lunch recess was announced and activists wanted to block the doors, Forman ordered that everyone leave the building with him. It would be more effective to begin the action in the afternoon, he said. But after lunch he never reappeared. His assistant told the activists that Forman had driven straight to O'Hare Airport, and was at that moment on his way to New York City! Shock and some demoralization hit folks.

Although the story wasn't pieced together until days later, it turns out that the CPUSA had changed its mind. Possibly their national leadership had sent down new directives. The CPUSA decided that the struggle should not center around defending the Black movement, but should be changed into a liberal "civil liberties" issue focusing on Dr. Stamler, the respected public health specialist. By "whitening" the issue, particularly given the fact that Dr. Stamler was a well-known medical researcher and was not a revolutionary of any kind, the CPUSA planned to mobilize a larger involvement by white liberals. And the CPUSA privately demanded that there be no violence, no civil disobedience, no action other than a peaceful picket line. Anything more, they said, would scare off the white liberals.

We do not know if the CPUSA ordered their "ally," Forman, to kill the SNCC action, or if under pressure he simply decided to abandon his own people. Within a few hours a protest campaign against the US Government, called for by SNCC, had been ripped off by the settler Communist Party USA. While the petty-bourgeois CPUSA had "alliances" with Black petty-bourgeois opportunists, that did not mean that they had any genuine alliance at all with the New Afrikan nation or its liberation struggle. The supposed "allies" were enemies in actual fact.

The young SNCC and CORE militants decided to go ahead with the action, even though the situation was totally disorganized. After all, disrupting US Congressional hearings could only be a righteous thing. Several days of chaotic arrest scenes followed, generating front page headlines. The Sit-Ins were mostly done by young high school students, both New Afrikan and Euro-Amerikan, with college New leftists, SNCC and CORE militants, and others taking part. There was payback by the police and Federal marshals, who had been unable to prevent the disruptions from taking place. Arrested demonstrators were worked over at length in a back hallway, out of public sight, with the pigs taking special pleasure in torturing several New Afrikan sisters while cuffed brothers were forced to watch.

The full dimensions of the CPUSA's takeover did not become clear until the arrests took place. 'Rads on the outside found out that there was no defense fund left. The CPUSA, which had been in control of the defense funds, said that they had spent the money on a large newspaper ad for a

THIRTY-FIRST YEAR NO. 34   Week of June 8 thru June 14, 1965   Published at 639 E. 71st St., Stewart 5-1040

LAUNCH WEEK OF PROTESTS

To March On Board; City Hall

By RICHARD TAYLOR SCOTT

WHAT HAS BEEN predicted as a summer of protests was launched with an appeal demonstration at McCormick Place last Thursday; appealing to President London B. Johnson to urge Mayor Daley to 'get rid of Willis' and an outdoor rally Sunday afternoon in Washington Park featuring 5th Ward Ald. Leon M. Despres and entertainer-civil rights fighter Dick Gregory.

Despres called the reappointment of Willis "an insult to all of us" and labeled the School Superintendent as a man whose "entire life has been devoted to hatred."

The outspoken alderman reflected upon the meetings at Harpers Ferry when W.E.B. Dubois and his followers founded the NAACP and started what has led to the present day movements. He called the Washington Park rally a "historic gathering" in this city and contended that "good education for all black children in the country" must be demanded.

HE CITED the freedom fighters of Mississippi, Selma, Birmingham, and concluded that "we will fight for freedom and equality for everyone in Chicago."

Dick Gregory berated the crowd with a barrage of indicting remarks, both humorous and stinging, aimed at Mayor Richard J. Daley. "Governor Wallace knows that Daley is the only northerner who could come to Alabama and run for governor — and win," said Gregory.

The tireless Gregory called for support of the school boycott scheduled for Thursday and Friday, June 10 and 11. He warned people not to listen to those who say it will hurt your child to leave him out of school

summer."

Gregory contended that the "big white folks" think Daley controls the Negro population of Chicago and he promised that all of that "is going to be changed this summer."

The entertainer took time out from his barrage against Daley, Willis and the white power structure to heap praise upon Ald. Despres. He called the 5th ward voice "brave, dedicated and sincere."

GREGORY'S voice softened and his admiration was abounding as he asserted: "If the day ever comes, in this revolution, when the Negro is throwing bricks, you (Despres) can walk in any black neighborhood and don't worry about catching any bricks." The crowd's applause seemed to second the motion.

Plans were announced for a "March on City Hall and the Board of Education," Thursday, June 10, assembling at the south parking lot of Soldier's Field at 10 a.m. The march has the support of community organizations throughout the city, including T.W.O., according to president Leonard Stevenson.

T.W.O. ISSUED a plea to the community, saying "Now is the time . . . join with every man, woman and child of this community" in Thursday's march and "remember — no school Thursday and Friday."

Literacy Project In Area

The Illinois State Employment Service announced the inauguration of the Adult, Basic Education, Prevocational, and Vocational Training Program, "Project 300," last week, May 28th. Training is

The Old And The New

JOINING HANDS in the middle are Stonewall Edwards, (left) self-styled humanitarian who first earned a reputation as a freedom fighter in Woodlawn and Garfield 'Dicky' Harris, (right) 6341 Greenwood, a young man who was arrested two times during the recent anti-HUAC demonstrations and is slowly but surely earning a reputation as Woodlawn's most active demonstrator. The demonstration above was an anti-Daley and Willis demonstration at McCormick Place, Thursday, June 3rd. Others on the photo are unidentified. (See special on 'Dicky' Harris on page 6.)

peaceful demonstration of their own. Forman's assistant explained to the activists that since they had not followed orders (by the CPUSA, that is), the "Movement" would not help them. No bail, no lawyers, no help of any kind would be furnished.

Two footnotes: The unpleasant publicity and the "riots" so angered Mayor Daley that he uncharacteristically invited HUAC to leave Chicago and not to return. And, in fact, the whole Southern HUAC tour was cancelled, rather than face the possibility of mass confrontations. Secondly, when two SNCC 'rads got out of jail they walked over to the office of the CPUSA official who had been in charge of the defense fund, and gave him a definite reminder to not come near the liberation movement again.

We should say several things here. The first is that defense funds supposedly raised to aid SNCC and the Southern movement were in reality only used to promote settler revisionism. **In other words, SNCC was raising funds to aid the settler CPUSA, not the reverse.** We can start to see what kind of political confusion the Formans had folks in, and why 'rads who didn't even know what was happening on their doorstep could not lead a revolutionary upsurge. The CPUSA, in fact, has **never given** money to the New Afrikan struggle. They only **invested** money out of which they made a political profit. "Solidarity" meant using the Formans and Angela Davises to raise hundreds of thousands of dollars, much of which the CPUSA used for itself. Causes like the United

Front of Cairo, defense cases like Martin Sostre, and so on, have funded the CPUSA and other settler organizations. Often over the bitter objections of ripped-off New Afrikans and other Third World revs.

James Forman, who was representative of a certain strata of Black petty-bourgeois radicals, went on from SNCC to new neo-colonial fiascos. After a passing alliance with the BPP during SNCC's dying days, Forman launched the Black Economic Development Conference (BEDC) in the Spring of 1969. This was a distorted version of reparations for 400 years of colonial enslavement. The BEDC's Black Manifesto was essentially a gigantic foundation grant request. Forman's illusionary program was that the Euro-Amerikan churches would give him hundreds of millions of dollars in "guilt money," which would supposedly be used to start a new "Black economy." Forman went on to the League of Revolutionary Black Workers, and played a role there in creating a faction that insisted on merging into the settler New Left.[33]

As a whole, we can see that the petty-bourgeois settler Left and petty-bourgeois Black radicals made private alliances between themselves during the 1960s. This false internationalism helped maintain a mis-leadership for the revolutionary struggle, promoted unhealthy and neocolonial attitudes, and left the young New Afrikan revolutionary movement ill-equipped to fight the co-optation of Black Power by the imperialists.

5. ENDING "THE DARK NIGHT OF SLAVERY"

In the beginning of the revolutionary crisis, the Black Nation found itself in a period where revolution was an objective possibility, but wherein false and primitive theories of **how** to get liberation led to setback after setback. This has not only been true for all other revolutionary movements in the continental Empire, but true for many other nations as well.

Even in Vietnam, which has been among the advanced guard in the World Revolution, what they call "the dark night of slavery" lasted close to seventy years. During those years the Vietnamese people heroically fought many battles, launched many uprisings, began many new revolutionary organizations. Only to be defeated time after time by the French colonial armies who had first invaded Vietnam in 1858. From 1885–1892 a series of local armed uprisings led by feudal intellectuals from the old ruling classes were defeated.

This led to a new trend, of looking abroad for new ways and in some cases for foreign help. Some Vietnamese tried to organize for bourgeois democracy on the French model, only to be repressed. Others pinned their hopes on the French Left taking over and decolonizing. Still others joined the Chinese bourgeois nationalist movement (Guomindang) and hoped that an independent China would free their country. Still

SAIGON
As South Vietnam collapses, evacuees struggle toward a U.S. helicopter atop the Pittman apartments in Saigon

others looked to Japan, as a new Asian power thought to be sympathetic on race lines. Others looked to the US for help, as a world power supposedly democratic and verbally critical of European colonialism.

In all cases, these many movements and organizations guided by unscientific theories about how to free their country met defeat year after year. It was not until Vietnamese communism began that the anti-colonial movement could work out a correct strategy. As the history of the Vietnamese Party notes: "… prior to 1920, no Vietnamese patriot had found out the light of national liberation in the dark night of slavery, neither was any patriotic, revolutionary organization capable of leading the people to victory. At this period, the Vietnamese revolution was faced with a grave crisis as regards the way to national salvation."[34]

Even the very self-reliant Vietnamese, at a confused stage in their history, looked heavily to others as the bearers of liberation. There was also much defeatism in these earlier periods, when repeated setbacks and other inadequacies had demoralized many. In particular this was true among the privileged Vietnamese classes, who were predisposed to be awed at European colonial power since they profited so much relatively within its occupation. Many petty-bourgeois Vietnamese preached that the French were just too strong for the small and weak Vietnamese nation to fight— better to seek reforms within the colonial system.

All this has certain parallels to the political situation within the New Afrikan liberation movement. This has manifested itself even within the armed organizations. The main problem facing the New Afrikan Nation today, as all other

oppressed peoples in the Empire, is the inability to find the correct path to liberation, and thus end "the dark night of slavery."

The most prevalent backward idea in the New Afrikan Liberation Movement has been defeatism. **Every national liberation movement has had to overcome this backward political position.** Even in China, the largest and one of the oldest nations on the earth, the Communists in the 1930s had to constantly fight defeatism among the people, among the national movement, and even among the army. Mao called this backward idea "the theory of national subjugation." So folks constantly hear in a thousand different voices, direct and indirect, that New Afrikan people are too few, too weak, too outnumbered to be able to themselves directly fight and defeat the US Empire. If New Afrikans foolishly dare to rise up then the vastly stronger White Amerika will simply commit genocide and wipe all New Afrikans out. Therefore, the theory of national subjugation goes, New Afrikan people must limit their strategies to those that win majority white approval or at least tolerance.

In the political debate in the early 1960s over first picking up the gun, Robert Williams spoke against the Black integrationists/assimilationists directly to this crucial issue. Williams wrote in 1962 in *Negroes With Guns*:

"The responsible Negro leadership is pacifist in so far as its one interest is that we do not fight white racists; that we do not 'provoke' or enrage them. **They constantly tell us that if we resort to violent self-defense we will be exterminated ...**

"This fear of extermination is a myth which we've exposed in Monroe. We did this because we came to have an active understanding of the racist system, and we grasped the relationship between violence and racism. The existence of violence is at the very heart of a racist system ... When people say that they are opposed to Negroes 'resorting to violence' what they really mean is that they are opposed to Negroes defending themselves and challenging the exclusive monopoly of violence practiced by the white racists ... When Afro-Americans resist and struggle for their rights they also possess a power greater than that generated by their will and hands. With the world situation as it is today, the most racist and fascist United States government conceivable could not succeed in eliminating 20,000,000 people."[35]

It is significant that Williams' political opponents, when pressed to explain how New Afrikans could protect themselves in a way that doesn't antagonize White Amerika, always fell back on the old, slavish idea that New Afrikans should look to white people—either the "white proletariat" or "concerned white liberals" or even the Federal government itself—as their protection. In other words, the oppressed should be dependent upon the oppressor. It is significant that those Blacks mentally enslaved by settler revisionism sounded no different from the upfront lackeys. One of the leading attackers against Williams and the armed self-defense movement was Claude Lightfoot, head of the "minority" department of the settler Communist Party USA, who also wrote in 1962:

"Another current to emerge recently is the movement around Williams, in Monroe, North Carolina. It also reflects a current born of desperation ...

"But it should be pointed out that armed struggle will not lead to Negro freedom. On the contrary, it would retard the fight for freedom because it would leave the struggle up to Negroes alone. It is this tendency of 'I'll walk alone' that underlies much of the confused direction the Williams forces advocate. But who else in America is prepared to take up arms for a cause—any cause?

"The main protection for Negroes in the South is to force the Federal Government to shoulder its responsibilities, as President Eisenhower was forced to do at Little Rock. This must be the direction. In this kind of struggle, we can muster allies throughout the country ..."[36]

This kind of slavish nonsense was from someone who called himself a "communist," but who had the kind of thinking 100% acceptable to imperialism. In general, the phony "Marxism-Leninism" practiced by petty-bourgeois careerists has always produced defeatism about New Afrikan liberation, however disguised. Robert L. Allen, for example, one of the leaders in the Black intellectual trend of Bourgeois "Marxism," editor of *Black Scholar* magazine, even went so far as to lie and falsely praise Malcolm X for his supposed defeatism. Allen, who was for years a staff member for the white Left *Guardian* newspaper, became a professor of Black Studies at San Jose State University. Malcolm, Allen lied, recognized that only white support could save New Afrikan people from genocide, and therefore Malcolm was actually working to **prevent** New Afrikan revolution from breaking out:

"As far as white workers were concerned, he had no faith at all that they could be anything but reactionary and racist. With beliefs such as these, it would be natural for Malcolm to hesitate to advocate that Blacks undertake anything more than self-defense. His major concern, wisely, was to prevent genocide, not encourage it. He knew that in a revolutionary situation only the presence of revolutionary forces outside the Black communities could prevent mass slaughter of the Black population. He saw no such forces in evidence, and therefore was forced to equivocate ..."[37]

In this unbelievable, lying rap, we are told (by a professor of Black Studies, of course) that Malcolm, too, believed that New Afrikan Revolution had to wait on the back burner. And not wait for anything New Afrikans might decide, no, wait for **white folks** to get ready to permit New Afrikan liberation! White people are again said to be the answer to the problems of the New Afrikan Nation. Well, if Malcolm X was so allegedly bent on "equivocating" and holding back the Rev, why did the CIA assassinate him?

We should start to see how important defeatism is, how it robs the liberation struggle of its independence, its hope for the masses, and its true vision of its tasks. It is not just liberalism and phony "M-Lism" that shelters defeatism. We can see this in phony "Pan-Afrikanism" as well. Pseudo-nationalists such as Stokely Carmichael have taken ideological refuge in a version of Pan-Afrikanism. This has allowed them to sound Afrikan-centered and nationalistic while still opposing any national independence for the oppressed right here. **I.e. this is militant integrationism disguised on a higher level.** Quite naturally, those who believe this also promote defeatism re-labeled as realism. Stokely has been upfront in saying that revolution in the US is a white thing, and New Afrikans must wait for revolution until the settler majority allows it (which would be a long wait indeed):

"For real socialist transformation to come to America, the white working class is the crucial element ... History has demonstrated to us the willingness of the Black man to work with his ally, the white working class ... Although the Black worker must be the vanguard, he must push the white worker out front. The Black worker must not move unless the white worker is moving."[38]

Again, we see across the political spectrum, among liberals, phony "M-L'ers," phony "Pan-Afrikanists," pseudo-nationalists, the same underlying politics: that New Afrikans will get genocidally wiped out if they push settler Amerika too far, and that only "majority" white support can shield New Afrikan people. **In other words, that white people are the answer.**

We can easily expose the falsehoods in this ideological slavishness. First, "the theory of national subjugation," that New Afrikans are too weak and outnumbered to militarily fight the colonial power. Time and again we hear this as a truism, so supposedly obvious that it needs no explanation. When we examine it, however, it blows away into dust. For example, if Amilcar Cabral had all the rebel fighters in Guinea-Bissau (which is a small nation with a population less than some major cities) frontally mass and charge the Portuguese machine-guns, it might well have been true that the liberation struggle would have been totally wiped out. If General Giap had the whole Vietnamese liberation army expose themselves and charge US bases, Saigon might be occupied right now. **But in fact People's War by the weak and small nations won, while the imperialist NATO powers lost.**

But couldn't the US have used H-bombs, poison gas, and its industrial/technological power to commit total genocide and wipe out Vietnam? Abstractly, perhaps. In reality, no. As Mao pointed out in 1945, atomic weapons once demonstrated in Japan could no longer be used by US imperialism against the Third World, since the people of the world would unite in horror against such dangerous barbarism. Hence, he said, their threat against China at that time was a "paper tiger." In the same way, People's War correctly fought uses many strategic factors, both military and political, to frustrate and immobilize the supposedly superior might of the imperialist nations.

This does not mean, of course, that any small or oppressed nation can automatically defeat any imperialist power. The dialectical process of constant change, of coming into being and going out of being, affects nations as well as other things. There are both many great empires and many small nations that have gone out of existence, just as many new nations are coming into being in this century. Once the entire Arab world, which today comprises many sovereign nation-states, was one colony of the large Turkish Ottoman Empire. Today Turkey is no empire but only a small nation, itself an oppressed neo-colony. There is no law that says that the US oppressor nation will continue to be a large nation. And there is no law that guarantees that New Afrika or Hawaii or the Navajo nation or any imperialist neo-colony will be independent in the future. This is up to the struggle, and up to the desires of the masses. Some peoples agree with Ho, that "Nothing is more precious than independence," and some peoples do not agree.

The key link to grasp here is that Vietnam proved that a weak nation can defeat a strong nation, and a small nation can defeat a large nation. This has changed the course of world history. Why, then, cannot Puerto Rico or the Philippines or New Afrika or Azania defeat the US oppressor nation? This exposes the assumption at the heart of defeatism within the New Afrikan liberation movement. Folks, even some professed nation-

alists, are still weak and hesitant about the New Afrikan Nation. They're uncertain that it is a separate, legitimate Nation. Too many revs keep thinking, if only unconsciously, that New Afrikan people are only a "minority" within the "majority" settler US oppressor nation. This "minority" thinking is strongly pushed by the oppressor, who always keeps labeling the oppressed as "minorities" **together** with Euro-Amerikan women. (If you listen to the oppressor, they are the "majority" even within the "minority.") It's easy to see how a "minority" within a nation might feel it impossible to win a war against its own "majority." But between nations, as Vietnam and other liberation struggles have shown, political consciousness is a bigger factor in the balance of power than population size, industry, weaponry, or size of armies. A larger problem might be that many Third World revs here, while wanting to get out of their oppression, don't entirely want to separate from the "good life" of the "Big House."

Consequently, when the New Afrikan urban guerrillas of the BLA swung into action in 1970–71, they found themselves quickly abandoned by the Black Movement. And not in any subtle way, either. New Afrikans as helpless victims and armed organization only for personal self-defense were acceptable to the Movement and its settler allies. The Black Movement refused to really support any of the urban guerrillas, either in deeds or for the most part even in words. New Afrikan guerrillas were not unaware of this, to say the least. In "Message to the Lumpen," the young BLA said:

"… when the lumpen first posed the alternative to organized reactionary violence of the ruling class, the lumpen found itself isolated … The other classes panicked and got as far away from the lumpen as possible … Now, while the world situation permits it we must make our move for the freedom and liberation of our people, realizing that nobody and nothing can stop us. To be successful, all we need to do is become fulltime revolutionaries. We have nothing better to do. No more of their programs for us … Field niggers have dreamed of this day since the first slave revolt was drowned in blood in Babylon. It's what haunts the dreams of every Indian alive."[39]

Yet what they discovered in practice was that most of the "Black Liberation Movement"—whether liberal, pseudo-nationalist, Black Power, phony "M-L," or phony "Pan-Afrikanist"—didn't want armed struggle and was convinced that liberation couldn't succeed. The urban guerrillas found that their own Movement was neither preparing the masses nor organizing for liberation. The vital relationship between the masses and the first seeds of armed revolutionary organization (necessarily small) had been cut—from within the Movement. Defeatism was a poison within the supposedly revolutionary "BLM."

Defeatism tugs at and undermines the liberation movement by slyly promoting the view that liberation can only come from others, in particular the old, colonialized view that white people are the answer to the problems of the

New Afrikan Nation. Revolutionary nationalists explicitly put down this idea. Yet, it isn't too hard to see it still lived on in disguised forms in the old '60s Movement. For example, the view was widespread that the New Afrikan revolution should be completely financed by contributions from liberal and radical Euro-Amerikans. New Afrikan people, it was claimed, were "too poor" to support their own Movement. We've all heard and read such things, and should admit what they mean.

Examples of this are not hard to find. For instance: in 1980 the African People's Socialist Party split. The split became a public controversy, with the majority of the Central Committee members led by Ajowa Ifateyo (sn Vicki Wells) and Aziza Ayoluwa expelling APSP Chairman Omali Yeshitela (sn Joseph Waller) on charges of alleged physical abuse of women. Yeshitela and his supporters, while not commenting on the specific events, counter-charged that the Ifateyo-Ayoluwa actions were part of a lesbian-FBI-COINTELPRO repressive operation against Black people.[40] We mention these issues only in passing, as background in a split in which the allegiance of Euro-Amerikan radical "allies" was very important.

The APSP had/has a Euro-Amerikan solidarity committee attached to it which played an all-important role inside the life of the organization. What that meant can be seen by the testimony of Ajowa Ifateyo. She has said in an interview that without the approval of this solidarity committee, which supported Chairman Yeshitela and withheld money from them, the majority of the APSP Central Committee was helpless, paralyzed:

"That was a real critical move at that time. The Party was heavily dependent on that money from the solidarity committee. The whole publication of the Party newspaper, *The Burning Spear*, depended on it. The solidarity committee also subsidized an entire African bookstore and the entire office rent and living space (the same building) of the national office.

"When it really slapped us in the face, it was totally unbelievable. Here were these white women going to take all this money ... the Party work came to a halt. There was nothing we could do. We had planned to publish a special issue of *The Burning Spear* to explain the whole struggle, but then we couldn't."[41]

It is really striking to hear a New Afrikan activist say that without Euro-Amerikan approval they were unable to even communicate with their own Nation, much less maintain an organization! False internationalism worked to produce a dependent mentality. There is no doubt that Euro-Amerikan "allies" were the central consideration for the APSP. Chairman Yeshitela was unafraid to publicly say that. He has explained the APSP national office's move to San Francisco as motivated by the need to find Euro-Amerikans:

"It was a struggle that was complicated by the tremendous poverty of our Party and of our people, so that often our struggle was composed equally of attempts to feed the members who constitute our Party, as well as to do the other work. Often our struggle was complicated by the most ridiculous need to pay a light bill in the office, by the most obscene need to pay the rent ...

"The decision to come to San Francisco was partially influenced by these difficulties ... We understood that we needed a rear base area. There are no mountains within the colonial territory to which we can escape, develop resources, repair our engines, and then return to attack our enemies. So, therefore, we had to create the mountain. From various utterances and signs of solidarity that we received from North American left forces in San Francisco, California, and from the evidence of the material resources that we could see here, we could see the ... possibility for creating our mountain here. We perceived the possibility of being able to bring leading Party forces to the San Francisco area, whose primary responsibility would be to develop unity with the North American forces in this area ... That's why we are in San Francisco, to build the mountain."[42]

White folks are said to be the Mountain. White folks are said to be the rear base area for the Black Revolution. National offices are moved several thousand miles, across the continent, in order to get closer to them. They are all-important. **Once again, white people are said to be the answer to the problems of the New Afrikan Nation.** And the thing is, that everyone who does this also adds that they are only carrying out **Malcolm's** legacy. Is that what Malcolm did?

Intervention by Euro-Amerikans in the affairs of the New Afrikan Nation is not a trick, played by sly white people on innocent New Afrikan leaders. Intervention is not a trick, but rather a relationship, an **alliance** between similar class forces in oppressor and oppressed nations. Some leaders, as we can see, are not innocent at all. They look for intervention, argue and recruit for intervention, and defend their cherished intervention as "allies" and "solidarity." Of course, when their schemes go wrong they simply blame it all on white folks. This has nothing to do with liking oppressors. After all, the drug addict may hate their addiction, but still find themselves going back to the Man for one more fix. This is not the fault of one leader or a hundred leaders as individuals. Defeatism and an attitude of dependence on others is an institutionalized condition throughout the colonial world, and can only be overcome by finally ending "the dark night of slavery" with proletarian class ideology. We remember that Stephen Biko said before his assassination:

"The Black man is subjected to two forces in this country. He is first of all oppressed by an external world through institutionalized machinery and through laws that restrict him from doing certain things, through heavy work conditions, through poor pay, through difficult living conditions, through poor education. These are all external to him. Secondly, and this we regard as the most important, the Black man in himself has developed a certain state of alienation ... Because of the ability of the white culture to solve so many problems ... You tend to look at it as a superior culture to yours. You tend to despise the **worker culture**, and this inculcates in the Black man a sense of **self-hatred** ..."[43]

Defeatism is **colonial** in that it is an oppressor nation view, an alien, imperialist view, rather than one that reflects the natural reality and interests of the oppressed nation. But it is simultaneously a class question. Defeatism represents the subjective and vacillating class nature of the neo-colonial petty-bourgeois, who are its social carriers. The neo-colonial petty-bourgeois are also drawn towards defeatism because of their own material reality as a class. They cannot overcome imperialism by themselves. **They are not the revolutionary class, the element of change.** In the modern age only the proletariat is the bearer of revolutionary science, of correct strategy for liberation of all the oppressed. Malcolm grasped the essence of this when he pointed out that only the grassroots provided rebellion, change, while the petty-bourgeois Black leadership always trailed ineffectually behind them.

6. ARMY WITHOUT PARTY

In January 1971 the public watched as a political split between Huey Newton and Eldridge Cleaver surfaced. It was announced that the Black Panther Party had split into two camps, the "Oakland faction" and the "Cleaver faction" or "East Coast faction." **Actually, the BPP was dying.** Its historic tasks had been accomplished. The contradictions within it broke through the old shell, smashing it to pieces. In the process came a new season of struggle. The Black Liberation Army was born out of the ruins of the old organization.

In keeping with the BPP's style, the split in their leadership erupted right on television. Since going into exile in 1968, Cleaver had set up an Intercommunal Section in Algiers, whose main job was diplomatic representation to socialist governments. With an ocean between them and changes coming down, rumors began to spread about political conflicts in the BPP leadership. To quiet those rumors Newton arranged to speak to Eldridge by long-distance telephone live on a San Francisco TV talk show. Huey was attempting to jam Eldridge into going along with his decisions right on television. To Newton's chagrin, Eldridge

attacked the Oakland headquarters' recent decisions and demanded the expulsion of Chief of Staff David Hilliard.[44] Newton was left to explain it all to the TV cameras. Later that day he called Cleaver in Algiers. Huey told Eldridge that his whole "fraction" was expelled from the Party. That call, too, was tape-recorded by them and later broadcast on US public radio, macho threats and all:

"EC: Hey man.

HN: Eldridge.

EC: What's happening?

HN: Well, you dropped a bombshell this morning.

EC: Yeah.

HN: Don't you think so?

EC: I hope so.

HN: Well, it was very embarrassing for me … Hello, you listening? The Intercommunal Section is expelled.

EC: … Right on, if that's what you want to do, Brother. But look here, I don't think you should take such actions like that.

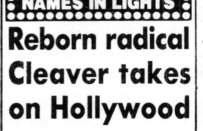

...

HN: And you know, I'd like a battle, Brother. We'll battle it out.

...

EC: Well, then I think you're a madman, too, Brother.

HN: OK, we'll battle like two bulls, we'll lock horns.

EC: We'll see then, OK?

HN: But I think I have the guns.

EC: I got some guns too, Brother.

HN: Alright, you put yours to work and I'll put mine to work, but I'm not a coward like you Brother ... you're a coward, you're a punk, you understand."[45]

•⌶⌶⌶⌶• •⌶⌶⌶⌶• •⌶⌶⌶⌶•

The internal crisis had been precipitated by the Oakland Central Office, desperately trying to stop the Party membership from going over to armed struggle. Public expulsions became regular features of *The Black Panther*, together with photographs of the purged members. In December 1970 the FBI busted a clandestine BPP guerrilla cell in Dallas, Texas. Fugitive Geronimo Pratt, who had organized the cell, was arrested along with Will Stafford, "Crutch" Holiday, and George Lloyd. Pratt was the BPP Deputy Minister of Defense for Southern California. To the Party's surprise, *The Black Panther* responded by announcing Geronimo's expulsion from the Party as a supposed traitor. Geronimo had been one of the most liked and respected leaders. He had led the five-hour defense of the LA BPP office on December 8, 1969, against police armed with automatic weapons, helicopters, and armored cars. One of the Panther 21 recalls:

"... I remember the response and reaction of the brothers and sisters, not only in the Party, but in the street when they picked up that edition of the paper that had in it the purge, the expulsion from the Party of Brother Geronimo and his branding as being a pig. This is like the straw that broke the camel's back, and that was the spark that set off the prairie fire. It would not be tolerated any longer.

"We started getting together on the East Coast to righteously move on the situation ... It started with brothers and sisters just relating to two tunes that were currently on the hit parade, 'Who's Gonna Take the Weight' by Kool and the Gang and 'Somebody's Watching You.' Brothers and sisters made it known that way, that they were tired of this sh—."[46]

Geronimo Pratt himself insisted that he had gone underground with the full knowledge of the Central Office. But Oakland had gotten unhappy with his plan to start guerrilla activity for a New Afrikan state in the South:

"As we, the Black Liberation Army, the military arm of the Black Panther Party, transcended ... that level of politics and moved to the stage of armed urban confrontation (Huey, Eldridge and Bobby Hutton—Oakland, 1967 to Los Angeles, 1969 shootout on Central Avenue), I observed the dastardly (cowardly, sneaky) reactions of many so-called leaders of our organization. Right before my departure to begin my underground mission it became even more obvious. I began to outline my plans to them, especially the mention of one Dixie Region State, they were sparked with astonishment and stood agape (mouths wide open) looking foolish."[47]

By the next month, January 1971, the NY Panther 21 prisoners were publicly expelled from the Party as well. The cause was their open letter of support to the Weather Underground. In it the imprisoned 'rads, who had been politically abandoned by Huey and the Central Office, strongly criticized certain unnamed "vanguard" parties. Everyone understood this was aimed at the Oakland leadership:

"We see how the pigs are working overtime to try and fuck things up—but we also see how much of the misdirection comes from these self proclaimed 'vanguard' parties themselves.

THE BLACK PANTHER, SATURDAY, JANUARY 23, 1971 PAGE 7

ON THE PURGE OF GERONIMO FROM THE BLACK PANTHER PARTY

The Black Panther Party is informing all Chapters, Branches, N.C.C.F.'s and the mass of People that we are purging from our ranks Elmer Gerard Pratt, more commonly known as Geronimo or "G".

In addition to committing flagrant violations of our Party's principles, this man ultimately showed that although he claimed allegiance and devotion to the struggle of the People from oppression and to the Black Panther Party, his devotion and allegiance was still to the ways and rules of the Pig Power Structure. When he left the Marine Corps' Special Forces (having trained Green Berets), the armed agency of the CIA, he joined the Black Panther Party. But he has proven beyond a doubt that he is as dedicated today to that Pig Agency as he was when he was in Vietnam, killing innocent Vietnamese women and children on various "search and destroy" missions.

It is certain that we were under an illusion that he had switched allegiances, for his lies (which he admitted he had been trained to tell) were extremely convincing. For the Black Panther Party did everything in our power to allow this man - who can no longer be considered such, for he lacks human compassion and understanding - to remain free from the vicious clutches of the pigs. As a result of our efforts, this jackanape informed the Central Committee of our Party of certain demands he had - namely money. He advised the Party that he had organized some other fools, that they were armed and that if his demands were not met, he would "move on" (assassinate) our Chief

Elmer Gerard Pratt, more commonly known as Geronimo or "G"

of Staff, David Hilliard. This nape further stated that he in fact didn't like the manner in which the Chief of Staff conducted himself or the Party's business, and that he felt he needed to be removed anyway. He also mentioned that once his forces were together, he would also "get rid of" (assassinate) our Assistant Chief of Staff, June Hilliard.

But, the most disgraceful, counter-revolutionary, piggish and dog-like thing this pig has done is to state openly that if the Party would not go along with his ideas, he would assassinate the Supreme Commander and Minister of Defense of the Black Panther Party, Huey P. Newton.

As if this were not sufficient, he used money he had obtained through and in the name of the Party to purchase alcohol and narcotics for the purpose of indulging himself and his stupid cohorts in nightly bourgeois, orgiastic revelry. (Without the direct eye of the Party's leadership, he maintained a personally pleasure-seeking life.)

During this period - that is, prior to the arrests in Dallas, Texas on last December 8th and after he left his obvious Party tasks to avoid capture by the pigs - during this period, Geronimo 1) violated many young Black sisters he met while moving from town to town, forcing them to submit to himself and the other fools; 2) left a wide trail for the pigs to follow, thereby, exposing the Party to the pigs, by letting most of the people he met know he was a member of the Black Panther Party; 3) harassed and intimidated many of the people with whom he came into contact, by demanding their aid under the threat of their lives; 4) purchased "Christmas" presents ("Christmas" being the high holiday of the pig capitalists, particularly the avaricious businessmen; and, the period during which the masses of People are exploited in the highest,), to send to his and the others' families and friends. In addition to the counter-revolutionary nature of this particular act, he would have provided additional exposure of their location - which was to have been clandestine (secret).

Finally, Geronimo and the others who are hereby purged - Will Stafford, Wilfred "Crutch" Holiday, and George Lloyd - attempted to organize other renegades from our Party and themselves into a counter-revolutionary, little rebel roving band, certainly not adhering to the Party's principles or orders, but also violating the masses of People themselves. They are like snakes who crawled into a baby's crib. And we expel them from our ranks, as we would such snakes. We have no word of good to say for them and have faith that the People will someday let these pigs like all other burn in the Fires of Reaction.

Let it be known, then, that Geronimo (Elmer Gerard Pratt), his wife Sandra Lane Pratt or Sandra Holmes or "Red" (who worked in concert with him), Will Stafford. Wilfred "Crutch Holiday and George Lloyd are forever purged and expelled from the Black Panther Party. Any Party member or community worker who attempts to aid them or communicate with them in any form or manner shall be considered part of their conspiracy to undermine and destroy the Black Panther Party.
ALL POWER TO THE PEOPLE

Huey P. Newton

HUEY P. NEWTON
SUPREME COMMANDER AND
MINISTER OF DEFENSE
BLACK PANTHER PARTY

How these 'omnipotent' parties are throwing seeds of confusion, escapism, and have lost much of their momentum by bad tactics—in fact terrible tactics, tripping out, pseudo-machoism, myrmidonism, dogmatism, region-alism, regimentation, and fear. Thus the situation out there has become a sort of the lost leading the blind."[48]

Huey Newton had a supposed loyal supporter placed close to Geronimo Pratt. This person warned Newton that Geronimo's armed cell was planning to correct Newton himself. This alarm triggered off the purge of Geronimo and his 'rads. But Newton's loyal supporter, Melvin "Cotton" Smith, was really an agent for the LA Police Department (later surfaced to testify at Panther trials). Huey was maneuvered by the FBI into issuing orders that Geronimo be "offed."

A jubilant FBI-COINTELPRO memo sent to FBI field offices on January 28, 1971, said that Newton was going **"to respond violently to any questions of his actions or policies ... The present chaotic situation within the BPP must be exploited."**[49] Families of BPP members opposed to Oakland received FBI visits, with "friendly warnings" that their sons and daughters might be killed soon. On March 8, 1971, Panther Robert Webb was shot down in a Harlem ambush by seven armed men, who were thought to be Huey's "guns." A situation developed which was reminiscent of the assassinations that followed Malcolm's split from the Nation of Islam. Supposed "Panthers killing Panthers" was used

to discredit the rev and confuse the masses. The relationship between politics and the gun was not as folks once thought.

For a while both factions operated publicly under the BPP name, each denying the legitimacy of the other. The Oakland-based Party was just a facade of its former self, already shrunken around anti-revolutionary politics. Huey had carried the logic of his "United Front Against Fascism" to the

---

PANTHER 21 TO THE WEATHER UNDERGROUND

We wish to make known to you that we feel an unrighteous act has been done to you by the self-proclaimed "vanguard" parties by their obvious neglect in not openly supporting you—by their obvious disregard of and silence on your righteous revolutionary actions. But they have all but ignored us also—so in that respect we are in similar waters. But we wish to inform you that the most revolutionary and progressive brothers that have met within the confines of a maximum security Babylon—along with us—have considered you one of the—if not the true—vanguard within the artificial boundaries of the United States of Amerikkka at this time. You related to action—the unequivocal truth—by which revolutionaries gauge each other.

Panther 21, January 1971

limits. In December 1970 the BPP had convened a so-called "Revolutionary People's Constitutional Convention" in Washington, DC, where it had hoped to lead the Euro-Amerikan liberals and radicals into rewriting the US Constitution! This flopped, being too silly even for the petty-bourgeoisie. On a theoretical level Newton had published his "Intercommunalism" theory that the world had evolved to the point where nations no longer existed. Folks began to wonder what world Huey was in?

In New York the revolutionary wing of the party quickly moved to reorganize itself. A Bronx office became the new Central Headquarters. To replace the old *Black Panther* newspaper, the revolutionary wing began publishing *Right On!* under the editorship of Safiya Asya Bukhari (sn Bernice Jones). For two years *Right On!* served as a voice of the armed struggle. It was both lively and politically serious, and unlike *The Black Panther*, maintained a healthy dialogue. Guerrilla actions were evaluated, 'rads on the inside helped to exchange views, news from Afrika and inside Babylon spread. Expropriations and other preparations had already begun. On May 21, 1971, a BLA unit corrected NYPD patrolmen Joseph Piagentini and Waverly Jones. That was a celebration of Malcolm's birthday. Other attacks on police and police stations followed. As did counter-attacks from the political police. Safiya recalls:

"When the split went down in the Black Panther Party, i was left in a position of Communications and Information Officer for the East Coast Party. It wasn't until much later that i was to find out how vulnerable that position was.

"Most of the members of the Party went underground to work with the Black Liberation Army (BLA). i was among those who elected to remain aboveground and supply necessary support. The murders of youths such as Clifford Glover, Tyrone Guyton, etc. by the police, and retaliation by the BLA with the assassination of pigs Piagentini and Jones and Rocco and Laurie, made the powers that be frantic, and they pulled out all the stops in their campaign to rid the streets of rebellious slaves."[50]

In the new political season Eldridge's theoretical leadership was quickly revealed to be as useless as Huey's. Cleaver had been happy to run for US President for the white anti-war folks, and happy to tie up the Party doing similar nonsense, so long as it promised to promote and protect him personally. But once he fled into exile, Cleaver found it more personally advantageous to pose as the leader of a guerrilla-based national liberation movement. At least temporarily. His lumpen class orientation remained constant throughout, however.

Eldridge had been deliberately hounded into leaving the country by the FBI, which would have taken him out instead if they'd had to. In September 1968, Eldridge had been convicted of manslaughter and had his parole revoked. But the court gave him 60 days in which to report for reimprisonment. The Panther squad of the San Francisco FBI had Cleaver under constant, heavy

KATHLEEN CLEAVER ADDRESSES BLACK G.I.'S IN W. GERMANY

surveillance. The Feds could have assassinated him any night. They wanted to pressure him, to herd him into reacting the way they'd wanted. Cleaver admitted:

"This reached the point where I was afraid to sleep in the same place twice. Whenever the FBI would discover one of my shelters, they would telephone and ask for me. Sometimes this would blow my mind. If I had gone through elaborate evasive tactics and made my way to what I considered to be a 'cool pad,' then the phone suddenly rang and someone asked for me, it was unsettling, to say the least. Sometimes they would say, 'Just checking,' or 'Thought you could shake us, didn't you Eldridge.'"[51]

The political police maneuvered Eldridge into running as a way of politically neutralizing him, and also of setting the BPP leadership up for the "Panthers killing Panthers" campaign. Eldridge said: "The tactic which the authorities used against me was to keep me under constant pressure ... They 'knew' me very well. I had been State raised: I had climbed up the ladder from Juvenile Hall in Los Angeles, starting at age 12, to Folsom Prison, making all the stops in between ... I had been studied, numbered, analyzed and psyched out much more than the average person in the movement."[52]

Once in exile Eldridge's options became very different. If he had claimed to be a reformer he would have gotten nowhere. Instead, Eldridge veered "left" and asked for hospitality as a guerrilla leader-in-exile of the New Afrikan national liberation movement. The Algerian Government responded generously. Eldridge and his section were given diplomatic passports, funds, a large house that was an official "embassy." Overnight, Eldridge was elevated to diplomatic status. But for Huey and Bobby Seale, who were still in prison, the line of building a reform movement around their legal defense made much more individual sense. Eldridge and Huey were two sides of the same lumpen coin, despite their political differences on the surface.

The incipient split was furthered by the fact that the CIA's *HTLINGUAL* program was monitoring all their communications, while the FBI was using their planted agents to promote violent disunity. Panther squad FBI Agent William Cohendet said about Cleaver's being hounded into exile: "We just helped the split along … I'm sure they would have split anyway because of the personalities of the men, and fleeing took away all his chance of doing anything. He was yelling in the desert out there."[53]

At first the split in the Party took the form of each wing trying to be the only legitimate BPP. The revolutionary wing presented itself as the true Party. In that situation, the Algiers section was a de facto political leadership. Not only because Eldridge was the most prominent theoretician in the old BPP, but because he, Kathleen Cleaver, and Field Marshall Donald Cox were members of the old Panther Central Committee. This was a source of legitimacy and continuity for the new organization.

Within a year that relationship changed. The East Coast BPP became just a small support apparatus, as the main organization was the new Black Liberation Army units. Moved by Carlos Marighella's scenario of the urban guerrilla "foco," the former BPP members now had no use for "superstar" leadership that refused to join the armed struggle on the ground. The emergence of the new BLA marked the end of Eldridge's leadership, although his theories continued as an unacknowledged influence in the revolutionary movement.

While Cleaver in exile was carefully draping himself in words like "Marxist-Leninist" and "communist," his revolutionary theory was a logical continuation of the BPP's original glorifica-

tion of the lumpen. Just like Huey, Eldridge took his political road to the limit. In the first days of the split, Eldridge defined the political differences as over simply getting down, and said that the original line of the Party was correct: "Once upon a time the Black Panther Party had no problem on that level. When the Party was a small organization, it wasn't a very well-known organization, **it didn't have any political prisoners around which we had to indulge in mass activity. It was just Panthers, pigs, and guns.**"[54]

By the following year Eldridge's theoretical analysis of the lumpen as the world revolutionary class had fully developed. Interestingly enough, his views were being put forward by the same Black Bourgeois "Marxists" who were playing

such a neo-colonial role in the movement. An issue of *Black Scholar* magazine on "The Black Masses" featured two major articles justifying the lumpen theory. The first was by Eldridge, "On Lumpen Ideology." In it he explicitly attacks Marxism and the proletariat:

"... Marxism has had disastrous effects upon the revolutionary movement. Marx, misunderstanding the basic condition of oppression, identified the proletariat, the working class, as the most revolutionary element of society ... In reality, the Working Class has become as much a part of the system that has to be destroyed as the capitalists. They are the second line of resistance, after the cops. The real revolutionary element of our era is the Lumpen ..."

According to Cleaver's very lumpen consciousness, economic production was unimportant. Soon technology/automation will throw almost all of the world forever out of work, he said. Work will be unnecessary for the lumpen. The only real question was dividing up the loot: "The basic demand of the Lumpen, to be cut in on Consumption in spite of being blocked out of Production, is the ultimate revolutionary demand. What is wrong with the way that this basic Lumpen demand has been set forth in the past is that it has come out as a sort of begging, ashamed of itself ... Brainwashed with the proletarian consciousness of the working class, the Lumpen has been made to feel that it does not have any rights ... We look forward to the day when all

work can be done by technological advances, which will be a good thing. But this doesn't mean we should be blocked out of Consumption."[55]

Eldridge's crackpot theory reflected his lumpen class view, in that the social program of his struggle was "Consumption'" without having to work. It was a social program that could only have come out of Babylon. By the time that article was published, Cleaver and most of the Algiers section had formally left the new BPP, ostensibly to build an international network for revolutionary news. Soon after that he was kicked out of Algeria, moved to France and became a self-professed "Social Democrat," and was on his greased slide into the pocket of the US Right Wing.

Cleaver's worthlessness as a political leader had larger ramifications. First, in that the ambiguity of class orientation that both he and Huey had used, lived on in both the revolutionary wing, and then in the BLA itself. The second is that his line in the split, which was that the original program of the Black Panther Party was fine and only needed to be carried out, became a fundamental assumption of the new BLA fighters. In other words, both the strengths and the weaknesses of the BPP were continued into the new armed front. And thirdly, that in proving worse than useless to the armed struggle, Cleaver only reinforced the growing disillusionment among the rank and file with "theoreticians," and with all political theory itself.

The new armed front was centered around the primacy of action. Its key slogan was **"Action is the Vanguard!"** And the main theoretical influ-

*George
Lester
Jackson
9·23·41 – 8·21·71*

ence was not Mao or Cabral, but the Brazilian pioneer of urban guerrilla warfare, Carlos Marighella. This narrow focus was not correct but was unavoidable in the situation. So many, many leaders and organizations had promised Revolution, spoken of Marxism-Leninism, threatened armed struggle—and then had backed down. Or sold out. Their own Party leadership had betrayed them. So the fighters put all their efforts into finally making the military breakthrough, "getting down," overcoming individual fears and hesitations, and becoming guerrilla hunters instead of just being the hunted victims. This long-awaited breakthrough was made, even without a revolutionary party or science, but at a certain price. In their "Progress Report On Our Struggle" at the end of 1971, the armed front said:

"We learned a lot from the dissension that came to light within the Black Panther Party.

"1) To guard against personalities.
The Party made Gods out of its old Central Committee ... Instead of stressing adherence to revolutionary principles adherence to leadership was stressed ...

"2) To stop theorizing and become practitioners.
... The Party got so hung up in theory that it forgot about educating through example, by practice (Action is the Vanguard).

"3) To implement the primary objective of the Black Panther Party which is to 'Establish Revolutionary Political Power for Black People.' We had become so hung up in being the Vanguard, that we'd forgotten about the Black community."[56]

In the 1972 message *Spring Came Early This Year*, the organization and politics of the guerrillas were laid out:

"Many people are asking what is the Black Liberation Army? ... The various guerrilla groups are entirely autonomous and decentralized and do not have to wait on orders coming from the 'High Command.' There are no political commissars to these guerrilla groups, nor do we have charismatic, superstar, long distance leaders dictating policies from afar ... Our leadership is a collective leadership. Whether the task is 'collecting a compulsory revolutionary tax' from a bank, or punishing a pig by death, everyone gets down together including the 'leader.' We relate to tactical and strategic principles and not to personalities. 'Our only obligation is to act.'

...

"The BLA understands the importance of the Mass Political Movement. We are not coming from a purely military viewpoint, undermining the importance of building a strong United Front. But we must go about this in a different way. The political apparatus will have to deal with the bourgeois nationalist and the 'tribal bureaucrats' in the struggles to build a united front. For us, a 'United Front is Fire Power,' is revolutionary action, and nothing else ..."[57]

The BLA rejected Huey Newton's strategy of reforming White Amerika in favor of guerrilla war—but in fact had no new strategy of their own. War is not a strategy. The small, "autonomous and decentralized" BLA units were preoccupied with tactical problems and actions; many fighters were understandably focused on developing their own personal resources, mental and physical, to become good soldiers. How would the revolutionary war be developed? How would final victory be won? There were, in reality, no answers to these questions. The fighters were a force that had no strategy, no long-range path, and was therefore living only day-to-day.

False internationalism seemed to be no problem, primarily because the settler New Left wanted nothing to do with the "adventurist" BLA. The BLA units did have some Latino, Asian, and Euro-Amerikan allies and 'rads. These were for the most part very modest relationships, built on practical assistance without any fanfare, or on common situations as fighters. But these relationships involved very few people. Attempts by BLA units to unite with the WUO, which was seen as a very important possibility, all failed. The problem of false internationalism was not resolved, but only deferred.

In those circumstances the armed struggle was viewed as only a quantitative thing, an accumulation of tactics. The liberation war was pictured as growing numbers of guerrillas from all nations doing a growing amount of destruction,

mounting up and up until "AmeriKKKa" finally collapsed under the weight. I.e., the revolutionary task was just to destroy. As the BLA's 1971 "Message to the Lumpen" said:

> "... Dreaming of trips from rags to riches, the lumpen had spent some time dreaming the All American Dream of the shoeshine boy growing up to be President. Now that they had been convicted of a felony, that dream was dead. The lumpen had to dream up new dreams ... From this point on, the Lumpen gives up everything, including all allegiances to the living. From now on, he makes all his deals with the dead ... The Lumpen takes an oath. To kill, to destroy, in order to make the necessary room in which to build ..."[58]

Armed struggle was seen only as a matter of killing and creating havoc to bring down the Enemy. Later, after liberation, would be time for building. That non-dialectical view was widespread in the 1960s, and reflected the ideological difficulties of all young revolutionary movements.

Some revisionists unfavorably contrasted the BLA of 1970–73 to the Vietnamese liberation armies that dealt such blows to US imperialism, saying that the BLA in comparison wasn't doing any real armed struggle at all. But everything must begin somewhere. Even the Vietnamese army was once only one squad of guerrillas without any training, learning how to fieldstrip make-shift weapons. In 1947, for example, the young Vietnamese Republic was fighting to oust the French occupation. They had already formed a recognized national government. It had been eighteen years since the founding of their communist party, and eighteen years since their modern armed struggle had been initiated by the unsuccessful Nghe-Tinh Soviet of 1930–31. Did they have, therefore, a crack professional army? No, that was something they were still struggling for. Central Committee member Truong Chinh pointed out to cadres at the time:

> "Our troops are not as well trained as those of the enemy; that is why we must learn rapidly from the experiences gained in every battle, study the enemy's methods, improve our own strategy and tactics ... **At present most of our soldiers only know how to fight bravely**"[59] (our emphasis—ed.)

The difficulties of starting something new cannot be underestimated. Especially when armed struggle is the question on the agenda. The urban guerrillas of the BLA did not have a communist party, did not have a correct political-military strategy, did not yet have a clear understanding of class and nation. But against counterinsurgency raids, assassinations, betrayal by the BPP leadership, and retreat by the broader movement, they advanced into the storm. There was little time for shortcomings to be fixed, since within three years the small network of guerrilla units was smashed, most of the fighters dead or in prison, the community base neutralized. While not dead by any means, the armed struggle had encountered severe setbacks.

WEATHER
ough Wednesday, cold-
Tuesday mid 30s, high
low Wednesday near 30
upper 30s. Reservoir
winds 12-16 knots.
High 61, low 44. Pearl
Jackson 12.0 foot, down

The Clarion-Ledger

Mississippi's Leading Newspaper For More Than A Century

TE — Army Master Sgt. Daniel Pitzer, a prisoner of the Viet Cong for four years, the ball to open the 1971 American season Monday in Washington. He was substituting for President Nixon, who was on the West Coast. Secretary of Defense Melvin Laird is at left and Robert Short, president of the Senators team, is at right. — AP Wirephoto.

'Hard' Drugs Availa
Hearing Here Indic

CHICAGO MAYOR CONFIDENT OF ELECTION TO 5TH TERM

CHICAGO (AP)—Mayor Richard J. Daley, in a confident and jocular mood, predicted on the final day of his campaign for a fifth term that he will win "a substantial victory" Tuesday over liberal Richard E. Friedman, a Democrat turned Republican.

Daley, who will be 69 in May, was heavily favored to win another four-year term in City Hall and to preserve a Democratic party winning streak that dates in 1927.

Both sides expect that voter turnout will exceed one million as it has in Daley's previous four elections. The weather forecast for Tuesday is warm and sunny.

Black 'Nation' Seeks Parley

BY THE ASSOCIATED PRESS

The Republic of New Africa Monday denied it was preaching "armed insurrection" in Mississippi and called no state officials to negotiate differences "for the benefit of both the citizens of the Republic of New Africa and ... of Mississippi."

Imari Abubakari Obadele, president of the RNA, said his organization planned to "secure complete sovereignty over our land—a territory which the present white government of the State of Mississippi also, but erroneously held" claims.

pasture as its new capital, were "heavily armed with rifles and sidegum which were ... openly brandished in a menacing fashion."

"This organization has distributed in Mississippi pamphlets containing graphic drawings of how to prepare molotov cocktails, simple flamethrowers, and methods of destroying the utility systems of towns, cities and counties" Summer charged.

DENIES CHARGES

Obadele denied the RNA had distributed such material and said "all our arms are of a defensive nature and deploy-ment". The presence of armed personnel on our territory represents no more threat to peace than the presence of armed personnel on the grounds of countless Mississippi corporations all over the state"

NO U.S. REPLY

"I'm still awaiting word from the federal government," he said, "and there is nothing to be settled at the state level. I don't ... authority to negotiate ...

Heroin, Coca
In Hinds Cir

By JEAN CULBERTSON
Clarion-Ledger Staff Writer

Heroin and cocaine, two of the so-called "hard" narcotics, are now available in Jackson.

"Sale of heroin" and "sale of cocaine" were criminal charges listed against three defendants who were arraigned Monday in Hinds County Circuit Court, among a record 24 alleged drug law violators.

All of the accused pleaded innocent at the hearing on these charges and other offenses ranging from "false pretense" for alleged food stamp fraud to seven capital cases—murder, rape, and armed robbery.

Two dozen food stamp violators were indicted by the Hinds County Grand Jury which was handed down on Friday; but they had not been served with captases by Monday so the names were withheld. Court house observers doubted the cases would come to trial in circuit court and speculated they might be remanded to a lower court.

Drug violation defendants, all of whom pleaded not guilty, were as follows:

— Herman Bailey, sale of marijuana.

— Willie Bradley, violation of narcotics laws;

— Vernon Brown, sale of LSD and sale of marijuana (hashish);

— Virtis Lanier, sale of heroin

— Alex Butler alias Edward Butler, sale of heroin;

— William D. Kimbrell, possession of marijuana;

— William David Kimbrell, sale of cocaine;

— William ...

astland Bills
d Security

... Senator
astland (D-Miss.)
... uced a legislative
... he said in ...
... to bolster the
... al security laws.
... airman of the
... al Security Subc-
... the six bills
...

wholly or partly by Federal funds;

— deny tax exemptions to subversive organizations or individuals, and;

— disallow tax donations to communist organizations.

In addition, the proposed Security Offense (A) would amend the criminal code in an effort to increase security. It ... of definitions of ...

FULGHAM NAMED ALDERMAN IN YAZOO CITY RUNOFF VOTE

YAZOO CITY—Charles E. "Blackie" Fulgham, owner and distributor for a vending machine company, won the post of Yazoo City alderman in Monday's runoff election.

In unofficial but complete returns, Fulgham received 1,803 votes to defeat Eugene Ward, a Negro, who received 988. Less than a hundred votes were write-ins for Paul Stewart who was eliminated in the preferential primary. These were eliminated as unconstitutional.

In the straw vote, unofficial returns for the proposed Urban Renewal project were 1,357 against and 927 for the new plan.

Boggs Attacks FBI; Mitchell Says Lie

WASHINGTON (AP)—"The ... state is you categorically ... of FBI that everything I said today was ... I do not speak lightly ... carefully ...

"I'm still awaiting word from the federal government," he said, "and there is nothing to be settled at the state level. I don't ... authority to negotiate ...

U.S. Senate
Iron Curtain

WASHINGTON (AP)—When they ... out a voice raised against it, the ...

Group Wants Its Own 5-State Black Nation

From Herald-Chicago Daily News Wire

CHICAGO — The chairman of the legislative session explaining the basic ... of the Republic of New ... a group that peti-... Washington this week and ... ablish its own nation in ... uthern states.

... will have nothing less ... ack minds taught in ... niversities owned by ... wn; black people ... the land owned by ...

... Negro in America ... to acquire several ... man continued: ... that feeling

the wall depicting a young happy Negro couple with ultra-modern, towering buildings in the background.

The Republic of New Africa is the most recently formed of several separatist sects that have sprung up in the hearts of northern big-city ghettos.

One member said it was an offshoot of the Malcolm X society in Detroit. Another said it was a secular version of the Black Muslims. The gathering resembled a third ...

Chicago-based group called the Hebrew-Israelites, or Black Jews.

The setting was a press conference in the middle of the three-day legislative session here.

About 40 persons, mostly in African dress, sat at desks at the second-floor conference room. The morning had been devoted to the question of taxation for the new nation and debate had centered on whether the new nation should ... per cent ...

income tax.

The press briefing was conducted by five persons sitting at the head conference table. Three men, apparently guards, stood be-

His voice had a ... conviction. His words reflected the dream of a utopian society for this country's black people.

The dream was illustrated ...

hind them with widely planted feet, a wooden black fist hanging around their necks.

"We must recognize," said the chairman, Raymond E. Willis, who is minister of finance in the ... the whole country ... state of revolution ... fact, what we are ... here is an alter ... chaos."

7. INDEPENDENCE
& DEPENDENCY

At the same time that the first, "embryonic form" of the Black Liberation Army was starting military action, the Provisional Government of the Republic of New Afrika (PG-RNA) was moving South to establish itself on the Land. It was not a coincidence that two major elements of any independence movement were being focused on then—army and provisional government.

Under the leadership of its President, Imari Obadele, the PG-RNA had made a controversial and hotly debated decision to move its center out of the Northern inner cities. The RNA President had argued that only by setting up a small but functioning government on the 5-State National Territory (Louisiana, Mississippi, Georgia, Alabama, South Carolina) would the revolutionary nationalist movement offer a real hope for the New Afrikan masses. The immediate plan was to buy farmland with New Afrikan tax monies, gradually expanding and defending the area controlled. A provisional capital would be set up, continent-wide elections held to legitimize the Provisional Government as elected representatives of the Nation, a broad program of economic co-ops, New Afrikan schools, self-defense units, and other separate institutions would restructure the existing communities into a new society. The slogan was **Free the Land!**

On March 28, 1971, 150 New Afrikans held a "nation time" ceremony, consecrating 20 acres of newly-purchased land just west of Jackson, Mississippi. The land was designated as the future capital of the Nation, named El Malik after Malcolm X (El Hajj Malik Shabazz). Fifteen new citizens took the "nation oath." President Imari Obadele officiated at a New Afrikan wedding ceremony. Uniformed men and women of the Black Legion, the regular military of the PG-RNA, patrolled the perimeter with rifles. Educational workshops, a meeting of the PG-RNA's People's Central Council, and other ceremonies filled the day. The RNA caravan of twenty cars and a bus was followed to and from the land by both Mississippi state and local police plus the FBI.[60]

The nation-building campaign was taken very seriously by the local settlers. Slave revolts have always been a part of their reality. Front-page newspaper stories in Jackson warned: **"BLACK 'NATION' SEEKS PARLEY."** Mississippi Attorney General A.F. Summer demanded that the US Government stop the RNA; and moaned about **"a new nation carved out of our state …"** Arrests and police raids began to take place both in Mississippi and in New Orleans. A few days before the land consecration ceremony, ten RNA citizen-activists were arrested in Bolton, Mississippi on stolen car charges. The same night, two other RNA citizen-activists were arrested on weapons and drug charges, after a "routine" stop and search of their car. The counterinsurgency machinery was being put into gear.

On August 18, 1971, a joint force of FBI and Jackson city police, equipped not only with riot shotguns and steel helmets but with a tank, attacked two PG-RNA residences in Jackson at 6:30 a.m. At the Lewis St. residence, police shouted over a bullhorn for the "Black bastards" to come out, and only seconds later firing began on the house with tear gas grenades and firearms. But return fire ripped up the overconfident attackers. Jackson police Lieutenant William Skinner was killed, another policeman and an FBI agent wounded. At the Lynch St. residence, President Imari Obadele walked out to confront the surrounding police, and surrendered without casualties. Eleven PG-RNA citizens were arrested, ultimately to face murder charges and Federal conspiracy charges.[61]

"Nation-time" was cut down. Counterinsurgency stopped yet another New Afrikan mass organizing campaign. While the PG-RNA had tried to avoid any legal pretexts for repression, the local authorities made it clear that the lack of pretexts was merely a slight inconvenience to them. Jackson Mayor Davis said: **"Every legal possibility for forcing the RNA out of Jackson had been explored, but that Wednesday was the first chance law-enforcement officers had to move in on the headquarters."** The so-called evidence against the RNA-11 defendants was so pitiful that at first the US Justice Department wanted to drop the charges. But FBI Chief J. Edgar Hoover insisted on prosecution. An FBI memo spoke to the political significance of the case: **"If this case is not vigorously pursued and the charges are dropped, publicity in this matter will be spread to all extremist organizations throughout the US by the RNA."**[62]

The nervousness of the settler authorities to slave insurrections on the National Territory was general, and not limited to the PG-RNA. This was proven by the Baton Rouge Massacre on January 10, 1972. On that day a small group of Muslims were conducting a street rally in front of the Temple Theater in Baton Rouge, Louisiana. A crowd gathered and car traffic was blocked. Led by Police Chief Edwin Bauer a force of police and sheriff's deputies attacked the New Afrikan crowd, clubbing and shooting. Some of the pigs apparently got in each other's lines of fire, for after the smoke had cleared no arms were found on any of the arrested Muslim brothers. Two New Afrikans and two sheriff's deputies were killed. Twelve New Afrikans were wounded. Fourteen police and deputies were wounded, as were three Euro-Amerikan TV newsmen and two Euro-American civilians. Louisiana National Guard with fixed bayonets guarded the downtown area for four days afterwards.[63]

The Southern expedition of the PG-RNA was part of an elaborate strategy for winning New Afrikan Independence, worked out and tirelessly explained by Imari Obadele. Unlike most of the nationalist community, he had puzzled out a step-by-step plan for national independence. It was this that gave his leadership such momentum. Imari had spent countless hours and miles explaining his strategy to RNA groups, at conferences

and in college forums, in the pages of magazines and in pamphlets like *WAR IN AMERICA: The Malcolm X Doctrine*. He summed it up in "The Struggle Is For The Land":

"... The essential strategy of our struggle for land is to array enough power (as in jui-jitsu, with a concentration of karate strength at key moments) to force the greatest power, the United States, to abide by international law, to recognize and accept our claims to independence and land ... Chief among these strategies is the **limited objective**, an essential element in preparing before this war for a peace settlement that is an African victory."[64]

Imari's "War in America" strategy was to catch the US Empire in the jaws of a threat, pressuring the Empire with the threat of unendurable disaster. And then use diplomacy to settle for: "not fifty states, or twenty-five states, or even ten states ... We are saying five states, taken together the poorest states in the nation ..." Imari predicted that giving up these few states would be acceptable to "the white American ... when he is forced to the point where giving up something will be a necessity." Of course, these five Black Belt states are the historic National Territory of the New Afrikan Nation, long populated by and economically developed by the New Afrikan people. As Imari pointed out:

"We have lived for over 300 years in the so-called Black Belt, we have worked and developed the land, and we have fought to stay there—against night riders and day courts, against cultural genocide and economic privation, against bad crops, and no crops. Against terror and ignorance ... we have met all the criteria for land possession required of us by international practice, international law."

This strategy visualized the new Nation initially growing within the present political system of the "u.s.a.," carefully following the imperialist laws, buying land, gradually taking over the entire Kush (the fertile Mississippi River Delta area of Mississippi and Louisiana). And from there organizing a plebiscite to declare itself the legitimate government of the 5-state area of New Afrika. Many folks thought this plan certain suicide for its organizers. Imari himself raised the point: "But are we naive enough to believe that ... this violent, racist United States ... will be successful in achieving laws which effect a peaceful plebiscite and the peaceful ceding of the land to New Africa?"

Imari Obadele (sn Richard Henry) was one of the remarkable "Henry brothers." The family, which in 1966 was named as the Urban League's "Family of the Year," included Dr. Walter Henry, Jr., chairperson of the Howard University Medical School; Attorney Milton Henry, former City Councilperson of Flint, Michigan and a prominent nationalist; and Rev. Lawrence Henry, a Baptist pastor in Philadelphia. Imari Obadele had worked as a journalist, and for some years was a technical writer for the US Army's tank facility near Detroit. He had become president of GOAL (Group On Advanced Leadership), a militant Civil Rights organization in Detroit which his brother Milton had helped lead. Imari became a "Malcolmite" following Malcolm's break with the Nation of Islam.

To understand where his views came from—really, what their framework was—we have to see that Imari was not one of the young 1960s radicals. He was of an older generation, influenced by the bourgeois nationalism of so many 1950s Afrikan independence movements. Reliance on diplomacy, lobbying at the UN, and establishing one's legal position as the true government-to-be were considered very important. After all, even such militant independence leaders as Kwame Nkrumah of Ghana and Julius Nyerere of Tanzania had been conceded power without ever having to fire a shot. This older generation of nationalism here in the "u.s.a." focused on building some outward forms of nationhood (elected officials, diplomatic plans, acting as statesmen, etc.). They confused the situation in Afrika with that of the settler "u.s.a.," the heart of world imperialism. US imperialism was not willing to dismember its central fortress, nor hand over nations here as a tactical concession.

The key to Imari's strategy were the two threats which he hoped to hold over White Amerika's head. The first was international alliances with friendly nations. Indeed, Imari believed that these alliances would be so powerful that they would immobilize the US Government. First among these would be a military alliance with China. Imari predicted that **"the possibility—however remote, however logistically difficult—that Chinese troops might, if asked by us, make an appearance in the battle area with us ..."** would force a settlement.[65] Especially since friendly Afrikan nations would at the same time be seizing US property. Even more potent, he wrote, would be: **"The presence of Chinese nuclear subs in the Gulf of Mexico, supporting Black people in Mississippi who have well made their case for independence and land before the United Nations ..."**[66]

Threat of nuclear war by China, together with the threat of invasion by their army, would give the new nation considerable military support. As Imari said: **"Alliance with China is therefore of utmost importance."**[67]

Today it may sound crazy, particularly to a younger generation that did not share those fast-changing times, to think that the Chinese government would risk war to assist New Afrikans. But there really were ties of solidarity then between the New Afrikan national liberation movement and the Chinese government of Mao Zedong. The Chinese government had proudly given refuge to Robert Williams and his family, as official guests of the People's Republic. Williams was given every material assistance in sending his revolutionary messages back to the "u.s.a." Moreover, Williams, who was elected as the first President of the PG-RNA, was officially recognized by the Chinese as a national liberation leader. The Mao Zedong government publicly supported New Afrikan revolutionary nationalism.

And if the US Government decided to attack the RNA anyway, there was still the second threat looming over them. That, according to Imari's strategy, was the so-called Second Strike capability of massive urban destruction in the North: "... There are over 120 major cities where the brothers have used the torch ... The Black man has, or can develop, the means for destroying white industrial capacity and—if need be—white Amerika in general as mercilessly as a missile attack."[68] That threat alone, Imari believed, could **"bring the United States, finally, to the Negotiating Table ..."**

There was a direct and inescapable link between this strategy and the successful repression of the PG-RNA. Previously we have seen how petty-bourgeois elements hostile to national liberation worked to disarm the masses through defeatism. But defeatism, like all ideas generated by the imperialist culture, is constantly around us as a part of daily life in Babylon—in schools, on television, in neo-colonial political theories, in bourgeois reform politics, and so on. Defeatism exists within the revolutionary movements as well, as an influence sometimes stronger and sometimes weaker. There is no air-tight seal around the movements that automatically keeps out imperialist infections; therefore, genuine revolutionaries as well are influenced by defeatism, sexism, individualism, and other views dominant in the oppressor society. We all have to struggle with this.

Backward and unscientific theories on how to win liberation not only lead to setback after setback, but they are unable to overcome neo-colonial influences. Imari's "War in America" strategy was conceived of to fight defeatism about the New Afrikan Nation, to make folks see how real the possibility of independence was. These noble intentions gave it a certain strength of purpose. **Yet, because of its unscientific character Imari's strategy itself was defeatist, and contained disarming attitudes within it.**

To begin with, Imari saw liberation coming not from New Afrikans but from others. In particular the People's Republic of China. If the world's largest nation is going to put nuclear missiles and its huge army on the line for you, then you hardly need to defeat imperialism yourself. Imari is explicit on this point, that only other nations and peoples can free New Afrikans. It is well known that China has always said that no nation should look to it or anyone else to win its revolution for them; Mao always argued that each nation must practice self-reliance in revolution. In addition, it is hardly desirable to ask other nations to engage in brinksmanship with World War III and a nuclear exchange. So the scenario of liberation by Chinese nuclear benefactors was always an illusion born of desperation.

Nor is it true that a host of friendly nations could put such pressure on US imperialism that it would give up the National Territory. No oppressed nation in history has had such a world chain of revolutionary alliances as Vietnam had. Those alliances were very important, but they couldn't replace the Tet Offensive. Our Vietnamese comrades had to overcome the largest air force bombardment in history, fight elite divisions of the US Army to a standstill, and then defeat a million-soldier puppet army. Imari's "Defense of International Alliances" was an illusion. However difficult the path, liberation cannot come from others.

That strategy embodied the stage of development, the contradictions, and the two-line struggle that characterized the movement as a whole. A plan that bravely set out to defy the greatest Empire in the world, was paradoxically built around the conviction that White Amerika was militarily all-powerful. Over and over, Imari warns his people that they cannot withstand **"destruction beneath certain and overwhelming Federal power."**[69] Guerrilla warfare in the Northern ghettoes is, he explains, not only militarily hopeless but might touch off settler genocide that would wipe out New Afrikan communities:

"First, thoughtful militants know that the Northern cities—where the warfare was fought for the first three years—are indefensible over the long run … The compactness of Black-occupied inner cities in the North lends these cities, once surrounded, to classic and brutal military sweeps. Indeed, with the Black man no longer an economic necessity in the United States—he is, in fact, for the white man, a decided inconvenience—the temptation to 'solve the problem' by wholesale slaughter in

Black communities under siege may be too great for the average white leader to resist."[70]

That is why the PG-RNA strategy in the South never actually planned to wage war against the US Government. President Imari Obadele warned that the Black Nation could never win militarily: "Separation is militarily possible, ultimately, because of diplomatic considerations ... Against the overwhelming power of the United States, against which no single state nor group of five states is sufficient ... Indeed, these alliances may prove our only guarantee of continued existence."[71] At most, he saw the PG-RNA military only doing a temporary holding action against US attack, until these other pressures would get Washington to the bargaining table.

Therefore, the PG-RNA military arm, the Black Legion or later New Afrikan Security Force, was designed to be a public, highly visible, "legal" militia. Black Legionnaires wore military fatigues and carried rifles and shotguns. Obvious sitting ducks for any US repression, they were planned primarily to fight small groups of Right-Wing civilian settlers. As Imari said: "Our biggest threat comes from the white civilian armies, the Ku Klux Klan ..."[72] Not from the FBI, CIA, and US Army.

So the "War in America" strategy was first a "legal" campaign. While President Imari believed that the US Government was "overwhelming," militarily invincible, he also believed that the supposed democratic safeguards of the US Constitution and the imperialist courts would protect the infant Republic of New Afrika. This was a good example of the contradictions in the movement at that time. For these reasons the PG-RNA built, politically and militarily, in a way that was dependent on bourgeois legality. Just as the BPP did. Looking back afterwards, Imari has recalled his thinking:

"Somehow, i think now, in the back of my mind there was a lingering belief that, with fearless and bright lawyers, it would be possible to use the contradictions in their law to defeat them even in their own courts ... I thought that if the Mississippi Supreme Court would not do it—and it did not—certainly the US Appeals Court or the US Supreme Court would do it.

"In my mind, in a recess, there must have lingered the phantom of a group of dispassionate appeals judges—white United States-ers, to be sure, but nonetheless fair and distant ... coolly weighing the facts and the crystal-clear law."[73]

The '60s revolutionary thinking didn't fully understand New Afrikan people's capacity to liberate themselves. It underestimated them while being too trusting in the imperialists. So Imari's strategy depended on liberation coming from others, while also depending on the imperialists to extend "democratic rights" to the anti-colonial Provisional Government. This is an example of how backward and unscientific revolutionary theories cannot overturn defeatism, dependency, and other neo-colonial views.

From this vantage point we can see the similarity (as well as the differences) between the

PG-RNA and the Black Panther Party. Both put forward a military strategy that was actually based on using threats to avoid combat. Both tried to build a "legal," highly visible, uniformed military. Both believed in the imperialist courts and bourgeois legal process as a vital protection for New Afrikans. Both saw their contradictions exposed in the savage process of US counterinsurgency.

The comparison is valuable for another reason. Many nationalists believed that the main pitfall was relating to Euro-Amerikans. For that reason many nationalists criticized the Black Panther Party's alliances with white radicals and liberals. Some nationalists in the '60s claimed that they couldn't get subverted, because they had no relations with white people. The PG-RNA itself originally had only minimal ties with Euro-Amerikans, primarily because settlers weren't too eager to relate to them. But instead of depending on white liberals or radicals for liberation, as the Oakland BPP did, the PG-RNA substituted a dependency on China and other Third World nations. The issue isn't white people; it is the dependency, and other backward viewpoints on how liberation can be won. Not whether one has or hasn't alliances. These problems in no way negated the historic contributions of the 1960s revolutionary organizations. The founding of the PG-RNA, for example, made the goal of independence from the oppressor society much clearer. It gave liberation a definite political shape, and refuted the lie that New Afrika wasn't an oppressed nation.

8. DIVIDING THE NATION VS. UNITING THE NATION

False and backward theories of how to get liberation, even revolutionary ones, counterpose class vs. nation and emphasize one at the expense of the other. It has often been feared that pushing proletarian ideology would lead to disunity. Yet, despite many years of forming Black united fronts along backward lines, under petty-bourgeois political leadership, there is still much potential unity but no developed unity. Even within revolutionary nationalist ranks, chaos and disunity abounds. **We say that the proliferation of false and backward theories about liberation promotes disunity and divides the New Afrikan Nation.** This can be proven.

Correct ideas must come from **conscious struggle**. In the 1960s the New Afrikan National Movement grew, progressing rapidly from Civil Rights to Black Power, nonviolence to armed self-defense, integrationism to revolutionary nationalism. In all cases powered by the irreconcilable contradictions of captive nations within the US settler empire. The New Afrikan masses pushed things ahead mightily by uniting in rebellions. The rebellions were "festivals of the oppressed," showing in practice the power of millions of New Afrikan people uniting against the oppressor. **Never since has there been so much New Afrikan unity.** And it came from the grassroots of the Nation.

The masses produced actual unity, and yet the Movement has never been able to recapture that elusive power. After the urban rebellions of 1967–68 peaked, the forward progress slowed and then stagnated. Because building revolutionary organization, building national unity and People's War, cannot be done by mass spontaneity alone. At that point new progress waited on conscious political development to end "the dark night of slavery." The new stage requires revolutionary science, which is a major task and a conscious struggle against all false and primitive political theories. Not only within others, but within ourselves. Which is why Biko correctly raises the importance of "the worker culture."

The old Movement helped usher in dramatic changes, unseen since the first Reconstruction of the 1870s. Many sacrificed in the struggle, many died or went to prison. The masses were thrown back. Yet it is also true that the colonial petty-bourgeoisie, even the radical protest leadership, has achieved significant class gains. Joseph McNeil was the leader of the first four Greensboro Woolworth sit-inners, whose arrests on Feb. 4, 1960, sparked off the whole Southern Sit-In Movement. Because of the gains of the struggle, McNeil could go on to become Major McNeil, US Air Force. He could become a B-52 navigator and take part in the terror bombings of North Vietnam (before leaving for an executive career with IBM).[74] John Lewis, former Chairman of SNCC, is now an Atlanta City Councilman. Ivanhoe Donaldson of SNCC is now an aide to Washington, DC Mayor Marion

Barry, Jr., Howard Fuller (aka Owusu Sadauki), once one of the main nationalist youth leaders of the Afrikan Liberation Support Committee, is now in the Cabinet of the Governor of Wisconsin. There are enough examples to fill a book.

Even though the colonial petty-bourgeois still suffers from oppression, the US ruling class has tried to slightly lift them up so that they can help keep order in the disintegrating urban "Bantustan." Bobby Rush, former Minister of Defense of the Illinois BPP and the man whose weaknesses set up Fred Hampton to be guarded by a police agent, is currently a member of the Illinois State Legislature. The contradictions can be seen in an obscene way in the "COINTELPRO" case of Amiri Baraka. In June 1979, NY police arrested Baraka for allegedly beating his wife outside a Greenwich Village nightspot. The Barakas said that the racist police took advantage of a non-violent argument to vamp on Amiri Baraka. A very large national defense campaign was waged. Baraka himself wrote a long, autobiographical appeal for Euro-Amerikan support in a New York City *Village Voice* article titled "Confessions of an Ex-Anti-Semite." Benefits were put on to raise funds for Baraka, who was said to be a victim of an "FBI COINTELPRO" operation.

Baraka was finally convicted in November 1979 of resisting arrest, and sentenced to **90 days** on Rikers Island. This was certainly not something that would have happened to a prominent Euro-Amerikan professor and author. It was put out that Baraka was a political prisoner. His

TV: Documentary Film Examines Amiri Baraka

...screen, no sound, just words, sol- words. They say that for two dec- ...Mr. Baraka has been "a major controversial figure in the politi- ...and cultural life of America," ...the documentary "cove... ...two weeks before his sente... ...ederal court on the charge... 're- ...ng arrest'" a few years a...

...t then to the outside of a co...fort- ...old house. Inside, a boy is prac... ...g on the drums, the sound invad-

Mr. Baraka of resisting arrest. A month later, he was sentenced to 90 days and ... ...Mrs. ...d her husband was "a p... ...prisoner." In fact, he was re... leased the next day pending an appeal of the conviction. If he stayed in jail, it was noted, he would be unable to at- tend a reception at the White House in honor of American poets.

The appeals process went on ... ...Colonial Co... ...ate Su- ...preme Court. The documentary, in...

Amiri Baraka sentenced to 90 days

supporters said that if he had to serve his 90-day sentence he might be assassinated by the State just like George Jackson. According to the press, what moved the judge, however, was Baraka's complaint that if he went to jail he would miss a White House reception with President Carter to which he had been invited.[75] So Baraka was first released on bail and later allowed to serve his 90 days only on the weekends, staying home during the week.

The colonial petty-bourgeois leaders compare themselves to Malcolm and George, but have been allowed to serve in the "Big House." Their fate is not assassination or long prison terms, but first pick of the table scraps and lighter blows. For them "things have never been better." But this is not true for the New Afrikan Nation as a whole, and for the oppressed classes within it. False lib- eration programs based on neo-colonialism have **widened** class contradictions within the Nation, and **further separated** the "haves" from the "have-nots."

This was not just **external** to the old Movement, but in fact **internal** to it. Perhaps the clearest, most significant example of how false and primitive theories divide the Nation and promote disunity is the widespread thesis that liberation is a male thing. **In particular, the old Movement slavishly echoed the oppressor opinion that New Afrikan women were "too strong" and that it was the task of New Afrikan men to hold down and weaken New Afrikan women.** So much of the old Movement worked with fanatical zeal to keep half the Nation effectively out of the Revolution. Many false and primitive theories were put out promoting male supremacy. It became fashionable in the media, in the Movement, and on the streets for men to degrade and exploit women. Terms like "bitches" and "whores" became how many men were convinced to talk about comrades and sisters. Young men so oppressed by the richest Empire the world has ever seen that they could not afford to support their children at all, were subtly told to abandon them without any second thoughts.

The attack on New Afrikan women was also directed at New Afrikan children, and at the social fabric of the Nation. New Afrikan women, after all, were supposedly too strong and needed to be pushed down. Much of the old Movement started to be corrupted by the social views of Daniel Patrick Moynihan, the CIA, and Hollywood—but re-labeled those views "Afrikan revolutionary," "communist," or "nationalist."

This trend was evident from the beginnings of the 1960s Civil Rights Movement. New Afrikan women were systematically restricted and excluded from expressing leadership. In the old Movement, many Black leaders were convinced that even colonialism was better than recognizing the legitimate strength of New Afrikan women. This was not an unconscious attitude. **Among pro-imperialist leaders the need to manipulate New Afrikan men into repressing New Afrikan women was very conscious.** Andy Young was upfront in admitting that he worked at that, even saying that Rev. Martin Luther King, Jr. was too influenced by his mother:

"We had a hard time with domineering women in SCLC, because Martin's mother, quiet as she was, was really a strong, domineering force in the family. She was never publicly saying anything but she ran Daddy King, and she ran the church and she ran Martin, and Martin's problem … was directly related to his need to be free of that strong matriarchal influence. This is a generality, but a system of oppression tends to strong women and weak men."[76]

Again and again we hear it implied that the strength of New Afrikan women comes from colonialism, and somehow helps weaken New Afrikan men. Any fool can see that the slavemaster never wanted any strong New Afrikans, and that the strength of New Afrikan women has come from their drive to ensure that New Afrikan people as a whole survive into freedom. If Andy Young is right that Mrs. King had a lot to do with Martin Luther King, Jr.'s role as a leader, it's easy to see why imperialism fears what New Afrikan women will do when they stand up. And act not through men but through themselves.

We should note that while Malcolm X had very traditional ideas about sex roles within the family and so on, he was always open about accepting the strength and co-leadership of New Afrikan women in the struggle. It was Malcolm, after all, who singled out Gloria Richardson of the Cambridge, Maryland Movement for praise as an outstanding grassroots leader, when she was under so much sexist attack. Malcolm's closest political advisor and his first real mentor was his sister Ella Collins. Muriel Feelings, a former OAAU member, recalls:

"Among the core of people in the OAAU, some of the most hard-working were women who had skills, good skills. He had no problems with women having ideas or asserting leadership. All he cared about was that things get done ... Perhaps Malcolm's attitude was a little bit unusual than that which typified, I really hate to say this, the nationalists, but he was a very open-minded person."[77]

In that period perhaps only Fanny Lou Hamer and Mae Mallory were accorded recognition for their leading roles. In most cases New Afrikan women were driven out of leadership, even if the organization had to be destroyed. Gloria Richardson was isolated and harassed, even being shouted down at a rally as a "castrator" by male CORE members. Ella Baker, who held together SCLC and SNCC in the early days, said: **"There would never be any role for me in a leadership capacity with SCLC. Why? First because I'm a woman ... And second ... I know that my penchant for speaking honestly ... would not be well tolerated."**[78] How many folks in the struggle have said that?

Gloria Richardson, Cambridge, MD.

Even the Organization of Afro-Amerikan Unity (OAAU), Malcolm's organization, was killed rather than accept women's co-leadership. Sister Ella Collins tried to hold the OAAU together after Malcolm's death, but too many men in the young organization dropped out rather than acknowledge a woman's leadership. Men became convinced that Malcolm's program was not that important.

That's how beneficial it was for imperialism to use false and primitive theories to divide the Nation. What was the cost of abandoning Malcolm's program and political momentum? As the struggle stagnated and lost its forward progress this issue became a non-issue to the old Movement. Folks talked privately about these problems, but in public everyone agreed that nothing was wrong—the king had clothes. This became completely out of hand.

To take one example, useful because it was public. In 1977 Joseph Waller (later name: Omali Yeshitela) of the Afrikan People's Socialist Party was taken into court by his ex-wife for not paying any child support for his three children. He was worried about adverse public reaction, especially since settler judges and newspapers in Florida liked to smear New Afrikan activists. Omali Yeshitela was a leading Civil Rights activist in

Ella Collins and Malcolm X

Florida during the 1960s. At the start of the Black Power period he led in forming JOMO—the Junta of Militant Organizations—which was repressed out of existence. Following that he formed the APSP in his hometown of St. Petersburg. It was one of the earliest Black socialist groups. Their program has evolved, and currently features a type of "Pan-Afrikanism" that denies any separate nationhood for New Afrikans in the "u.s.a."

So his party issued a "Special Free Edition" of their newspaper, *The Burning Spear*, solely devoted to Waller's argument that his wife was an unwitting tool of "FBI COINTELPRO."[79] He said that the whole thing might have been "taken by the state on its own initiative …" Joseph Waller said that even if he had any child support money he wouldn't use it for his own children, or any New Afrikan children, since his publishing activities as a New Afrikan leader took priority for him. Everyone understands how if a rev is in prison, underground, temporarily tied up with a special project, etc. they may not be materially able to help his or her family. But would Malcolm X have said that supporting his children was not his responsibility **especially because** he was a New Afrikan leader? Would Malcolm have published a "special free issue" of a newspaper and passed out thousands of copies, all to denounce his ex-wife in public? If you decide not to support your children and your ex-wife demands financial help, do you cry for public sympathy as a victim of "FBI COINTELPRO"?

In the first place, such false and primitive views espoused by the colonial petty-bourgeoisie and lumpen do not unite the New Afrikan Nation but divide it. Communism recognizes the importance of women's liberation in really freeing the masses for revolution and nation-building. How can any of the oppressed be "too strong"? Where do such views come from? Did they come from the holds of the slave ships? Did they come from the plantations where "Moses" Tubman was staging guerrilla prison-breaks? Did they come from the millions of New Afrikan children whose survival has so often depended upon the strength of New Afrikan women? Did they come from the heroic tradition of the BLA where Safiya and Assata played such a role? Where can such ideas come from, if not from the oppressor, however well-disguised?

Secondly, the question has even deeper ramifications. New Afrikan women are not just roles within a household. In their work holding together families and communities they maintain a communal tradition within the long time in Babylon. To repress and politically restrict New Afrikan women is to disorganize the proletariat and its surviving independent culture. There can be no liberation without women's liberation, no proletarian leadership without women's co-leadership. That's why Vietnam could survive the sea of fire and throw off the most repressive Empire in world history.

The old Movement **divided** the Nation in that it had no program for the proletarian masses, only a program of promotions and careerism for the colonial petty-bourgeoisie. In the exact same way it had no real social program for liberation, since without Women's Liberation all social programs became only different versions of capitalism. That's why some "nationalists" preach the social doctrine of Daniel Patrick Moynihan and the CIA, and think it "Afrikan."

The other side of the same imperialist maneuver was to promote bourgeois feminism as the answer for New Afrikan women. The Ford Foundation, *Ms.* magazine, government agencies, etc. all push this. New Afrikan men are hit with staggering joblessness as imperialism is screening them out of the workforce. On the other hand, New Afrikan women who have some education have been given jobs that a generation ago were reserved for white women—retail sales clerks, bank tellers, typists and clerks for major corporations. These are lower-level jobs, of course, although a handful of "exceptional" New Afrikan women are allowed to become professionals and supervisors. New Afrikan women are being told to think of themselves and their careers first, just as their settler "sisters" do. This bourgeois feminism seeks to assimilate New Afrikan women as individuals into the oppressor culture—how to get in the corporate "fast track" for promotion, how to wear the latest Euro-styles of "designer" clothing, etc. It tries to disunite the Nation by telling New Afrikan women to find their political future in the white women's movement or in imitating it. This imperialist strategy only feeds on the backwardness of a liberation movement that tries to deny women's liberation.

IX. Nyack—The Road to Nowhere

There is a nodal point that marks the final playing out of the contradictions of neo-colonial politics within the 1960s revolutionary movements. **That point was the founding of the Revolutionary Armed Task Force (RATF).** By nodal point we locate where the quantitative development of a thing becomes qualitative, dominant or characteristic of the whole. In RATF neo-colonialism finally became dominant. The New Afrikan elements within RATF had turned away from the New Afrikan proletariat to merge with an element of the petty-bourgeois Euro-Amerikan New Left. And those Euro-Amerikans fled from the criticisms, political struggle, and difficulties of their own movement to instantly elevate themselves as the only whites "heavy" enough to be within the New Afrikan Liberation Movement. Instead of communist politics—which instructs that problems are solved by **"going deeper, down into the oppressed masses"**—RATF tried to relaunch the armed struggle by petty-bourgeois integrationism. Not surprisingly, RATF also represented the FBI's most successful penetration of the New Afrikan Independence Movement.

RATF became front-page news with the failure of its $1.6 million Brinks expropriation attempt near Nyack, NY on October 20, 1981. Within hours it was being flashed coast-to-coast as an extraordinary event. A merger of elements of the old Black Liberation Army and elements from the old Weather Underground Organization surfaced in the national news. The bourgeois press reacted in a predictable way: the *Readers Digest*, for example, called its round-up article on RATF, "Terror Network, USA." And the *New York Times* headlined its main story "Behind the Brink's Case: Return of the Radical Left." The Times centered on the personal stories of the arrested **"former Black Panther and Weather Underground leaders, now in their middle 30s, who returned suddenly and dramatically to public attention after a decade in which their names had been largely forgotten."[1]**

Peter Middleton is a traitor. He was nothing before the New Afrikan Independence Movement gave him a life and he is a dead man now. The movement made him a doctor and taught him how to heal the ravages of colonial terror against the Black Nation. He fought drugs. The movement taught h... how to prepa... Black people for war to be healthy, strong, able to defend the... ...the Nation.

2...

The special importance of the Nyack action to us is that it was a nodal point. RATF represented a last attempt to make the exhausted politics of the '60s work, by boldly combining the remaining resources of several small organizations, New Afrikan and settler, into one more military-political offensive. Although each represented only a small element in their respective movements, their alliance exposed fundamental problems. While organizational remnants may go through the motions of repeating over and over again what hasn't worked before, to us the failure of RATF is the end of an entire, undeveloped way of approaching revolution. It proves more conclusively than any words can the need for new, deeper, and more developed politics.

There are several reasons why the Nyack case and RATF have not been publicly evaluated by the movements (as opposed to limited circulation critiques by participants). In general, the '60s movements have usually been reluctant to put out any serious analysis of military work. The usual reason given is security. We strongly disagree here. The political-military situation is obscured with smoke—artificial smoke. Movements are told almost nothing about the real situation, no real political-military programs are put forward, no serious explanations or criticisms of setbacks are made. **On the other hand, the State knows far, far too much.** The revolutionary organizations have few secrets from the State, just from the people. This is what is mistakenly called "security." We believe that the artificial smoke, which is now only the cover for bad politics, must be blown away.

The other reason for keeping the Nyack action smoke-screened was the widespread fear of demoralizing people in already-weakened movements. **In other words, cadres try to hold things together by "putting a good face on things."** New Afrikan revolutionary nationalists politically associated with RATF have certainly tried to do this in the past. After the main Brinks trials in 1983, which ended in the defendants being convicted with long sentences, and after the public existence of the flippers and informers was widespread, the *New Afrikan* (journal of the PG-RNA) ran major stories proclaiming the trial as a victory. Headlines read **"New Afrika Wins!"** and **"After US-Brinks' Defeat."**[2] At a Los Angeles meeting on August 21, 1982, a representative of the National Committee to Defend New Afrikan Freedom Fighters tried to downplay Nyack as just one incident:

"And finally, Brothers and Sisters, let's not dwell on the negative. Because if we've been looking at, in any way, what has been happening in the press, even the crackers themselves have to acknowledge that although what happened in October of '81 may not have been a success, our Brothers and Sisters, our combatants have had numerous successes prior to that event. Now you gonna tell me, you gonna abandon the struggle because of one setback?"[3]

That is an example of what can go wrong with "putting a good face on things." Everyone can appreciate the need for revs to keep morale up, to orient folks positively to moving forward. But

if you can't tell the basic truth to the people, you aren't giving correct leadership. Nyack was not just "one" setback amidst a growing stream of military successes. **It exposed a major political defeat.** What that political defeat was, how it happened, its relationship to the respective strategies of one group of Euro-Amerikan fighters, an element in the Black Liberation Movement, and the imperialist security forces, is too important to the future not to bring into the daylight.

By mid-1983 Euro-Amerikan RATF combatants Judy Clark and David Gilbert, together with the May 19th Communist Organization, had struggled to reach a self-criticism of their initial "… stand through the first year and a half that claimed October 20th as a victory, promoted a multi-national model of the Revolutionary Armed Task Force, and fought against doing serious self-criticism in the face of mounting losses and the emergence of traitors and corruption within the ranks."[4] We can see that the problems involved in RATF went far beyond the usual security or tactical errors. That is, Nyack was not primarily a matter of a tactical setback, but rather a strategic one.

WHAT WAS RATF?

RATF was a "Black–White" alliance, under New Afrikan leadership, whose immediate political goal was to take over direction of the revolutionary nationalist movement. New Afrikan cadre and fighters were veterans of the BPP, PG-RNA, and BLA, struggling to survive and turn their 1971–73 defeats around. The Euro-Americans were from WUO and the NY pfoc, which became the May 19th Communist Organization. The correct part of their intentions were to reverse the past flightism of their Movement, to finally act fully in solidarity with national liberation fighters. Unfortunately, that was only a part of it.

The New Afrikan leadership involved believed strongly in revitalizing the urban guerrilla forces that relate to one faction of the Provisional Government-Republic of New Afrika. But they blamed the low state of both the PG-RNA itself and the armed movement on the then-current leaderships. They held RNA President Imari Obadele's strategy of "prematurely" setting up a nation-building center in the Deep South as primarily responsible for the setbacks of the early 1970s and the PG-RNA's loss of momentum. Similarly, they felt that the existing BLA-CC structure, much of which was inside the kamps, to be righteous but hopelessly misled. In both cases they believed that the incumbent PG-RNA and BLA-CC leaderships were incompetent at best, roadblocks to the Black Revolution.* Their highest priority, then, was to remove these obstacles, as they saw them, to revitalizing things. RATF was not just a series of armed actions, but actions guided by and serving a definite political tendency, the faction of the PG-RNA that is at present part of the New Afrikan People's Organization, in its efforts to gain hegemony within the movement. May 19th Communist Organization chose to ally itself to one faction against the rest of the liberation movement.

---

* There has been some confusion over the BLA. Confusing statements have been put out that the Black Liberation Army is divided into different "wings," one of which is in support of the PG-RNA (and was in RATF). This is apt to create misimpressions. Originally, the BLA was composed of "autonomous and decentralized" units, with a variety of different political views. In the mid-1970s a "Call to Consolidate" was issued, to create a unified organization. The majority of the BLA who accepted consolidation formed the BLA-CC (Coordinating Committee). The minority who did not agree with consolidation formed a completely separate group. We use the term BLA to refer to the "autonomous and decentralized" units before the Call was issued, BLA-CC to refer to the consolidated structure of the 1970s, and BLA-RATF to refer to the minority who united with the ex-WUO people. Contrary to any misimpressions, the BLA-CC did support the PG-RNA but was not involved in the factional struggle within it. It is misleading to think of the BLA as one organization with different "wings."

There was considerable criticism of RATF's integrated composition within the nationalist community, once it became known after the arrests. In its defense, RATF and its New Afrikan supporters justified the relationship as a limited, practical necessity in fighting the armed white right. This, incidentally, is the same line used in the mid-1970s by the old WUO, which tried to justify itself by falsely claiming to be initiating clandestine operations against the Klan and other white supremacist groups. As one RATF supporter put it:

"I am for National Liberation for Black people but I am also not a fool. Now if we're serious, if we're serious about talking about dealing with the Ku Klux Klan, if we're talking about dealing with these white paramilitary organizations, then we know we have to have intelligence. Show me somebody Black that's gonna infiltrate the Ku Klux Klan, huh? We have to

have intelligence. The role of allies are to perform those tasks that are difficult that we cannot perform. Our white allies have been doing this."[5]

That, of course, wasn't true. Over five years of practice was the proof. The New Afrikan–led RATF struck no blows at the armed white right or at killer cops. **"Our white allies" were recruited primarily to strike at other New Afrikans.** Euro-Amerikan funds, public support, lawyers, defense committees, petty-bourgeois privileges and connections, were all considered and used as factional advantages in a drive to defeat other political tendencies and finally assume overall leadership of the revolutionary nationalist movement. May 19th Communist Organization used the excuse of "following Third World leadership" to isolate themselves from criticism both from other white people and from other New Afrikans.

So RATF was not just a matter of a few Euro-Amerikan combatants joining a New Afrikan guerrilla unit. Far from it. The entire East Coast pfoc, renamed the May 19th Communist Organization, was incorporated into one wing of the PG-RNA and placed under nominal New Afrikan command. Integrating the New Afrikan movement was incorrect, and it was very different from supposedly having "white allies" infiltrate the KKK for you. It wasn't the Klan that was infiltrated.

Under RATF's strategy the Euro-Amerikan May 19th Communist Organization quickly became ever-present in their new movement. Settler anti-imperialists marched in Harlem demonstrations, spoke at Harlem political meetings, became behind the scenes support staff, and played an active role in opposing other New Afrikan political tendencies. Just like the old Communist Party USA in the 1930s.

EVALUATING RATF'S MILITARY WORK

For five years RATF led a charmed life, as the saying goes. Major expropriations and other actions were pulled off. On November 2, 1979, RATF removed Assata Shakur from a New Jersey prison in one of the most important military actions of the 1970s. Three days later a large Black rally for Black Human Rights at the UN Building listened to Assata's tape-recorded message of solidarity from underground. RATF seemed to have made a breakthrough. By combining New Afrikan fighters with Euro-Amerikan organization, which furnished initial funds, obtained vehicles and weapons, set up safehouses, did tactical intelligence, and helped drive vehicles during actions, the BLA-RATF seemed to have found the key that earlier BLA units lacked. **Even the Government confirmed this, saying publicly that integrating the BLA made it much more powerful.** One Justice Department investigator later praised RATF in a typical comment: "By acting together they were more of a menace than we realized."[6]

That all changed sharply on October 20, 1981, when RATF was setback in its attempted $1.6 million Brinks expropriation near Nyack, NY. Four RATF members were captured while leaving the scene that day. Those arrests made RATF front-page news coast-to-coast, since one of the four was famed Weather Underground fugitive Kathy Boudin. **Within hours RATF began unraveling under rapid-fire blows from the FBI.**

On October 23, 1981, two RATF fighters were overcome by police in a Queens shoot-out. One, Mtayari Shabaka Sundiata, was killed.

Like falling dominoes, Nyack triggered a series of setbacks and arrests, with each new FBI advance producing the intelligence for the next wave of arrests. Within hours of the attempted expropriation, FBI forces began cracking RATF safehouses. People who had had contact with RATF began receiving FBI visits. It soon became obvious that the security forces had extensive knowledge of RATF, including lists of telephone numbers called, supporters' names, and so on. On January 21, 1982, Kuwasi Balagoon was captured by the FBI's "Joint Terrorist Task Force" in the Bronx, NY.

There was a brief tactical slowdown in the FBI offensive as they set up the next round of arrests. For four months the FBI maneuvered to let the aboveground RATF members use FBI-tapped telephones and FBI-bugged meeting rooms. On March 26, 1982, the FBI raided the Black Acupuncture Advisory Association of North America (BAAANA) in Harlem, and associated residences all over NYC. More RATF members and supporters were arrested. During this period RATF tried mobilizing mass support for defense campaigns, and was surprised to find that it had very little. By that point RATF as a New Afrikan military operation was finished, having been crushed with relative ease by the FBI.

The defense campaign was undercut by the well-publicized defection of captured New

Afrikans: Tyrone Rison, Ema Rison, Peter Middleton, Solomon Brown, Yvonne Thomas. It was a new thing in the Black Liberation Movement for so much betrayal to take place. In case after case—the RNA-11, the Wilmington 10, the Panther 21, the many BLA units that were cracked, etc.—New Afrikans historically have withstood setbacks and imprisonment without giving way. Even in enemy hands, the public steadfastness of fighters Sekou Odinga and Kuwasi Balagoon and the courage of patriots such as Yaasmyn Fula and Shaheem Jabbar was in that heroic tradition. But it is still true that the amount of betrayal in RATF was a shocking exception from this culture of resistance. It also became publicly known that part of RATF had been involved in cocaine use and dealing. Despite its early show of strength, despite its endorsements from Euro-Amerikan Anti-Imperialists, RATF was decayed at its heart.

A handful of May 19th Communist Organization fugitives continued as best they could, although in relative isolation. Again, like dominoes falling in a row, the May 19th fugitives fell in the Winter and Spring months of 1984–85. Susan Rosenberg and Tim Blunk in New Jersey, in November 1984. Marilyn Buck and Linda Evans on May 11, 1985, in New York. And finally, Alan Berkman and Elizabeth Duke in Pennsylvania on May 25, 1985. Because of the political isolation of the armed struggle at this time, the security forces have also been able to use proliferating Grand Jury investigations to force activists and supporters into prison on contempt charges, bypassing the necessity for criminal charges and trials.

The failed Brinks expropriation of October 20, 1981, was the point at which the political initiative openly passed from RATF into the hands of the security forces. How could one tactical setback produce such a change?

RATF, for all its apparent armed successes, was very brittle. It was a hollow structure that collapsed under the first blow. This was not technical but political; not tactical but strategic. Much criticism has centered on the many security lapses. While important (and also equally present in other organizations today) these were effects rather than a cause. The problem was that RATF believed that the old revolutionary politics of the 1960s could still be made to work. **They believed that the defeat of the '60s Movements was because their politics were never fully applied, due to the combination of white flightism and Black lack of resources.** By adding these two missing factors while combining their respective strengths, RATF believed that the defeats could be reversed. RATF was the most backward, neo-colonial aspect of the old '60s politics in action.

RATF was not just a "Black–white" alliance. It was a **class** alliance of people who, though from different nations, shared petty-bourgeois/lumpen class politics. Just as in the 1930s, when the revisionist Black intelligentsia chose to unite with the settler petty-bourgeois inside the Communist Party USA—as opposed to uniting with their own proletarian and peasant classes. Why did some New Afrikan leaders want to build on this isolated handful of Euro-Amerikan middle-class people? The millions of the Black proletariat have every skill and physical resource needed to sustain the liberation struggle—knowledge, cars, arms, apartments, intelligence, access to technology, etc.—plus the life-or-death need to find an answer outside Babylon.

Further, Marxism-Leninism is not an abstract philosophy or a set of rules. It is the revolutionary science of a specific class, the world proletariat, and its development in a national situation is only possible as part of the political development of that proletariat. In turning away from the New Afrikan proletariat, the New Afrikan leadership of the RATF affirmed their non-communist, neo-colonial politics. They were unable to reach the Black proletariat because they had antagonistic class goals. They united in RATF with the people who they had the most in common with, petty-bourgeois/lumpen from the oppressor nation.

RATF was **not** a clandestine organization in the Marxist-Leninist sense (although it was armed and illegal). **Its organizational and political**

focus was aboveground. While a small number of fighters (and Kathy Boudin) were clandestine fugitives, a larger number of RATF members and even leaders were aboveground. **Nor were they anonymous.** They were well-known, under their true identities, as leading activists and supporters of one faction of the nationalist movement and the BLA-RATF. Their New Afrikan activities were centered in one very "hot" Harlem nationalist health facility, while their Euro-Amerikan activities were centered in the equally "hot" May 19th Communist Organization. Neither the people nor the politics, nor the relationships, were at all hidden from view.

In a classic example of one style of work that emerged from the '60s, by day May 19th leaders were the most public white supporters of urban guerrilla warfare (BLA, RAF, FALN, etc.) in New York City, and by night they slipped away to **be** the guerrillas they supported during the day. If that didn't fool the security forces in 1968, why should folks have thought the state would be fooled in 1980? Judy Clark, for example, was put forward by the PG-RNA in their newspaper, the *New Afrikan*, as an exceptional white woman. She toured the country making speeches supporting RATF and one tendency of the PG-RNA. Was anyone who followed the struggle surprised that she was in RATF? There is nothing **clandestine** in a serious sense about such a primitive, "radical chic" style of work that clearly relied on being exceptionally privileged.

THE EFFECTS OF POLITICAL BACKWARDNESS

The political backwardness of the RAFTF was the deciding factor in all areas of its practical work. While RATF and its supporters promoted itself as **"a qualitative advance in the military response to US imperialism,"** and put RATF forward as the revolutionary leadership for all struggles in the continental US Empire, RATF's shared politics were actually very backward.[7] This can be seen in the 1983 Euro-Amerikan self-criticisms around RATF, which were certainly the product of much painful examination and struggle. While those self-criticisms accept responsibility for some errors, they still shy away from admitting what they really did. Limited self-criticism is still used as a tactic, if only unconsciously, to ward off taking responsibility for the political defeat. To hide its real meaning.

The political line of the 1983 self-criticisms by Clark and Gilbert, as well as the May 19th Communist Organization, was simple: 1. Accept criticism for mistakenly intervening within the BLM, trying to join it as exceptional white people rather than struggling to change the settler movement. They do not admit to having to learn from other white people, or to having to **change themselves**. Nor do they admit to the opportunistic game they played, where they proclaimed some New Afrikans as the supreme leadership of the New Afrikan Nation—and then those same New Afrikans turned around and returned the favor, proclaiming the May 19th-WUO folks as the leading white revolutionaries.

2. Completely separate from the first point, vague statements that "the revolutionary movements" have to overcome unspecified "internal weaknesses" to deal with traitors, drug use, and pimping-prostitution of women. **Which** movements, **who** within these movements, and **what** weaknesses is never said. This is clearly a touchy matter for RATF people. In their self-criticism, Clark and Gilbert treat this awkward subject with self-protective vagueness: "Over the past two years, corruption in the revolutionary movements—the use and tolerance of drugs and pimping—has come to light; and a new revolutionary morality is being fought for ... Prostitution, pimping and the tolerance of both are counter-revolutionary—they work against our ability to build revolutionary struggle."[8]

While the Euro-Amerikans appeared, on the surface, to nominally accept some responsibility by the repeated use of the plural phrase "the revolutionary movements," that was not true. Their real position was to place the blame on the BLM and criticize themselves **only** for being liberal in not raising criticisms of the BLM—i.e., "clean hands." Since the only publicly reported cases of flipping, drug use, dealing, and pimping involved Blacks, to be vague was to support the belief that these degenerations were solely a Black phenomenon. Their vagueness and lack of self-criticism played right along with the imperialist media campaign that portrays New Afrikans as all pimps,

violent criminals, dope dealers—"animals" in the popular settler expression. Euro-Amerikan RATF supporters were heard to put out pointed comments like: **"At least none of the white people have become informers"**—implying their moral superiority compared to the BLM.

Two things are true: that the New Afrikan Liberation Movement has not 50% responsibility, not shared responsibility ("the revolutionary movements"), but 100% responsibility for **all** political weaknesses and moral degenerations within its own ranks—which unfortunately includes RATF; that the Euro-Amerikan "allies" do not have clean hands in this matter, and have 100% responsibility for the degeneration in their own ranks. Even the attempted evasions are transparent: "The use and tolerance of drugs and pimping ... has come to light; a **new** revolutionary morality is being fought for." What "new" morality do they mean? Is it "new" to communism that selling drugs, pimping, and the sexual exploitation of women is a crime? Was it "new" to Harriet Tubman in 1860? Was it "new" to Malcolm in 1960? Was it "new" to Ho Chi Minh? Who was it "new" to besides RATF and the May 19th Communist Organization? To see that these politics are very, very backward in revolutionary terms is not difficult.

We have to go back and **unite** the two, disjointed parts in their 1983 self-criticism: settler "Anti-Imperialist" intervention inside the BLM and security weaknesses and "moral corruption." It's clear from all descriptions of the flippers and informers that the BLA-RATF had an excessive number of weak, confused, and opportunistic people inside it. The number of the traitors, in relation to just one unit, was qualitatively significant. Peter Middleton, who had a long history with this grouping, was revealed to be a cocaine addict who was embezzling movement funds. Tyrone Rison is a lumpen mercenary who while in the US Army tortured Vietnamese women. Yvonne Thomas, the wife of Mtayari Shabaka Sundiata, was said to have long been mentally ill. And so on. In every oppressed community under imperialist occupation there are damaged people, there are politically unenlightened people, there are people who for various reasons are only tactically or temporarily siding with the Movement, etc. That was true in Ali Aponte's Casbah in 1955, as well as in Harlem in 1985. That these people exist around and in the struggle is simply the real world.

But how did a unit with so many treacherous or damaged people get to be thought of as "a qualitative advance in the military response to US imperialism" (to quote May 19th)? The small New Afrikan nucleus that started RATF had their roots in the Black Panther Party, the RNA, and the early armed struggles. Like so many others, they were stranded after the 1971–73 defeats by the unresolved class contradictions of their Movement, which had left the armed struggle in disarray.

Imperialism's neo-colonial counter-offensive in the 1960s had struck most heavily at the New Afrikan proletariat, tearing up and dislocating neighborhood after neighborhood. In the chaos, warlordism grew to fill the social vacuum. The large monies from the growing narcotics trade became, as in old China, the material basis for layers of mercenary armed groups parasitic on the masses. Stranded fighters increasingly found the "street force," the source of their new recruitment in the 1960s, tied up in warlord organizations. At the same time so much of the petty-bourgeois leadership was using the neo-colonial road to escape the ghetto, personally and politically.

In those circumstances many stranded fighters reduced themselves to surviving as just another small armed group within the overall subculture of warlordism. Expropriations for personal funds together with drug dealing became major activities. Political drift and the individualistic erosion of warlordism took their toll on some individuals. Just as in warlord China at the turn of the century, at a time when the masses of armed men and amount of armed violence is at an all-time high within the Nation, the liberation struggle is in disarray and has relatively few forces. The stranded fighters, like all other sectors of the Black Nation, needed the rise of New Afrikan communism to resolve these contradictions.

There was no offensive on the part of the one New Afrikan faction prior to RATF because they were mostly just trying to stay alive, politically and personally. There was not enough organized support in the community to sustain them in an exchange of blows with the State (i.e. there were small handfuls of fighters, but there was no revolutionary infrastructure among the people to sustain guerrilla operations). This is not just weakness, but a sign of transition between old and new and the inability of the old movement to meet the demands of the masses.

In this period many revs complain, if only privately, about the lack of support from the people. A superior attitude is adopted towards the masses, such as: "We're out here fighting, risking ourselves for you, but you aren't supporting us the way you should." This is one-sided and subjective as a position. In many ways this lack of support is also a positive element in change. **Sometimes when the Movement doesn't have enough popular support that's because the masses are right not to give it.** Sometimes that's a message from the grassroots. RATF, to use one example, didn't need support from the masses. First, they needed to either clean their own house or go out of business.

BLA-RATF's political center was at a drug abuse clinic, they preached to the people how drugs were imperialist counterinsurgency to poison the New Afrikan Nation—yet some of them secretly took part in and/or condoned cocaine use and dealing. One standard for the New Afrikan Nation and a second, degenerate standard for the New Afrikan petty-bourgeois/lumpen elite. Why should the New Afrikan masses have supported such a mess?

Whether or not that small New Afrikan armed nucleus would have made any inner transformation is moot, since the intervention of the May 19th Communist Organization short-circuited any such possibilities. That small nucleus never was forced to transform themselves or die politically. Because when their leadership recruited May 19th to join them, it provided

an alternative, artificial answer to their practical dilemma. With a complete Euro-Amerikan organization providing money, safehouses, cars, weapons, intelligence, assistance at armed actions—to say nothing about arranging public forums after the actions—**what did BLA-RATF need the New Afrikan Nation for?** RATF could freewheel totally away from the rest of the revolutionary nationalist movement, including other fighters, and the masses of the New Afrikan Nation. The withholding of support by New Afrikans, including other revs, no longer could restrain and temper a small armed group that was still politically confused.

So what the May 19th people called being "allies" was actually substituting themselves for the New Afrikan Nation. An arrogant and foredoomed conceit. By helping to launch a guerrilla offensive with such an imaginary foundation they only created another certain military defeat, another certain political victory for the State security forces. **RATF was an artificial construct, alien to the New Afrikan masses, that boosted an unstable group into the spotlight as a supposed armed vanguard.** False internationalism helped put Tyrone Rison into the position to betray so much. What united RATF was not internationalism, but shared false internationalism. Thus, settler intervention within the New Afrikan liberation movement, neo-colonial attitudes within the Movement, poor security, weak military organization, and abuses of revolutionary morality are not separate problems, but interrelated aspects of the same backward politics.

POLITICAL DEFEAT AT THE HANDS OF THE STATE

The amateurishness that has plagued all revolutionaries in the US Empire was shown in the political defeat of the Revolutionary Armed Task Force. We mean no put-down by the use of the word "amateur"; it is a scientific description of revolutionaries who have not succeeded in reaching a **professional** revolutionary level. Communists define professional revolutionaries by one measure—ability to combat the political police. RATF was totally out-planned and out-maneuvered by the State security forces, despite the courage and fighting ability of individual RATF fighters. **The FBI had a superior grasp of strategic political-military factors, and was playing a deeper political game.** Which was how they could not only wipe RATF out militarily, but inflict a stinging political defeat.

Often setbacks, even major ones, are turned around by the struggle. The imprisonment of Leonard Peltier, for example, has become an international rallying point to build greater support for the Native Amerikan struggle. But in this case weakness cannot be turned around without a full understanding of how revolutionary amateurishness and neo-colonial attitudes are linked, and how they led to a political-military defeat at the hands of the State security apparatus.

RATF hoped that its growing public visibility, their record of pulling off action after action, would be powerful armed propaganda to help relaunch themselves. Instead, at the end of the contest, it was the FBI that had scored a dramatic political-military blow and walked off with everything:

1. The State security forces used the crushing of RATF to falsely put themselves forward as all-powerful. For five years they had withheld their fist, waiting as RATF built up its image. By 1981 RATF was claiming to be the only armed vanguard of the New Afrikan Liberation struggle. Much of the nationalist movement and most of the settler anti-imperialist supporters backed RATF, which had removed Assata Shakur and carried her endorsement. So when the imperialist security forces defeated RATF in rapid-fire blows after October 20, 1981, it was dramatic propaganda. Not only that RATF was militarily overcome in well-publicized arrests and raids, but that the State security forces crushed RATF so quickly, so easily and decisively. "The bigger the build-up, the bigger the let-down."

2. FBI exposure of the moral corruption within RATF was perhaps the most damaging political blow. It was a propaganda coup to be able to smear the New Afrikan Independence Movement and the BLA as being associated with cowards, traitors, confused people, drug dealing, and pimping. **This was worth any price to the imperialists.** To degrade the Revolution of its moral superiority, its integrity in the eyes of the masses, is the worst blow of all. The enemy knows this. That is why the FBI tried unsuccessfully in

the 1960s to portray Rev. Martin Luther King, Jr. as a "moral degenerate." That's why "Hill St. Blues," "Miami Vice," Hollywood movies, imperialist media in general all portray revolutionaries as vicious "terrorists." When RATF failed to maintain proletarian standards of morality while at the same time pushing itself forward as **the** armed vanguard, it was only blindly playing the FBI's game. As were all those who supported RATF.

3. Once the State publicized **who** made up RATF it was an automatic setback. **The grassroots of the New Afrikan Nation has never asked for and has never supported these alliances of New Afrikan men and settler women.** No matter how well-intentioned, such distorted alliances have both sexist and neo-colonial aspects. The May 19th Communist Organization, which was primarily women, recreated the customary male-dominated movement only with New Afrikan men instead of white men. There was a pattern of such alliances in the 1960s and 1970s, in many solidarity committees and anti-imperialist groups, as radical white women broke with white men but not with patriarchal ways of seeing the world.

4. Playing on political weaknesses, the State security apparatus got the most celebrated defendant to disavow armed struggle explicitly and the BLM implicitly. Defendants who refused to turn their backs on the liberation struggle, such as David Gilbert and Judy Clark, were given extremely heavy sentences (ranging up to 75 years). But Kathy Boudin, the most famous of all the Brinks defendants, worked out a deal for a heavy but lesser sentence. In return for some leniency, she had to express public remorse over the deaths of police and guards, plead guilty, and disassociate herself from armed struggle. This confession was heavily publicized in TV news, newspapers, and the white Women's Movement press. Her lawyer explained their decision as "pragmatic."

EXCEPTIONAL WHITE PEOPLE

As her trial neared, Kathy Boudin's defense began one of those media blitzes that WUO/radical chic do so well. The plan was to win settler public acceptance of her as a nice, middle-class white woman who accidentally got involved in Black violence because of her youthful humanitarianism. *Mademoiselle*, the upper-class fashion magazine, ran a five-page story presenting her in a very mushy, sympathetic light. *Mademoiselle*'s interviewer and Kathy, talking in the Goshen jail, found out that they had so much in common:

"Her cheekbones are high, her lips chiseled, her hair short, a little tousled. No makeup. Her voice is very low. 'You look like someone from my generation,' she says. 'How old are you?'

"We have things in common: my father was a biochemist, a professional like hers. I was in Harvard's student and women's movements when she was organizing the welfare mothers in Cleveland. I finished graduate school; she

started law school ... Her eyes rest on me warmly as I talk. She is still, very attentive. Her smile—a kind of encouraging smile ... The talk turns to books—as it often does when talking with friends, although in this context even so small a thing is charged with significance. 'Yes, I read here a lot,' says Kathy. Mainly books by black women writers like *The Color Purple*, by Alice Walker. She's loaned them to the other women and to some of the guards ..."[9]

When questioned on it, Boudin refused to express support for either the BLA or Kuwasi Balagoon's statement that the Brinks action wasn't robbery but a revolutionary expropriation. She did willingly tell *Mademoiselle*, however, that even before her arrest she had already decided to surface, to return—as she put it—to **"her own people."** A similar, although much more political, sympathetic eleven-page interview in the liberal *Village Voice* was important in that it set forth her position of **"feeling terrible about the loss of lives,"** both police and New Afrikan, as well as being concerned about the **"suffering"** of the policemen's families. The *Washington Post* ran a major interview as well. This media blitz was a carefully orchestrated campaign using her family's exceptional connections. It paid off, impressing her trial judge and playing a role in his decision to let her repent.[10]

This opportunistic vacillation characterized her part of the Brinks defense. On the one hand, Kathy Boudin did not want to become an informer and give up her standing as a revolutionary. On the other hand, she claimed the right to maneuver around politically and make whatever deals with the State she could to get some sentence reduction. In the final deal she agreed to plead guilty and repent in return for a 20 years to life sentence (first parole in 18 years). She also took (and passed) an NYPD lie detector test to back up her claim to have never in her whole life engaged in violence against the Government. While she admitted to being captured fleeing the expropriation, she stressed to the court that unlike the others: "I was unarmed throughout."

In addition to repeating her position of repenting the deaths, Boudin had to recite aloud in court a statement jointly worked out with the State: "I have led a life of commitment to political principles, and I think I can be true to those principles without engaging in violent acts."*[11]

The State security apparatus was quite satisfied with that. It was good propaganda for them to have a prominent settler radical, underground for 12 years, publicly beg them to be considered nonviolent. The security forces always like to make a display of weak people. And Kathy Boudin's new image as a submissive white woman, respectful of imperialist authority, was used politically against the other defendants. The imperialist media gleefully played up her "sorrow" over police losses and her deliberate distancing herself from the other "terrorist" defendants.

The rest of May 19th did not deal with this vacillation. In large measure because it was just one side of a common position. **All three of the Euro-Amerikan Nyack defendants insisted on their personal right to be exceptional white people.** Judy Clark and David Gilbert actually claimed to be Prisoners-of-War. By late 1983 they were criticizing themselves for having stuck to that unreal position for a year and a half, until pressure from the liberation movement forced them to see how untenable it was.[12] Kathy Boudin was just a different version of being an exceptional white person: one who could be a WUO fugitive for years, but also be conveniently nonviolent; one who claimed that everything she did was motivated by her love for Black people, but who also was free to give the State propaganda against them.

None of these exceptional white people were willing to criticize each other, no matter how wildly different their stances, as their relationship was built on mutual self-protection. For years other Euro-Amerikans had told May 19th

---

* Typical of her vacillating stand, on her next court appearance for sentencing Boudin read a statement saying: "I was there out of my commitment to the Black liberation struggle, and its underground movement. I am a white woman who does not want the crimes committed against Black people carried out in my name." She and her supporters are trying to use this after-the-deal statement to maintain her image as a radical.

how misdirected their interventionism was. But May 19th claimed to be so exceptional as an organization that it didn't need to learn from other Euro-Amerikans or even answer their political criticisms. Just like the WUO.

On their part, Judy Clark and David Gilbert have now admitted the error of claiming for so long to be POWs, and have placed that error as originating in their thinking of themselves as exceptional white people working within the New Afrikan Liberation Movement. **We need to help deepen that self-criticism.** They said:

"We changed our positions as a result of a larger process of struggle to open up the errors of our strategy and line … Addressing these errors made us look at the problems of our defining ourselves as POWs. As New Afrikans organizing around the case argued to us, our position of multi-nationalism undercut the anticolonial character of their struggle."[13]

This was a very limited self-criticism; one that was still grudging and self-protective, holding onto the backward politics of Nyack. While no one except a few misguided people ever thought that Judy Clark and David Gilbert were really POWs,

this question is too important to handle carelessly. The political struggle by New Afrikan liberation fighters to gain recognition of their status as POWs is not a personal question. Recognition of POW status is recognition of the existence of the New Afrikan Nation and its War of Independence. For two Euro-Amerikans to jump up and tell the world that they, too, are POWs just muddied the waters around the issue. Judy Clark and David Gilbert treated being POWs as a revolutionary prestige symbol, as being "heavy." Being a POW says nothing about someone personally, just that they are a captured citizen/soldier of the Nation. Which these two captured comrades definitely were not.

This was not an innocent error on their part. It was not due to lack of simple understanding. **Nor was it honest ignorance on the part of their New Afrikan "allies," who shared their errors.** Judy Clark and David Gilbert say nothing about them, still trying to cover up the neo-colonial nature of the relationship. The question of **who** are POWs, the respective definition of POWs and political prisoners, was not a brand new issue in 1981. It was not a mystery.

What makes this error so heavy is that during the mid-1970s the New Afrikan prison movement and the BLA-CC struggled through precisely these definitions of POWs and political prisoners. Major documents were written on this subject. Those comrades did this out of necessity, to give greater clarity to their Movement and to prevent the individualistic confusions that RATF willfully

fell into. So for Judy Clark and David Gilbert to make that error—and stubbornly refuse to see it for a year and a half—meant that they knowingly refused to listen to the political guidance of the Movement. They only reconsidered when their New Afrikan "allies," who were feeling the heat from the grassroots, urged them to. But the rest of the liberation movement was so unimportant to Clark and Gilbert that they could willfully ignore its political decisions—even though, as they admit, they were operating **within** the New Afrikan movement. **"Allies"** shouldn't look the same as **"divide-and-conquer."**

The fact is that the rank-and-file of the revolutionary nationalist movement **never** approved of integrating their movement, and never approved of RATF. And the grassroots never approved of any of this. This is well known.

So Judy Clark and David Gilbert were still not seeing the main point in their error—**that they were involved in neo-colonial politics against the wishes of most of the nationalist movement and the grassroots of the New Afrikan Nation.** Sliding your way illegitimately into another nation's liberation movement, disregarding the political guidelines of revolutionary activists, fighters, and prisoners, refusing to heed or even answer any criticism except from your selected "allies" is nothing but neo-colonialism. That it comes from Anti-Imperialists is only worse. What does that have to do with the heritage of Malcolm? The primary error is not with confused Euro-Amerikans, but is the unresolved neo-colonial influences in the liberation movement. Alliances based on these politics are so disastrous not because alliances are wrong, per se, but because these are cases of **false internationalism.**

Judy Clark, David Gilbert, and others had struggled to reverse the flightism of WUO, and cross the line into armed struggle. That they did so is an achievement. Unfortunately, they and May 19th as a whole did not overcome the WUO's neo-colonialism, but only continued it onto a higher level. It is so important to criticize their errors (while it is relatively unimportant to criticize the errors of a Bob Avakian or Irwin Silber), because these are weaknesses still embedded within the Revolution.

AMATEUR STRATEGY & NEO-COLONIALISM

The Revolutionary Armed Task Force's inability to withstand the political police, their amateur strategy of **non-clandestine** armed struggle with politically un-reliable forces, had its roots in neo-colonial attitudes. While their New Afrikan leadership was not inexperienced, being veterans of the armed struggle, no amount of practical expertise can make up for neo-colonial misorientation.

RATF's amateur strategy was based on the thesis that the defeat of the '60s Black Liberation Movement was the fault of apathetic Euro-Amerikans. By 1977 they were putting forward the line that the 1971–73 BLA defeats were **mainly** due to lack of Euro-Amerikan radical support. **In other words, that white supporters were the decisive factor in the New Afrikan Revolution.** Basing their military strategy around this neo-colonial error led to terrible consequences.

To evaluate RATF we need see not only its own strategy, but the **interrelated strategy** of the State security forces. Some comrades have advanced the hypothesis that RATF was a "pseudo-gang"—a State-controlled dummy guerrilla unit—and that it was no accident that so many traitors and confused people were incorporated in it. While we have no evidence that this is so, it is beyond any doubt that RATF was at least a State-tolerated and monitored counterinsurgency operation. What is called an **"encapsulated gang."** We should explain more fully what this is.

"Pseudo-gang" tactics were systematized and popularized by General Frank Kitson of the British Army, during the suppression of the 1952–56 Kenyan Revolution. But they were by no means invented there. "Pseudo-gang" use in counterinsurgency has an extensive history. In the 1946 Huk rebellion in the Philippines, CIA experts formed "Force X," one of the most famous "pseudo-gangs."[14] The CIA's "Force X" even included real wounded men, and briefly penetrated the Huk underground to identify sympathizers, set up traps for real guerrillas, and visibly commit criminal acts while posing as guerrillas. "Force X" specialized in stealing from peasants and abusing women, while supposedly being guerrillas.

A "pseudo-gang" is made up of traitors and mercenaries, who use the cover of being an entire guerrilla unit to penetrate the struggle and disrupt it from within. Sometimes only imperialist agents make up the dummy unit; in some circumstances the "pseudo-gang" recruits honest new revolutionaries and honest sympathizers as an even deeper layer of cover.

In its most sophisticated form, this becomes the "encapsulated-gang." That starts with a genuine revolutionary cell or unit, with a bona fide record in the movement, **which has mistakenly let the State security apparatus completely encapsulate it in a bubble of surveillance.** As the "encapsulated-gang" goes about its work, maintaining contacts and communications, the State security forces use it as a guide dog to map the underground. Knowing the unit's plans and activities, it is easy for the security forces to arrange for informers to be at the right times and places to be recruited into it. No one doubts the legitimacy of the **"encapsulated-gang,"** since its leading members have a solid history in the Revolution. Unaware revolutionaries become as agents and don't even know it.

The next-to-final step is for the security forces to permit the "contaminated" unit some successes to boost their image and lull any suspicions (while at the same time perhaps arranging setbacks for political rivals), so that they can play a more leading role in the struggle. The security forces actually want this "encapsulated-gang," which provides invaluable intelligence and which can be wiped out at any time, **to play as central a role as possible.** "Contamination" is promoted.

Permitting the State's "encapsulated-gang" to kill some soldiers or police, or bomb things, or even pull off a big armed action, is a cheap price to pay for infecting the heart of a revolutionary movement. This is true in all penetration operations. There are many examples: On October 8, 1969, Brazilian guerrillas took over an airliner with 44 people aboard and escaped to Cuba. It turned out that the CIA secretly knew all about this major action beforehand. With the prior approval of US National Security Advisor Henry Kissinger, the CIA had permitted the Brazilian guerrillas to successfully pull off the action. This further set up the position of their agents, who on November 4, 1969, finally trapped and killed Carlos Marighella, the famed guerrilla leader.[15] A hijacking in return for Carlos Marighella was a good trade for the CIA

It is **necessary** for the imperialist security forces to permit or even arrange for their "encapsulated-gang" to do successful actions. Otherwise the unit would be discredited or arrested. **The stakes are quite high in these operations.** In the Fall of 1957 the FLN, the Algerian national liberation front, bombed the French military headquarters in the most heavily guarded area of Algiers. This action received great publicity and was joyfully received by the hard-pressed Movement. Coming as it did right after bitter setbacks, the death of guerrilla organizer Ali Aponte and the setback of the FLN guerrillas in the city of Algiers, this action signaled an attempted comeback.

The new FLN Military Commander for the East Algiers Zone (Casbah), "Safy-le-Pur," was one of the few surviving guerrilla veterans in the city. His new actions, daring and well-publicized, confirmed his leadership. Soon many new people were recruited, as the urban guerrilla underground was rebuilt out of the ranks of sympathizers. **Only, the entire East Algiers FLN unit was an "encapsulated-gang."** "Safy-le-Pur" had survived because he was a traitor working for French intelligence. He was the one who had betrayed Ali Aponte. To promote the role of the "encapsulated-gang" and give it necessary cover, French intelligence had permitted the bombing of their own headquarters.[16] It was a cheap price

to pay for an "encapsulated-gang" operation that eventually took the lives of literally thousands of Algerian patriots.

The point is that the imperialist security forces are capable of sophisticated tactics and strategies, boldly carried out with considerable deception. That, after all, is their job.

None of this was really understood by the RATF leadership, who were concentrating on trying to make their own strategy work. RATF was not just a physical alliance, not just a simple joining of forces. It was itself a special political-military strategy, a child born of the 1971–73 BLA defeats. The one small unit of New Afrikan fighters that would initiate RATF found themselves stalemated by 1975. Underground they were only a surviving handful. Aboveground they were more numerous, but still small, with a precarious base in Harlem community health work. **But they knew that the FBI understood who and what they really were, and was keeping track of them.** As veterans of the Black Panther Party, the RNA security forces, and the first BLA units themselves, the aboveground people were well known to the State and were still among the "hottest" people in New York City.

They had learned the hard way from the BLA setbacks in 1971–73 that their very small forces with a small network of known supporters was not capable of withstanding a full FBI counter-offensive. Around them they had seen small units of isolated BLA fighters, usually recently released from prison, just go into activity and get wiped

out. That was a dead-end that only burned up scarce fighters. Yet without taking the political-military offensive again, they foresaw that the armed movement would just grow weaker and fewer in a downward spiral. That was the trap that RATF was designed to burst out of.

The new strategy that would be embodied in RATF grew out of the relationship between those New Afrikan fighters and East Coast elements of the Prairie Fire Organizing Committee (pfoc) and former WUO members. These New Afrikan revolutionaries had envied the relative immunity from repression that settler radicals had. WUO's long record of going without casualties or even arrests was noted. They saw how the FBI's harassment of anti-war activists (including WUO members) was reined in by the liberal Establishment, with media scandals and even demotions of FBI officials. To them the amount of privilege that settler liberals and radicals had was so great as to force the State security apparatus to keep "hands off," for fear of more Watergate type public explosions. The ability of Euro-Amerikan radicals like Judy Clark to get some public support for lawsuits against past FBI COINTELPRO break-ins and surveillance, only further convinced them that they were on the right road.

RATF's strategy was to take advantage of that settler privilege in two ways. The first was to form an integrated "Black–white" military unit, **which the FBI would inescapably know about but would have to keep away from.** Kathy Boudin and Judy Clark would be a shield for the

BLA-RATF, using their settler privilege to supposedly hold off repression. Second, bringing as large a part of the ex-WUO under New Afrikan leadership as possible, forming a settler front that would mobilize liberals against any anti–New Afrikan counterinsurgency drive by the State. **The New Afrikan RATF leadership believed that petty-bourgeois settler "allies" could evenly counterbalance the power of the settler political police.** The reformist strategy of Huey Newton and the Oakland BPP, of dependency on white allies to survive repression, had never been overturned, and now infected even armed struggle. Old politics still helped shape new alliances, however unconsciously.

Holding off the FBI—together with the plentiful resources that settler organizations would provide the BLA-RATF fighters—would hopefully give them space and momentum to establish stronger roots. This particular unit had for years tried to set up ties with the WUO, and with the breakup of WUO in 1977 was at long last starting to recruit anti-imperialists. By 1978 the entire May 19th Communist Organization was nominally under the direction of New Afrikans.

This was **not** a clandestine relationship. Far from it. **The very RATF strategy called for settlers and New Afrikans to organizationally intertwine as closely as possible and as publicly as possible—to warn the FBI off.** By 1978 the New Afrikan RATF leadership felt certain their risky strategy, which was admittedly very unpopular within their Movement, was working.

They summed it up: **"The FBI is afraid of us because they know we control May 19th."** A more amateurish understanding of the political-military situation is hard to imagine.

By that point RATF, which was seemingly successful in an escalating series of armed actions, was living in a fools' paradise. Aboveground RATF people would organize armed struggle support rallies as public leaders, and then slip away to work on the next armed action. Nothing was really clandestine. The ritualistic pretense of security in such a fools' paradise was like a narcotic, making some feel stronger as they got weaker. It is possible that traitors helped maintain the political confusion. **In any case, the amateurish misestimation that "The FBI are afraid of us" directly sprang from a neo-colonial awe of the magical power of white people—and the neo-colonial error that white people are the answer to the problems of the New Afrikan Nation.**

THE OTHER SIDE OF PROTRACTED WAR

The political-military disaster of the Revolutionary Armed Task Force was in a long-term sense healthy, like a hard blow awakening revolutionaries out of their amateurish games and daydreams. It is possible that the State security forces made a major miscalculation around RATF, showing too much of their real methodology. Perhaps the enemy became over-confident, thinking that people would never catch on to how they work despite repeated beatings.

What imperialism is doing is simple—it is called **protracted war.** Whether revolutionaries do it or not, the State security apparatus is right now conducting war 365 days a year, year in and year out. This is currently a **one-sided war**, with all the political strategy, military offensives, and total command of the battlefield being held by only one side. **A one-sided war is still a war.** Just because people are not together or ready doesn't mean that the State security forces are going to call a time-out. Although they always like revs to think that they are not really active whenever revs don't see them. **"Out of sight, out of mind"** is the motto of the amateur revolutionary.

The imperialist security apparatus has been through many wars. Including many losing wars that forced them through harsh lessons. They have continually learned and reshaped themselves. While ten years after the Fall of Saigon we still haven't learned the first thing from the Vietnamese Revolution—as judged by practice, which never lies. Literally not the first thing.

It is past time to leave the fools' paradise, past time to master the real world of protracted war, with all its complexities and deceptions. **For the security apparatus is never going to be hospitable enough to hand over their secrets.** On the contrary, not only does the enemy try to conceal their methods and plans (as any serious

army would), but they try to get revs to have misconceptions about them. Even the liberated FBI COINTELPRO documents only brought to daylight a tiny fraction of the enemy's activities and distorted some (which is why past COINTELPRO revelations cannot be leaned upon as a crutch).

In the first place, it is the dominant petty-bourgeois/lumpen politics of the old movements that has kept us from learning even the simplest tricks of the enemy. Like a political lobotomy. What are called "security violations" or "errors" are not really errors in the usual sense of the word. Done every day by hundreds of activists in dozens of units and organizations, these "errors" are simply established, unofficial policy of the movements. It has been our consistent policy, year after year, to refuse to see even the oldest, simplest maneuver of the security forces. Thus, understanding the enemy can only develop while simultaneously struggling to understand ourselves and overturning our bad politics.

We can prove this by examining practice. What is the oldest, most simple-minded tactic that the security forces use? One of them, in any case, must be the old trick of infiltration by the male military vet who supposedly now wants to join the Rev and use his weapons savvy in doing "heavy" stuff. Haven't we all heard of this many times?

Let us mention just a few of the better-known cases of this tactic: In February 1968 "Yedwah Sudan," an airborne veteran, joined the NY BPP and quickly became a leading Bronx BPP activist. He was really NYPD rookie Ralph White, who tried to set up the Panther 21 for various bombings and assassination conspiracies. In October 1964 Larry Grathwohl joined the Cincinnati WUO collective, claiming the usual Vietnam vet rap. He, too, was an agent, and arranged Linda Evans' 1970 arrest (she was the first of the WUO fugitives to be caught by the FBI). The FBI and local police used this fairly primitive tactic dozens of times in the 1960s and early 1970s against every movement around. They used it because the cover story both fit what the Movement wanted to hear, and because the "heavy" Vietnam Vet act gave plausible cover to reactionary men who obviously had questionable politics but were talking up armed conspiracies.

Did revs learn from all these well-publicized cases? Well … The "Revolutionary Committee of the WUO" built its West Coast military cell in 1976 around two FBI agents, one of whom played the by now classic role of the Vietnam vet weapons expert. At the same time the New Afrikan nucleus of BLA-RATF was recruiting another "heavy" Vietnam vet combat expert to help do expropriations—name: Tyrone Rison. And in 1981, yet another "heavy" veteran joined a New Afrikan collective that was publishing "an illegal newspaper." This veteran specialized in weapons training and trying to set up more expropriations—name: Howard Bonds. Can we see any pattern here?

Howard Bonds became the Government's star witness at the 1985 trial of the New York 8+. The defendants were members of the Sunrise Collective, which conducted political study classes at the Harlem Fightback Center, did community organizing, and secretly published *Arm the Masses*. *ATM*, according to NY 8+ defendant Omowale Clay, was **"an illegal newspaper. It was an underground newspaper."** One

The NY 8+

liberal newspaper report on the case stated: "**When you examine the profile of Bonds that emerged at the trial, it matches up with the classic COINTELPRO double agent. Bonds approached Chimurenga** [defendant Coltrane Chimurenga—ed.] **in 1981 professing military expertise. His function within the group became weapons procurement and training ... According to Wareham,** [defendant Roger Wareham—ed.] **Bonds disdained the rest of the group's dedication to study of political theory and always sought to engage them in adventurous activity."** FBI pre-arrest surveillance records admit that Bonds made daily drug buys and spent many nights at the expensive sex club Plato's Retreat. In part because Bonds was discredited, the NY 8+ won a trial victory, with only seven months of community service for weapons and false ID charges. One defendant, Jose Rios, was acquitted completely. His former 'rads now believe that Bonds is a self-serving mercenary, who either was always an informer or who flipped months before the arrests.

If someone claimed to be a mathematician but didn't know that 1+1=2, we might wonder. Yet it's unfortunately "normal" that those who fight the State security apparatus, don't know one single thing (literally) about security. It's a costly clown show, where year after year the State agents can sucker revs in with the same, tired-out, simpleminded tactics. Folks who are righteous veterans of firefights, folks experienced with the BPP and WUO, folks who went to Harvard, who have law degrees, don't know that "1+1=2" in political-

military terms. Practice is the proof of amateurishness and everything else. We are sharp here not in a personal sense, but because it is absolutely time as the No. 1 priority to end all such revolutionary backwardness.

This police tactic is just a minor thing in and of itself. What is important is an unofficial **policy** of being fools for the same simple tricks, taking beating after beating, year after year. Isn't that unnatural? "Custeristic"? What it proves is that this is not a matter of individual errors, of "street smarts," of knowing the past famous cases of infiltrators, or of better technique. The fundamental ideological view of the old '60s movements is the cause—which is why these "errors" are so universal and so persistently hard to stamp out.

In this particular example, the State security forces are taking advantage of our **petty-bourgeois subjectivism, manifested in revs' insistence on seeing things as they wish them to be, rather than as they really are.** Because Vietnam veterans made important contributions to the '60s revolutionary organizations, folks started hoping that they were an easy solution to practical needs. The common fantasy is that recruiting ready-made fighters and ready-made experts will be a free short-cut to building. **And folks are willing to have little or no political standards for such "heavy" fighters.** The imperialist security forces feed upon our amateur fantasies. (But Attica and Marion are very real.) This example also shows how deeply folks still believe that People's War is a "macho man" exercise, where the eagerness to engage in violence is all there is. That's why **in practice** folks couldn't tell the difference between revolutionary fighters and imperialistic mercenaries. It looked the same. **"Macho, macho man …"**

When we become objective instead of subjective, we can readily see that the State security forces have certain developed tactics, short-term strategies, and long-term strategies. All of which they attempt to conceal from our eyes. That the security apparatus too has its own contradictions and limiting conditions. This is too long a discussion for us to go into here, but it is still necessary to keep this generalization in mind.

It is not the long-range strategy of the security apparatus to wipe out all revolutionary opposition. **For the simple reason that they do not believe that this is possible.** For example: a classified counterinsurgency analysis by an official in the FBI's Latin Amerikan division concluded that revolutionary opposition was a permanent fixture, because the mass discontent that produced it could never be avoided in capitalist societies ("even in the United States"). This is an objective recognition on their part. Nor is it just part of the FBI that has this view. In 1976 the US Justice Department's Task Force on Disorders and Terrorism concluded:

"A substantial segment of the community is not merely politically apathetic but surprisingly naive in its beliefs and reactions. This segment is easy prey for extremists and is materially influenced by the apparent suc-

cesses of radical action. Civil authorities cannot afford to ignore the existence and attitudes of this passive mass or wait until it has thrown its support in a crisis to those seeking change by violent means."[17]

In other words, the professionals in the State security apparatus recognize that revolutionary discontent is continually being reborn and sustained within the **masses**, and therefore that its total eradication is not practical. Their long-range strategy is thus one of **controlling and indirectly managing** the inevitable revolutionary opposition. That is, they recognize and adapt in their own way to the necessarily **protracted** nature of the conflict. For this **information** is their primary necessity, the alpha and omega of counterinsurgency. Given the superior resources of the imperialist State, anything and anyone they know about fully (names, locations, etc.) they can neutralize. Their strategy involves trading conditional tolerance for numbers of already-known revolutionaries (who are being observed) in order to ensure a continuing flow of information about all new people and developments.

Such deceptions have a long history, being standard operating procedures of the Russian Czarist Okhrana (secret political police). Whenever the Okhrana broke up a local underground revolutionary collective (the Russians called them "circles") they always let at least one rev "escape." This survivor was kept under surveillance so that when a new underground group was built, he or she would lead the Okhrana to it. The Russian underground called these people **"breeders."** The same idea expanded becomes the "encapsulated-gang."

When we point out that the enemy works to keep their methods and plans a secret, this is not just because they don't want us to know. They are also constrained by the general political situation. The US is not yet Kenya, Algeria, or Vietnam before independence, where open war without limitations could be waged. Regular "pseudo-gangs" are in theory illegal in the US, since the Government is not supposed to have its own security officers rob banks, do jailbreaks, shoot police, and plant bombs. Their use here has meant several alterations, all directed at concealment: the use of "encapsulated-gangs," using lumpen mercenaries instead of security officers to infiltrate, and never admitting that any operation existed at all. This has meant that mercenary agents planted in the "encapsulated-gang" must conceal their role—either "escaping" or pretending to turn traitor only **after** the group is arrested, as Howard Bonds and the FBI did after the arrests of the New York 8+.

In their RATF operation the State security apparatus depended upon both tactical and strategic deception. For their "encapsulated-gang" operation to work, the FBI's "Joint Terrorist Task Force" had to keep the RATF cadre lulled and unaware. The lengths to which they went was shown by their line around the April 20, 1981, shooting in Queens that left two police down (one dying). The two officers were cut down in

a barrage of 9 mm bullets, after stopping a van for questioning. Their assailants fled the scene. Police allegedly identified the two fighters involved by fingerprints and witnesses.

Within hours the NYPD had put out a nationwide alert for Abdul Majid (sn Anthony LaBorde) and Basheer Hameed (sn James York). Both had long political records, and had in the past been accused by authorities of being in the BLA. Early news reports featured sensationalistic police speculation that a BLA operation was involved, either an ambush or shooting to protect fugitive Assata Shakur (who the police had conjectured was possibly in the van). **This created a problem for the political police.** A renewed spotlight on the BLA in general—plus public demands for an "anti-terrorist" campaign—might jolt RATF awake and stir folks into fleeing the trap. So the FBI and NYPD put on an act to lull everyone, putting out that the shooting wasn't political and that **they thought the BLA didn't even exist anymore!**

At a press conference the night of the incident, NY Chief of Detectives James T. Sullivan, backed up by FBI officials, told the press with a straight face: **"The BLA came to an end in the early 1970s."** He even said that Federal authorities had **"no indications"** of any "BLA" activity anywhere in the US. When wounded police officer John Scarangella finally died on May 1, 1981, the police and FBI once again used a press conference to put out the same reassurance that they had **"no indications"** of any "BLA" activity.[18]

That was amazing. Over a year since Assata Shakur had been liberated from prison, followed by public BLA-RATF support meetings in various cities playing the tape-recorded message from Assata, the State security forces were clumsily pretending that they knew nothing about any "BLA." But their flimsy deception worked. RATF remained confident that there was no cause for alarm. Things were going well on the road to Nyack.

However clumsy, these tactical deceptions worked within the larger context of the security forces' strategic deceptions. RATF cadre just could not see the warning lights, because action after action was successful. **They mistakenly thought the job of the State security apparatus was to stop them from doing actions;** so if they were pulling off expropriations and prison breaks then the FBI must be powerless to stop them. As though the political police were just cops on the street. **Those cadre were still under the conditioning of the colonial/criminal mentality.***

The political police have long-range concern for **political goals**. They don't care primarily about bank-jobs, prison escapes, hijackings, or symbolic bombings *per se*. The CIA/FBI/etc. are concerned about winning protracted war, not about small skirmishes along the way. If you will help them stage a front-page propaganda show trial, help them morally discredit the BLA, help them deepen splits in the liberation movement, help them appear all-powerful, then they'll be glad to let you stage some actions before your arrests. And the security forces will be especially glad to let you attract all the new (and old) people possible into their trap.

The State security apparatus knows that the breakup of the US Empire is a possibility. They know that oppressed masses have moved from protest to rebellion, putting armed struggle to the forefront, and that when US imperialism's neo-colonial scheme breaks down liberation war will break out on a higher level. **In their own way, they have faith in the masses.** More, perhaps, than we do. For our movements do not really yet believe that the masses are the element of liberation. That's why there are still no actual plans for the breakup of the Empire, no beginnings of laying the roots of socialism among the masses. What we can learn from RATF is that ending backwardness means understanding armed struggle in a communist way. **In the real world, "Rambo" is scared of Madame Binh.**

---

* See "Transforming the Colonial/Criminal Mentality," *Notes From a New Afrikan POW Journal Book One*. Also in: James Yaki Sayles, *Meditations on Frantz Fanon's Wretched of the Earth: New Afrikan Revolutionary Writings*, Kersplebedeb 2010

LESSONS

1. It is necessary to sum up the past after each particular period—not to dwell in it, but precisely to be able to move sure-footed into the future. We have all heard of athletes who are haunted by a losing match or game, replaying it over and over in their minds. Some folks are still haunted by the setbacks of the '60s movements, replaying it over and over, bitterly blaming others for the defeats, trying the same moves all over again hoping that the page of history can be rewritten. We as communists must reach a consolidated understanding of the past period, so that its lessons can be used in the new period of rebuilding. Sum up the past to leave the past.

2. We have seen that false internationalism has been a significant factor in the world struggle. While false internationalism exploits the genuine respect for proletarian unity that exists, it is not merely a trick. False internationalism is an opportunistic alliance between petty-bourgeois–minded elements of different nations. In pre-liberation China false internationalism was used to promote very different policies at different times—from the disarming of the masses in 1926–27 to the reckless military adventurism of 1934–35. What was consistent was their inner political content. Each involved unrealistic subjectivism and opportunism. Each promoted a certain petty-bourgeois clique at the expense of the Revolution (but in its name).

There are two kinds of neo-colonialism present in the world. The first and more obvious kind is represented by the Marcos Regime in the Philippines, the former Shah of Iran, Andy Youngs and Jesse Jacksons. That is, national pseudo-bourgeois and petty-bourgeois who are openly pro-imperialist and pro–US Empire. They stand for some kind of independence but only within the framework of being puppets for imperialism. The second kind of neo-colonialism is by far the more dangerous. It is the neo-colonialism **within** the revolution. Even the strongest liberation movement can lose in the two-line struggle within its ranks. The temporary victory of the capitalist roaders in China is an inescapable example. In our own movements, even in armed units, there are neo-colonial elements, trends of thought, policies. False internationalism that has plagued the '60s revolutionary movements here in the US is neo-colonial in essence.

False internationalism, no matter how "nationalist" or "Marxist" its outward dress, inevitably promotes slavish attitudes of the supposed superiority of oppressor nations, of the imperialistic way of doing things, etc. This may be done crudely—such as the treacherous replacement of Mao Zedong by the European revolutionary tourist Otto Braun. It may be done more subtly: the Revolutionary Armed Task Force, for example, took the line that "Black–White" political integration was good so long as selected New Afrikans gave the orders instead of settlers. But RATF's basic principle was the slavish idea that **white people are the answer to the problems of the New Afrikan Nation.** In this type of relationship the oppressor nation acts as a Rear Base Area

318

for opportunism within the national liberation movement (and vice-versa). False internationalism confronts us with this choice—slavishness or self-reliance.

3. It is not enough to just change one wrong policy. To end backwardness we must overturn the entire petty-bourgeois/lumpen way of life and thought of the old movements. The '60s style of political work promoted individualism, to use one example. For fifteen years revolutionary organizations here in the US Empire have correctly criticized individualist politics. The progress has been less than spectacular, however. May 19th and ex-WUO people were determined to reverse the history of flightism of the Anti-Imperialist tendency. And they did cross the line into armed activity. But they did so as individuals (exceptional white people), joining the New Afrikan liberation movement, **leaving** their own movement and leaving it unchanged. Ten years after it all began with the split inside the WUO, there is still the same approximate amount of Euro-Amerikan support for armed struggle that there was a decade ago. Almost zero. The Euro-Amerikan movement is still primarily flightist.

4. Because people are still circling around under the guidance of petty-bourgeois/lumpen class politics, all the talk of building revolutionary culture is still just lip-service. WUO, as we saw, spoke of revolutionary culture but kept being drawn to the most reactionary aspects of the alternative culture—opposing Women's Liberation and allying itself with the patriarchal drug subculture. **Picking up the gun in no way changes this.** RATF and May 19th Communist Organization proved that by continuing the same policy as the WUO.

The Women's Movement, for all its weaknesses and settleristic limitations, was at the center of cultural change in the US oppressor nation. Because that was where the spark of Women's Liberation had been struck. Like WUO and the rest of the patriarchal settler Left, pfoc and May 19th paid lip-service to Women's Liberation while opposing it.

May 19th related to the Women's Movement only in an opportunistic way. They always sought to recruit radical women out of the women's community, turned to it as the only community in White Amerika that would give them a hearing (the full meaning of that fact never penetrated their arrogance), but only wanted to take and never to give. Although May 19th and pfoc congratulated themselves as the supposed communist leadership for white women, they led no new struggles to strengthen the Women's Movement, contributed no new ideas or strategies, and made no secret of the fact that they considered themselves above other white women. It is not a surprise that such a backward, slavish attitude should lead them into association with the reactionary drug subculture, dope dealing, FBI agents, traitors, and the oppression of New Afrikan women. Their thoughtless approach to armed struggle was as a macho playground. Revolutionary armed struggle, whether its forces be large or small, seeks to encourage and represent the most rebellious mass political currents, the most honest and serious-thinking sectors of society. To be practical about revolutionary military work demands this understanding.

5. The fact that RATF marked a nodal point where neo-colonialism was clearly dominant in the armed movement, reminds us again that the fundamental struggle is between socialism and capitalism. Too often words like "socialism" or "armed struggle" get ritualistically tossed around by folks who don't even know what they mean. Key concepts get demeaned and robbed of their serious meaning.

Socialism is not a type of government that goes into effect the day after the Revolution, as many believe. Neither is capitalism merely a society with private ownership of capital and a ruling class that embodies this. Capitalism is the dominant world culture, a prevalent way of organizing social life, of solving problems, a distinctive structure of thought. As a human system it is many hundreds of years old, has absorbed within it older social systems such as patriarchy, slavery, and feudalism, and has spread to root itself within many different nations and peoples.

Socialism in comparison is very new and still in its historical infancy. **We can win state power but we cannot "win" socialism.** Socialism is also a certain structure of relations between people, a certain culture, a certain ideology and way of solving problems. It must be built, developed, created, and understood, particularized to the needs of specific nations and peoples. As we know, social-

ism is the class rule of the proletariat. It is the social system of the proletarian class. The modern proletariat is the newest world class, still centuries away from assuming fully developed form anywhere in the world. As a class the proletariat has, like all other classes, definite characteristics—modern-thinking, communal, scientific, leading the oppressed of the world. To be a socialist is to be a partisan of one particular world class.

There are only two great, opposing class systems and ideologies in the world—capitalism and socialism. If we are not thinking and living in a socialist manner, then irregardless of what we may subjectively think, we are thinking and living in a capitalist way. **We can only go one way or the other.** There is no third choice or halfway ground. Because capitalism is so much more established, older everywhere, rooted in "the daily habits of millions," we can only "win" socialism by struggling to self-consciously build it in all aspects of life.

Those who do not struggle, consciously struggle, to become fully socialist in their thought will inevitably remain capitalistic in their thought. Those who do not consciously struggle to become fully socialist in their way of life are inevitably drawn backward to neo-colonialism and patriarchy. That is the most important lesson of the RATF experience. If we can pick up that understanding, then the losses and sacrifices of the revolutionaries involved in RATF will have contributed in full.

THE STRUGGLE NEVER ENDS

Men learn and reach correct judgments only by experience. To test a certain line of action is not to make a mistake but to take the first step toward discovering the correct line. If that test proves that certain line to be wrong, the test itself was correct, was experiment in search of correctness, and therefore necessary. There are no controlled conditions in the great laboratory of social science.

I have not always reasoned in this way. Until 1932 I sat like a judge, mercilessly condemning "mistakes" and beating recalcitrants into line like a drill sergeant. When I saw men killed and movements broken because of stupid leadership and stupid following, a fury possessed me. I could not forgive. When Han and another Korean party leader were on trial in Shanghai in 1928, I did not care whether they were spies and traitors, but I felt earnestly that they deserved any punishment for their objective criminal stupidity in having a party organization so weak that the Japanese could arrest a thousand men in a few days.

For myself, I no longer condemn a man by asking what is good or what is bad, what is right or what is wrong, what is correct or what is mistaken. I ask what is value and what is waste, what is necessary and what is futile, what is important and what is secondary. Through many years of heartache and tears, I have learned that "mistakes" are necessary and therefore good. They are an integral part of the development of men and of the process of social change. Men are not so foolish as to believe in words; they learn wisdom only by experiment. This is their safeguard and their right. He knows not what is true who learns not what is false. The textbook of Marxism and Leninism is written not in ink but in blood and suffering. To lead men to death and failure is easy; to lead men to victory is hard.

Kim San

Endnotes

I. The Importance of National Struggles to Communism: the european experience

1. V. I. Lenin, "Discussion on Self-Determination Summed Up," *On the National Question and Proletarian Revolution* (Moscow, 1972), pp. 142–148.

2. Ibid.

3. Michael Futrell, *Northern Underground* (London, 1963), pp. 51–65.

4. Ibid.

5. Ibid.

6. Ibid.

II. False Internationalism in China

1. V. I. Lenin, "Preliminary Draft of Thesis on the National and Colonial Questions" (June 5, 1920), *Lenin on the National and Colonial Questions, Three Articles* (Peking, 1966), p. 23.

2. James Pinckney Harrison, *The Endless War, Fifty Years of Struggle in Vietnam* (NY, 1982), p. 67.

3. General account of development of Chinese Revolution and Comintern in 1923–35 period drawn from:
Han Suyin, *The Morning Deluge, Mao Tsetung and the Chinese Revolution 1893–1954*. Boston, 1972.
Agnes Smedley, *The Great Road*. NY, 1956.
Stuart Schram, *Mao Tse-Tung*. Baltimore, 1967.
Helen Foster Snow, *The Chinese Communists, Sketches and Autobiographies of the Old Guard*. Westport, 1972.
Edgar Snow, *Red Star Over China*. NY, 1938.
John E. Rue, *Mao Tse-Tung in Opposition 1927–1935*. Stanford, 1966.
E. H. Carr, *The Interregnum 1923–1924*. Baltimore, 1969.

4. Agnes Smedley, *The Great Road* (NY, 1956), p. 148.

5. Mao Tsetung, "On the Ten Major Relationships," *Peking Review*, Jan. 1, 1977.

III. Afrikan Anti-Imperialism in the 1930s

1. Mark Naison, "Marxism and Black Radicalism in America: The Communist Party Experience," *Radical America*, May–June 1971.

2. Nell Painter & Hosea Hudson, "Hosea Hudson: A Negro Communist in the Deep South," *Radical America*, July–August 1977.

3. James W. Ford & Harry Gaines, *War in Africa* (NY, 1935), pp. 28–29.

4. Agnes Smedley, *Battle Hymn of China* (NY, 1943), pp. 108–109.

5. Agnes Smedley, *The Great Road* (NY, 1972), p. 333.

6. Ford & Gaines, p. 29.

7. Dennis Mack Smith, *Mussolini's Roman Empire* (NY, 1976), pp. 78–81.

8. Ibid.

9. Ibid.

10. Brice Harris, Jr., *The United States and the Italo-Ethiopian Crisis* (Stanford, 1964), p. 44.

11. Smith, p. 87.

12. John P. Diggins, *Mussolini and Fascism: The View From America* (Princeton, 1972), pp. 287–312.

13. Ibid.

14. Ibid.

15. Ibid.

16. Smith, p. 307.

17. Claude McKay, *Harlem: Negro Metropolis* (NY, 1940), pp. 200–201.

18. Diggins, op. cit.

19. *Congressional Record*, 74th Congress, 2nd Session, Vol. 80, Pt. 1, pp. 2219–2221.

20. William R. Scott, "Black Nationalism and the Italo-Ethiopian Conflict 1934–1936," *Journal of Negro History* (1977), pp. 118–134.

21. *Negro Liberator*, March 15, 1935.

22. Ibid.

23. Ibid.

24. Ford & Gaines, pp. 30–31.

25. Mark Naison, *Communists in Harlem During the Depression* (NY, 1983), pp. 155, 175.

26. *Negro Liberator*, Sept. 2, 1935.

27. Vittorio Vidotto, *The Italian Communist Party From Its Origin to 1946* (Bologna, 1975), pp. 314–322.

28. Ibid.

29. McKay, p. 189.

30. *Negro Liberator*, March 15, 1935.

31. Naison, p. 196.

32. Mao Tsetung, *On Protracted War* (Peking, 1967), p. 3.

33. Ford & Gaines, pp. 28–29.

34. *On Protracted War*, pp. 20–21.

35. Smith, p. 81.

36. Harris, Jr., pp. 140–142.

37. Naison, p. 196.

IV. Settler "Communism"

1. Information on French revisionism regarding Algerian liberation drawn from: Konrad Melchers, "Racist Communism—How the French Communist Party Tried to Sabotage the Algerian Revolution," *Ikwezi*, March 1980; Alistair Horne, *A Savage War of Peace* (London, 1977), pp. 23–28.

2. *Rectify Errors and Rebuild the Party, Congress of Re-establishment*, Communist Party of the Philippines, Dec. 26, 1968. Published by the Filipino Support Group, London, 1977, p. 13.

3. Alfredo B. Saulo, *Communism in the Philippines* (Manila, 1969), pp. 32–35. *Rectify Errors* … , pp. 4–5.

4. For general discussion of this line, see: Amado Guerrero, *Philippine Society & Revolution*. Oakland, 1969.

5. Claude McKay, *A Long Way From Home* (NY, 1970), pp. 164–166.

6. Richard O. Boyer, *The Dark Ship* (Boston, 1947), p. 269.

7. Peter Kwong, *Chinatown, NY Labor & Politics, 1930–1950* (NY, 1979), pp. 119–128.

8. Ibid.

9. Ibid.

10. Ibid.

11. Karl Yoneda, "100 Years of Japanese Labor in the US," in *Roots: An Asian American Reader* (Los Angeles, 1971), pp. 150–158.

12. Michi Weglyn, *Years of Infamy* (NY, 1976), pp. 121–123.

13. Naison, pp. 5–8. Unless otherwise noted this work is the source for the data in this section.

14. Harry Haywood, *Black Bolshevik* (Chicago, 1978), pp. 121–130.

15. Ibid.

16. *Crisis*, June 1934.

17. Ben Stolberg, "Black Chauvinism," *Nation*, May 15, 1935.

18. Letter to the Editor from Sterling A. Brown, Ralph J. Bunche, Emmet E. Dorsay, E. Franklin Frazier, *Nation*, July 3, 1935.

19. Letter to the Editor from James S. Allen, *Nation*, July 3, 1935.

20. "The Question Box," *Negro Liberator*, July 1, 1935.

21. Richard Wright, *American Hunger* (NY, 1983), p. 113.

22. Naison, pp. 193–195.

23. William R. Scott, op. cit.

24. Claude McKay, *Harlem, Negro Metropolis* (NY, 1940), pp. 185–216.

25. Naison, pp. 196–197.

26. McKay, *Harlem Metropolis.* p. 216.

27. Mark Naison, "Marxism and Black Radicalism in America: The Communist Party Experience," *Radical America*, May–June 1971, p. 19.

V. Freedom Now!

1. David L. Lewis, *King: A Critical Biography* (Baltimore, 1971), p. 90. Unless otherwise indicated, this book is the general source for all quotations and background information in this section.

2. Reese Cleghorn, "Epilogue in Albany: Were the Mass Marches Worthwhile?" *The New Republic*, July 20, 1963.

3. Ibid.

4. "Secret Talk in Capital On Georgia," *New York Post*, August 4, 1962.

5. Howard Zinn, *SNCC: The New Abolitionists* (Boston, 1964), pp. 211–212. "The Albany Cases," *The Nation*, April 20, 1964.

6. Zinn, op. cit.

7. Interview with member of National CORE staff.

8. While this is made clear in Lewis op cit., Aldan D. Morris' *The Origins of the Civil Rights Movement: Black Communities Organizing for Change* quotes Dr. King directly on this point.

9. El Hajj Malik El Shabazz, "Message to the Grass Roots," in George Breitman, ed., *Malcolm X Speaks* (NY, 1966), pp. 3–17.

10. Daniel S. Davis, *Mr. Black Labor* (NY, 1972), p. 148.

11. El Hajj Malik El Shabazz, "God's Judgement of White America (The Chickens Are Coming Home to Roost)," in Benjamin Goodman, ed., *The End of White World Supremacy, Four Speeches by Malcolm X* (NY, 1971), p. 146.

12. *Report of the National Advisory Commission on Civil Disorders* (NY, 1968), pp. 35–38.

13. Ibid.

14. Breitman, ed., p. 194.

15. John O. Killens in "Talking Book: Oral History of a Movement," *Village Voice*, February 26, 1985.

16. Breitman, ed., p. 85.

17. Ibid., p. 212.

326

VI. Vietnam Catalyst

1. Irving Louis Horowitz, *The Struggle Is the Message: Organization and Ideology of the Anti-War Movement* (Berkeley, 1970), p. 105.

2. Daniel S. Davis, *Mr. Black Labor* (NY, 1972), pp. 126–130.

3. Lewis, pp. 249–250.

4. Ibid., p. 260.

5. Ibid., pp. 304–305.

6. Committee On Un-American Activities, US House Of Representatives, *Guerrilla Warfare Advocates in the United States*, Washington, 1968, pp. 17–18.

7. Lewis, p. 303; Robert W. Mullen, *Blacks in America's Wars* (NY, 1973), p. 68.

8. Lewis, p. 296.

9. Ibid., pp. 312 and 357.

10. Ibid., pp. 311 and 304.

11. Committee On Un-American Activities, op. cit., p. 21.

12. Horowitz, p. 15.

13. Neil Miller, "Coming of Age in the '80s," *In These Times*, Oct. 17–23, 1984.

14. Kirkpatrick Sale, *SDS* (NY, 1973), pp. 632–643.

15. David Siff, "Judgement at Madison," *University Review*, March 1974.

16. Ibid.

17. House Committee, op. cit., pp. 40–46.

18. Ibid.

19. Mullen, pp. 77–79.

20. Myra MacPherson, *Long Time Passing: Vietnam and the Haunted Generation* (Garden City, 1984), pp. 552–571.

21. Mullen, pp. 81–84.

22. David F. Addlestone & Susan Sherer, "Race in Viet Nam," *Civil Liberties*, February 1973.

23. Ibid.

24. MacPherson, op. cit.

25. Fred Halstead, *Out Now!* NY, 1978, p. 637.

26. Dr. Armando Morales, *Ando Sangrando (I Am Bleeding): A Study of Mexican American-Police Conflict* (La Puente, 1972), pp. 570–575.

VII. The Birth of Euro-Amerikan Anti-Imperialism

1. "About LSM," *LSM News*, Vol. 3, Issue 2, Summer 1976.

2. Don Barnett, *Toward an International Strategy* (Richmond, 1972), pp. 15–16.

3. Don Barnett, "LSM: Problems in Theory, Strategy & Practice," *LSM News*, Vol. 1, No. 3, December 1974.

4. Ibid.

5. Karen Ashley, Bill Ayers, Bernardine Dohrn, John Jacobs, Jeff Jones, Gerry Long, Howie Machtinger, Jim Mellen, Terry Robbins, Mark Rudd, Steve Tappis, "You Don't Need a Weatherman to Know Which Way the Wind Blows," in Harold Jacobs, ed., *Weatherman* (NY, 1970), pp. 51–90.

6. Bill Ayers, "A Strategy To Win," in Jacobs, pp. 183–195.

7. Jacobs, p. 509.

8. Senate Internal Security Subcommittee, *The Weather Underground, Report of the Senate Internal Security Subcommittee* (Washington, 1975), pp. 11–12.

9. Senate Internal Security Subcommittee, p. 28.

10. George Tyler, "Weather Underground: Driving down a dead end street," *Unity*, Nov. 6–19, 1981.

11. *The Weather Underground*, p. 40.

12. Karen Ashley, et al.

13. Jacobs, p. 509.

14. "Tape From Bernardine Dohrn (November 1976)," in *The Split of the Weather Underground Organization* (Seattle, 1977), pp. 33–35.

15. "Stormy Weather," in Jacobs, p. 346.

16. Jacobs, p. 516.

17. "New Morning—Changing Weather," *East Village Other*, Dec. 22, 1970.

18. "Open Letter to the Weather Underground from the Panther 21," *East Village Other*, January 19, 1971.

19. WUO, *Prairie Fire* (S.F., 1974), p. 1.

20. Ibid., pp. 134–136.

21. Ibid., pp. 10–11.

22. Ibid., p. 145.

23. Ibid., p. 10.

24. Ibid., pp. 115–117.

25. Ibid., pp. 28–34.

26. Ibid., pp. 139–140.

27. Ibid., p. 30.

28. Sale, pp. 636–638.

29. Revolutionary Committee, "Criticism of the Central Committee," in *The Split of the Weather Underground Organization*, pp. 25–32.

30. Celia Sojourn and Billy Ayers, *Politics in Command*. n.d.

31. As an example of the major criticisms of the Hard Times Conference, see: *A Single Spark: Internal Newsletter of the prairie fire organizing committee*, No. 1, May 1976.

32. Stephen Brook, *New York Days, New York Nights* (NY, 1985), pp. 148–152.

33. Revolutionary Committee, "WUO Public Self-Criticism," in *The Split* … , p. 18.

34. "New Morning—Changing Weather," op. cit.

VIII. Black Power and New Afrikan Revolution

1. El Hajj Malik El Shabazz, "The Black Revolution," in George Breitman, ed., *Malcolm X Speaks* (NY, 1966), pp. 45–57.

2. *Report of the National Advisory Commission on Civil Disorders* (NY, 1968), p. 56–69.

3. Ibid., pp. 128–129.

4. Ibid., p. 129.

5. Lewis, p. 385.

6. *Vietnam GI*, May 1968 and August 1968.

7. Fred Halstead, *Out Now!* NY, 1978, p. 386.

8. Robert F. Williams, *Negroes With Guns* (NY, 1962), p. 111.

9. See: A. Muhammad Ahmad, *History of RAM*. Chicago. n.d., and
Committee On Un-American Activities, US House Of Representatives, *Guerrilla Warfare Advocates in the United States* (Washington, 1968), pp. 16–24.

10. Ibid.

11. *Chicago's American*, October 16, 1968. A. Muhammad Ahmad, pp. 31–33.

12. Yuri Kochiyama, *Fishmerchant's Daughter: Yuri Kochiyama, An Oral History* (NY, 1982), pp. 9–10.

13. Lowell Bergman & David Weir, "Revolution On Ice," *Rolling Stone*, September 9, 1976.

14. "The CIA As An Equal Opportunity Employer," *The Black Panther*, June 7, 1969.

15. Stokely Carmichael, "What We Want," in Bradford Chambers, ed., *Chronicles of Black Power Protest*. NY, 1969. (Originally published in *New York Review of Books*, September 22, 1966.)

16. Robert L. Allen, *Black Awakening in Capitalist America* (NY, 1970), p. 161.

17. Stokely Carmichael & Charles V. Hamilton, *Black Power: The Politics of Liberation in America* (NY, 1967), p. 44.

18. Chambers, p. 224.

19. Allen, pp. 136–137.

20. Ibid., p. 165.

21. *The Extended Family— A Tribal Analysis of US Africanists: Who They Are; Why to Fight Them.* Africa Research Group, Cambridge, 1970. p. 12.

22. Allen, pp. 144–148.

23. Ibid., pp. 228–229.

24. Imari Abubakari Obadele, *Free the Land!* Washington, 1984.

25. Allen, p. 139.

26. Imari Obadele. "The Struggle Is for the Land," *Black Scholar*, Feb. 1972. *History of RAM*, p. 33.

27. Gene Marine, *The Black Panthers*, NY, 1969. For the sake of convenience, unless otherwise noted this book by a member of the *Ramparts* magazine staff, based on interviews with Newton and Seale, is the source for quotations and events in this section.

28. Bergman & Weir, op. cit.

29. *Look For Me in The Whirlwind* (NY, 1971), p. 296.

30. Eldridge Cleaver, *The Land Question*. Mimeo 8 p. pamphlet, n.d.

31. *The Black Panther*, June 7, 1969.

32. Based on interviews with former members of SNCC and CORE.

33. For a highly critical view of Forman's role in the LRBW, see A. Muhammad Ahmad, *The League Revolutionary Black Workers*.

34. Commission for the Study of the History of the Party, *50 Years of Activities of the Communist Party of Vietnam* (Hanoi, 1980), pp. 13–17.

35. Robert F. Williams, *Negroes With Guns* (NY, 1962), p. 114.

36. Claude Lightfoot, *Turning Point in Freedom Road* (NY, 1962), p. 17.

37. Allen, pp. 34–35.

38. "Historic ALSC Conference Discussed: Which Road For Black People?" *The African World*, Vol. IV, No. 5, July 1974.

39. "Message to the Lumpen," *Right On!*, November 15, 1971.

40. *Big Mama Rag*, April 1984, Vol. 12, No. 4. Political Bureau of the Central Committee of the APSP, "Party Bulletin," *The Burning Spear*, March 1984.

41. "Ajona Ifateyo: Speaking Up Front," *Off Our Backs*, November 1984.

42. Omali Yeshitela, *Not One Step Backward!* Oakland, 1982, pp. 160–162.

43. Donald Wood, *Biko*. London, 1978.

44. "Panther Party Split Deepens," *Guardian*, March 13, 1971.

45. "On Contradictions Within the Black Panther Party," *Right On!*, April 3, 1971.

46. *Right On!*, April 3, 1971.

47. Elmer Geronimo Pratt, "The New Urban Guerrilla," *Right On!*, May 17, 1971.

48. *East Village Other*, January 19, 1971.

49. Bergman & Weir, op. cit.

50. Safiya Asya Bukhari, "Coming of Age: A New Afrikan Revolutionary," *Notes From a New Afrikan POW Journal*, Book 7.

51. Bergman & Weir, op. cit.

52. Ibid.

53. Ibid.

54. *Right On!*, April 3, 1971. This comes from a transcript of a tape-recorded political education class, said to have been held by the Algiers Section on January 31, 1971.

55. Eldridge Cleaver, "On Lumpen Ideology," *The Black Scholar*, Nov.–Dec., 1972.

56. "On the Progress of the Black Liberation Struggle," *Right On!*, Jan. 1–31, 1972.

57. *break de chains*, NY, 1973, National Committee for the Defense of JoAnne Chesimard and Clark Squire, pp. 11–16.

58. *Right On!*, November 15, 1971.

59. Truong Chinh, "The Resistance Will Win," in *Selected Writings*. Hanoi, 1977. p. 168.

60. Jan Hillegas, "Republic of New Afrika meeting harassed," *Guardian*, April 10, 1971.

61. *Chicago Sun-Times*, August 19, 1971. *Right On!*, February 29, 1972.

62. *Right On!*, February 29, 1972. "FBI Frame-Up," *Guardian*, February 22, 1978.

63. *Right On!*, February 29, 1972.

64. Imari Abubakari Obadele, "The Struggle Is For The Land," *Black Scholar*, February 1972.

65. Imari Abubakari Obadele, *The Eight Strategic Elements For Success of a Black Nation in America.* 10 p. mimeo pamphlet. n.d. Speech to the Third Annual Black Power Convention, Philadelphia, September 1968.

66. Imari Abubakari Obadele, *War in America: The Malcolm X Doctrine*. Detroit, 1968, revised edition, p. 57.

67. Ibid.

68. *Eight Strategic Elements...*, op. cit.

69. *War in America*, p. 52.

70. Ibid., p. 21.

71. Ibid., p. 55–57.

72. "The Struggle Is For The Land," op. cit.

73. Imari Abubakari Obadele, *Free The Land!* Washington, 1984, pp. 224–225.

74. Melvin Wolff, *Lunch at the 5&10* (NY, 1970), pp. 185–186.

75. *NY Times*, June 28, 1983.

76. Paula Giddings, *Where and When I Enter* (NY, 1984), p. 313.

77. "Talking Back: Oral History of a Movement," *Village Voice*, February 26, 1985.

78. Giddings, p. 311.

79. *Burning Spear*, "Special Free Edition," November 1977.

IX. Nyack—The Road to Nowhere

1. Eugene H. Methvin, "Terror Network, USA," *Readers Digest*, December 1984.
M. A. Farber, "Behind the Brink's Case: Return of the Radical Left," *NY Times*, February 16, 1982.

2. *The New Afrikan*, Vol. IX, No. 3, December 18 adM (1983).

3. *Arm The Spirit*, No. 14, Fall 1982.

4. Judy Clark & David Gilbert, "The Verdict Is Still Out—Evaluation of the Trial Stand & Strategy," *Resistance*, Vol. 2, No. 3, Oct./Nov. 1983.

5. *Arm The Spirit*, Vol. IX, No. 3, December 18 adM (1983).

6. *Wall Street Journal*, July 26, 1984.

7. "RICO—Test Case for Counterinsurgency, 1983," *Resistance*, No. 1, April 1983.

8. Clark & Gilbert, op. cit.

9. Ellen Cantarow, "Kathy Boudin in Jail: The Years of Living Dangerously," *Mademoiselle*, April 1984.

10. Jane Lazarre, "Conversations With Kathy Boudin," *Village Voice*, Feb. 14, 1984.
James Ferron, "Lie Detector Test Led to Brinks Guilty Plea," *NY Times*, April 28, 1984.

11. *Friends of Kathy Boudin Newsletter*, Issue 2, July 1984.
Ferron, op. cit.

12. Clark & Gilbert, op. cit.

13. Ibid.

14. Robert B. Asprey, *War in The Shadows: The Guerrilla in History* (Garden City, 1975), pp. 756–57, 884–85.

15. Victor Marchetti & John D. Marks, *The CIA and the Cult of Intelligence* (NY, 1980), pp. 211–212.

16. Alistair Horne, *A Savage War of Peace* (London, 1977), p. 259.

17. National Advisory Committee on Criminal Justice Standards and Goals, *Report of the Task Force on Disorders and Terrorism* (Washington, 1976), p. 41.

18. *NY Times*, April 21, 1981; May 2, 1981.

Bibliography

A Single Spark: Internal Newsletter of the prairie fire organizing committee, No. 1, May 1976.

Addlestone, David F. and Susan Sherer. "Race in Viet Nam," *Civil Liberties*, February 1973.

Africa Research Group. *The Extended Family— A Tribal Analysis of US Africanists: Who They Are; Why to Fight Them*. Africa Research Group, Cambridge, 1970.

Ahmad, A. Muhammad. *History of RAM*. Chicago. n.d.,

--------- *The League Revolutionary Black Workers*.

Allen, James S. Letter to the Editor, *Nation*, July 3, 1935.

Allen, Robert L. *Black Awakening in Capitalist America*. NY, 1970.

Arm The Spirit, No. 14, Fall 1982.

Arm The Spirit, Vol. IX, No. 3, December 18 adM (1983).

Ashley, Karen, Bill Ayers, Bernardine Dohrn, John Jacobs, Jeff Jones, Gerry Long, Howie Machtinger, Jim Mellen, Terry Robbins, Mark Rudd, Steve Tappis, "You Don't Need a Weatherman to Know Which Way the Wind Blows," in Harold Jacobs, ed., *Weatherman*. NY, 1970.

Asprey, Robert B. *War in The Shadows: The Guerrilla in History*. Garden City, 1975.

Ayers, Bill. "A Strategy To Win," in Jacobs.

Barnett, Don. "LSM: Problems in Theory, Strategy & Practice," *LSM News*, Vol. 1, No. 3, December 1974.

--------- *Toward an International Strategy*. Richmond, 1972.

Big Mama Rag, April 1984, Vol. 12, No. 4.

Bergman, Lowell and David Weir. "Revolution On Ice," *Rolling Stone*, September 9, 1976.

Boyer, Richard O. *The Dark Ship*. Boston, 1947.

break de chains, NY, 1973, National Committee for the Defense of JoAnne Chesimard and Clark Squire.

Breitman, George ed. *Malcolm X Speaks*. NY, 1966.

Brook, Stephen. *New York Days, New York Nights*. NY, 1985.

Brown, Sterling A., Ralph J. Bunche, Emmet E. Dorsay, E. Franklin Frazier. Letter to the Editor, *Nation*, July 3, 1935.

Bukhari, Safiya Asya. "Coming of Age: A New Afrikan Revolutionary," *Notes From a New Afrikan POW Journal*, Book 7.

Burning Spear, "Special Free Edition," November 1977.

Cantarow, Ellen. "Kathy Boudin in Jail: The Years of Living Dangerously," *Mademoiselle*, April 1984.

Carmichael, Stokely and Charles V. Hamilton, *Black Power: The Politics of Liberation in America*. NY, 1967.

Carmichael, Stokely. "What We Want," in Bradford Chambers, ed., *Chronicles of Black Power Protest*. NY, 1969. (Originally published in *New York Review of Books*, September 22, 1966.)

Carr, E. H. *The Interregnum 1923–1924*. Baltimore, 1969.

Chicago Sun-Times, August 19, 1971.

Chicago's American, October 16, 1968.

Clark, Judy and David Gilbert. "The Verdict Is Still Out—Evaluation of the Trial Stand & Strategy," *Resistance*, Vol. 2, No. 3, Oct./Nov. 1983.

Cleaver, Eldridge. "On Lumpen Ideology," *The Black Scholar*, Nov.–Dec., 1972.

--------- *The Land Question*. Mimeo 8 p. pamphlet, n.d.

Cleghorn, Reese. "Epilogue in Albany: Were the Mass Marches Worthwhile?" *The New Republic*, July 20, 1963.

Commission for the Study of the History of the Party, *50 Years of Activities of the Communist Party of Vietnam*. Hanoi, 1980.

Committee On UnAmerican Activities, US House Of Representatives. *Guerrilla Warfare Advocates in the United States*, Washington, 1968.

Communist Party of the Philippines. *Rectify Errors and Rebuild the Party, Congress of Re-establishment.* Dec. 26, 1968. Published by the Filipino Support Group, London, 1977.

Congressional Record, 74th Congress, 2nd Session, Vol. 80, Pt. 1.

Crisis, June 1934.

Davis, Daniel S. *Mr. Black Labor*. NY, 1972.

Diggins, John P. *Mussolini and Fascism: The View From America*. Princeton, 1972.

Dohrn, Bernardine. "Tape From Bernardine Dohrn (November 1976)," in *The Split of the Weather Underground Organization*. Seattle, 1977.

East Village Other, January 19, 1971.

El Shabazz, El Hajj Malik. "God's Judgement of White America (The Chickens Are Coming Home to Roost)," in Benjamin Goodman, ed., *The End of White World Supremacy, Four Speeches by Malcolm X*. NY, 1971.

--------- "Message To The Grass Roots," in George Breitman, ed., *Malcolm X Speaks*. NY, 1966.

--------- "The Black Revolution," in George Breitman, ed., *Malcolm X Speaks*. NY, 1966.

Farber, M. A. "Behind the Brink's Case: Return of the Radical Left," *NY Times*, February 16, 1982.

Ferron, James. "Lie Detector Test Led to Brinks Guilty Plea," *NY Times*, April 28, 1984.

Ford, James W. and Harry Gaines. *War in Africa*. NY, 1935.

Friends of Kathy Boudin Newsletter, Issue 2, July 1984.

Futrell, Michael. *Northern Underground*. London, 1963.

George Tyler, "Weather Underground: Driving down a dead end street," *Unity*, Nov. 6–19, 1981.

Giddings, Paula. *Where and When I Enter*. NY, 1984.

Goodman, Benjamin ed. *The End of White World Supremacy, Four Speeches by Malcolm X*. NY, 1971.

Guardian. "FBI FrameUp," *Guardian*, February 22, 1978.

--------- "Panther Party Split Deepens," *Guardian*, March 13, 1971

Guerrero, Amado. *Philippine Society & Revolution*. Oakland, 1969.

Halstead, Fred. *Out Now!* NY, 1978.

Han Suyin. *The Morning Deluge, Mao Tsetung and the Chinese Revolution 1893–1954*. Boston, 1972.

Harris, Brice, Jr., *The United States and the Italo-Ethiopian Crisis*. Stanford, 1964.

Harrison, James Pinckney. *The Endless War, Fifty Years of Struggle in Vietnam*. NY, 1982.

Haywood, Harry. *Black Bolshevik*. Chicago, 1978.

Hillegas, Jan. "Republic of New Afrika meeting harassed," *Guardian*, April 10, 1971.

Horne, Alistair. *A Savage War of Peace*. London, 1977.

Horowitz, Irving Louis. *The Struggle Is The Message: Organization and Ideology of the AntiWar Movement*. Berkeley, 1970.

Ifateyo, Ajona. "Ajona Ifateyo: Speaking Up Front," *Off Our Backs*, November 1984.

Killens, John O. "Talking Book: Oral History of a Movement," *Village Voice*, February 26, 1985.

Kochiyama, Yuri. *Fishmerchant's Daughter: Yuri Kochiyama, An Oral History*. NY, 1982.

Kwong, Peter. *Chinatown, NY Labor & Politics, 1930–1950*. NY, 1979.

Lazarre, Jane. "Conversations With Kathy Boudin," *Village Voice*, Feb. 14, 1984.

Lenin, V. I. "Discussion on Self-Determination Summed Up," *On the National Question and Proletarian Revolution*. Moscow, 1972.

--------- "Preliminary Draft of Thesis on the National and Colonial Questions" (June 5, 1920), *Lenin on the National and Colonial Questions, Three Articles*. Peking, 1966.

Lewis, David L. *King: A Critical Biography*. Baltimore, 1971.

Lightfoot, Claude. *Turning Point in Freedom Road*. NY, 1962.

LSM News. "About LSM," *LSM News*, Vol. 3, Issue 2, Summer 1976.

MacPherson, Myra. *Long Time Passing: Vietnam and the Haunted Generation*. Garden City, 1984.

Mao Tsetung. *On Protracted War*. Peking, 1967.

--------- "On the Ten Major Relationships," *Peking Review*, Jan. 1, 1977.

Marchetti, Victor and John D. Marks. *The CIA and the Cult of Intelligence*. NY, 1980.

Marine, Gene. *The Black Panthers*, NY, 1969.

McKay, Claude. *A Long Way From Home*. NY, 1970.

--------- *Harlem: Negro Metropolis*. NY, 1940.

Melchers, Konrad. "Racist Communism—How the French Communist Party Tried to Sabotage the Algerian Revolution," *Ikwezi*, March 1980.

Methvin, Eugene H. "Terror Network, USA," *Readers Digest*, December 1984.

Miller, Neil. "Coming of Age in the '80s," *In These Times*, Oct. 17–23, 1984.

Morales, Dr. Armando. *Ando Sangrando (I Am Bleeding): A Study of Mexican American–Police Conflict*. La Puente, 1972.

Morris, Aldan D. *The Origins of the Civil Rights Movement: Black Communities Organizing for Change*.

Mullen, Robert W. *Blacks in America's Wars*, NY, 1973.

Naison, Mark. *Communists in Harlem During the Depression*. NY, 1983.

--------- "Marxism and Black Radicalism in America: The Communist Party Experience," *Radical America*, May–June 1971.

Nation. "The Albany Cases," *The Nation*, April 20, 1964.

National Advisory Committee on Criminal Justice Standards and Goals. *Report of the Task Force on Disorders and Terrorism*. National Advisory Committee on Criminal Justice Standards and Goals, Washington, 1976.

Negro Liberator. "The Question Box," *Negro Liberator*, July 1, 1935.

--------- March 15, 1935.

--------- Sept. 2, 1935.

New York Post. "Secret Talk in Capital On Georgia," *New York Post*, August 4, 1962.

New York Times, April 21, 1981.

--------- May 2, 1981.

--------- June 28, 1983.

Obadele, Imari Abubakari. "The Struggle Is For The Land," *Black Scholar*, February 1972.

--------- *Free The Land!* Washington, 1984.

--------- *The Eight Strategic Elements For Success of a Black Nation in America.* 10 p. mimeo pamphlet. n.d.

--------- "The Struggle Is for the Land," *Black Scholar*, Feb. 1972.

--------- *War in America: The Malcolm X Doctrine.* Detroit, 1968, revised edition.

Painter, Nell and Hosea Hudson. "Hosea Hudson: A Negro Communist in the Deep South," *Radical America*, July–August 1977.

Panther 21. "Open Letter to the Weather Underground from the Panther 21," *East Village Other*, January 19, 1971.

--------- *Look For Me in The Whirlwind.* NY, 1971.

Political Bureau of the Central Committee of the APSP, "Party Bulletin," *The Burning Spear*, March 1984.

Pratt, Elmer Geronimo. "The New Urban Guerrilla," *Right On!*, May 17, 1971.

Report of the National Advisory Commission on Civil Disorders. NY, 1968.

Resistance. "RICO—Test Case for Counterinsurgency, 1983," *Resistance*, No. 1, April 1983.

Revolutionary Committee, "Criticism of the Central Committee," in *The Split of the Weather Underground Organization*.

--------- "WUO Public SelfCriticism," in *The Split of the Weather Underground Organization*.

Right On! "Message to the Lumpen," *Right On!*, November 15, 1971.

--------- "On Contradictions Within the Black Panther Party," *Right On!*, April 3, 1971.

--------- "On the Progress of the Black Liberation Struggle," *Right On!*, Jan. 1–31, 1972.

--------- April 3, 1971.

--------- February 29, 1972.

--------- November 15, 1971.

Rue, John E. *Mao TseTung in Opposition 1927–1935*. Stanford, 1966.

Sakai, J. *Settlers: The Mythology of the White Proletariat from Mayflower to Modern*. Oakland and Montreal, 2014.

Sale, Kirkpatrick. *SDS*. NY, 1973.

Saulo, Alfredo B. *Communism in the Philippines*. Manila, 1969.

Sayles, James Yaki. *Meditations on Frantz Fanon's Wretched of the Earth: New Afrikan Revolutionary Writings*, Montreal, 2010.

Schram, Stuart. *Mao Tse-Tung*. Baltimore, 1967.

Scott, William R. "Black Nationalism and the Italo-Ethiopian Conflict 1934–1936," *Journal of Negro History*, 1977.

Senate Internal Security Subcommittee. *The Weather Underground, Report of the Senate Internal Security Subcommittee*. Washington, 1975.

Siff, David. "Judgement at Madison," *University Review*, March 1974.

Smedley, Agnes. *Battle Hymn of China*. NY, 1943.

--------- *The Great Road*. NY, 1972.

Smith, Dennis Mack. *Mussolini's Roman Empire*. NY, 1976.

Snow, Edgar. *Red Star Over China*. NY, 1938.

Snow, Helen Foster. *The Chinese Communists, Sketches and Autobiographies of the Old Guard*. Westport, 1972.

Sojourn, Celia and Billy Ayers, *Politics in Command*. n.d.

Stolberg, Ben. "Black Chauvinism," *Nation*, May 15, 1935.

The African World. "Historic ALSC Conference Discussed: Which Road For Black People?" *The African World*, Vol. IV, No. 5, July 1974.

The Black Panther. "The CIA As An Equal Opportunity Employer," *The Black Panther*, June 7, 1969.

The New Afrikan, Vol. IX, No. 3, December 18 adM (1983).

Truong Chinh. "The Resistance Will Win," in *Selected Writings*. Hanoi, 1977.

Vidotto, Vittorio. *The Italian Communist Party From Its Origin to 1946*. Bologna, 1975.

Vietnam GI, August 1968.

--------- May 1968.

Village Voice. "Talking Back: Oral History of a Movement," *Village Voice*, February 26, 1985.

Wall Street Journal, July 26, 1984.

Weather Underground Organization, *Prairie Fire*. S.F., 1974.

--------- "New Morning—Changing Weather," *East Village Other*, Dec. 22, 1970.

Weglyn, Michi. *Years of Infamy*. NY, 1976.

Williams, Robert F. *Negroes With Guns*. NY, 1962.

Wolff, Melvin. *Lunch at the 5&10*. NY, 1970.

Wood, Donald. *Biko*. London, 1978.

Wright, Richard. *American Hunger*. NY, 1983.

Yeshitela, Omali. *Not One Step Backward!* Oakland, 1982.

Yoneda, Karl. "100 Years of Japanese Labor in the US," in *Roots: An Asian American Reader*. Los Angeles, 1971.

Zinn, Howard. *SNCC: The New Abolitionists* (Boston, 1964), pp. 211–212.

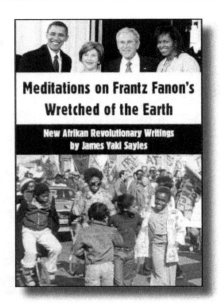

Meditations on Frantz Fanon's Wretched of the Earth: New Afrikan Revolutionary Writings
JAMES YAKI SAYLES • 978-1-894946-32-2
399 PAGES • $20.00

One of those who eagerly picked up Fanon in the '60s, who carried out armed expropriations and violence against white settlers, Sayles reveals how, behind the image of Fanon as race thinker, there is an underlying reality of antiracist communist thought. "This exercise is about more than our desire to read and understand Wretched (as if it were about some abstract world, and not our own); it's about more than our need to understand (the failures of) the anti-colonial struggles on the African continent. This exercise is also about us, and about some of the things that We need to understand and to change in ourselves and our world." —James Yaki Sayles

Settlers: The Mythology of the White Proletariat from Mayflower to Modern
J. SAKAI • 978-1-62963-037-3
456 PAGES • $20.00

The United States is a country built on the theft of Indigenous lands and Afrikan labor, on the robbery of the northern third of Mexico, the colonization of Puerto Rico, and the expropriation of the Asian working class, with each of these crimes being accompanied by violence. In fact, America's white citizenry have never supported themselves but have always resorted to exploitation and theft, culminating in acts of genocide to maintain their culture and way of life. This movement classic lays it all out, taking us through this painful but important history.

Amazon Nation or Aryan Nation: White Women and the Coming of Black Genocide
BOTTOMFISH BLUES • 978-1-894946-55-1
168 PAGES • $12.95

The two main essays in this book come from the radical women's newspaper Bottomfish Blues, which was published in the late 1980s and early '90s; while a historical appendix on "The Ideas of Black Genocide in the Amerikkkan Mind" was written more recently, but only circulated privately. These texts provide raw and vital lessons at the violent crash scene of nation, gender, and class, from a revolutionary perspective.

Night-Vision: Illuminating War and Class on the Neo-Colonial Terrain
BUTCH LEE AND RED ROVER • 978-1-894946-88-9
264 PAGES • $17.00

bell hooks: "Night-Vision was so compelling to me because it has a spirit of militancy which reformist feminism tries to kill because militant feminism is seen as a threat to the liberal bourgeois feminism that just wants to be equal with men. It has that raw, unmediated truth-telling which I think we are going to need in order to deal with the fascism that's upon us." A foundational analysis of post-modern capitalism, the decline of u.s. hegemony, and the need for a revolutionary movement of the oppressed to overthrow it all.

The "Dangerous Class" and Revolutionary Theory

J. SAKAI • 9781894946902
307 PAGES • $24.95

The "Dangerous Class" and Revolutionary Theory starts with the paper of that name, on the birth of the modern lumpen/proletariat in the 18th and 19th centuries and the storm cloud of revolutionary theory that has always surrounded them. Going back and piecing together both the actual social reality and the analyses primarily of Marx but also Bakunin and Engels, the paper shows how Marx's class theory wasn't something static. His views learned in quick jumps, and then all but reversed themselves in several significant aspects. While at first dismissing them in the Communist Manifesto as "that passively rotting mass" at the obscure lower depths, Marx soon realized that the lumpen could be players at the very center of events in revolutionary civil war. Even at the center in the startling rise of new regimes.

*The second part takes over on the flip side of the book, in the detailed paper **Mao Z's Revolutionary Laboratory and the Role of the Lumpen Proletariat**. This, too, is ground-breaking work. If the major revolutionary theory we have about the lumpen was first roughly assembled in 19th century Europe, these ideas weren't put to the test then. As Sakai points out, the left's euro-centrism here prevented it from realizing the obvious: that the basic theory from European radicalism was first fully tested not there or here but in the Chinese Revolution of 1921–1949. Under severely clashing political lines in the left, the class analysis finally used by Mao Z was shaken out of the shipping crate from Europe and then modified to map the organizing of millions over a prolonged generational revolutionary war. One could hardly wish for a larger test tube, and the many lessons to be learned from this mass political experience are finally put on the table.*

In addition, there are also two lively Addendums: The first is an informal correspondence, a back and forth of questions raised by an early draft of The "Dangerous Class" and Revolutionary Theory, between the book's editor and J. Sakai. It starts with the question of how to place the traditional gay community in this?

The second Addendum is a reprint of J. Sakai's 1976 covert intelligence paper, "U.S. Experiment Using Black 'Gangs' to Repress Black Community Rebellions" (circulated under the earlier title "The Lumpenproletariat and Repression"). There is both an extensive Foreword explaining the politics and circumstances that led to this paper, as well as an Afterword explaining how the education paper was used and some critical reaction to it.

The Red Army Faction, A Documentary History
Volume 1: Projectiles for the People

ANDRÉ MONCOURT AND J. SMITH

FOREWORDS BY U.S. POLITICAL PRISONERS
BILL DUNNE AND RUSSELL "MAROON" SHOATS
ISBN: 978-1-60486-029-0
736 PAGES • $34.95

For the first time ever in English: all of the manifestos and communiqués issued by the RAF between 1970 and 1977. From Andreas Baader's prison break, through the 1972 May Offensive and the 1975 hostage-taking in Stockholm, to the desperate, and tragic, events of the "German Autumn" of 1977. Separate thematic sections address the context from which the RAF emerged and within which it managed to repeatedly renew its base of support and carry out its daring anti-imperialist attacks.

The Red Army Faction, A Documentary History
Volume 2: Dancing with Imperialism

ANDRÉ MONCOURT AND J. SMITH

INTRODUCTION BY WARD CHURCHILL
ISBN: 978-1-60486-030-6
480 PAGES • $26.95

This work addresses a period in which the RAF regrouped and reoriented itself, with its previous 1970s focus on freeing its prisoners replaced by a new anti-NATO line. Includes details of the RAF's operations, and its communiqués and texts, from 1978 up until its 1984 offensive. Changes in both the guerilla and the radical left are addressed during what was a period of resurgent protest and political violence in West Germany.

KER SPLE EBE DEB

Since 1998 Kersplebedeb has been an important source of radical literature and agit prop materials.

The project has a non-exclusive focus on anti-patriarchal and anti-imperialist politics, framed within an anticapitalist perspective. A special priority is given to writings regarding armed struggle in the metropole, the continuing struggles of political prisoners and prisoners of war, and the political economy of imperialism.

The Kersplebedeb website presents historical and contemporary writings by revolutionary thinkers from the anarchist and communist traditions.

Kersplebedeb can be contacted at:

Kersplebedeb
CP 63560
CCCP Van Horne
Montreal, Quebec
Canada
H3W 3H8

email: info@kersplebedeb.com
web: www.kersplebedeb.com
            www.leftwingbooks.net

Kersplebedeb

CPSIA information can be obtained
at www.ICGtesting.com
Printed in the USA
BVHW010559120921
616597BV00004B/36